fushigi yûgi™

The Mysterious Play
VOL. 18: BRIDE

Story & Art By
YUU WATASE

FUSHIGI YÛGI
THE MYSTERIOUS PLAY
VOL. 18: BRIDE
SHÔJO EDITION

STORY AND ART BY YUU WATASE

Editor's Note: At the author's request, the spelling of Ms. Watase's first name has been changed from "Yû," as it has appeared on previous VIZ Media publications, to "Yuu."

English Adaptation/William Flanagan
Touch-up & Lettering/Bill Spicer
Touch-up Assistance/Walden Wong
Design/Hidemi Sahara
Editor/Frances E. Wall

Managing Editor/Annette Roman
Director of Production/Noboru Watanabe
Vice President of Publishing/Alvin Lu
Sr. Director of Acquisitions/Rika Inouye
Vice President of Sales & Marketing/Liza Coppola
Publisher/Hyoe Narita

© 1992 Yuu WATASE/Shogakukan Inc. First published by Shogakukan Inc. in Japan
as "Fushigi Yugi." New and adapted artwork and text © 2006 VIZ Media, LLC.
The FUSHIGI YÛGI logo is a trademark of VIZ Media, LLC. All rights reserved.
The stories, characters and incidents mentioned in this publication are entirely fictional.

Printed in the U.S.A.

Published by VIZ Media, LLC
P.O. Box 77010
San Francisco, CA 94107

Shôjo Edition
10 9 8 7 6 5 4 3 2 1
First printing, April 2006

www.viz.com
store.viz.com

CONTENTS

STORY THUS FAR

In the winter of her third year of middle school, Miaka was whisked away into the pages of a mysterious old book called THE UNIVERSE OF THE FOUR GODS and began a dual existence as an ordinary schoolgirl in modern Japan and a priestess of the god Suzaku in a fictional version of ancient China. Miaka fell in love with Tamahome, one of the Celestial Warriors of Suzaku responsible for the protection of the priestess. Miaka's best friend Yui was also sucked into the world of the book and became the priestess of Seiryu, the bitter enemy of Suzaku and Miaka. After clashing repeatedly with the corrupt and vengeful Seiryu Celestial Warriors, Miaka summoned Suzaku and vanquished her enemies, reconciled with Yui, and saved the earth from destruction. In the end, Suzaku granted Miaka one impossible wish: for Tamahome to be reborn as a human in the real world so that the two lovers would never again be separated.

Miaka enters Yotsubadai High School and plans to settle into a normal life with her beloved, who is now a real man named Taka Sukunami. But Suzaku returns to give Miaka a new mission: she must reenter THE UNIVERSE OF THE FOUR GODS and find seven special stones that contain Taka's memories from his former life as Tamahome…or her soulmate could disappear forever! With the help of the reunited Warriors of Suzaku, Miaka and Taka are able to recover four of the stones. But the demon-god Tenkô says he will stop at nothing to thwart their quest, and his minions repeatedly terrorize Miaka and Taka! Tenkô manages to steal all the stones they had collected, and the remaining stones are mysteriously destroyed. This devastates Taka, and he is on the verge of giving up all hope of continuing to live in the real world with Miaka when he notices another disturbing omen—he no longer has a reflection in the mirror. Tasuki attempts to comfort Taka, but he is also alarmed at this new development. He runs outside in grief…only to be greeted by Tamahome himself!

THE UNIVERSE OF THE FOUR GODS is based on ancient Chinese legend, but Japanese pronunciation of Chinese names differs slightly from their Chinese equivalents. Here is a short glossary of the Japanese pronunciation of the Chinese names in this manga:

CHINESE	JAPANESE	PERSON OR PLACE	MEANING
Hong-Nan	Konan	Southern Kingdom	Crimson South
Yong-Shua	Yôsui	Tenkô's Servant	Evil Commander
Mang-Chen	Bôshin	Crown Prince	Spreading Dawn
Tao-Hui	Dôkun	Chiriko's Name	Bright Path
Lai Lai	Nyan Nyan	A demigod	Daughter (x2)
Daichi-san	Daikyokuzan	A mountain	Greatest Mountain
Tai Yi-Jun	Taiitsu-kun	Emperor of Heaven	Preeminent Person
Lian	Ren	Lian-Fang	Collect

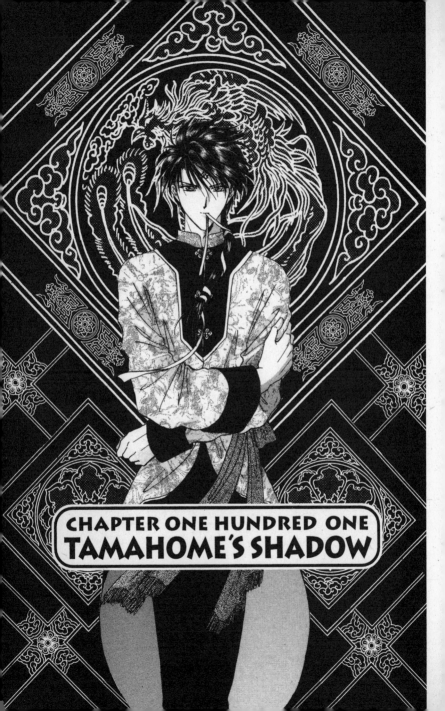

CHAPTER ONE HUNDRED ONE
TAMAHOME'S SHADOW

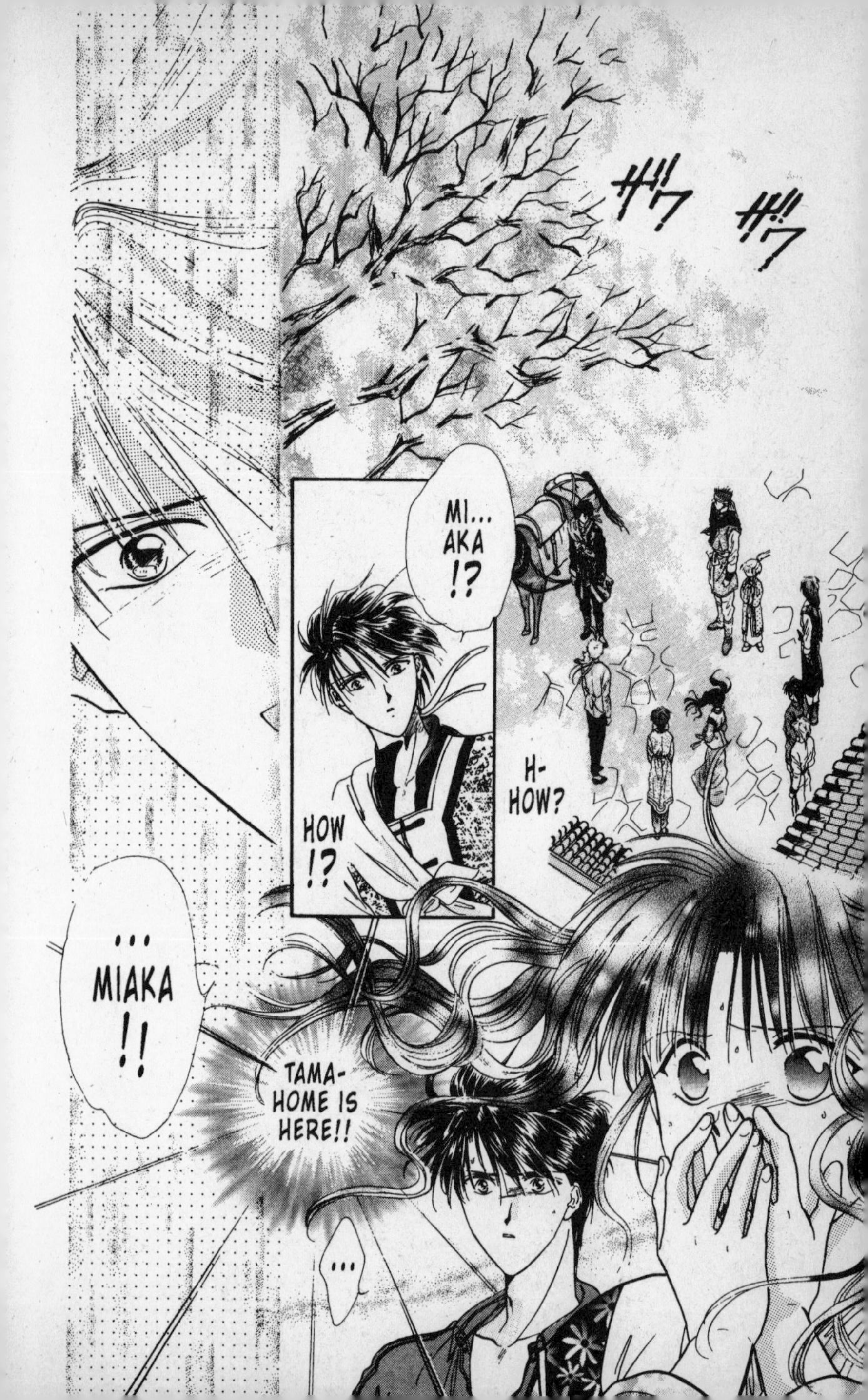
ザワ ザワ
H- HOW?
MI... AKA !?
HOW !?
TAMA-HOME IS HERE!!
...
... MIAKA !!

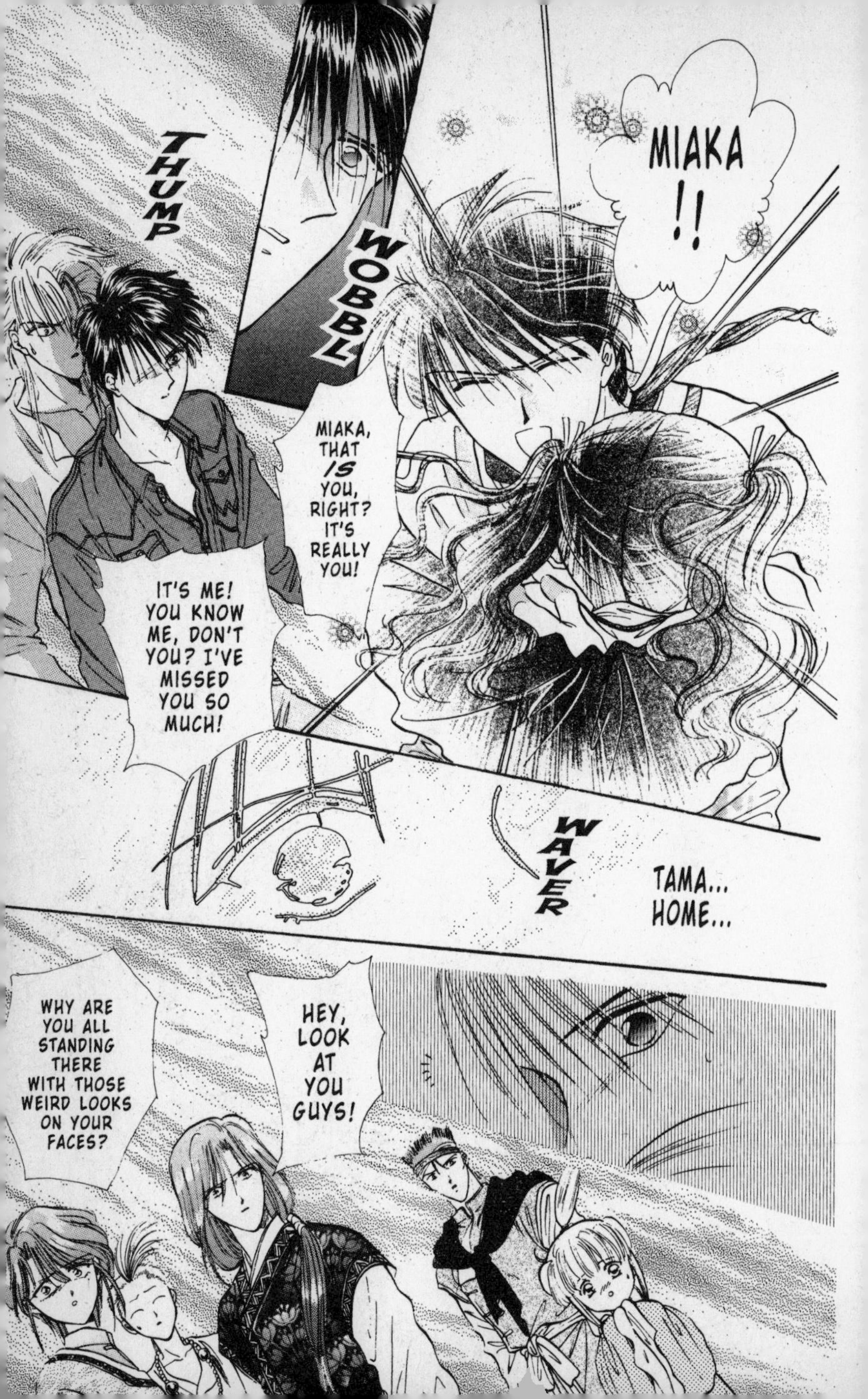
MIAKA !!
MIAKA, THAT IS YOU, RIGHT? IT'S REALLY YOU!
IT'S ME! YOU KNOW ME, DON'T YOU? I'VE MISSED YOU SO MUCH!
WOBBL
THUMP
TAMA... HOME...
WAVER
HEY, LOOK AT YOU GUYS!
WHY ARE YOU ALL STANDING THERE WITH THOSE WEIRD LOOKS ON YOUR FACES?

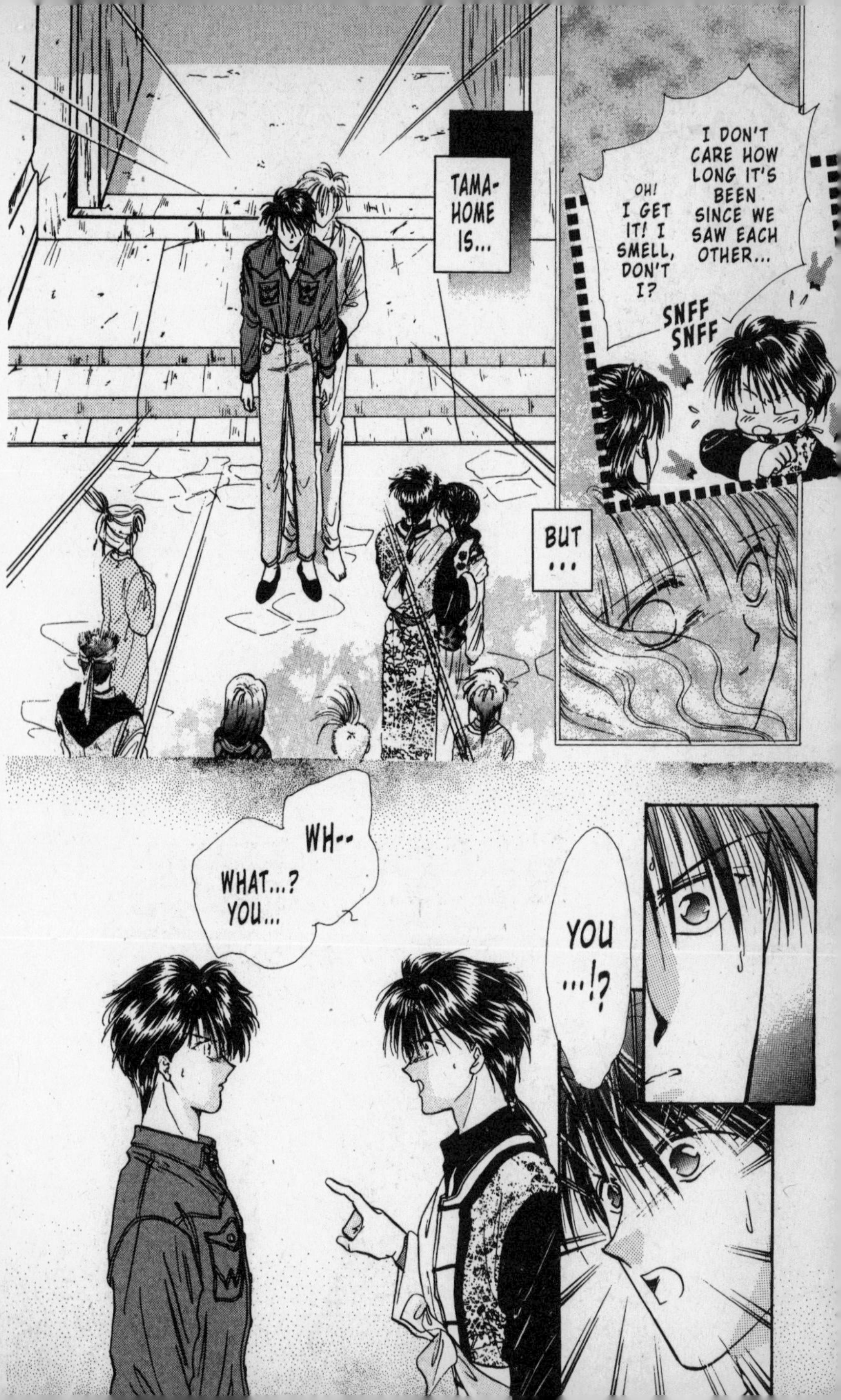
I DON'T CARE HOW LONG IT'S BEEN SINCE WE SAW EACH OTHER...
OH! I GET IT! I SMELL, DON'T I?
SNFF SNFF
BUT...
TAMA-HOME IS...
YOU...!?
WH--
WHAT...? YOU...

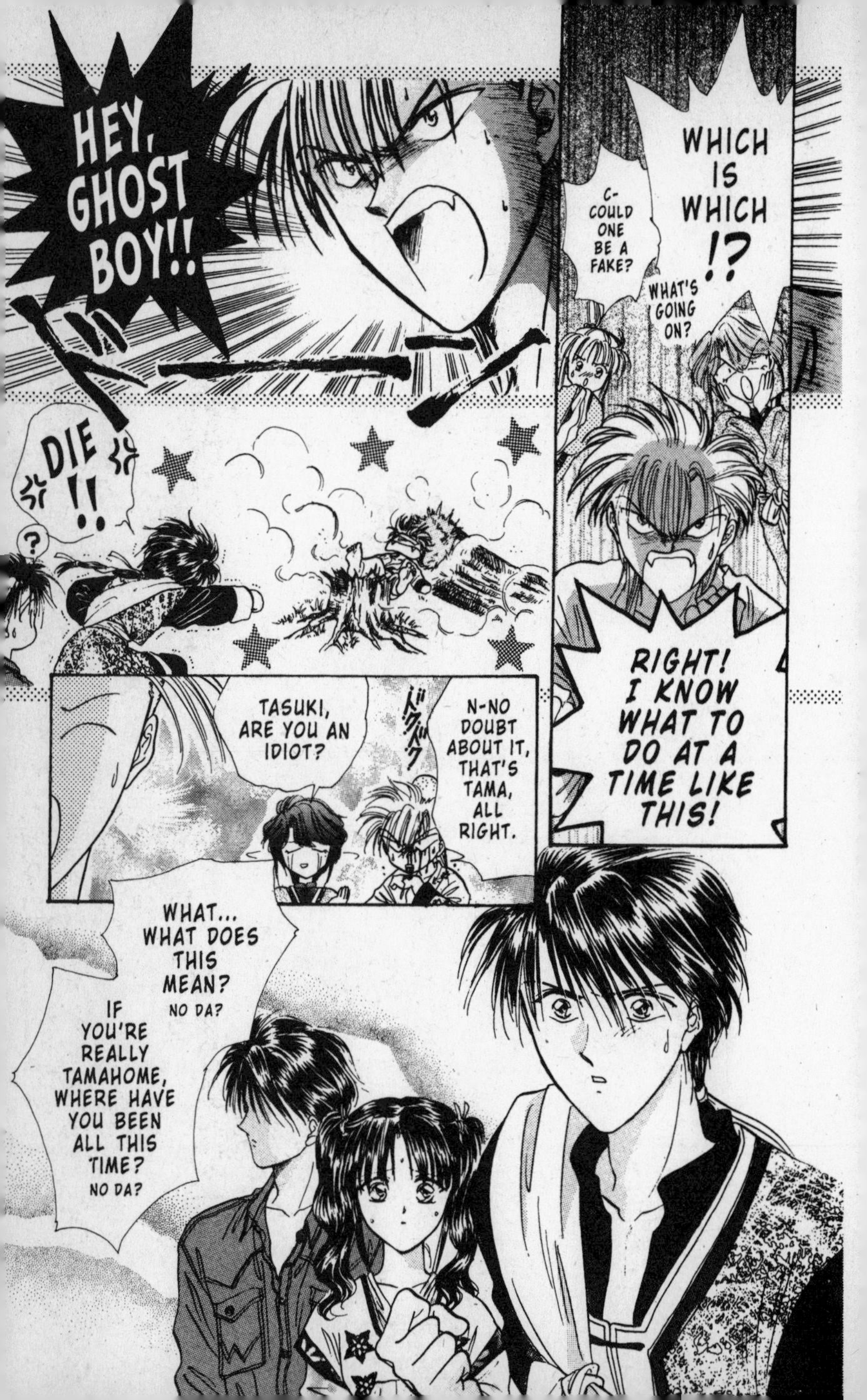
WHICH IS WHICH!?
C-COULD ONE BE A FAKE?
WHAT'S GOING ON?
RIGHT! I KNOW WHAT TO DO AT A TIME LIKE THIS!
HEY, GHOST BOY!!
DIE!!
?
N-NO DOUBT ABOUT IT, THAT'S TAMA, ALL RIGHT.
TASUKI, ARE YOU AN IDIOT?
WHAT... WHAT DOES THIS MEAN? NO DA?
IF YOU'RE REALLY TAMAHOME, WHERE HAVE YOU BEEN ALL THIS TIME? NO DA?

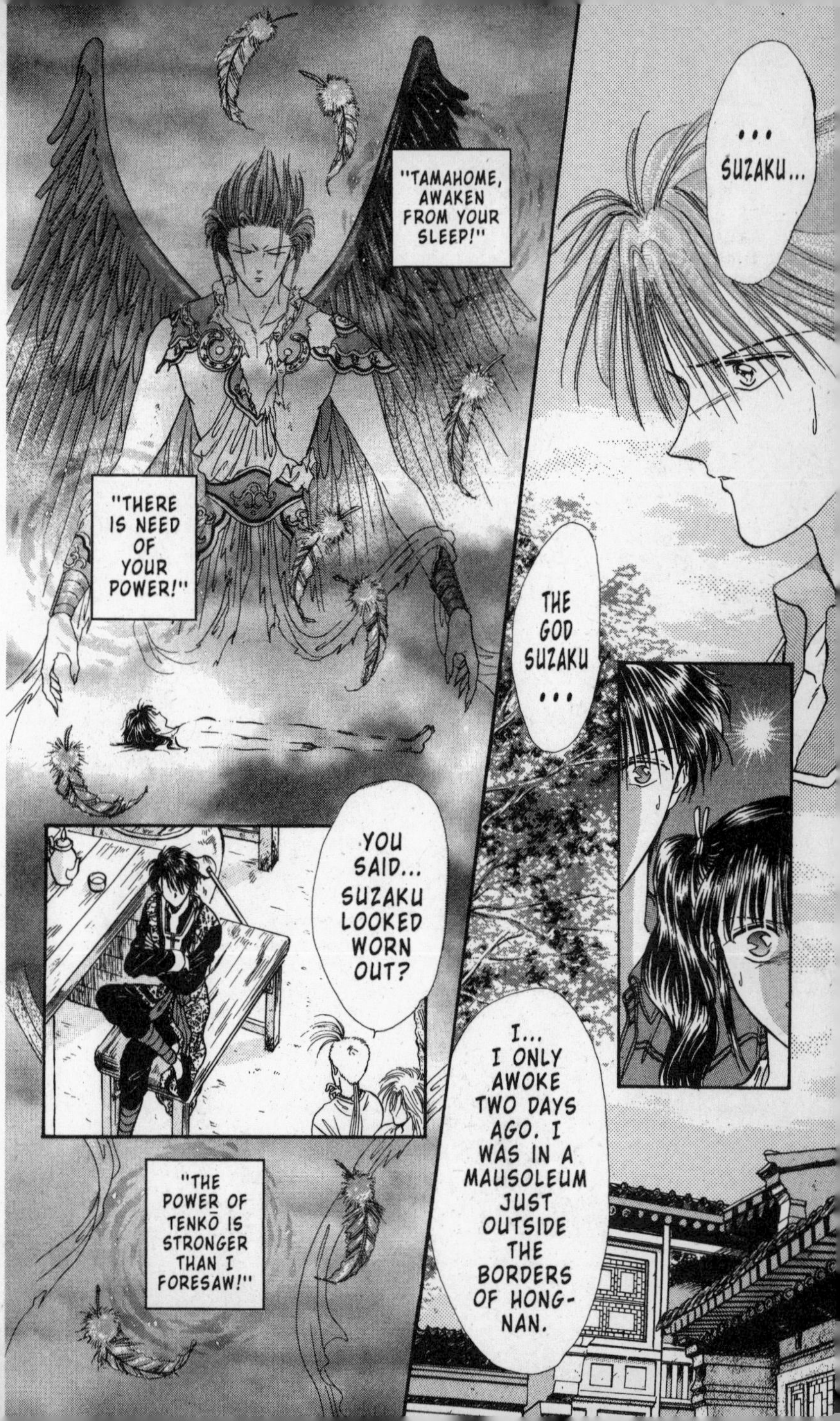
... SUZAKU...
THE GOD SUZAKU ...
I... I ONLY AWOKE TWO DAYS AGO. I WAS IN A MAUSOLEUM JUST OUTSIDE THE BORDERS OF HONG-NAN.
"TAMAHOME, AWAKEN FROM YOUR SLEEP!"
"THERE IS NEED OF YOUR POWER!"
YOU SAID... SUZAKU LOOKED WORN OUT?
"THE POWER OF TENKŌ IS STRONGER THAN I FORESAW!"

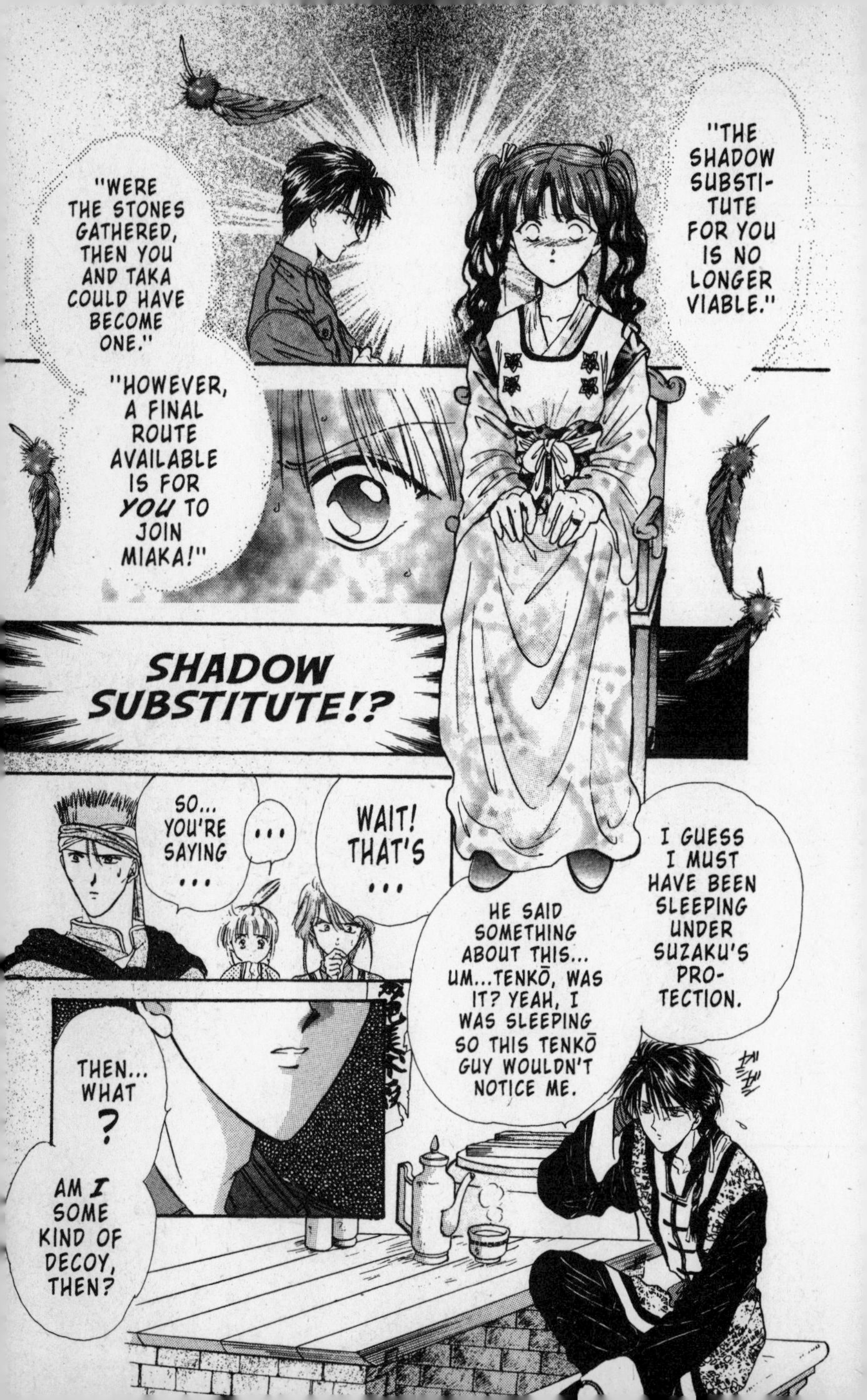
"THE SHADOW SUBSTITUTE FOR YOU IS NO LONGER VIABLE."
"WERE THE STONES GATHERED, THEN YOU AND TAKA COULD HAVE BECOME ONE."
"HOWEVER, A FINAL ROUTE AVAILABLE IS FOR *YOU* TO JOIN MIAKA!"
SHADOW SUBSTITUTE!?
I GUESS I MUST HAVE BEEN SLEEPING UNDER SUZAKU'S PROTECTION.
HE SAID SOMETHING ABOUT THIS... UM...TENKŌ, WAS IT? YEAH, I WAS SLEEPING SO THIS TENKŌ GUY WOULDN'T NOTICE ME.
WAIT! THAT'S ...
...
SO... YOU'RE SAYING ...
THEN... WHAT ?
AM *I* SOME KIND OF DECOY, THEN?

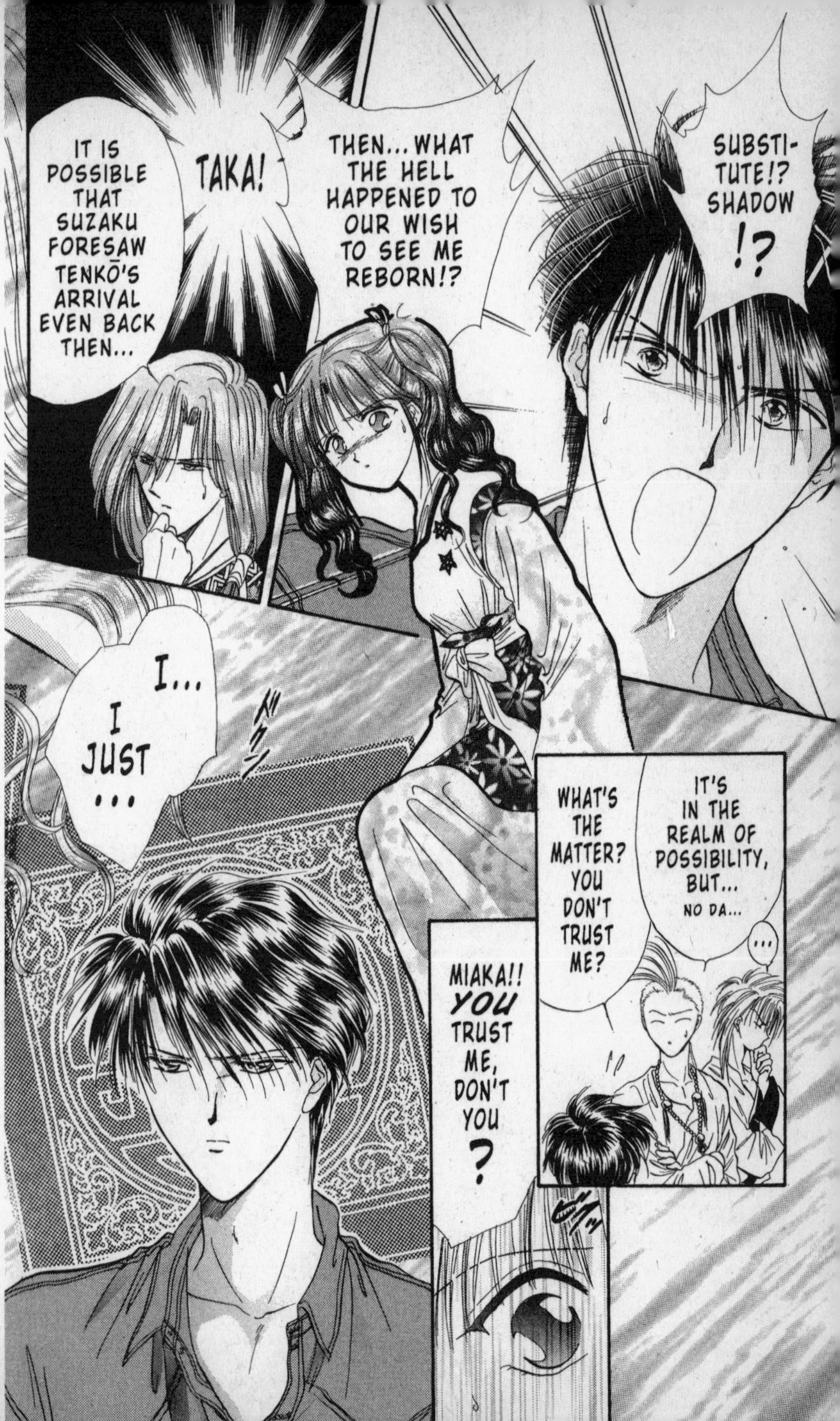
SUBSTITUTE!? SHADOW!?
THEN... WHAT THE HELL HAPPENED TO OUR WISH TO SEE ME REBORN!?
TAKA!
IT IS POSSIBLE THAT SUZAKU FORESAW TENKŌ'S ARRIVAL EVEN BACK THEN...
IT'S IN THE REALM OF POSSIBILITY, BUT... NO DA...
...
WHAT'S THE MATTER? YOU DON'T TRUST ME?
MIAKA!! YOU TRUST ME, DON'T YOU?
I... I JUST...

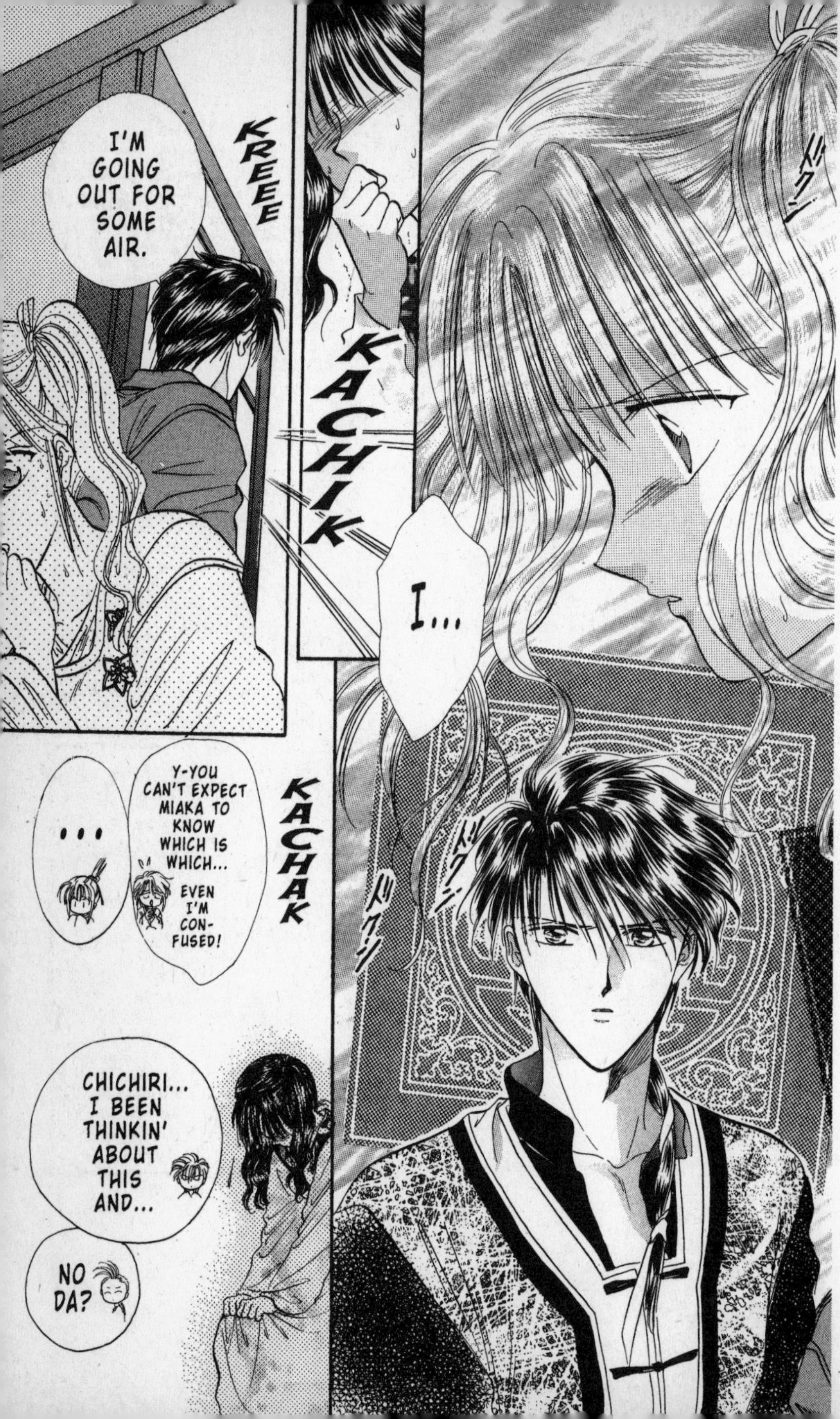
I...
KACHIK
KREEE
I'M GOING OUT FOR SOME AIR.
KACHAK
Y-YOU CAN'T EXPECT MIAKA TO KNOW WHICH IS WHICH... EVEN I'M CONFUSED!
...
CHICHIRI... I BEEN THINKIN' ABOUT THIS AND...
NO DA?

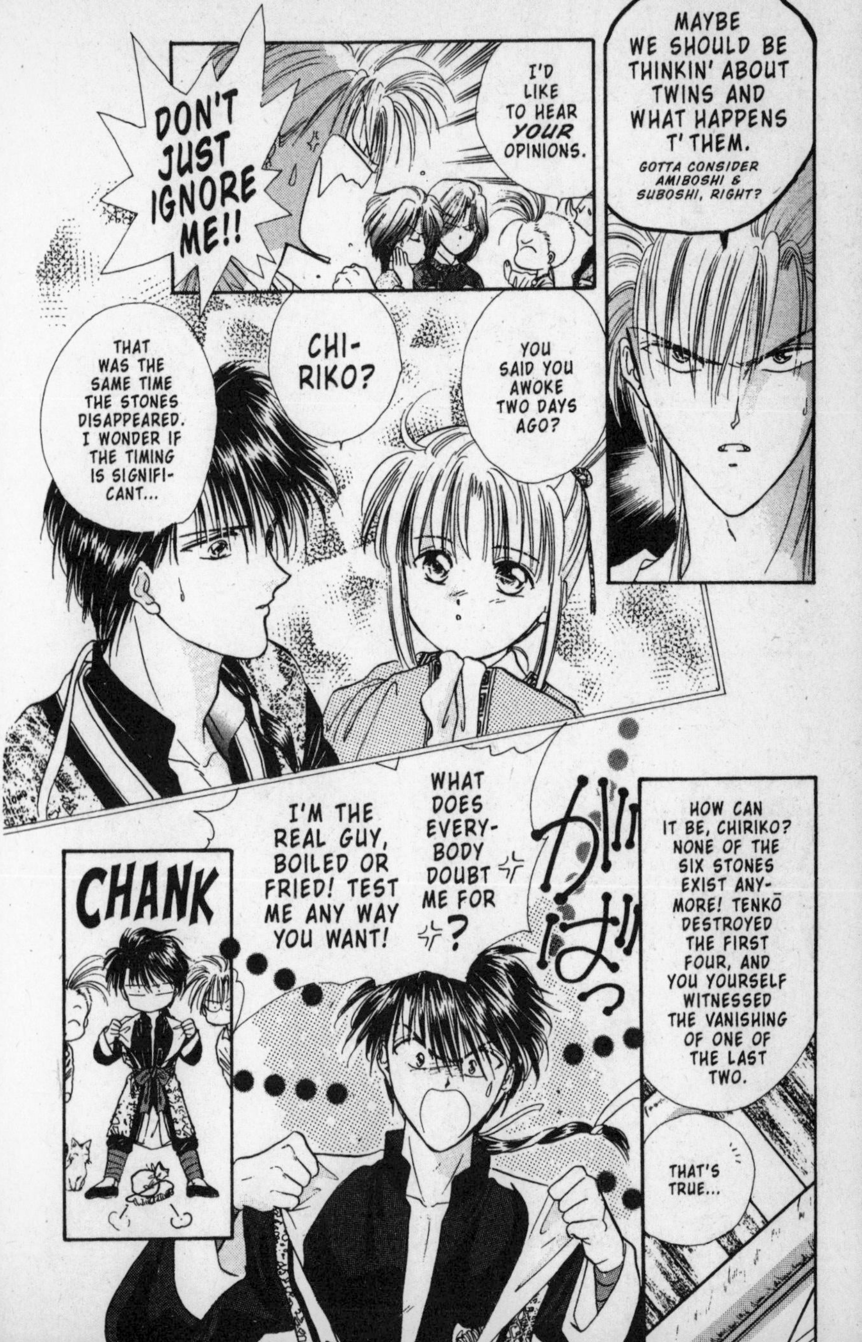
MAYBE WE SHOULD BE THINKIN' ABOUT TWINS AND WHAT HAPPENS T' THEM.
GOTTA CONSIDER AMIBOSHI & SUBOSHI, RIGHT?
I'D LIKE TO HEAR *YOUR* OPINIONS.
DON'T JUST IGNORE ME!!
YOU SAID YOU AWOKE TWO DAYS AGO?
CHI-RIKO?
THAT WAS THE SAME TIME THE STONES DISAPPEARED. I WONDER IF THE TIMING IS SIGNIFI-CANT...
HOW CAN IT BE, CHIRIKO? NONE OF THE SIX STONES EXIST ANY-MORE! TENKŌ DESTROYED THE FIRST FOUR, AND YOU YOURSELF WITNESSED THE VANISHING OF ONE OF THE LAST TWO.
THAT'S TRUE...
WHAT DOES EVERY-BODY DOUBT ME FOR?
I'M THE REAL GUY, BOILED OR FRIED! TEST ME ANY WAY YOU WANT!
CHANK

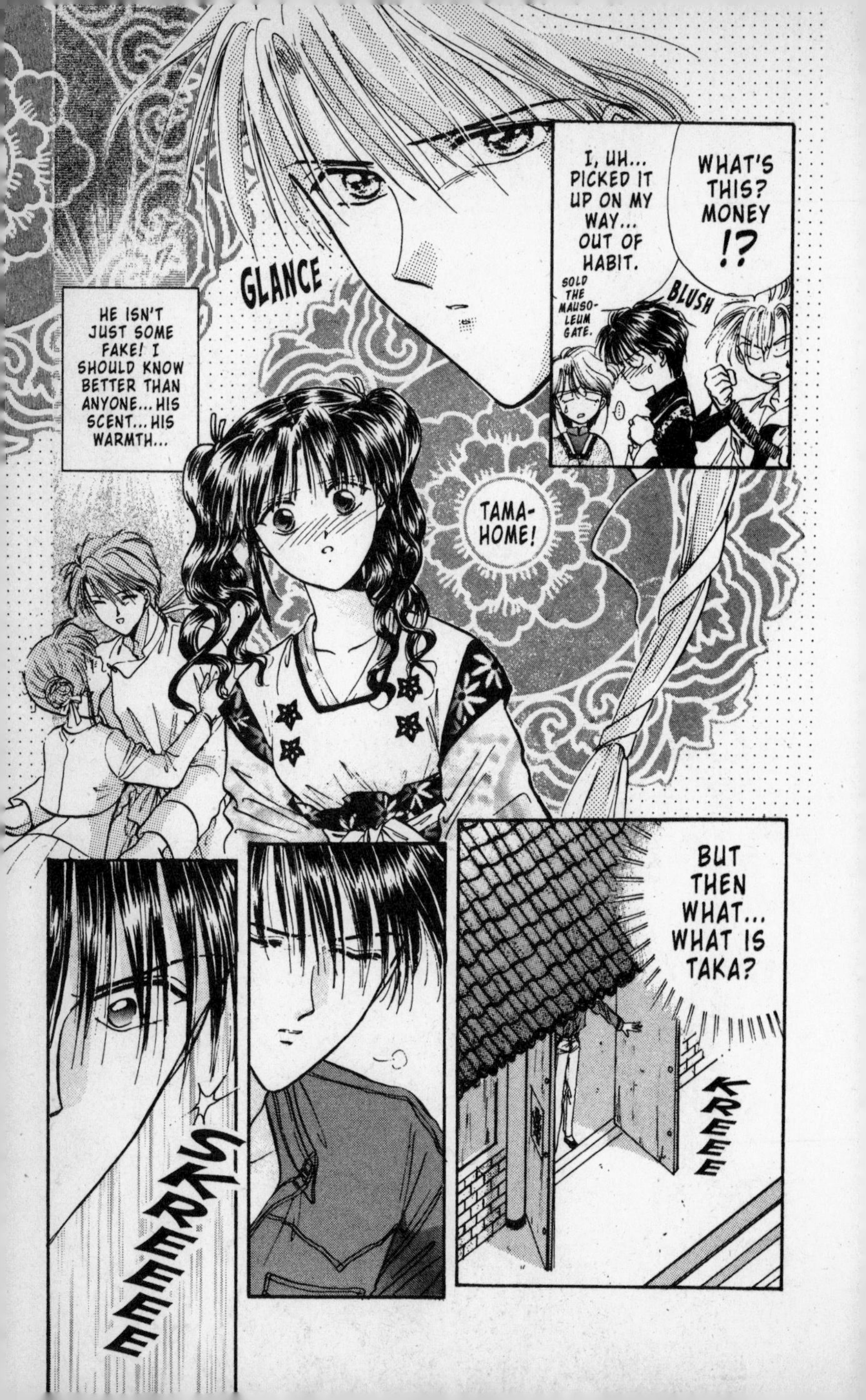
WHAT'S THIS? MONEY !?
I, UH... PICKED IT UP ON MY WAY... OUT OF HABIT.
BLUSH
SOLD THE MAUSOLEUM GATE.
GLANCE
HE ISN'T JUST SOME FAKE! I SHOULD KNOW BETTER THAN ANYONE... HIS SCENT... HIS WARMTH...
TAMA-HOME!
BUT THEN WHAT... WHAT IS TAKA?
KREEE
SKREEEE

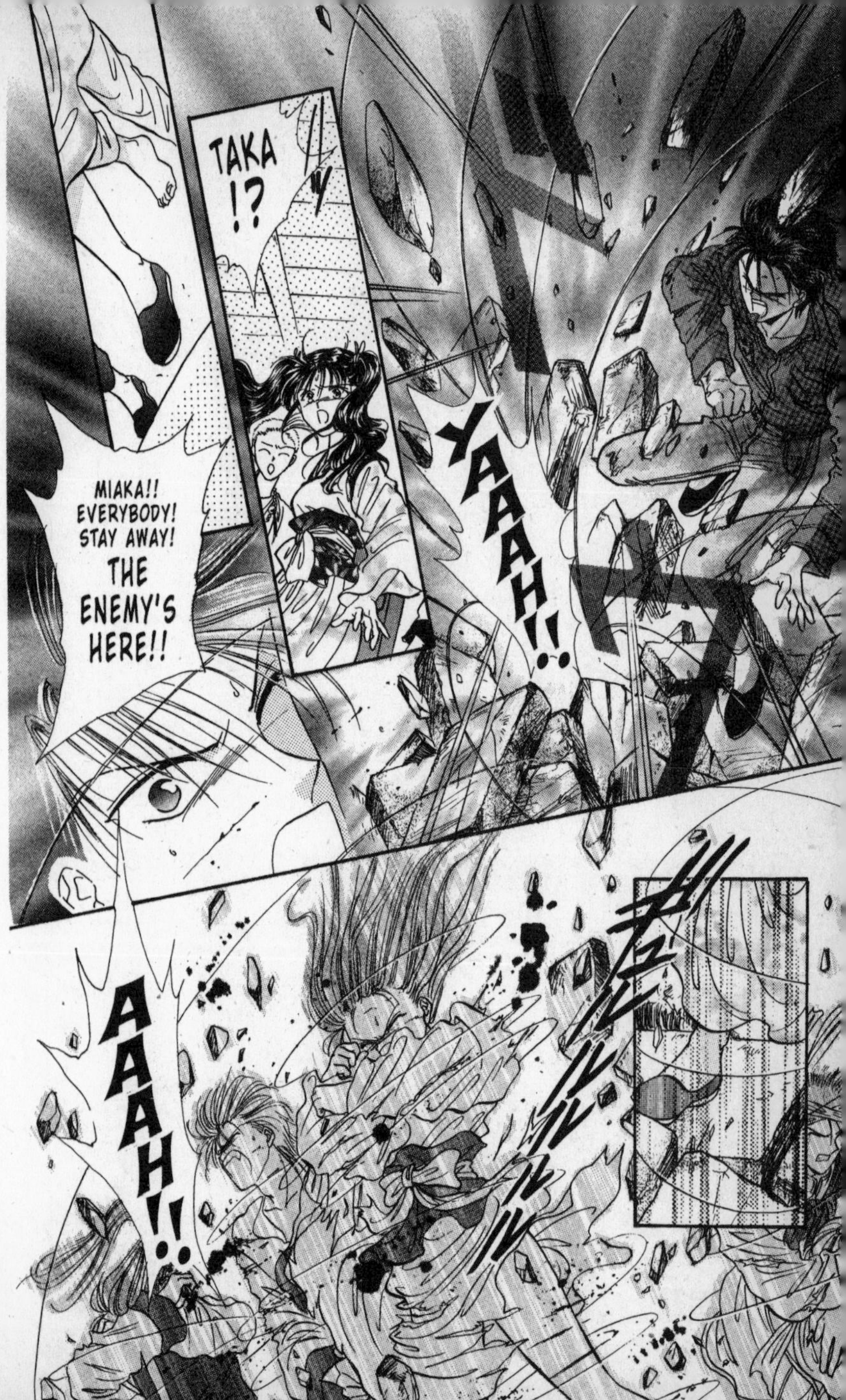
YAAAAH!!
TAKA !?
MIAKA!! EVERYBODY! STAY AWAY!
THE ENEMY'S HERE!!
AAAAH!!

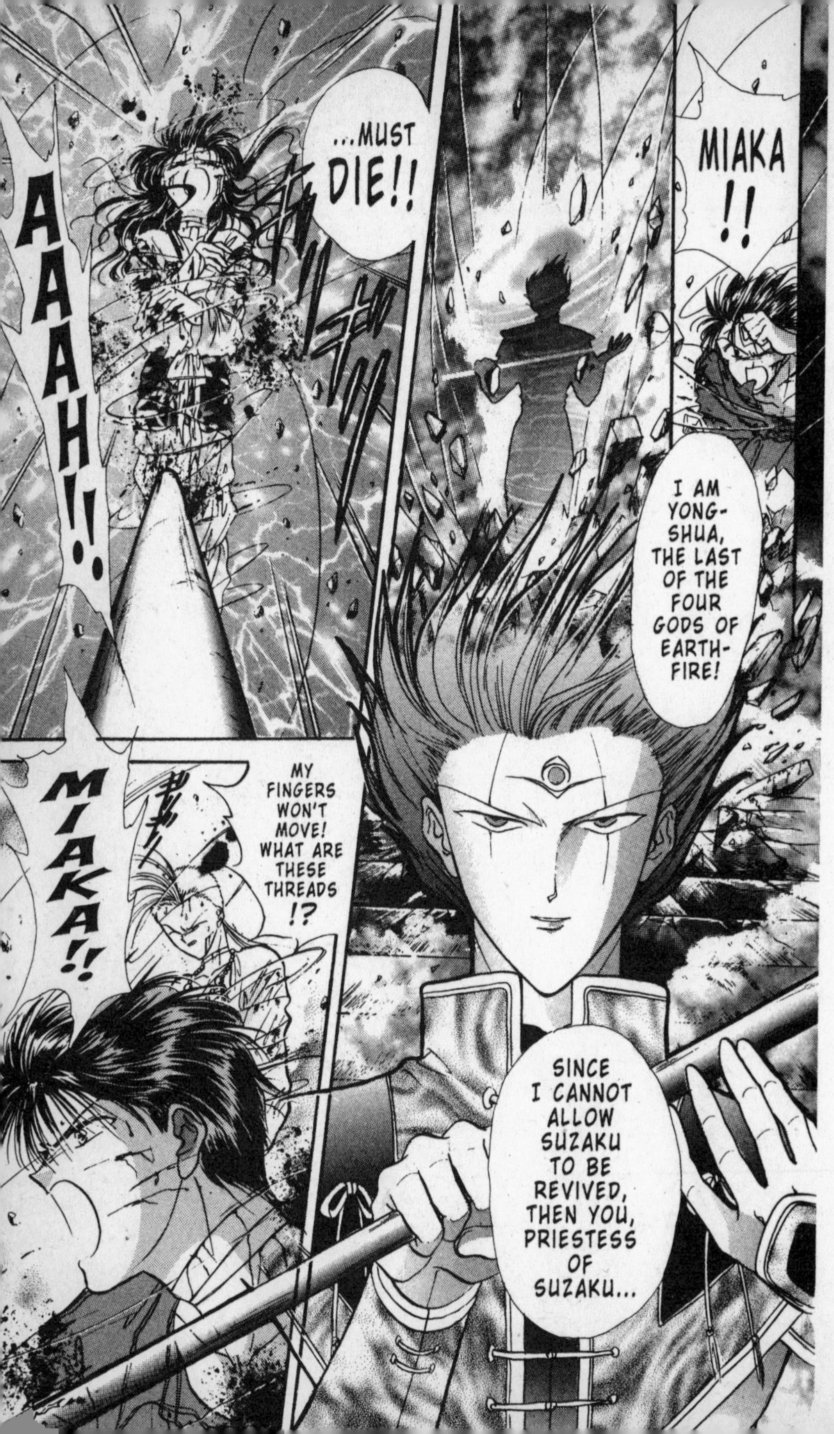
MIAKA!!
I AM YONG-SHUA, THE LAST OF THE FOUR GODS OF EARTH-FIRE!
SINCE I CANNOT ALLOW SUZAKU TO BE REVIVED, THEN YOU, PRIESTESS OF SUZAKU...
...MUST DIE!!
AAAH!!!
MIAKA!!
MY FINGERS WON'T MOVE! WHAT ARE THESE THREADS!?

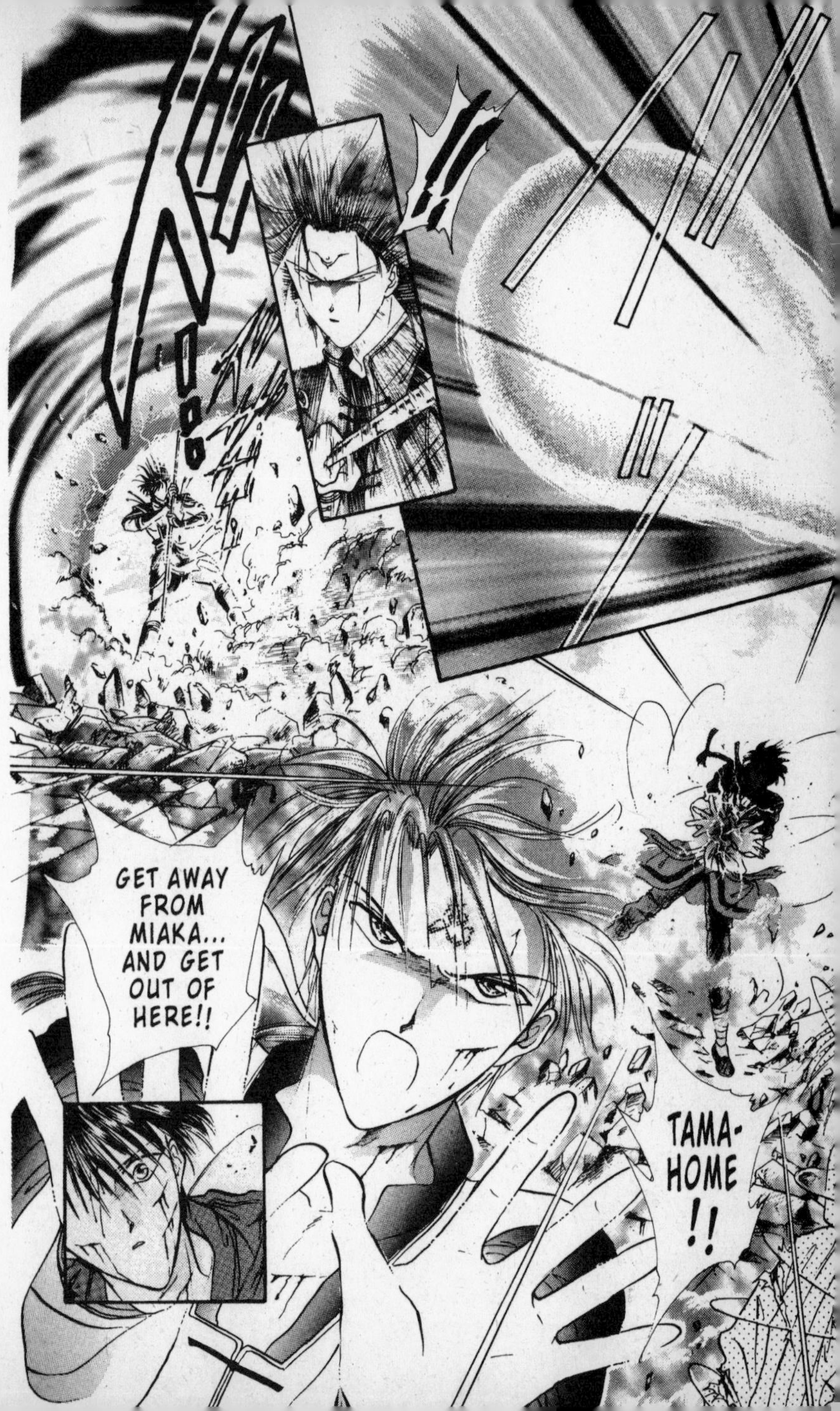
GET AWAY FROM MIAKA... AND GET OUT OF HERE!!
TAMA-HOME !!

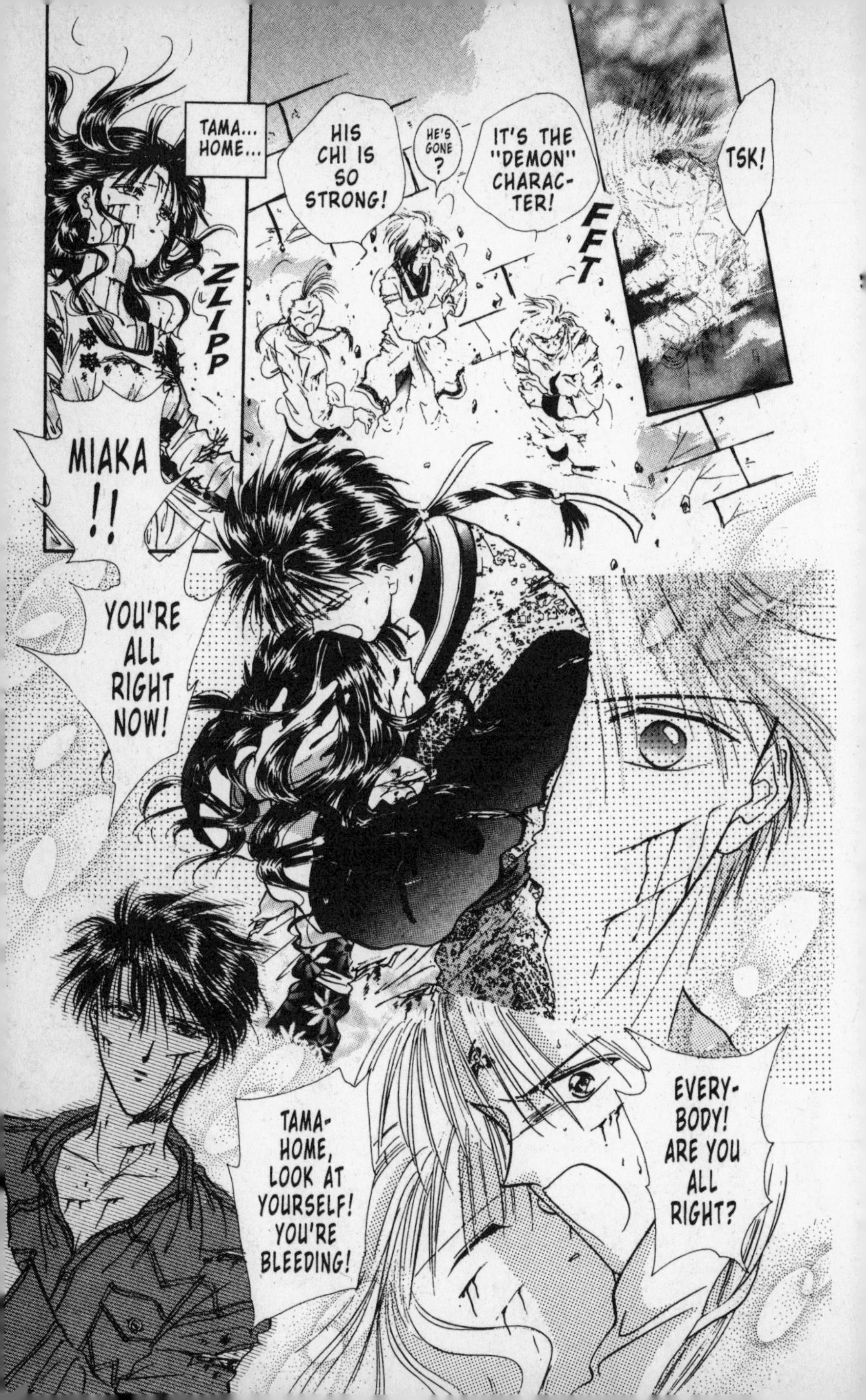
TSK!
IT'S THE "DEMON" CHARACTER!
HE'S GONE ?
HIS CHI IS SO STRONG!
FFT
TAMA... HOME...
ZZLIPP
MIAKA !!
YOU'RE ALL RIGHT NOW!
EVERY-BODY! ARE YOU ALL RIGHT?
TAMA-HOME, LOOK AT YOURSELF! YOU'RE BLEEDING!

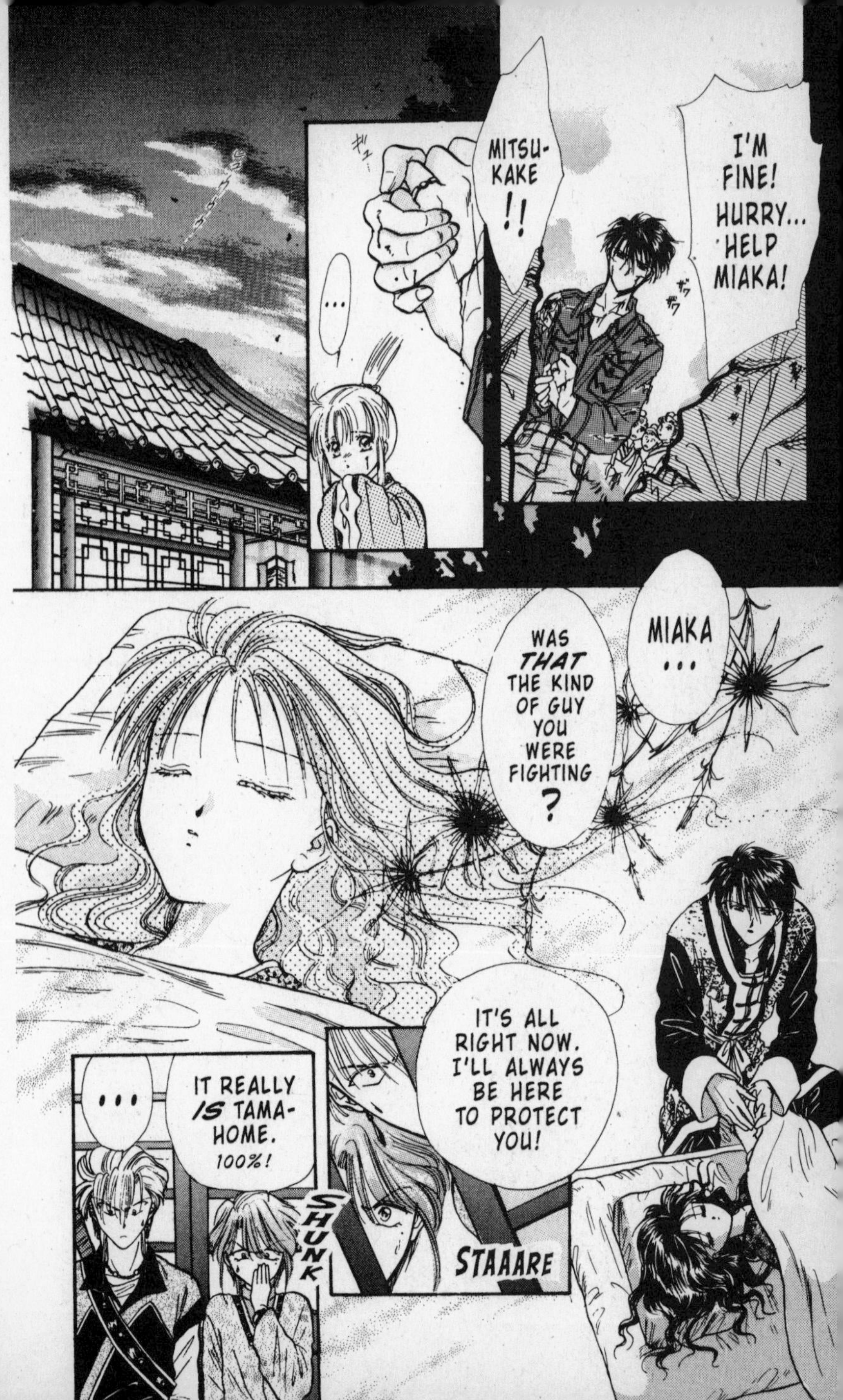
I'M FINE! HURRY... HELP MIAKA!
MITSU-KAKE !!
...
MIAKA...
WAS THAT THE KIND OF GUY YOU WERE FIGHTING?
IT'S ALL RIGHT NOW. I'LL ALWAYS BE HERE TO PROTECT YOU!
STAAARE
SHUNK
IT REALLY IS TAMA-HOME. 100%!
...

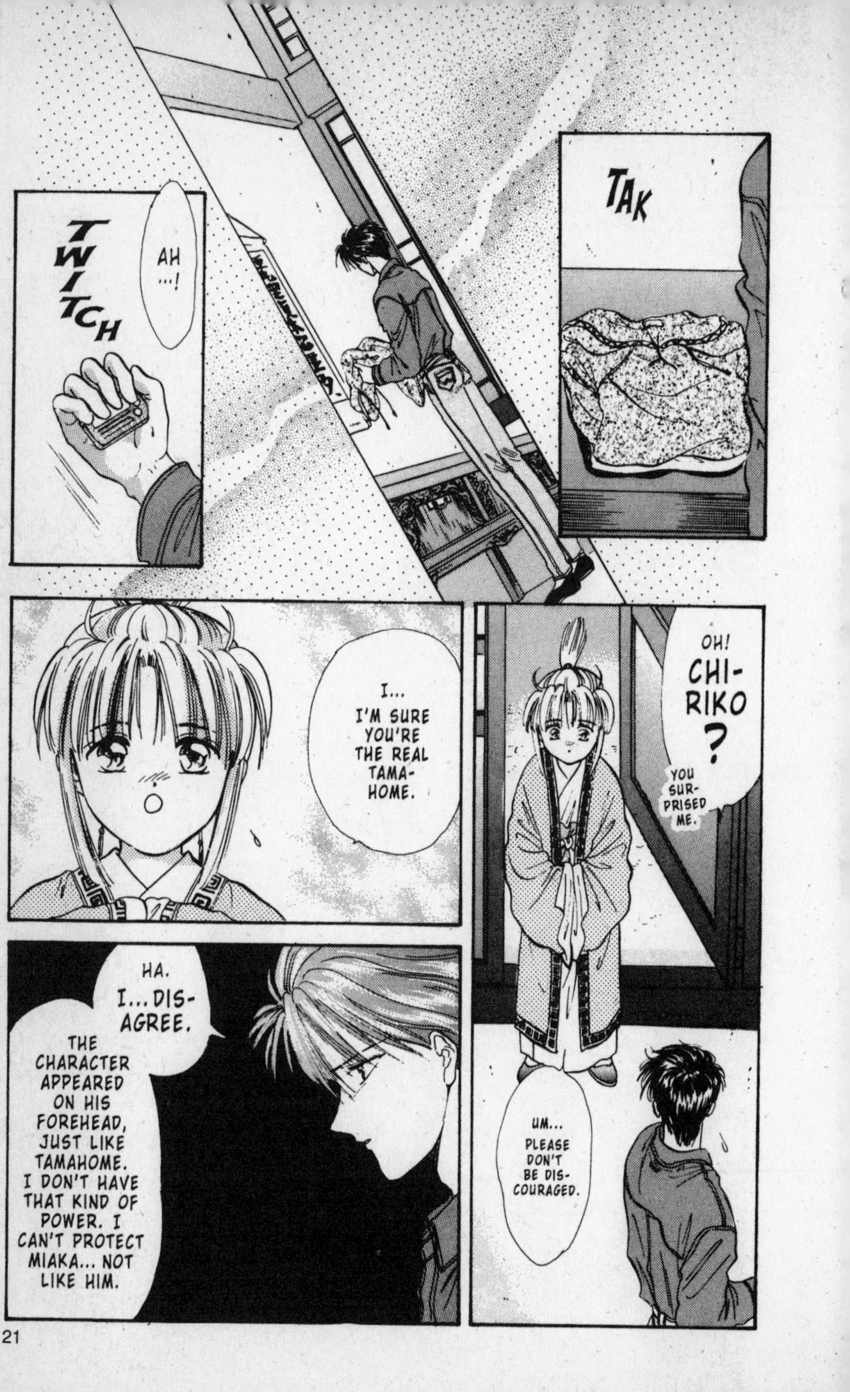
TAK
AH ...!
TWITCH
OH! CHI-RIKO?
YOU SUR-PRISED ME.
I... I'M SURE YOU'RE THE REAL TAMA-HOME.
HA. I... DIS-AGREE.
THE CHARACTER APPEARED ON HIS FOREHEAD, JUST LIKE TAMAHOME. I DON'T HAVE THAT KIND OF POWER. I CAN'T PROTECT MIAKA... NOT LIKE HIM.
UM... PLEASE DON'T BE DIS-COURAGED.

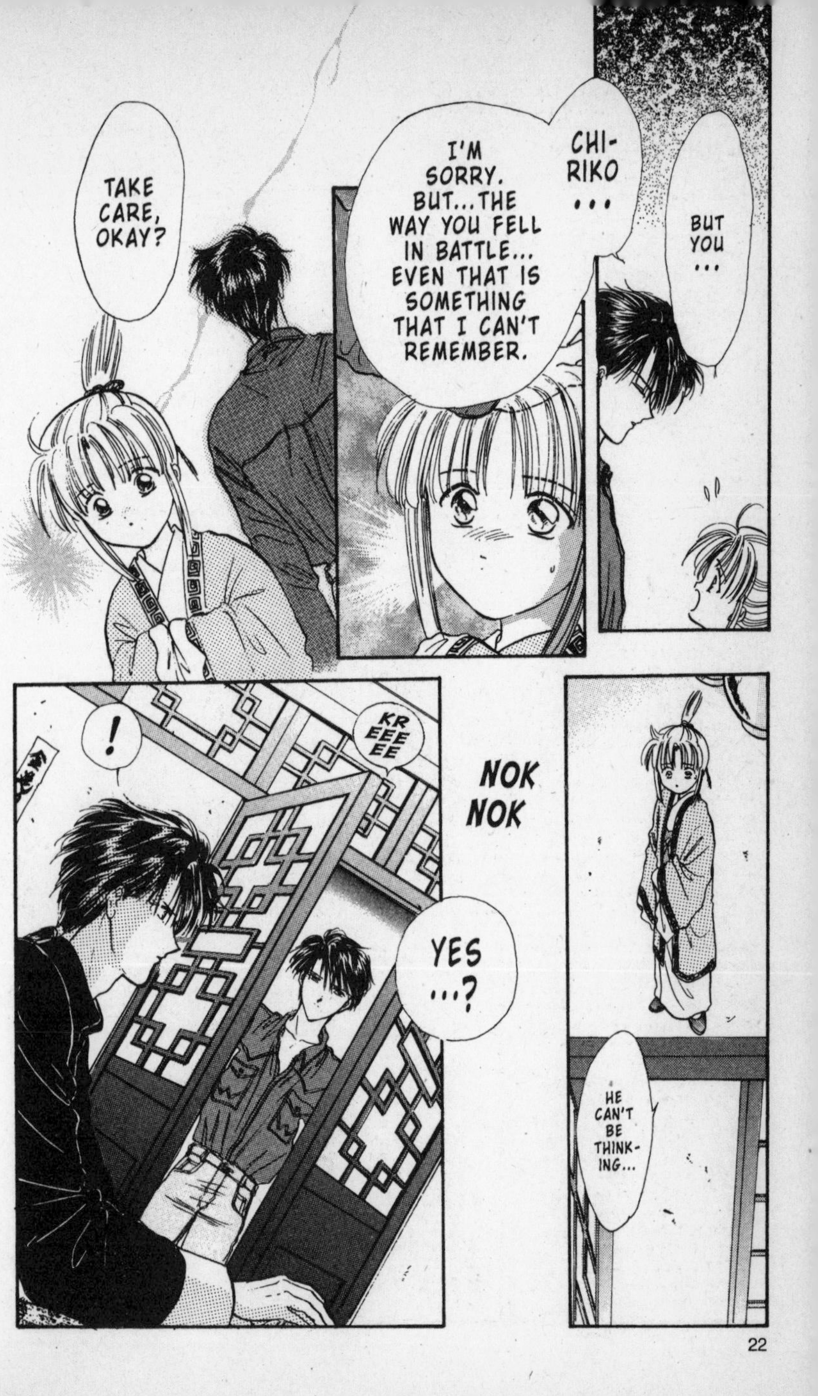
BUT YOU...
CHI-RIKO...
I'M SORRY. BUT...THE WAY YOU FELL IN BATTLE... EVEN THAT IS SOMETHING THAT I CAN'T REMEMBER.
TAKE CARE, OKAY?
HE CAN'T BE THINK-ING...
NOK NOK
KREEEEEE
!
YES...?

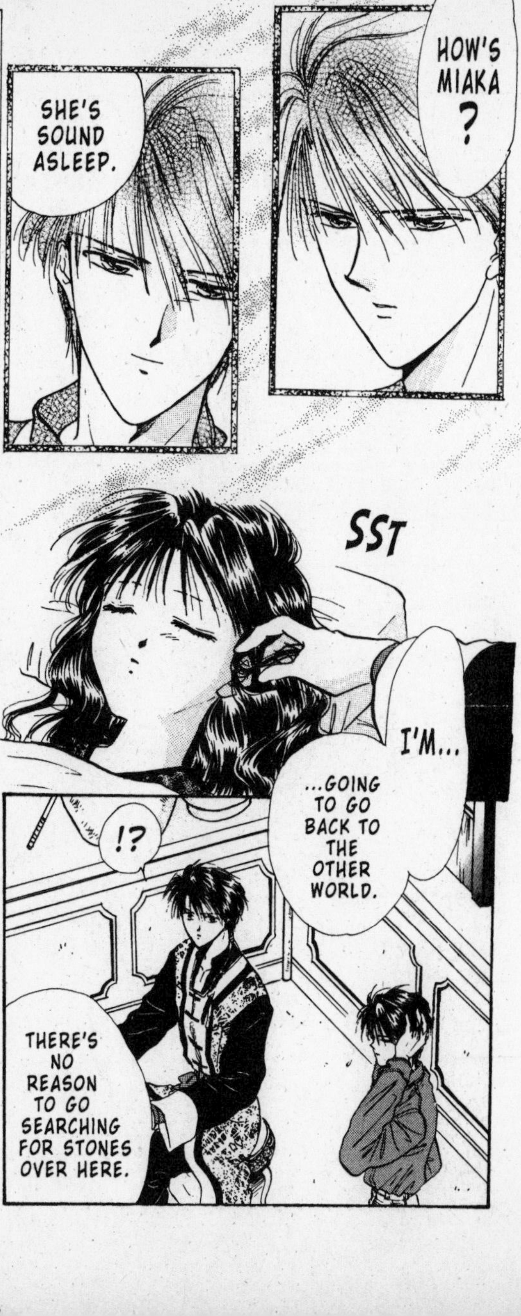
HOW'S MIAKA ?
SHE'S SOUND ASLEEP.
SST
I'M...
...GOING TO GO BACK TO THE OTHER WORLD.
!?
THERE'S NO REASON TO GO SEARCHING FOR STONES OVER HERE.

WHAT THE HECK!?

FUSHIGI YŪGI has reached its final volume!!
...And because of this, when it ended its run in the magazine, I received a whole lot of tear-stained letters. I can only pass along my thanks and my love to the fans. Speaking of endings... the anime! "Why is it only part 1!?" Well, it was only one year from beginning to end. I'm just thankful that it had a chance to end well. It impressed me in many ways, but as the creator, I have to say that I sure learned from it!
I met so many wonderful professional people, and it was a year that really bore fruit for me!
They had episodes in the anime that I never got the chance to draw (stuff with Keisuke and Tetsuya, and with Tatara and Suzuno...), and they were able to do scenes that surpassed my imagination! They even said, "Can we do it this way?" and asked my opinion on scenes! I was so happy! Before production started, everyone around me was warning me, "Don't get your hopes up too high!" When I think of that now, I can only wonder, "What was I so worked up about?" ☺ But everybody on the staff should get all the credit! The producers (all of them), the directors, the voice actors... everybody talked it over and tried really hard to wrestle with the concepts and come up with the best way to bring them to the screen. I was inspired to do that more myself! ☺ The colors were so beautiful! They struggled over Chichiri's hair and the backgrounds... I, as creator, heard many different opinions from the fans, but on the whole, I'd say that the production was really great! From the bottom of my heart, I think everyone on the staff was just wonderful! Although I'm not quite sure exactly what some of them do... but I really would like to thank the entire staff, one by one, for their contribution. Thank you so much, everyone! It's kind of strange, but when I watched the very final episode, I felt such peace of mind. (I felt like begging to be the anime director's disciple.) It made me question whether I was actually the creator behind this anime!! I was so amazed at the results! I'm so happy with it! Really! Rent it if you have to, but see it! *There are OAVs too! The people of Studio Pierrot took the scenes I had in my heart and animated them! I have absolutely no regrets!*

And that's good, right?

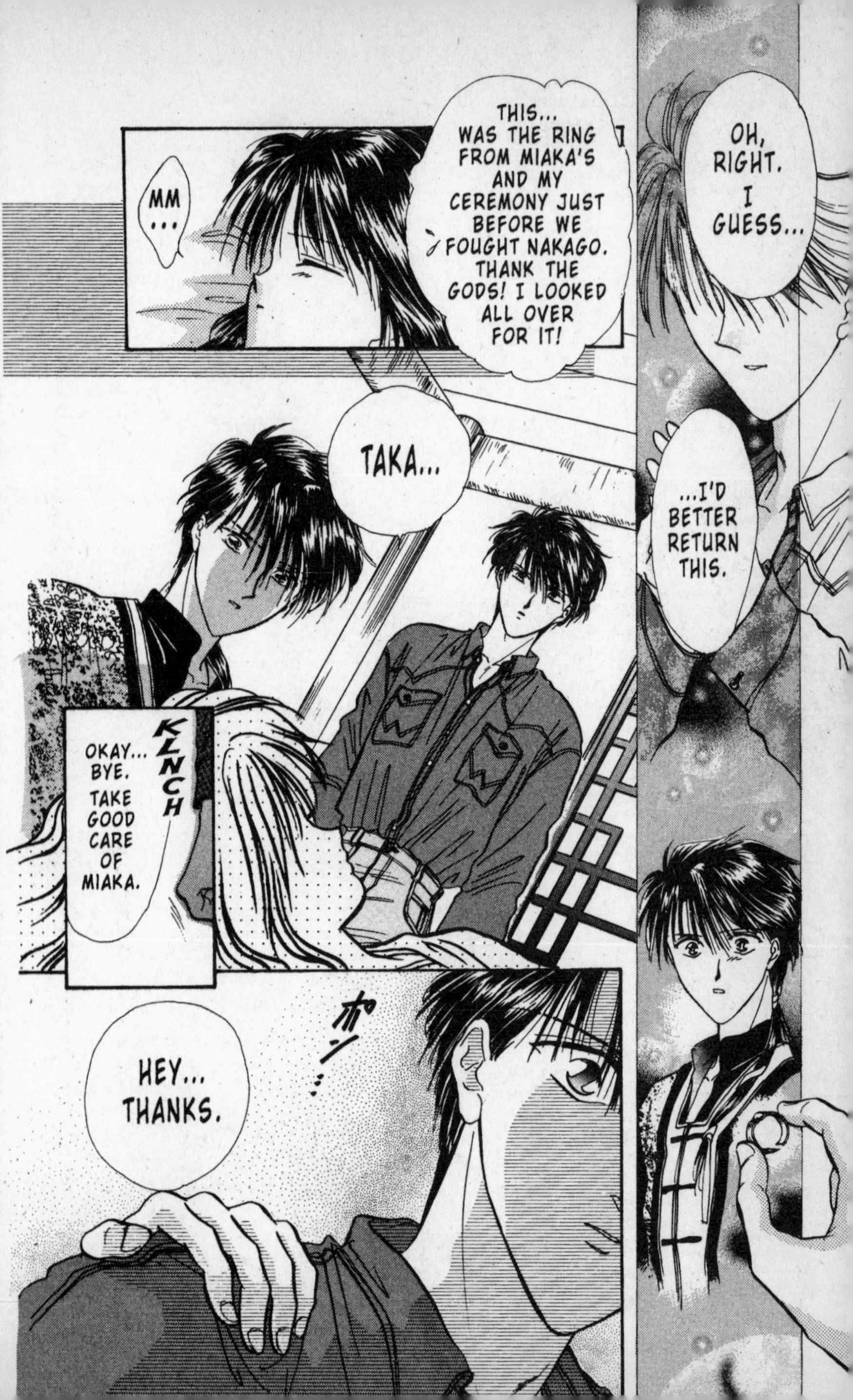
OH, RIGHT. I GUESS...
...I'D BETTER RETURN THIS.
THIS... WAS THE RING FROM MIAKA'S AND MY CEREMONY JUST BEFORE WE FOUGHT NAKAGO. THANK THE GODS! I LOOKED ALL OVER FOR IT!
MM...
TAKA...
KLNCH
OKAY... BYE. TAKE GOOD CARE OF MIAKA.
ポン…
HEY... THANKS.

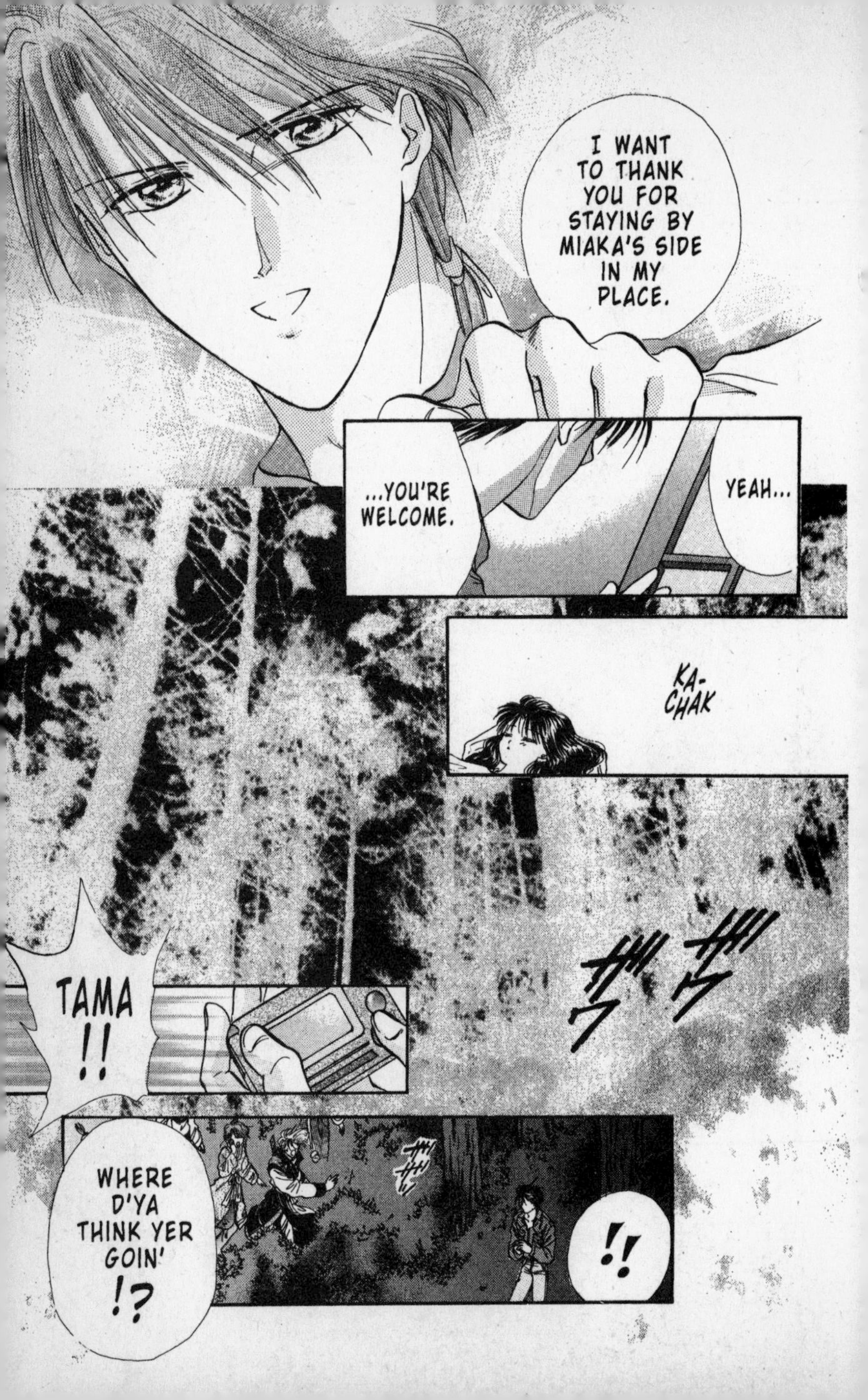
I WANT TO THANK YOU FOR STAYING BY MIAKA'S SIDE IN MY PLACE.
YEAH...
...YOU'RE WELCOME.
KA-CHAK
TAMA!!
!!
WHERE D'YA THINK YER GOIN'!?

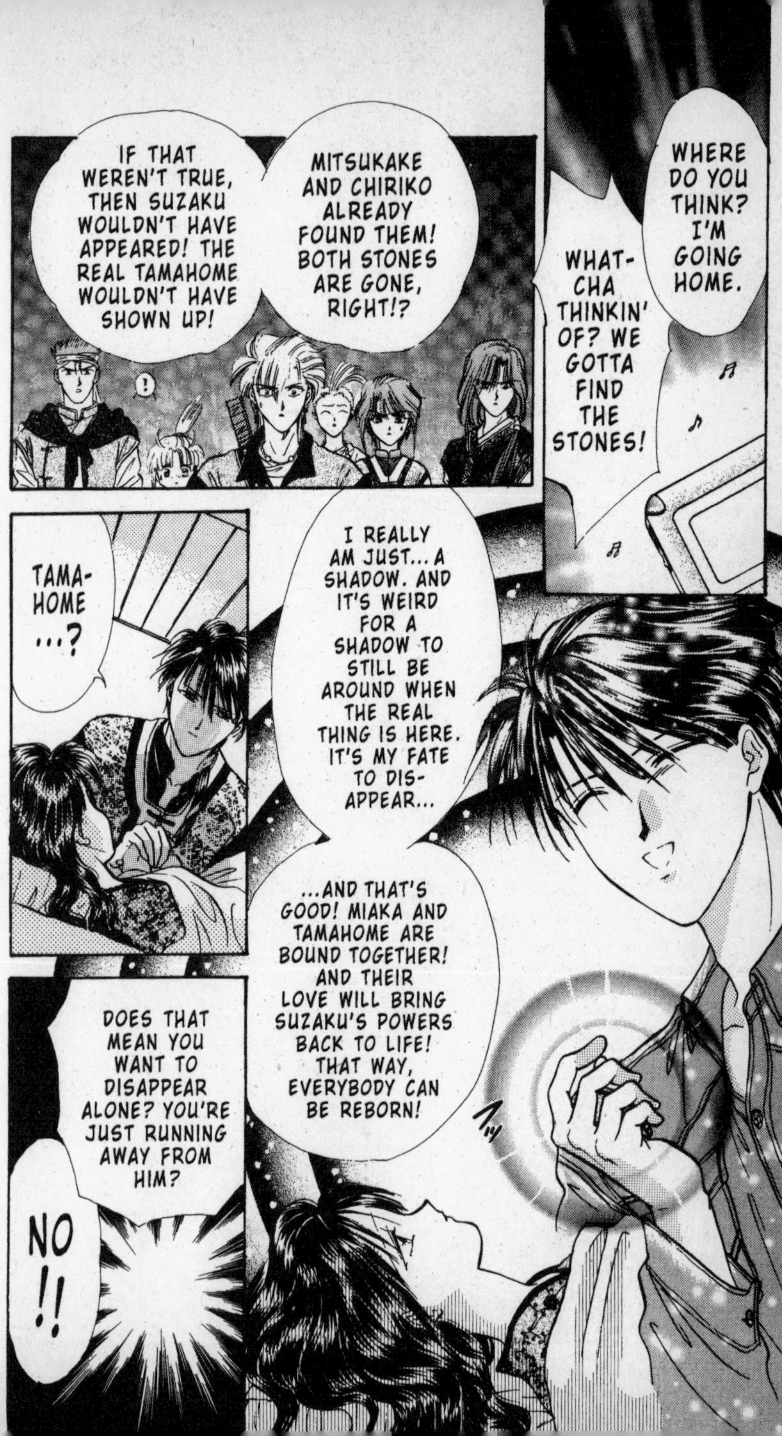
WHATCHA THINKIN' OF? WE GOTTA FIND THE STONES!
WHERE DO YOU THINK? I'M GOING HOME.
MITSUKAKE AND CHIRIKO ALREADY FOUND THEM! BOTH STONES ARE GONE, RIGHT!?
IF THAT WEREN'T TRUE, THEN SUZAKU WOULDN'T HAVE APPEARED! THE REAL TAMAHOME WOULDN'T HAVE SHOWN UP!
!
I REALLY AM JUST... A SHADOW. AND IT'S WEIRD FOR A SHADOW TO STILL BE AROUND WHEN THE REAL THING IS HERE. IT'S MY FATE TO DISAPPEAR...
...AND THAT'S GOOD! MIAKA AND TAMAHOME ARE BOUND TOGETHER! AND THEIR LOVE WILL BRING SUZAKU'S POWERS BACK TO LIFE! THAT WAY, EVERYBODY CAN BE REBORN!
ハッ
TAMAHOME...?
DOES THAT MEAN YOU WANT TO DISAPPEAR ALONE? YOU'RE JUST RUNNING AWAY FROM HIM?
NO!!

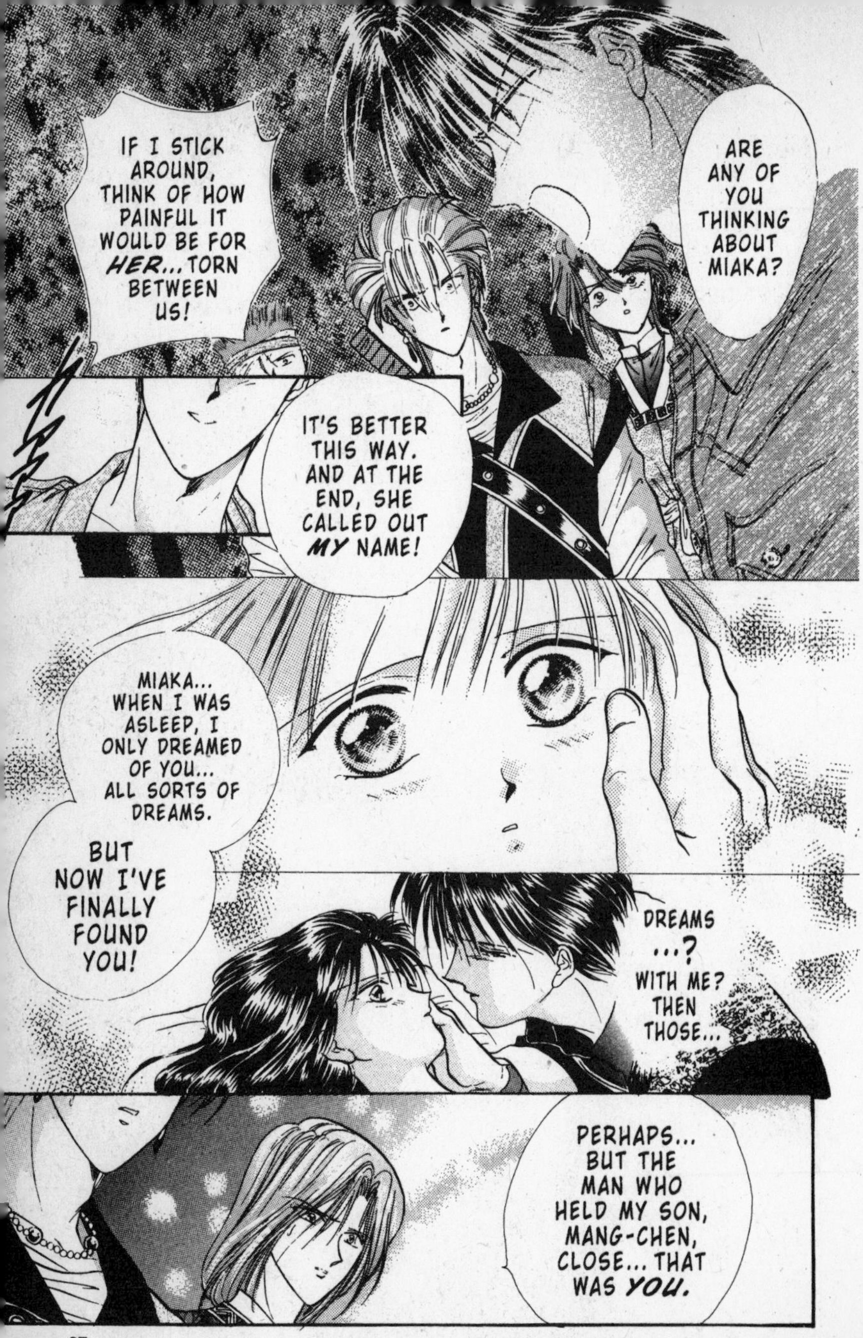
ARE ANY OF YOU THINKING ABOUT MIAKA?
IF I STICK AROUND, THINK OF HOW PAINFUL IT WOULD BE FOR *HER*... TORN BETWEEN US!
IT'S BETTER THIS WAY. AND AT THE END, SHE CALLED OUT *MY* NAME!
MIAKA... WHEN I WAS ASLEEP, I ONLY DREAMED OF YOU... ALL SORTS OF DREAMS.
BUT NOW I'VE FINALLY FOUND YOU!
DREAMS ...? WITH ME? THEN THOSE...
PERHAPS... BUT THE MAN WHO HELD MY SON, MANG-CHEN, CLOSE... THAT WAS *YOU*.

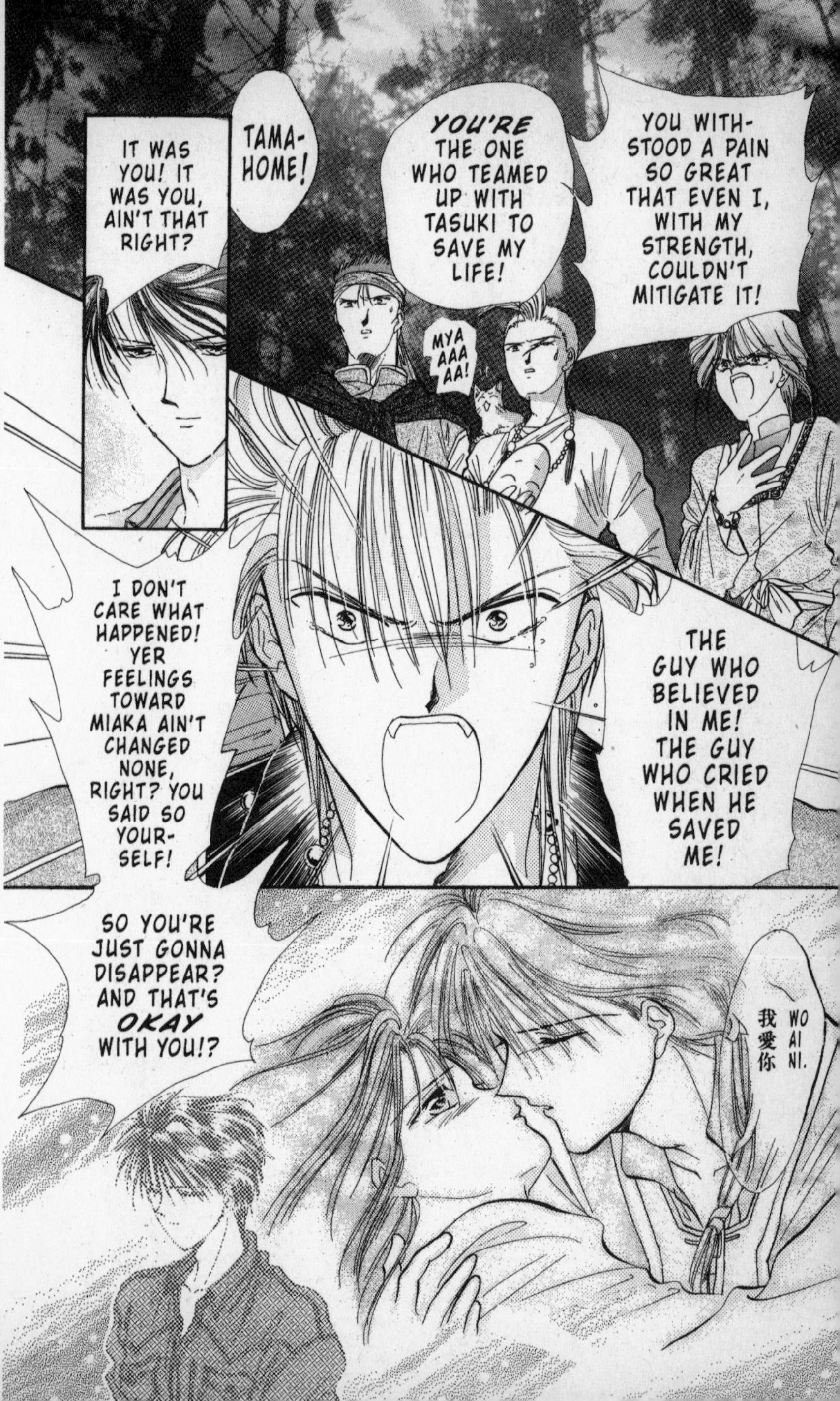
YOU WITH-STOOD A PAIN SO GREAT THAT EVEN I, WITH MY STRENGTH, COULDN'T MITIGATE IT!
YOU'RE THE ONE WHO TEAMED UP WITH TASUKI TO SAVE MY LIFE!
TAMA-HOME!
MYA AAA AA!
IT WAS YOU! IT WAS YOU, AIN'T THAT RIGHT?
THE GUY WHO BELIEVED IN ME! THE GUY WHO CRIED WHEN HE SAVED ME!
I DON'T CARE WHAT HAPPENED! YER FEELINGS TOWARD MIAKA AIN'T CHANGED NONE, RIGHT? YOU SAID SO YOUR-SELF!
WO AI NI. 我愛你
SO YOU'RE JUST GONNA DISAPPEAR? AND THAT'S *OKAY* WITH YOU!?

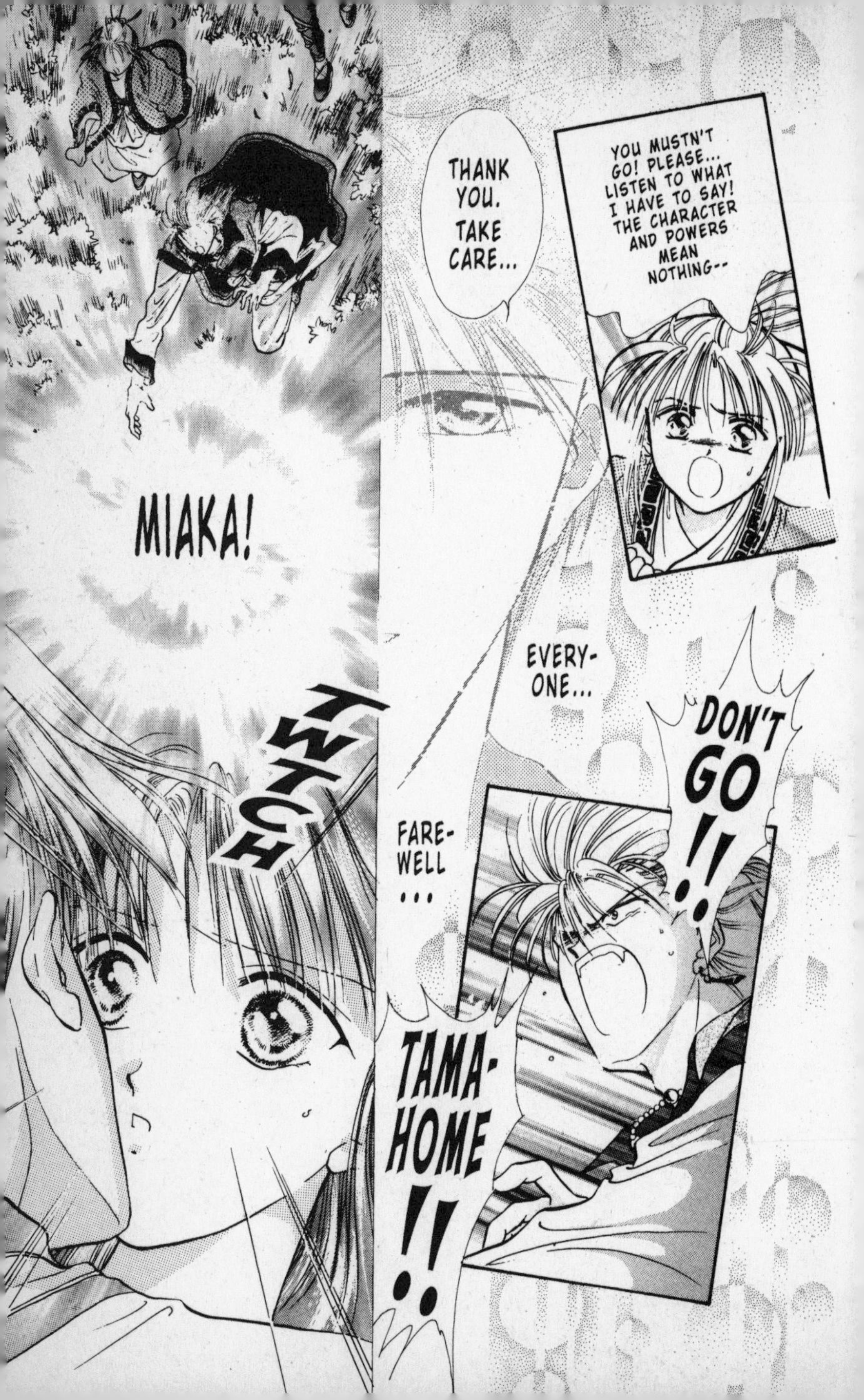
YOU MUSTN'T GO! PLEASE... LISTEN TO WHAT I HAVE TO SAY! THE CHARACTER AND POWERS MEAN NOTHING--
THANK YOU. TAKE CARE...
EVERY-ONE...
DON'T GO!!
FARE-WELL...
TAMA-HOME!!
MIAKA!
TWITCH

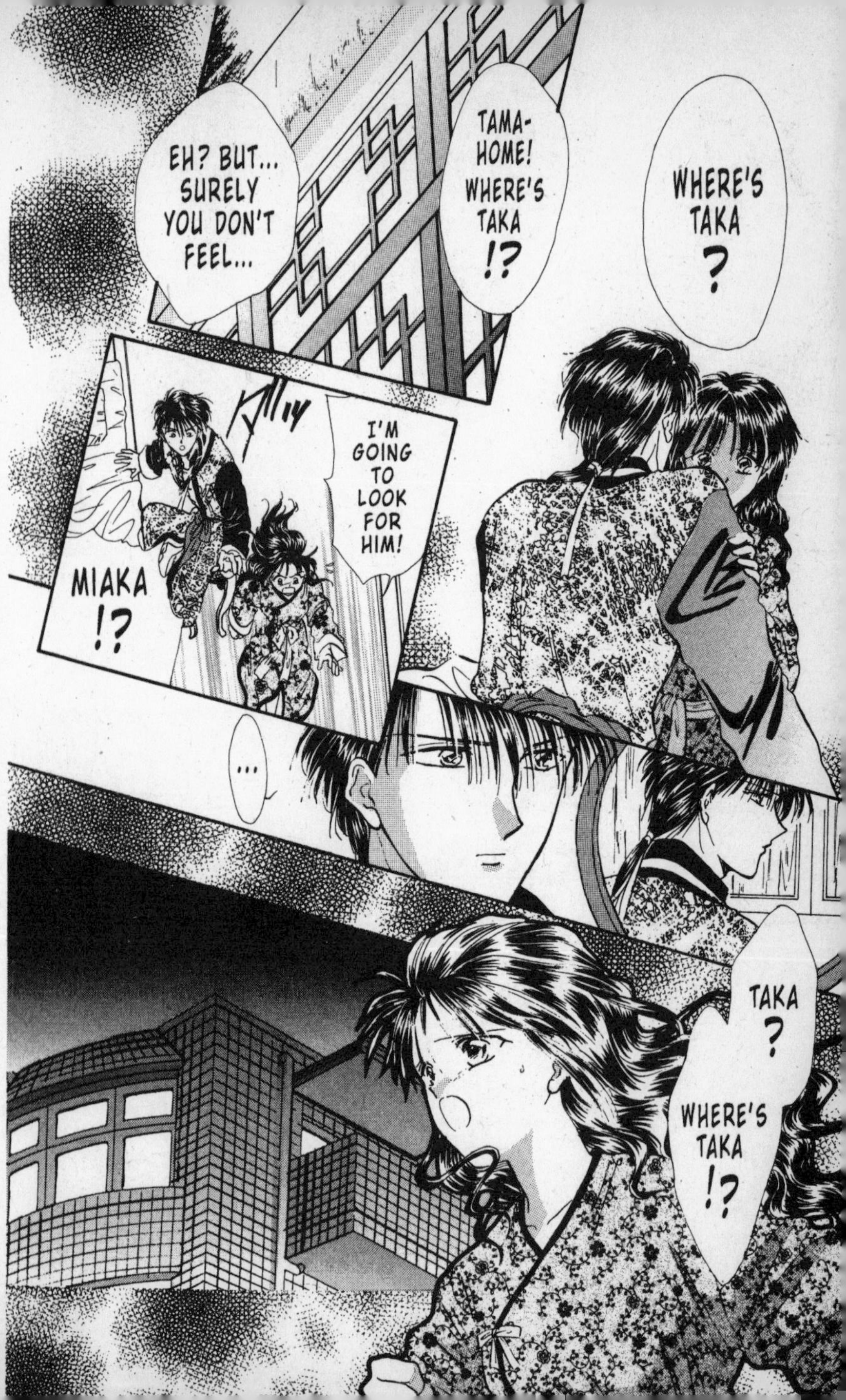
WHERE'S TAKA?
TAMA-HOME! WHERE'S TAKA!?
EH? BUT... SURELY YOU DON'T FEEL...
I'M GOING TO LOOK FOR HIM!
MIAKA!?
...
TAKA?
WHERE'S TAKA!?

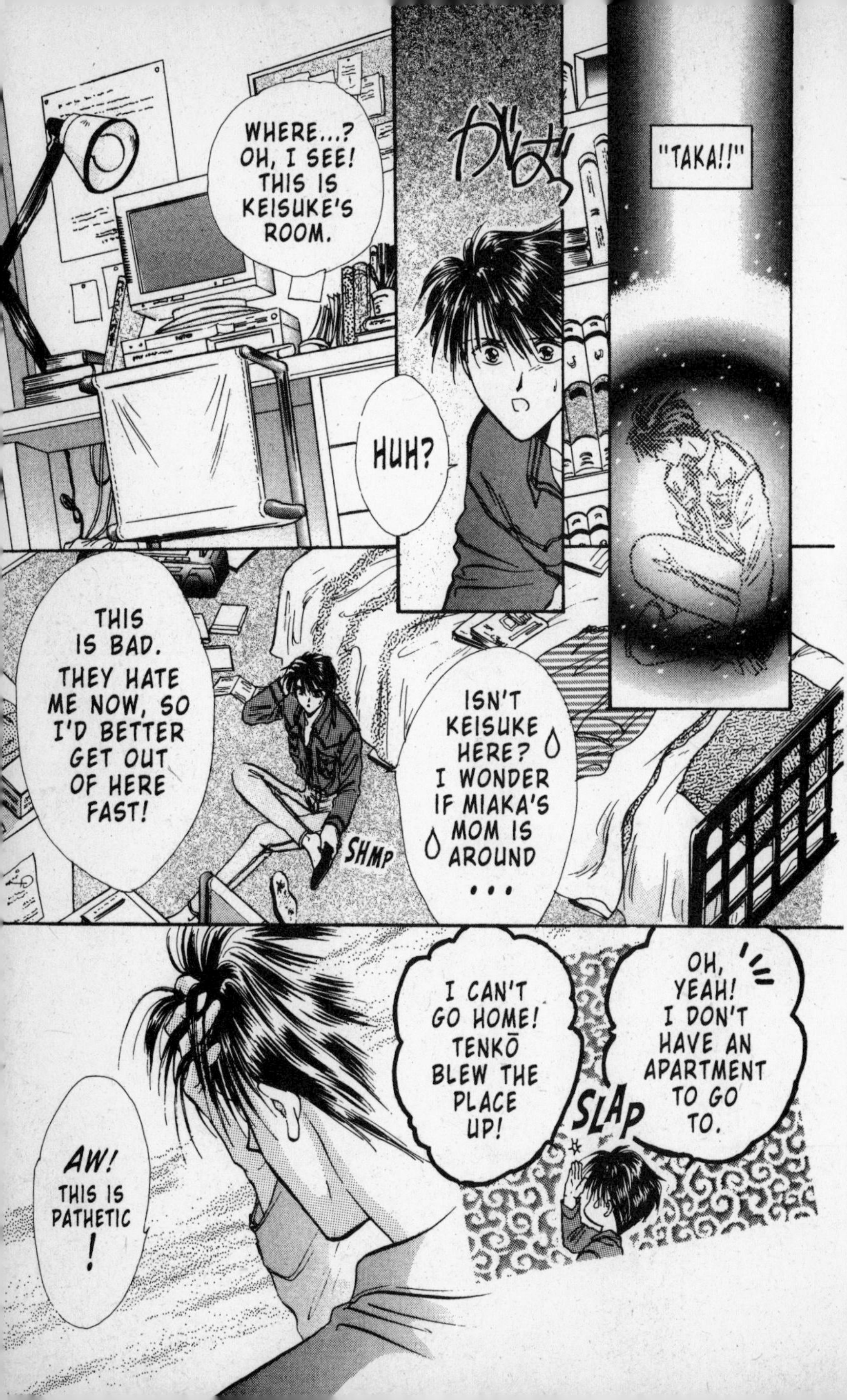
"TAKA!!"
がばっ
HUH?
WHERE...? OH, I SEE! THIS IS KEISUKE'S ROOM.
ISN'T KEISUKE HERE? I WONDER IF MIAKA'S MOM IS AROUND...
SHMP
THIS IS BAD. THEY HATE ME NOW, SO I'D BETTER GET OUT OF HERE FAST!
OH, YEAH! I DON'T HAVE AN APARTMENT TO GO TO.
SLAP
I CAN'T GO HOME! TENKŌ BLEW THE PLACE UP!
AW! THIS IS PATHETIC!

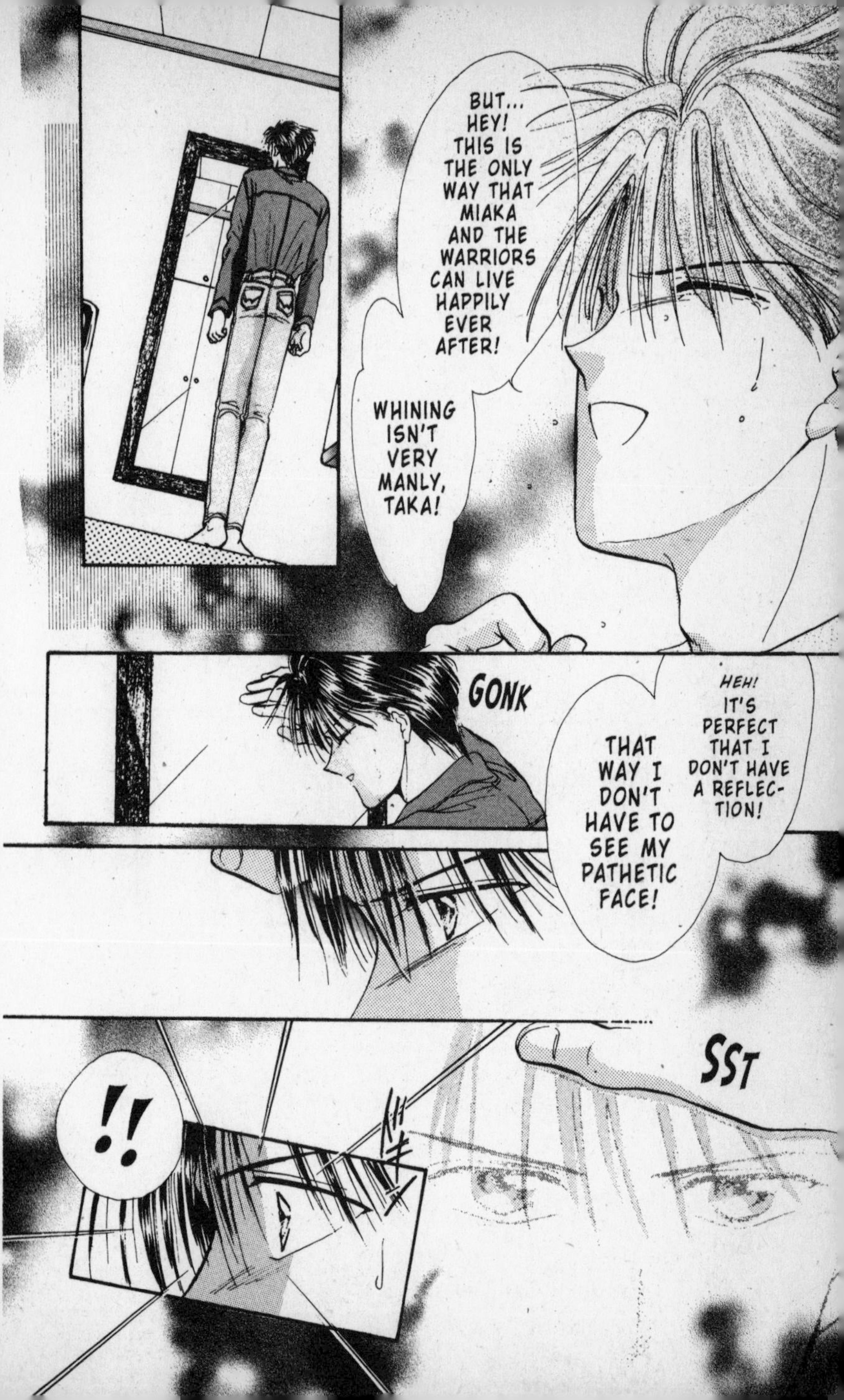
BUT... HEY! THIS IS THE ONLY WAY THAT MIAKA AND THE WARRIORS CAN LIVE HAPPILY EVER AFTER!
WHINING ISN'T VERY MANLY, TAKA!
GONK
HEH! IT'S PERFECT THAT I DON'T HAVE A REFLEC-TION!
THAT WAY I DON'T HAVE TO SEE MY PATHETIC FACE!
SST
!!

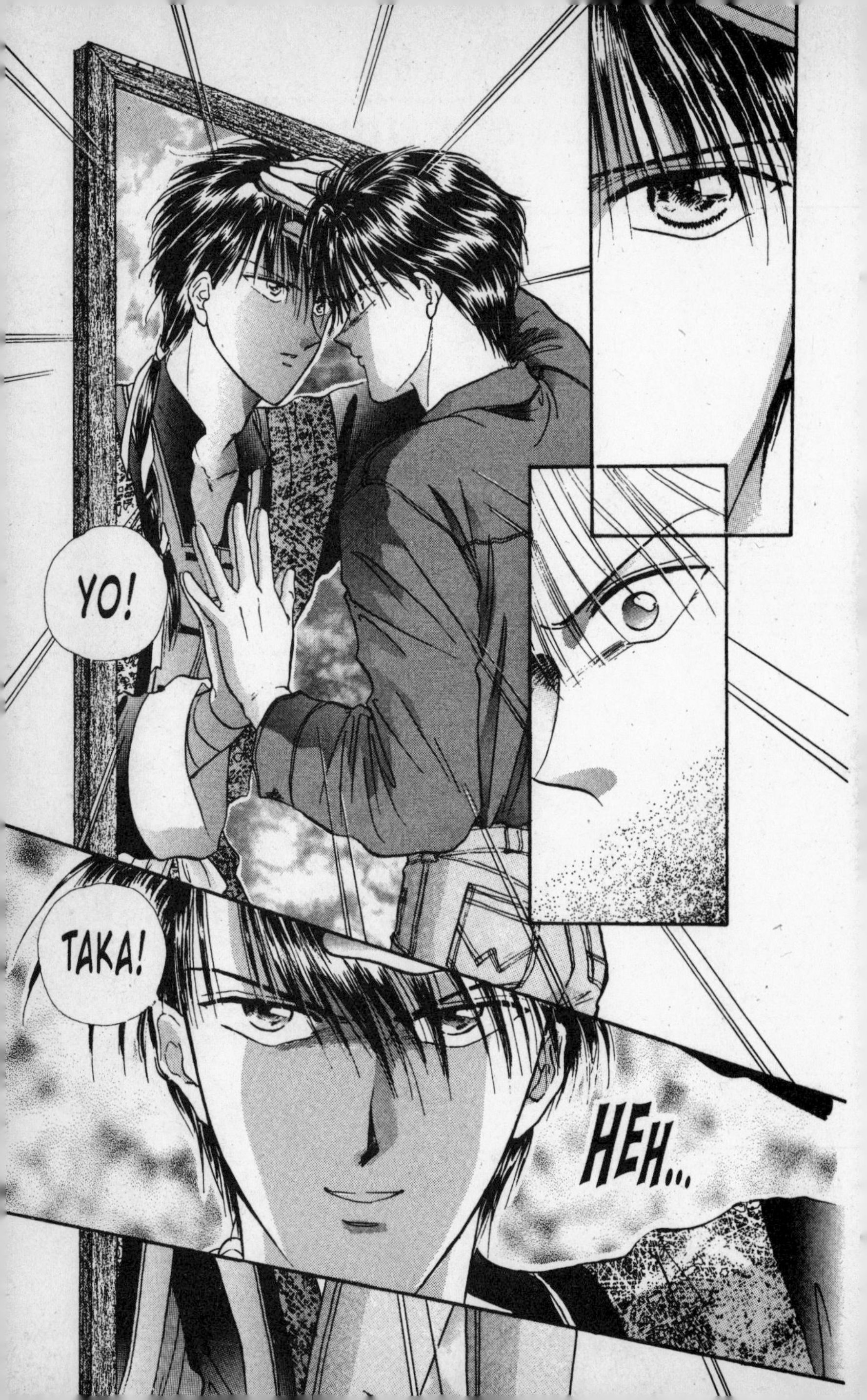
YO!
TAKA!
HEH...

CHAPTER ONE HUNDRED TWO
SOULS SEEKING THEIR MATES

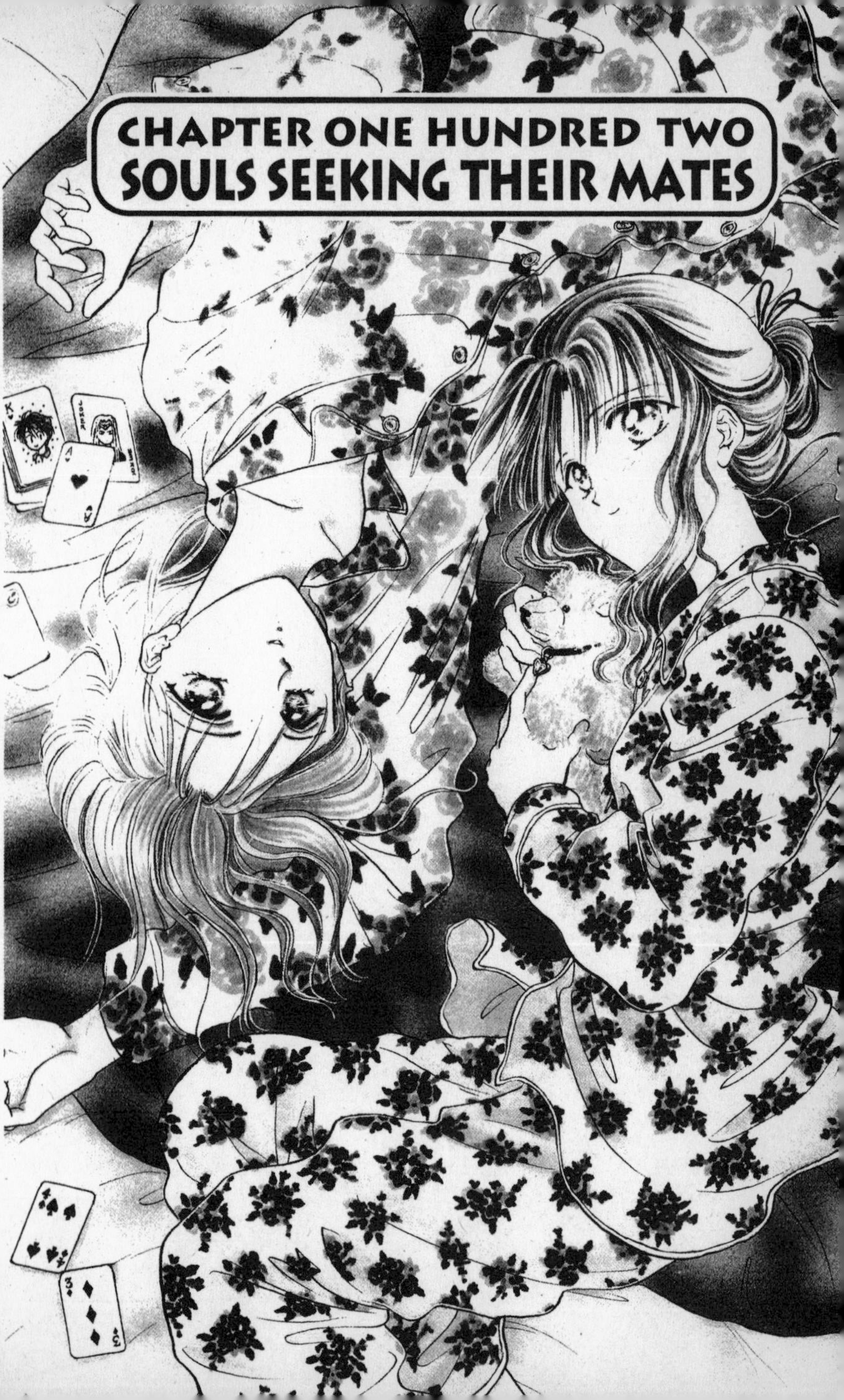

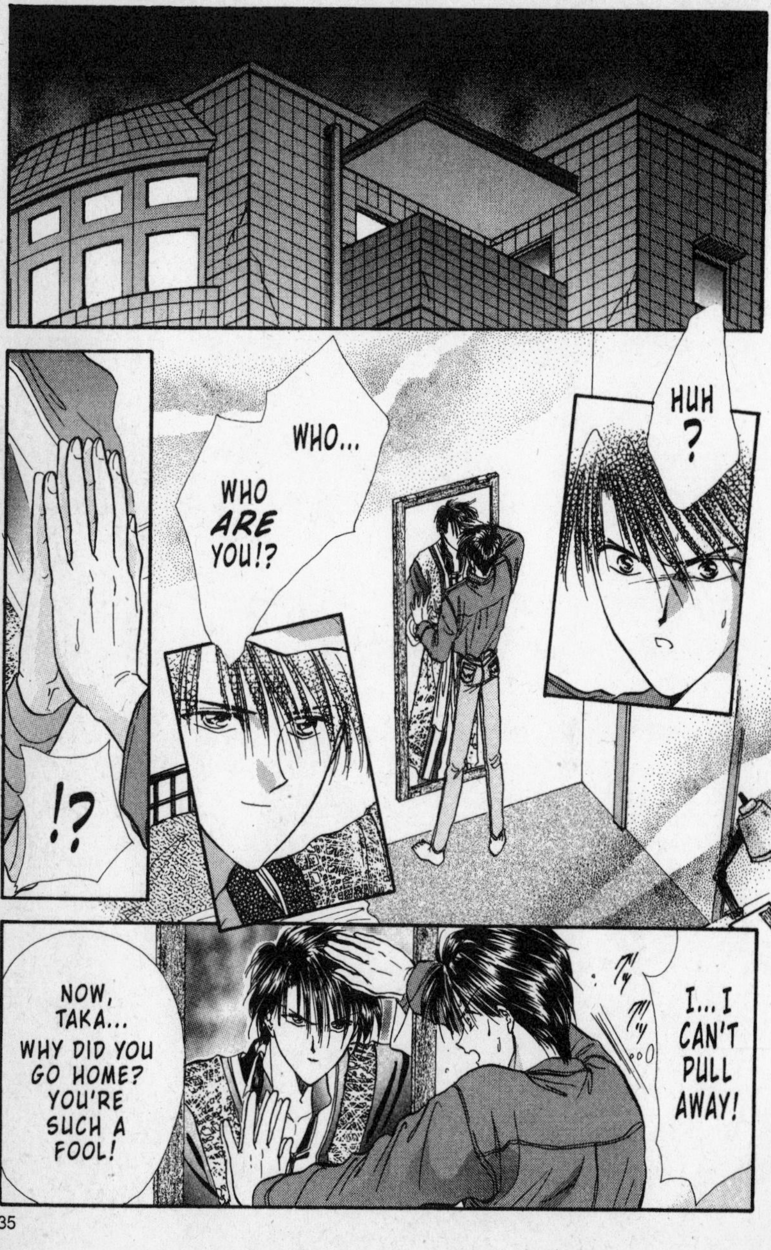
HUH ?
WHO...
WHO ARE YOU!?
!?
I... I CAN'T PULL AWAY!
NOW, TAKA... WHY DID YOU GO HOME? YOU'RE SUCH A FOOL!

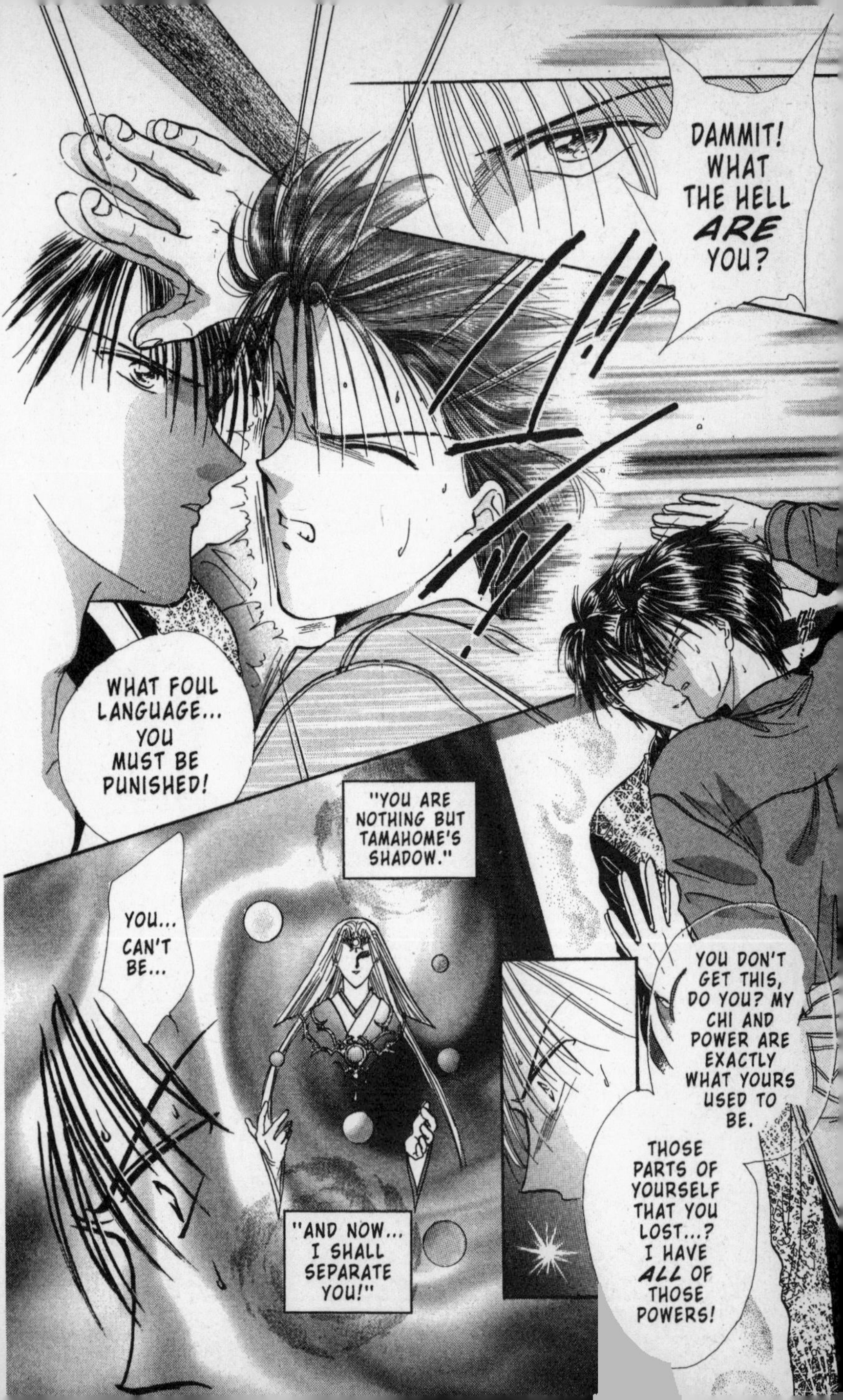
DAMMIT! WHAT THE HELL *ARE* YOU?
WHAT FOUL LANGUAGE... YOU MUST BE PUNISHED!
YOU DON'T GET THIS, DO YOU? MY CHI AND POWER ARE EXACTLY WHAT YOURS USED TO BE.
THOSE PARTS OF YOURSELF THAT YOU LOST...? I HAVE *ALL* OF THOSE POWERS!
"YOU ARE NOTHING BUT TAMAHOME'S SHADOW."
YOU... CAN'T BE...
"AND NOW... I SHALL SEPARATE YOU!"

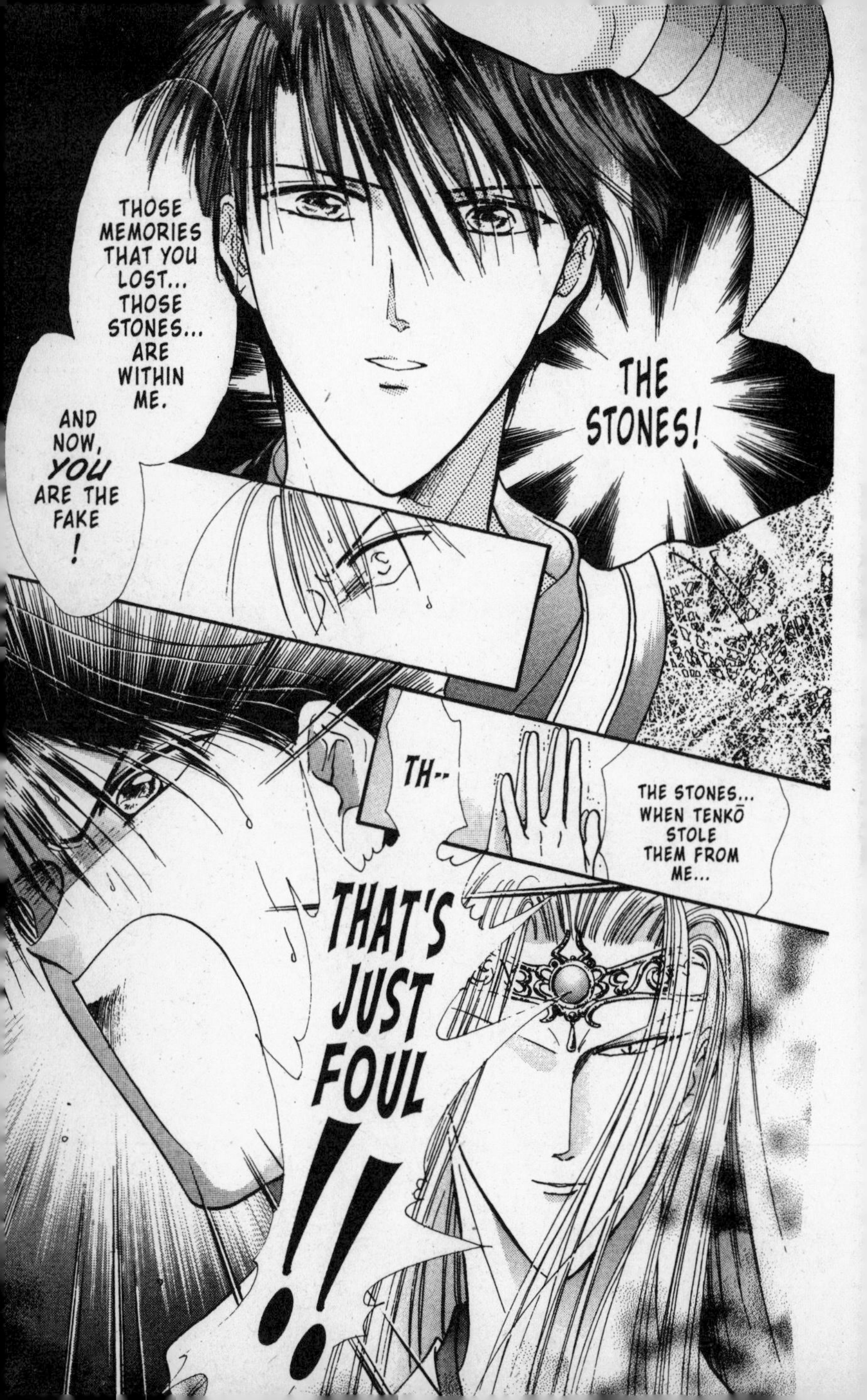
THOSE MEMORIES THAT YOU LOST... THOSE STONES... ARE WITHIN ME.
THE STONES!
AND NOW, *YOU* ARE THE FAKE!
TH--
THE STONES... WHEN TENKŌ STOLE THEM FROM ME...
THAT'S JUST FOUL!!

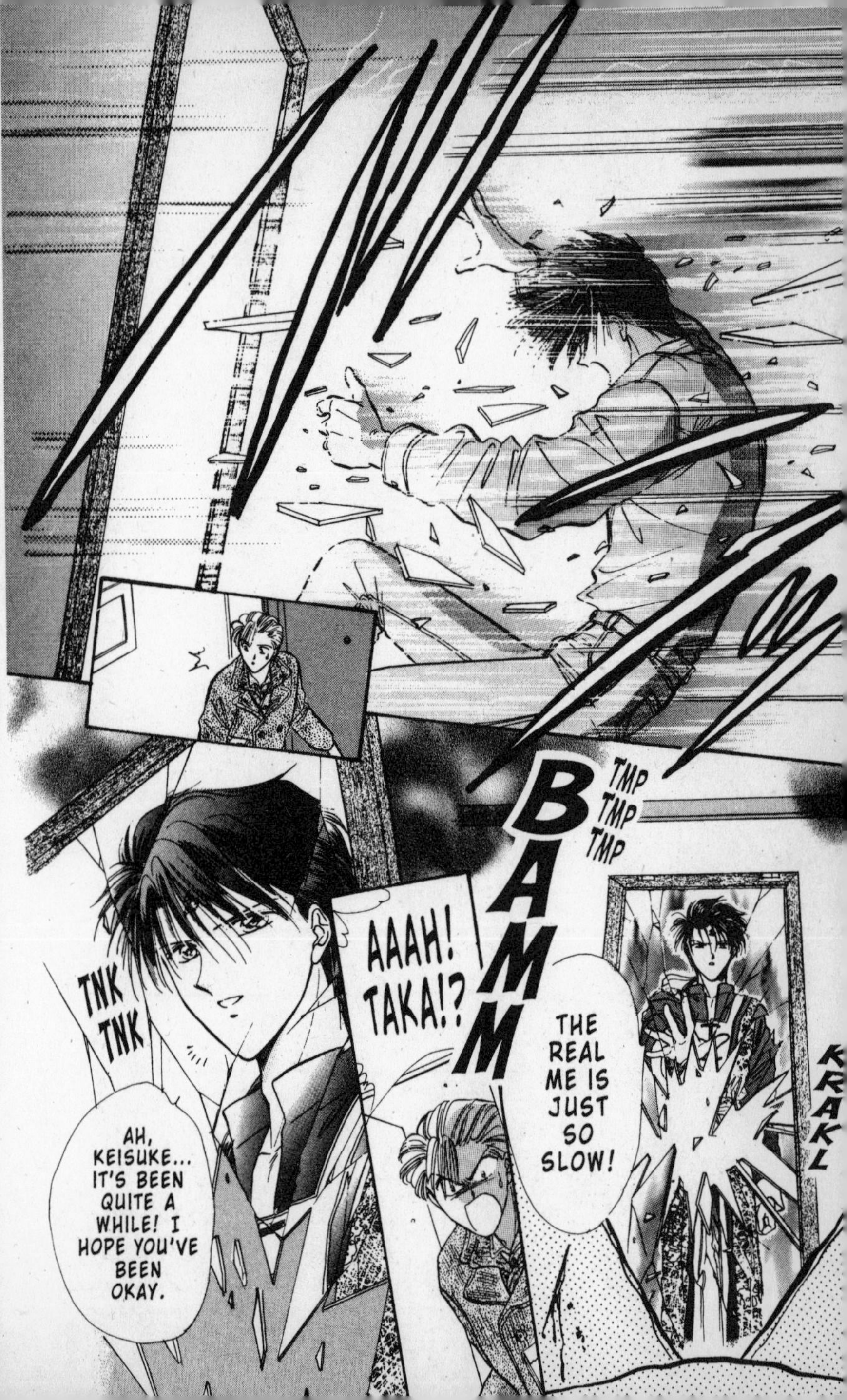
TMP TMP TMP
BAMM
KRAKL
THE REAL ME IS JUST SO SLOW!
AAAH! TAKA!?
TNK TNK
AH, KEISUKE... IT'S BEEN QUITE A WHILE! I HOPE YOU'VE BEEN OKAY.

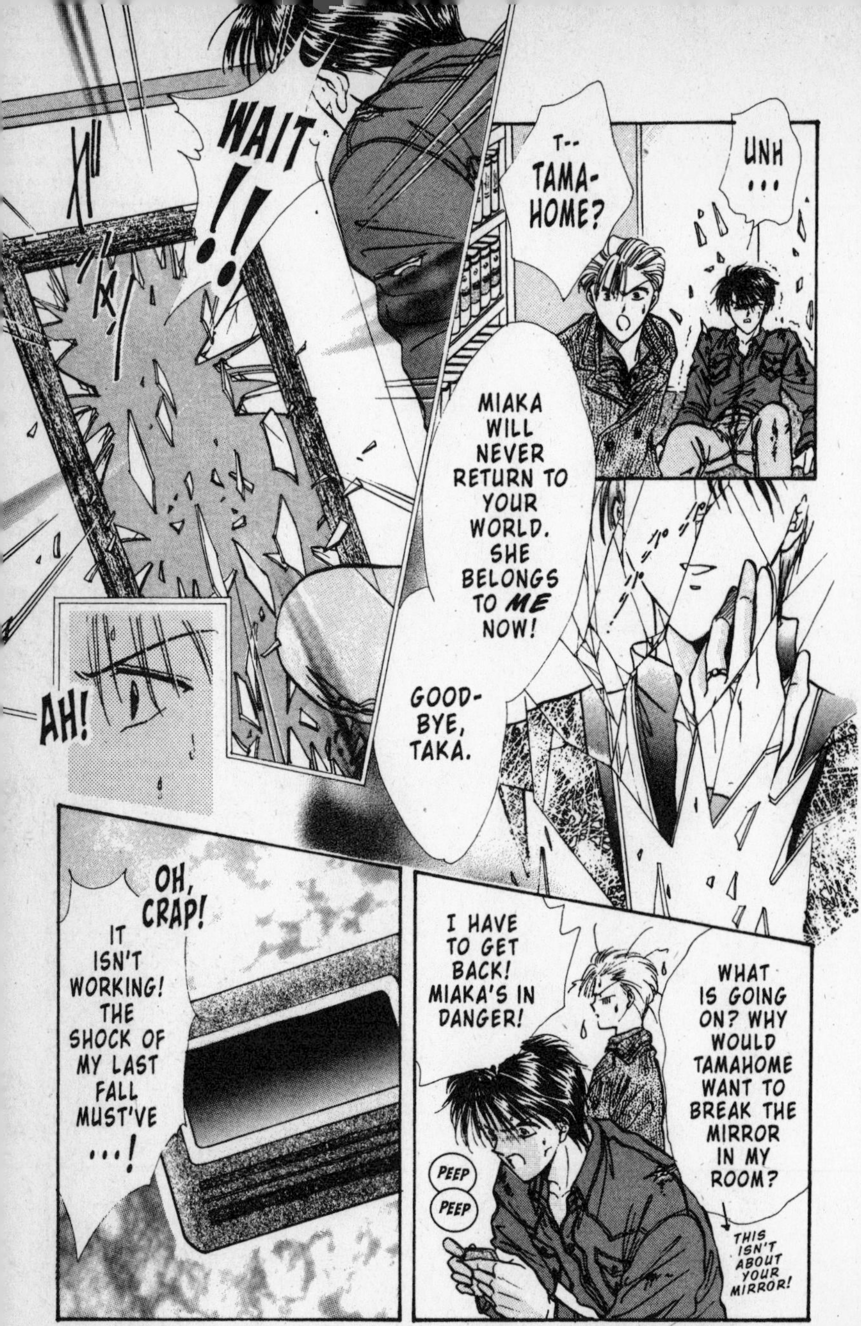

UNH ...
T-- TAMA-HOME?
MIAKA WILL NEVER RETURN TO YOUR WORLD. SHE BELONGS TO *ME* NOW!
GOOD-BYE, TAKA.
WAIT!!
AH!
WHAT IS GOING ON? WHY WOULD TAMAHOME WANT TO BREAK THE MIRROR IN MY ROOM?
I HAVE TO GET BACK! MIAKA'S IN DANGER!
PEEP
PEEP
THIS ISN'T ABOUT YOUR MIRROR!
OH, CRAP!
IT ISN'T WORKING! THE SHOCK OF MY LAST FALL MUST'VE ...!

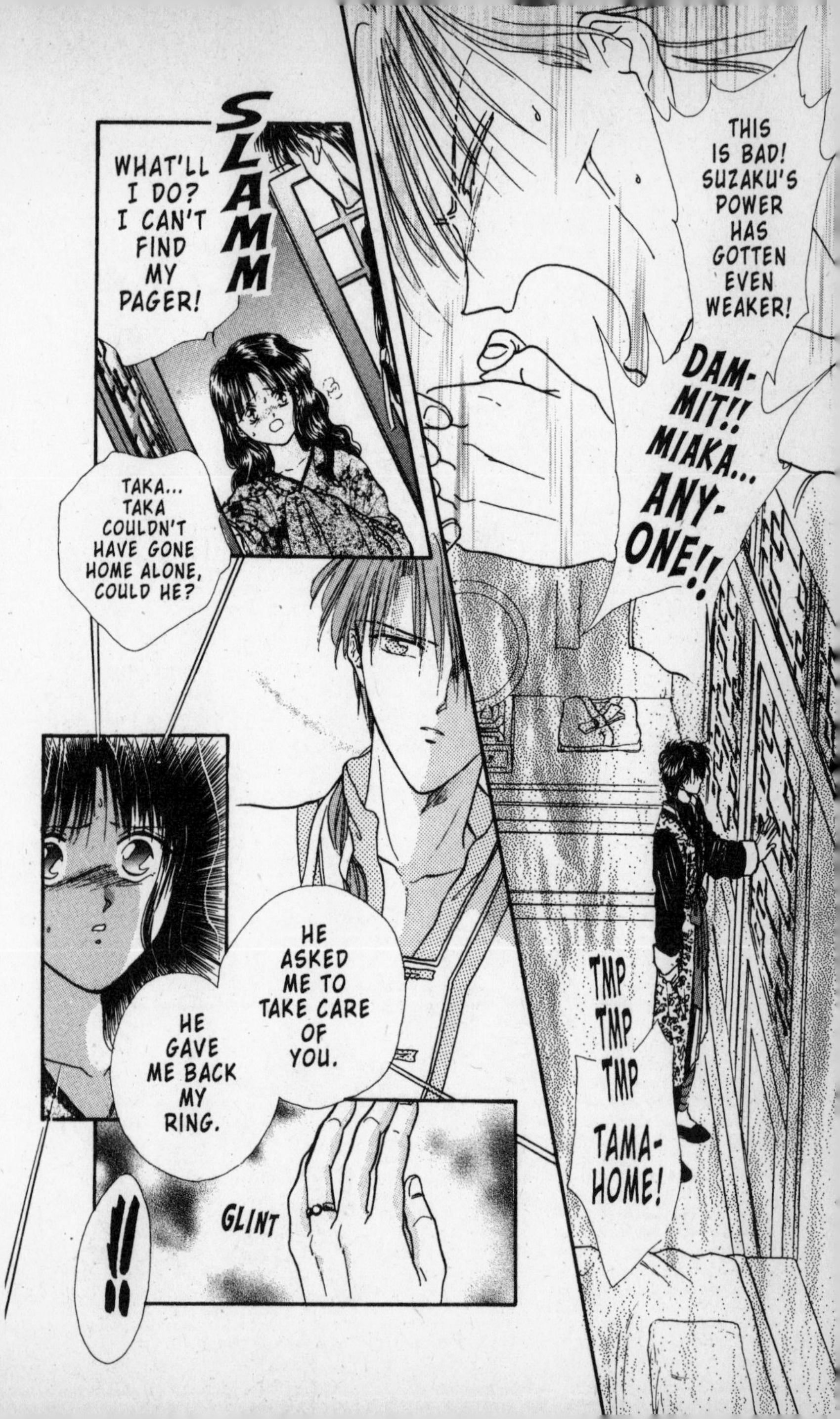
THIS IS BAD! SUZAKU'S POWER HAS GOTTEN EVEN WEAKER!
DAM-MIT!! MIAKA... ANY-ONE!!
TMP TMP TMP
TAMA-HOME!
SLAMM
WHAT'LL I DO? I CAN'T FIND MY PAGER!
TAKA... TAKA COULDN'T HAVE GONE HOME ALONE, COULD HE?
HE ASKED ME TO TAKE CARE OF YOU.
HE GAVE ME BACK MY RING.
GLINT
!!

THE *FUSHIGI YŪGI* TRENDS AND COUNTERMEASURES CORNER (?)

※ ONLY FOR THOSE WHO HAVE READ ALL THE WAY TO THE END!!

I really like Taka. (To be blunt.) At first, the Tamahome fans would say things like, "There's something not the same about him," or, "It's like he's a completely different person," etc., but I like him! I know I've talked a lot about Nakago and Tasuki, and said a lot of other things, but now that the end is here, I consider Taka to be one of the most important characters I've ever created. Love^2!!

(There are spoilers ahead, folks!)

Tamahome and Taka are the same, but different. Why? It's because Taka changed between his existence as Tamahome and becoming Taka. Sure, the change of names and situations took care of some of it, but there was also the change of Tamahome (the boy) to Taka (the man). By the way, when Taka first appeared minus his stones (memories), the first reaction to him was that he seemed less "human" and more like a "doll" or "puppet." Some people said that he didn't have his "spirit" anymore. That's only natural--he was made by Suzaku. He had no memories. Taka was pretty much a blank slate inside. And in some ways, for a young girl (Miaka), that was an ideal situation. He's an older guy, cute and gentle. What is a "human" anyway?

(Speaking of dolls, the most recent fans may not know about this but there was a Chichiri doll created for some UFO-Catcher-style crane machine games, and I was credited as designer! *It was made for a Shōjo Comics event.*)

Anyway, I'd like all of you to read the books and see Taka's growth. Do you see the change? No, I don't mean that his hair got longer! *No? You don't see it? Waaaaaah!*

× × ×

And so, I played Part 2 as if the main character was Miaka, but actually it was Taka! The adult will never again be the child. The most important thing wasn't gathering those stones! It was going through the experiences that will finally allow Taka to accept himself as Taka. Also, the people around him have to accept him as well. That's the kind of story this is!! On the other hand, *Fushigi Yūgi* has always been a work that built on the feelings of its readers. *Or something like that... right?*

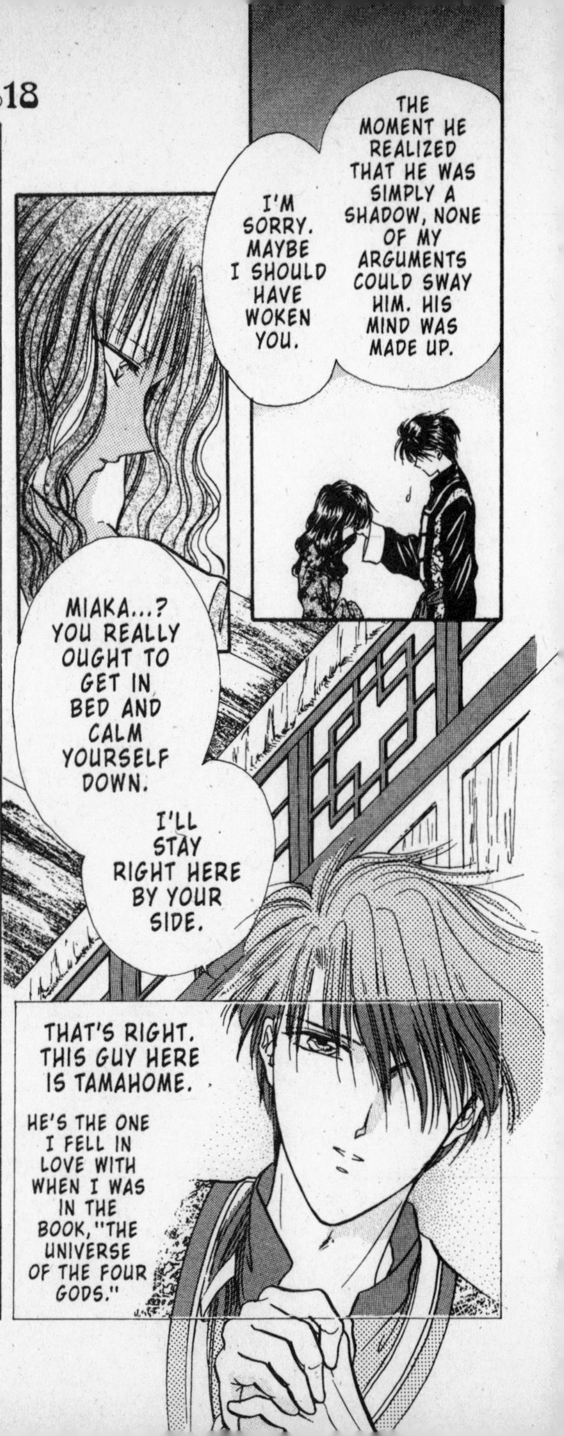
THE MOMENT HE REALIZED THAT HE WAS SIMPLY A SHADOW, NONE OF MY ARGUMENTS COULD SWAY HIM. HIS MIND WAS MADE UP.
I'M SORRY. MAYBE I SHOULD HAVE WOKEN YOU.
MIAKA...? YOU REALLY OUGHT TO GET IN BED AND CALM YOURSELF DOWN.
I'LL STAY RIGHT HERE BY YOUR SIDE.
THAT'S RIGHT. THIS GUY HERE IS TAMAHOME.
HE'S THE ONE I FELL IN LOVE WITH WHEN I WAS IN THE BOOK, "THE UNIVERSE OF THE FOUR GODS."

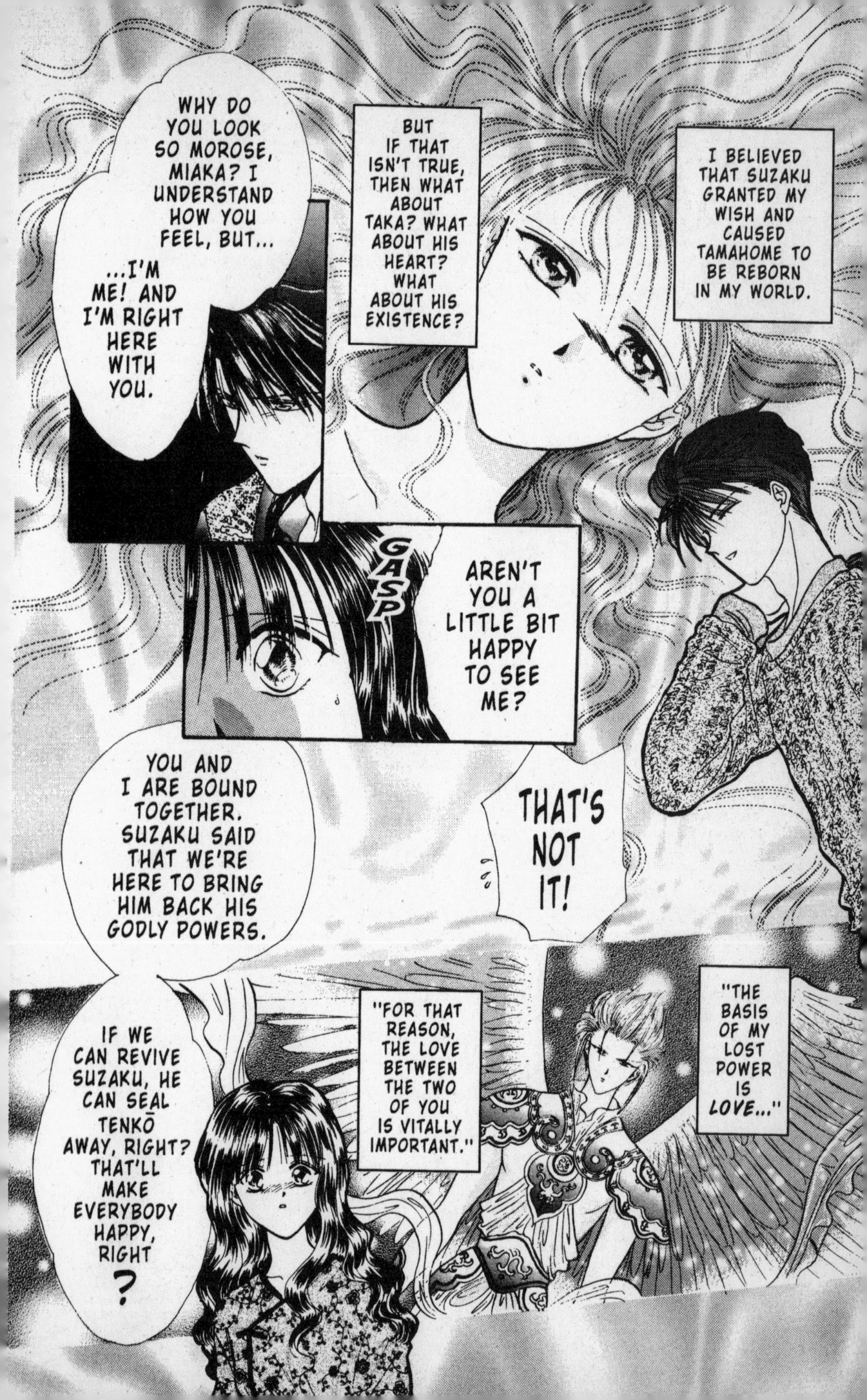
I BELIEVED THAT SUZAKU GRANTED MY WISH AND CAUSED TAMAHOME TO BE REBORN IN MY WORLD.
BUT IF THAT ISN'T TRUE, THEN WHAT ABOUT TAKA? WHAT ABOUT HIS HEART? WHAT ABOUT HIS EXISTENCE?
WHY DO YOU LOOK SO MOROSE, MIAKA? I UNDERSTAND HOW YOU FEEL, BUT...
...I'M ME! AND I'M RIGHT HERE WITH YOU.
AREN'T YOU A LITTLE BIT HAPPY TO SEE ME?
GASP
THAT'S NOT IT!
YOU AND I ARE BOUND TOGETHER. SUZAKU SAID THAT WE'RE HERE TO BRING HIM BACK HIS GODLY POWERS.
"THE BASIS OF MY LOST POWER IS *LOVE*..."
"FOR THAT REASON, THE LOVE BETWEEN THE TWO OF YOU IS VITALLY IMPORTANT."
IF WE CAN REVIVE SUZAKU, HE CAN SEAL TENKŌ AWAY, RIGHT? THAT'LL MAKE EVERYBODY HAPPY, RIGHT ?

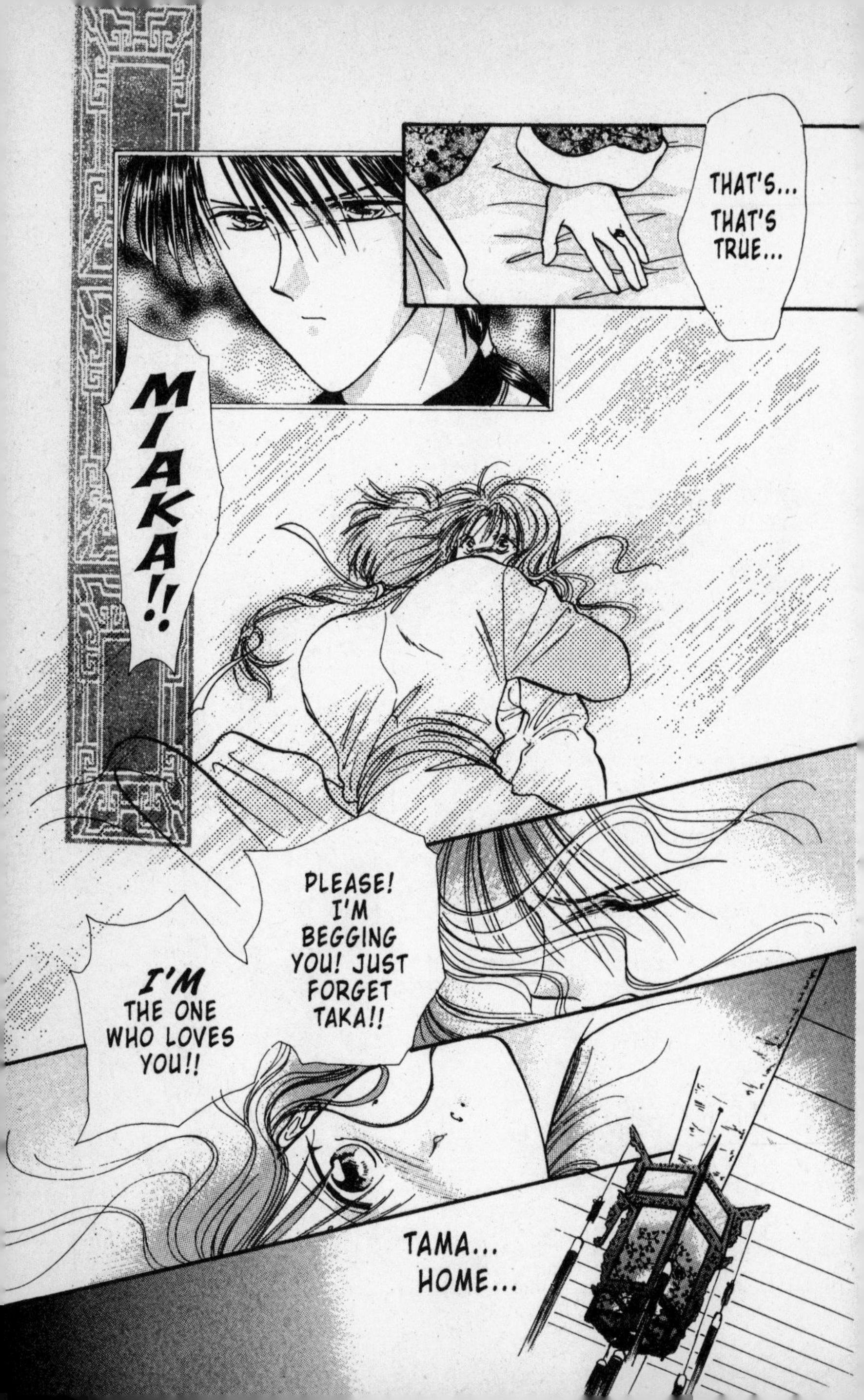
THAT'S... THAT'S TRUE...
MIAKA!!
PLEASE! I'M BEGGING YOU! JUST FORGET TAKA!!
I'M THE ONE WHO LOVES YOU!!
TAMA... HOME...

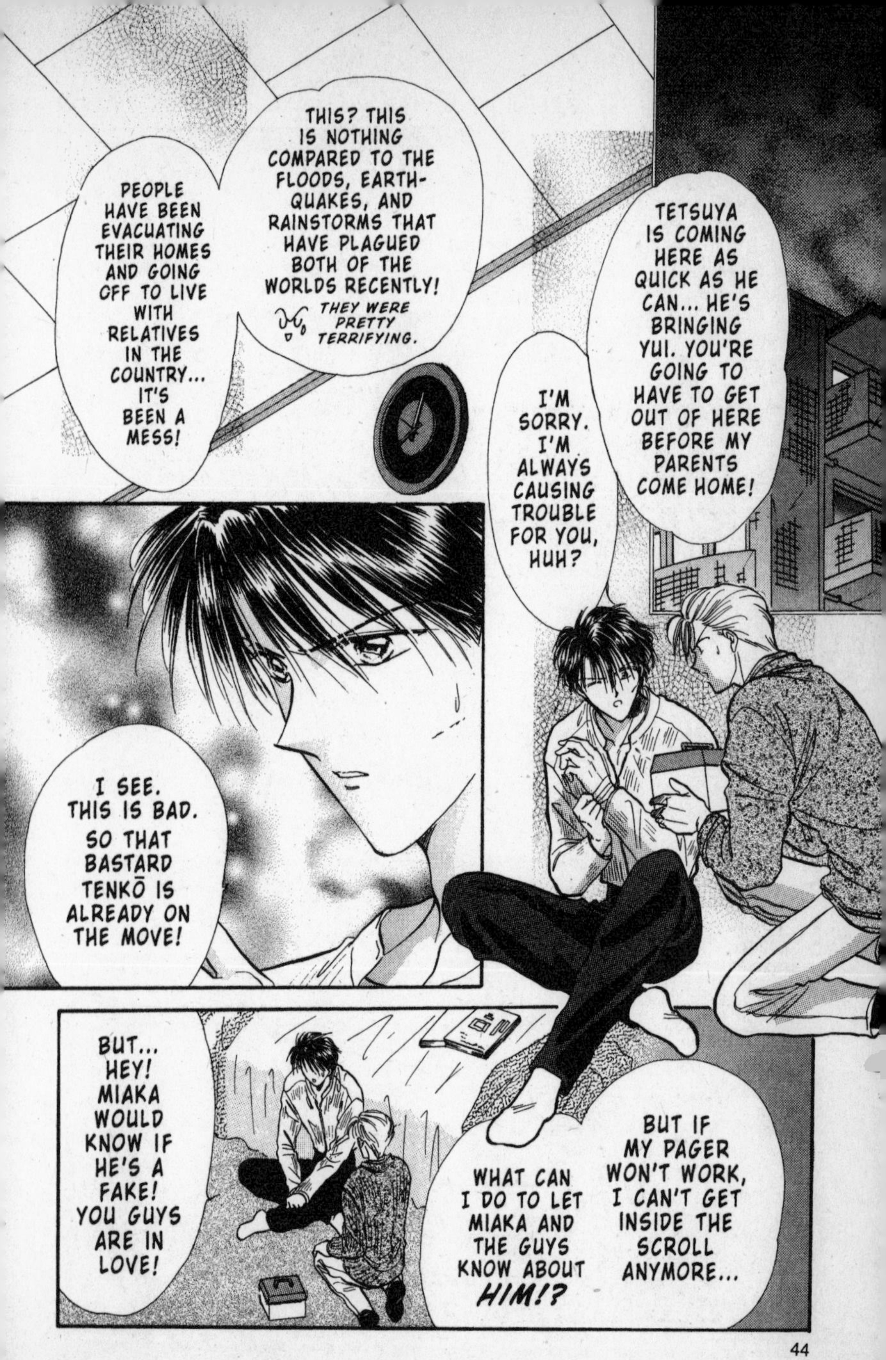
TETSUYA IS COMING HERE AS QUICK AS HE CAN... HE'S BRINGING YUI. YOU'RE GOING TO HAVE TO GET OUT OF HERE BEFORE MY PARENTS COME HOME!
I'M SORRY. I'M ALWAYS CAUSING TROUBLE FOR YOU, HUH?
THIS? THIS IS NOTHING COMPARED TO THE FLOODS, EARTH-QUAKES, AND RAINSTORMS THAT HAVE PLAGUED BOTH OF THE WORLDS RECENTLY!
THEY WERE PRETTY TERRIFYING.
PEOPLE HAVE BEEN EVACUATING THEIR HOMES AND GOING OFF TO LIVE WITH RELATIVES IN THE COUNTRY... IT'S BEEN A MESS!
I SEE. THIS IS BAD. SO THAT BASTARD TENKŌ IS ALREADY ON THE MOVE!
BUT IF MY PAGER WON'T WORK, I CAN'T GET INSIDE THE SCROLL ANYMORE...
WHAT CAN I DO TO LET MIAKA AND THE GUYS KNOW ABOUT *HIM!?*
BUT... HEY! MIAKA WOULD KNOW IF HE'S A FAKE! YOU GUYS ARE IN LOVE!

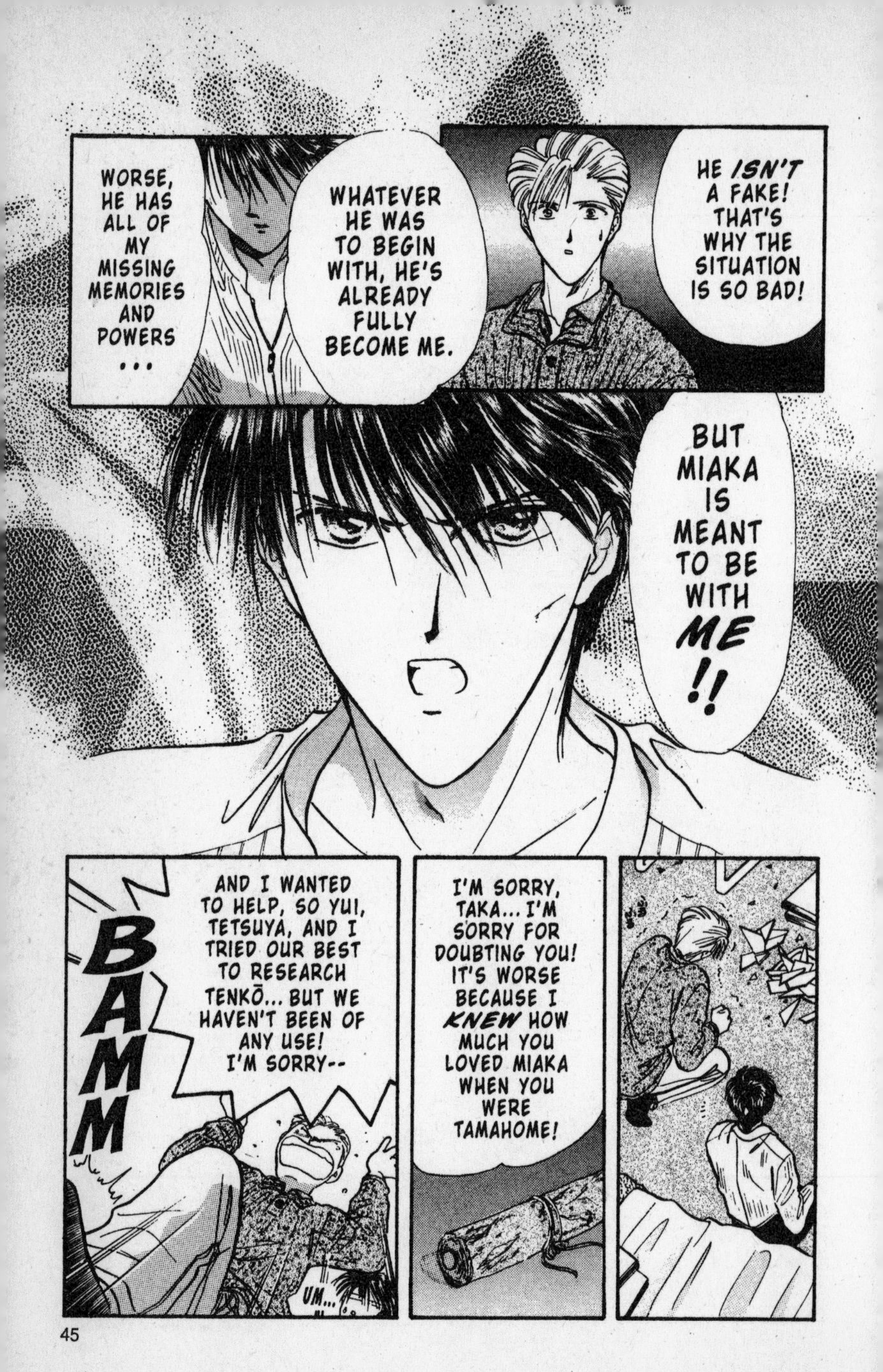
HE *ISN'T* A FAKE! THAT'S WHY THE SITUATION IS SO BAD!
WHATEVER HE WAS TO BEGIN WITH, HE'S ALREADY FULLY BECOME ME.
WORSE, HE HAS ALL OF MY MISSING MEMORIES AND POWERS . . .
BUT MIAKA IS MEANT TO BE WITH *ME* !!
I'M SORRY, TAKA... I'M SORRY FOR DOUBTING YOU! IT'S WORSE BECAUSE I *KNEW* HOW MUCH YOU LOVED MIAKA WHEN YOU WERE TAMAHOME!
AND I WANTED TO HELP, SO YUI, TETSUYA, AND I TRIED OUR BEST TO RESEARCH TENKŌ... BUT WE HAVEN'T BEEN OF ANY USE! I'M SORRY--
BAMM
UM...

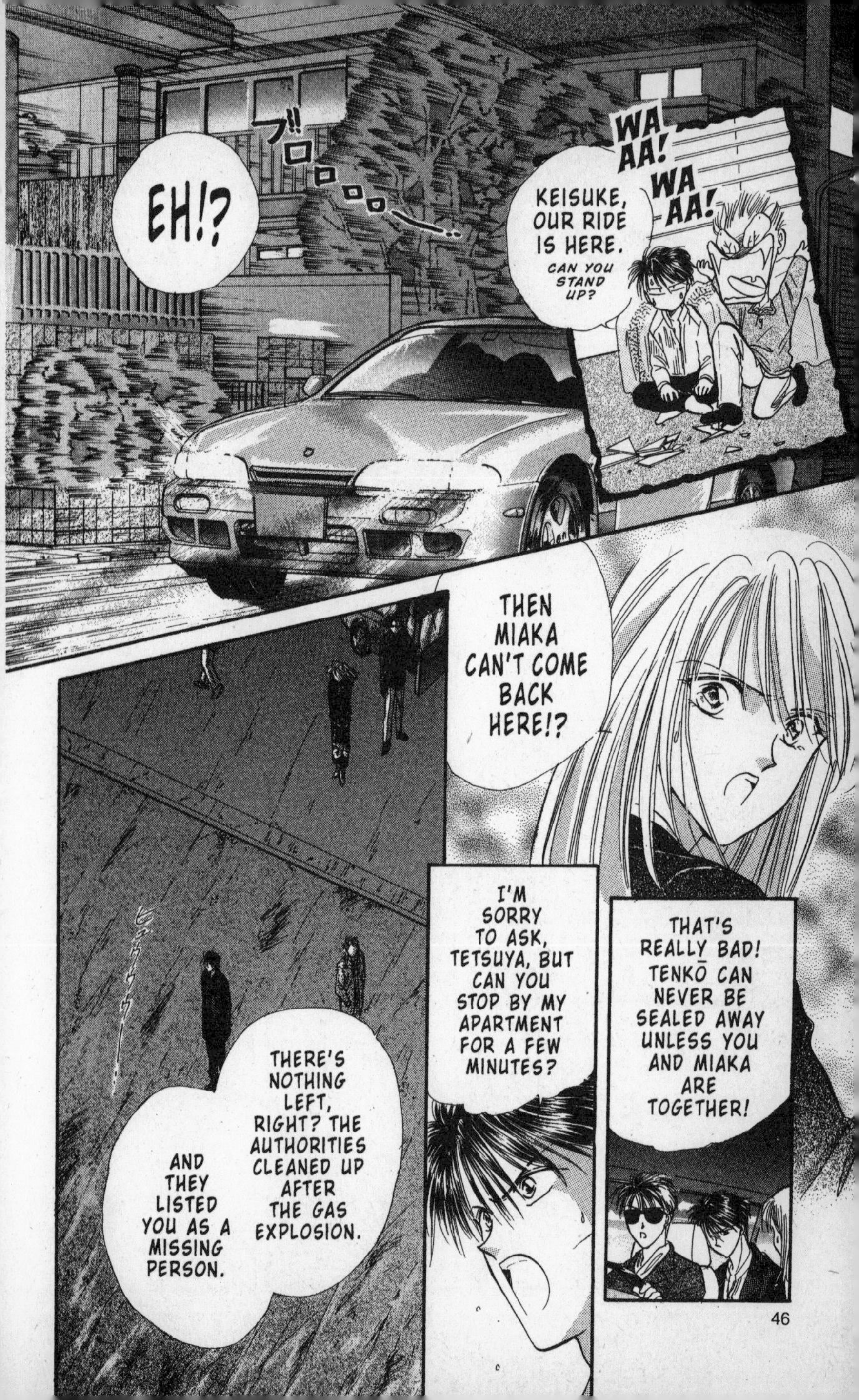
WA AA! WA AA!
KEISUKE, OUR RIDE IS HERE.
CAN YOU STAND UP?
ブ!! ロロロロー
EH!?
THEN MIAKA CAN'T COME BACK HERE!?
THAT'S REALLY BAD! TENKŌ CAN NEVER BE SEALED AWAY UNLESS YOU AND MIAKA ARE TOGETHER!
I'M SORRY TO ASK, TETSUYA, BUT CAN YOU STOP BY MY APARTMENT FOR A FEW MINUTES?
THERE'S NOTHING LEFT, RIGHT? THE AUTHORITIES CLEANED UP AFTER THE GAS EXPLOSION.
AND THEY LISTED YOU AS A MISSING PERSON.

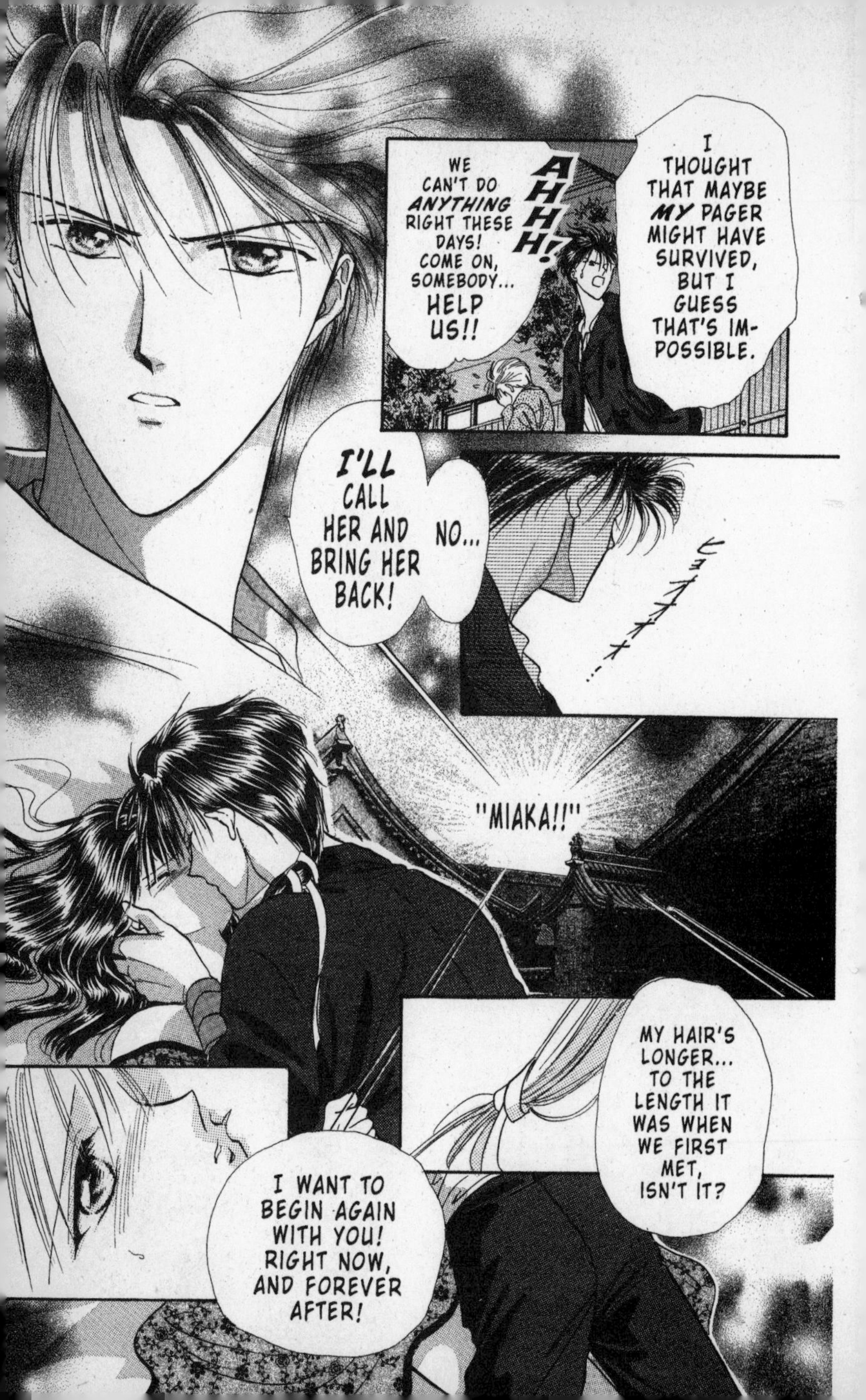
I THOUGHT THAT MAYBE MY PAGER MIGHT HAVE SURVIVED, BUT I GUESS THAT'S IMPOSSIBLE.
AHHHH!
WE CAN'T DO ANYTHING RIGHT THESE DAYS! COME ON, SOMEBODY... HELP US!!
NO...
I'LL CALL HER AND BRING HER BACK!
"MIAKA!!"
MY HAIR'S LONGER... TO THE LENGTH IT WAS WHEN WE FIRST MET, ISN'T IT?
I WANT TO BEGIN AGAIN WITH YOU! RIGHT NOW, AND FOREVER AFTER!

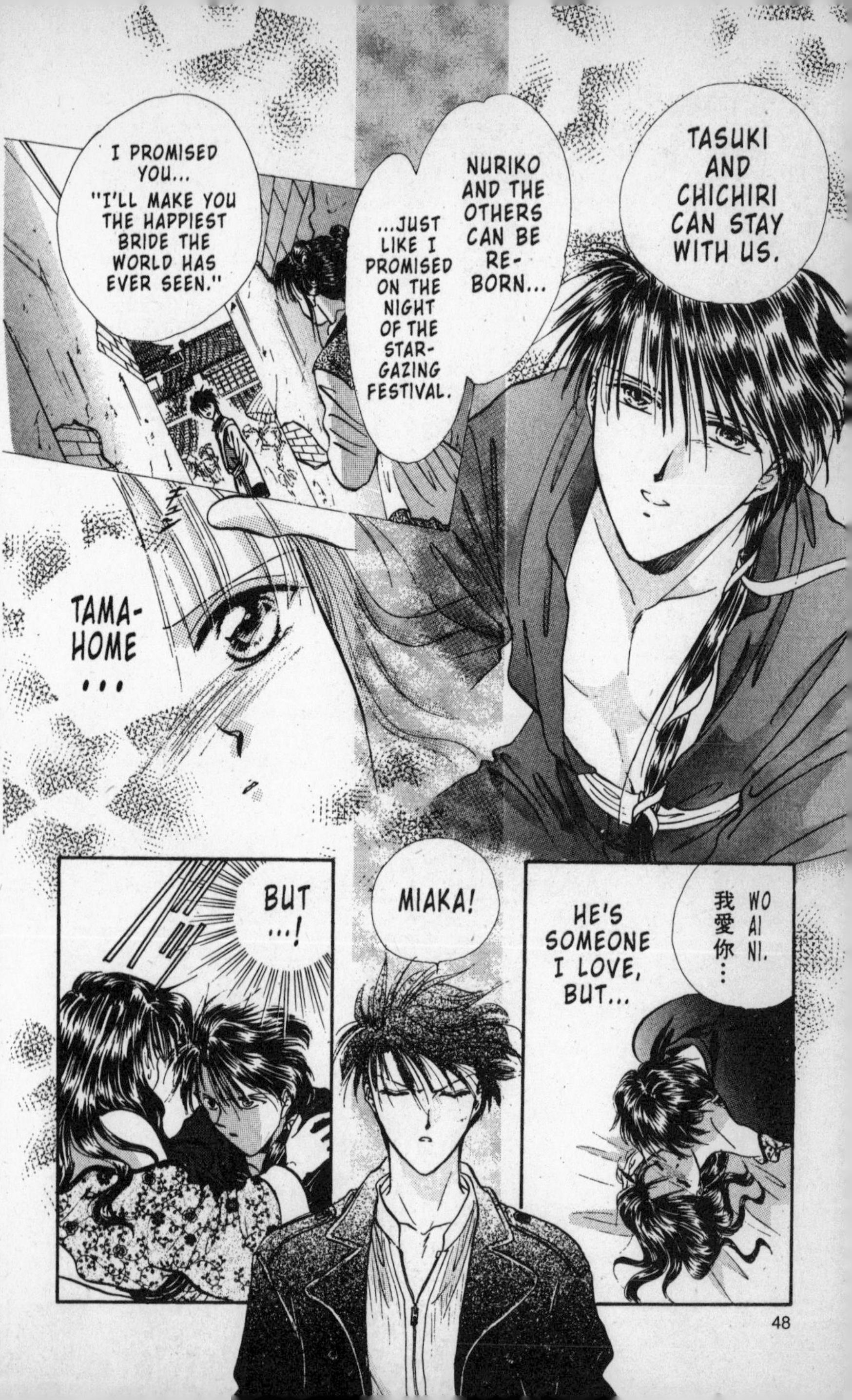
TASUKI AND CHICHIRI CAN STAY WITH US.
NURIKO AND THE OTHERS CAN BE RE-BORN...
...JUST LIKE I PROMISED ON THE NIGHT OF THE STAR-GAZING FESTIVAL.
I PROMISED YOU... "I'LL MAKE YOU THE HAPPIEST BRIDE THE WORLD HAS EVER SEEN."
TAMA-HOME ...
我愛你… WO AI NI.
HE'S SOMEONE I LOVE, BUT...
MIAKA!
BUT ...!

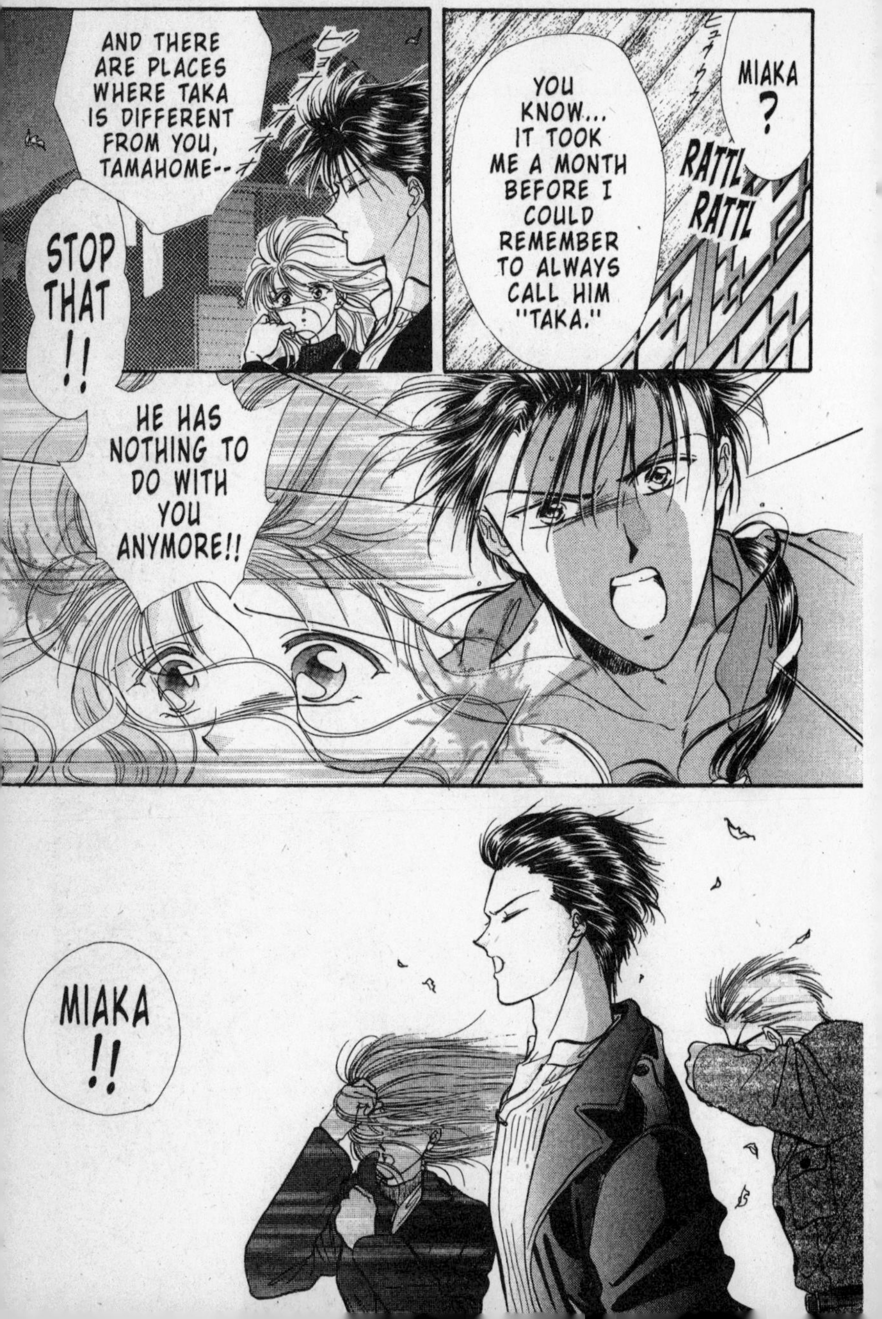
MIAKA ?
RATTL RATTL
YOU KNOW... IT TOOK ME A MONTH BEFORE I COULD REMEMBER TO ALWAYS CALL HIM "TAKA."
AND THERE ARE PLACES WHERE TAKA IS DIFFERENT FROM YOU, TAMAHOME--
STOP THAT !!
HE HAS NOTHING TO DO WITH YOU ANYMORE!!
MIAKA !!

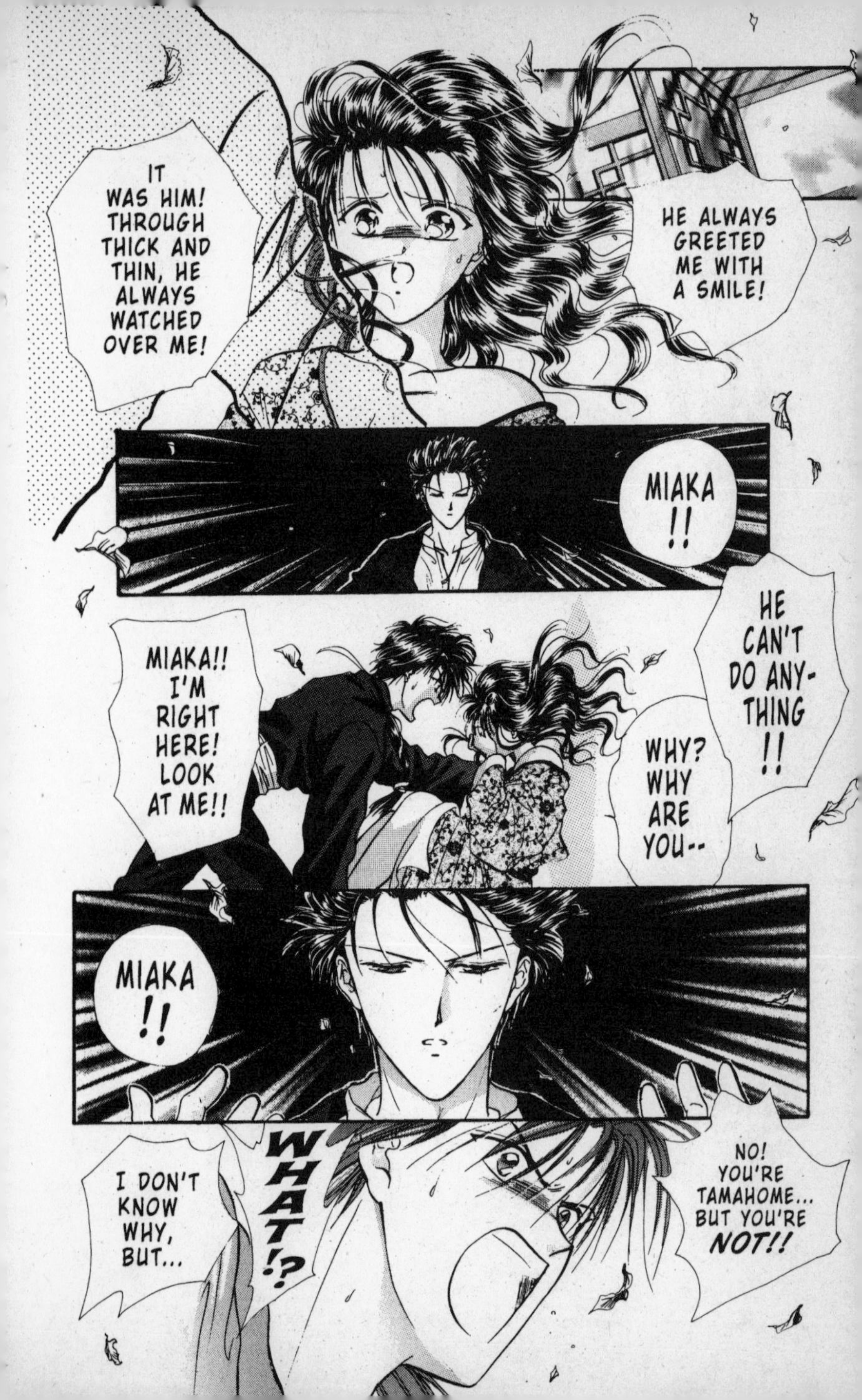
HE ALWAYS GREETED ME WITH A SMILE!
IT WAS HIM! THROUGH THICK AND THIN, HE ALWAYS WATCHED OVER ME!
MIAKA!!
HE CAN'T DO ANY-THING!!
WHY? WHY ARE YOU--
MIAKA!! I'M RIGHT HERE! LOOK AT ME!!
MIAKA!!
NO! YOU'RE TAMAHOME... BUT YOU'RE NOT!!
WHAT!?
I DON'T KNOW WHY, BUT...

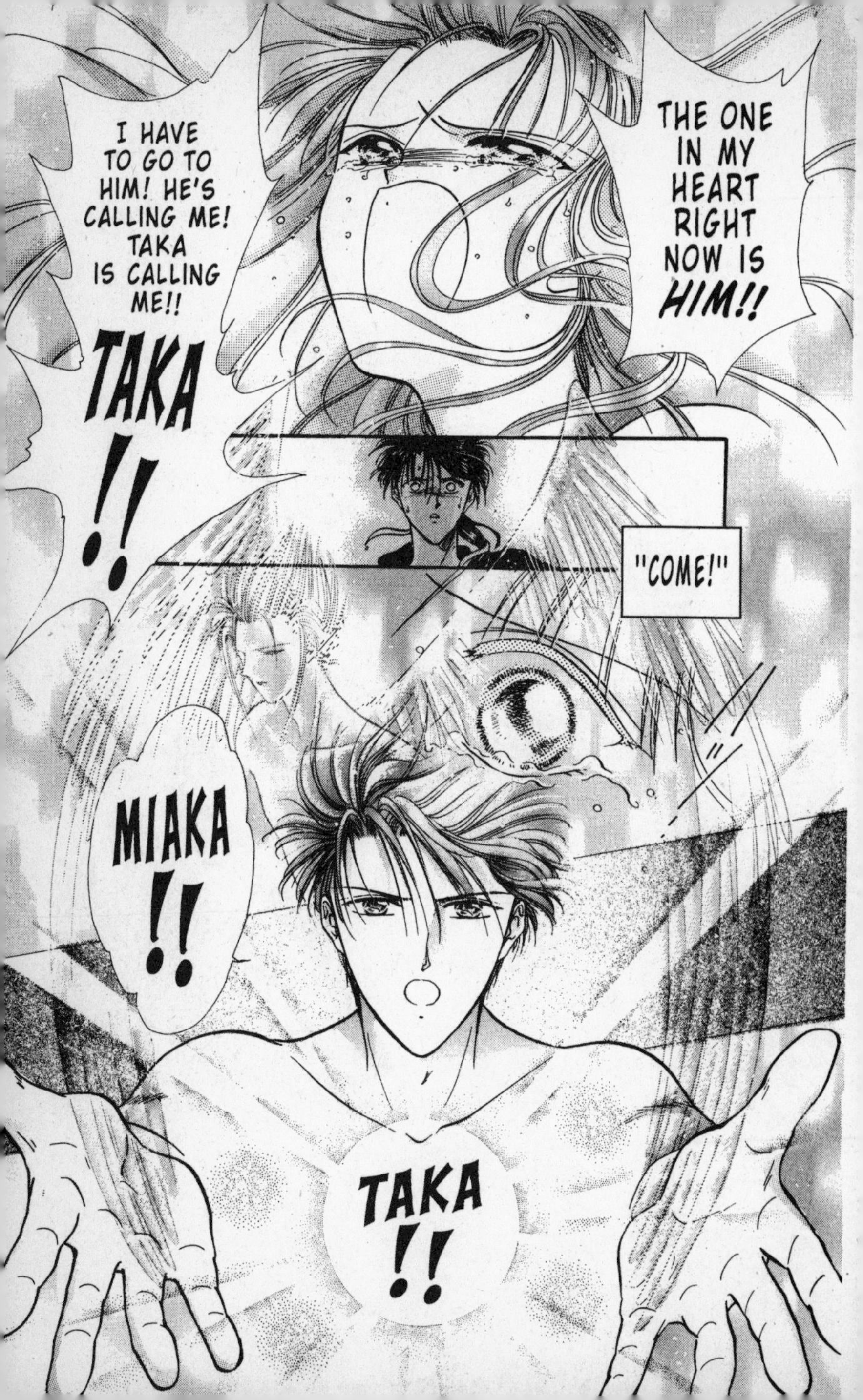
THE ONE IN MY HEART RIGHT NOW IS HIM!!
I HAVE TO GO TO HIM! HE'S CALLING ME! TAKA IS CALLING ME!!
TAKA!!
"COME!"
MIAKA!!
TAKA!!

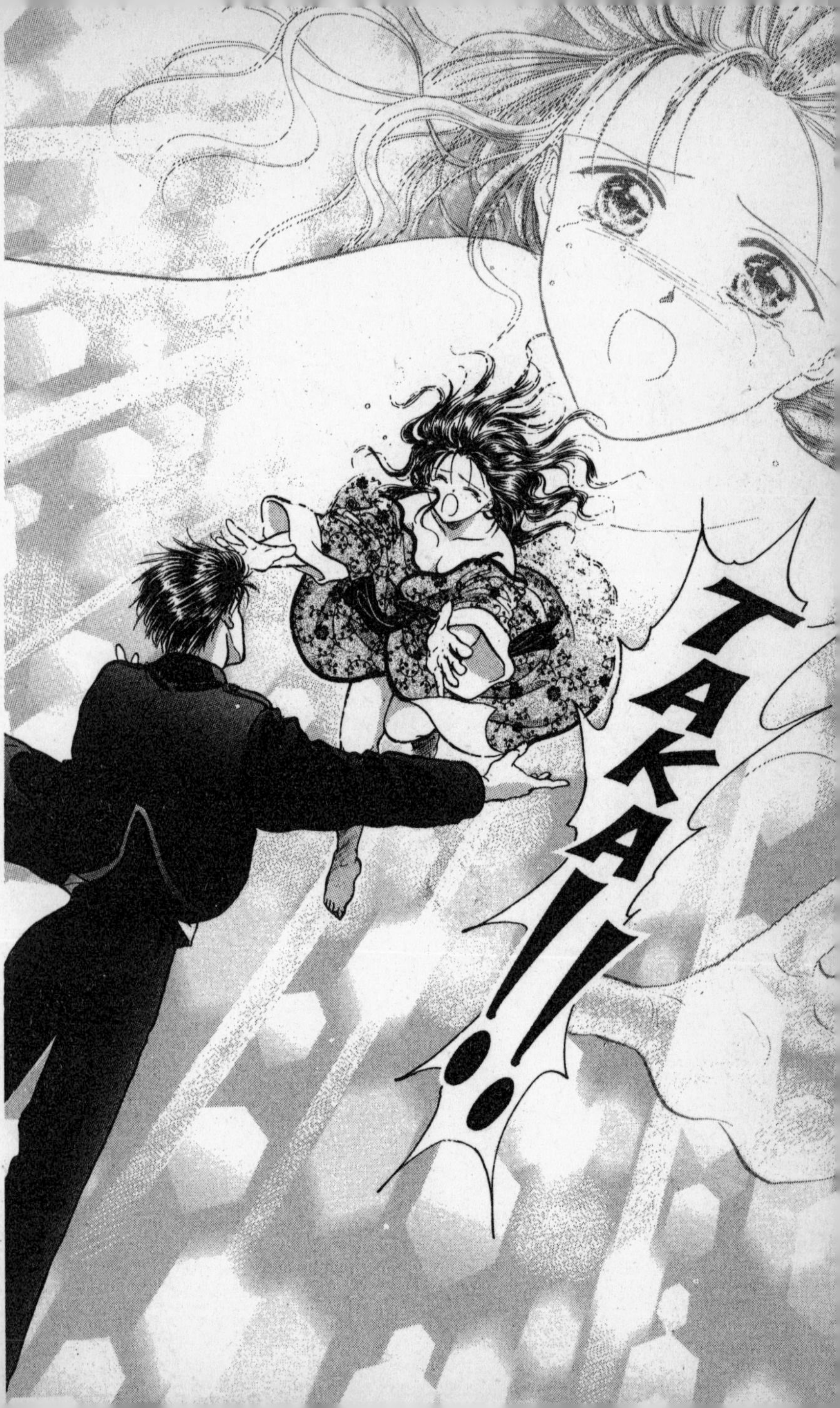
TAKA!!

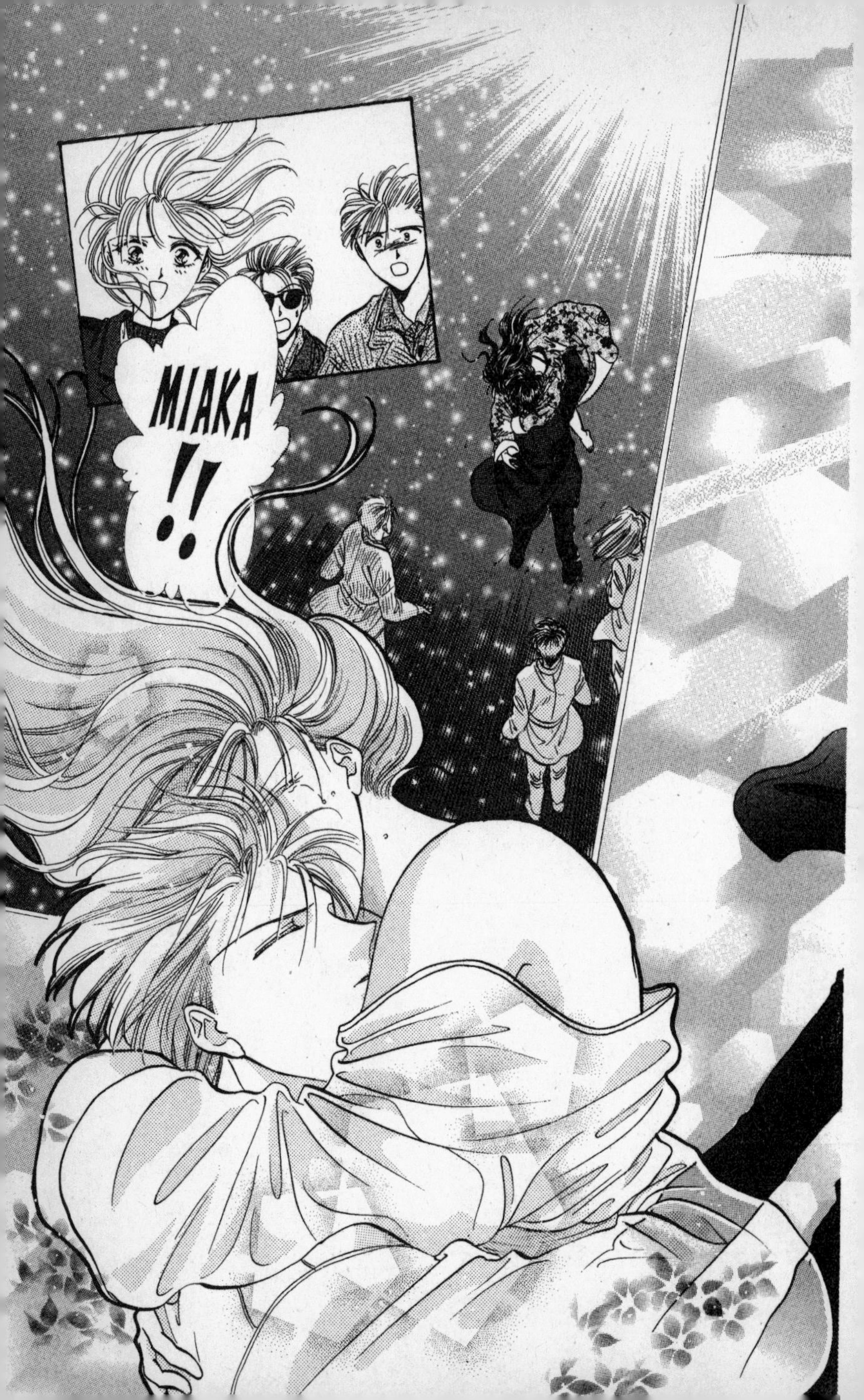
MIAKA !!

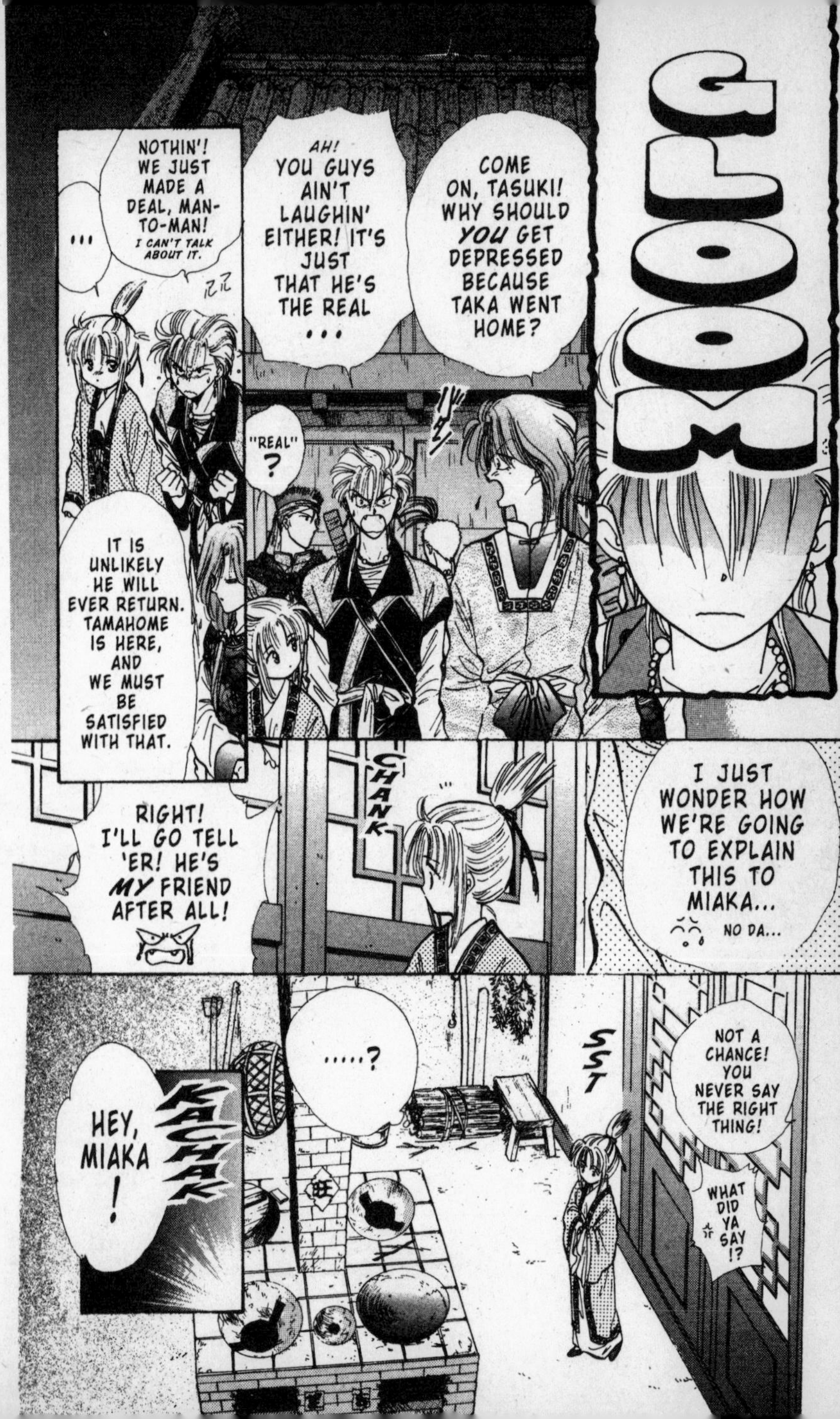
GLOOM
COME ON, TASUKI! WHY SHOULD *YOU* GET DEPRESSED BECAUSE TAKA WENT HOME?
AH! YOU GUYS AIN'T LAUGHIN' EITHER! IT'S JUST THAT HE'S THE REAL ...
"REAL" ?
NOTHIN'! WE JUST MADE A DEAL, MAN-TO-MAN! I CAN'T TALK ABOUT IT.
...
IT IS UNLIKELY HE WILL EVER RETURN. TAMAHOME IS HERE, AND WE MUST BE SATISFIED WITH THAT.
I JUST WONDER HOW WE'RE GOING TO EXPLAIN THIS TO MIAKA...
NO DA...
CHANK
RIGHT! I'LL GO TELL 'ER! HE'S *MY* FRIEND AFTER ALL!
SST
NOT A CHANCE! YOU NEVER SAY THE RIGHT THING!
WHAT DID YA SAY !?
.....?
KACHAK
HEY, MIAKA !

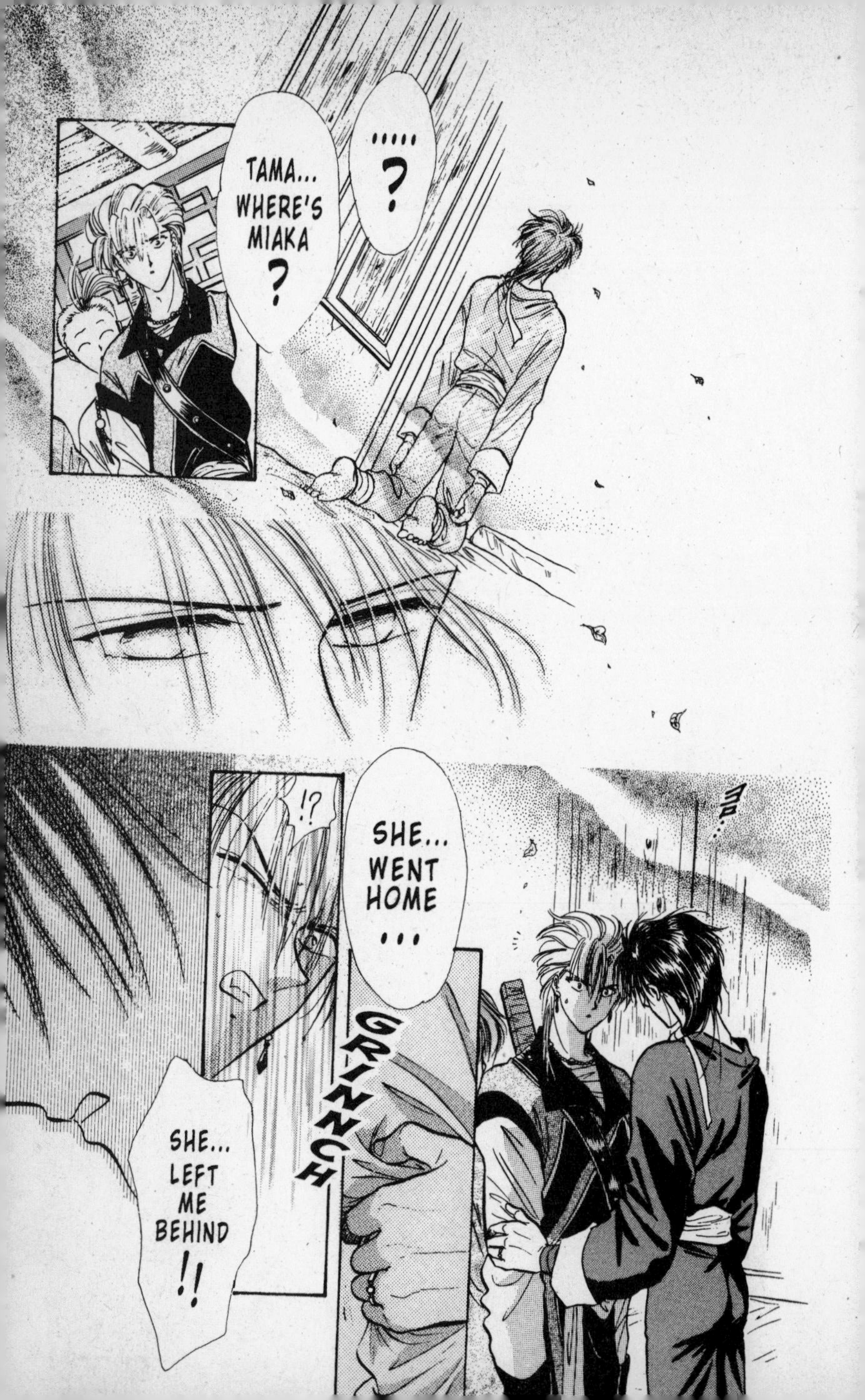
.....?
TAMA... WHERE'S MIAKA?
SHE... WENT HOME...
!?
GRINNCH
SHE... LEFT ME BEHIND!!

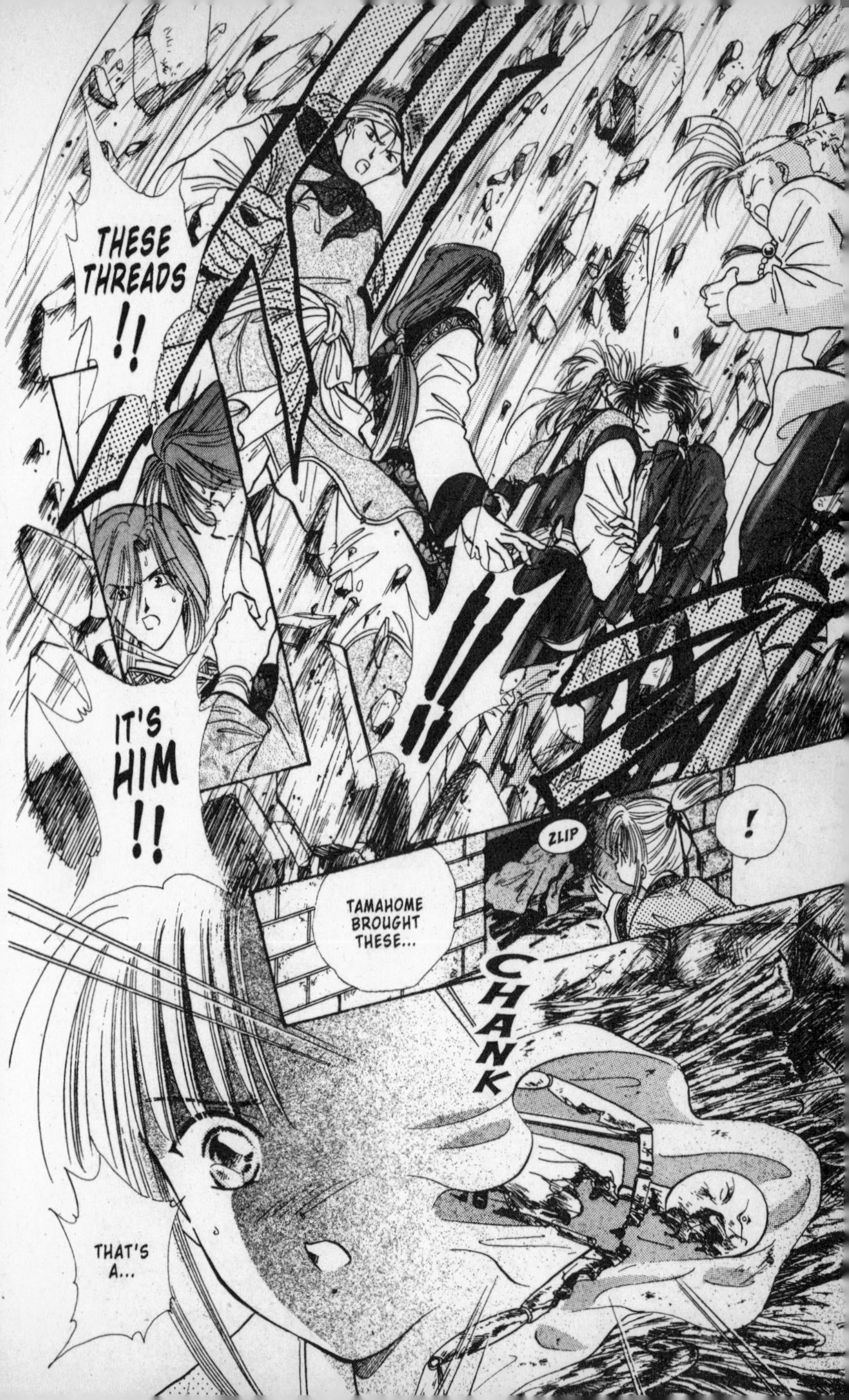
THESE THREADS!!
IT'S HIM!!
!
ZLIP
TAMAHOME BROUGHT THESE...
CHANK
THAT'S A...

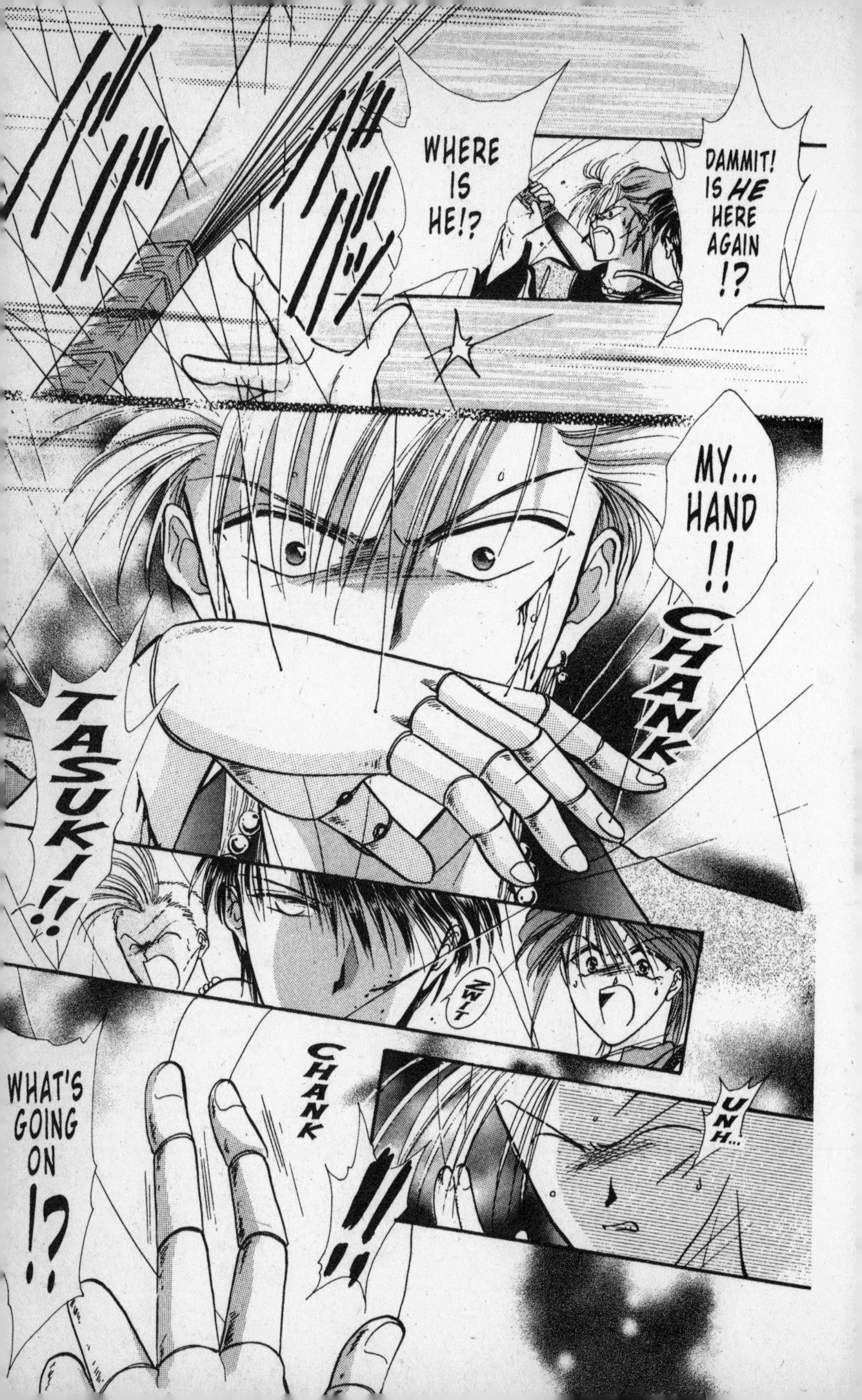
DAMMIT! IS HE HERE AGAIN!?
WHERE IS HE!?
MY... HAND!!
CHANK
TASUKI!!!
ZWIT
UNH...
CHANK
WHAT'S GOING ON!?

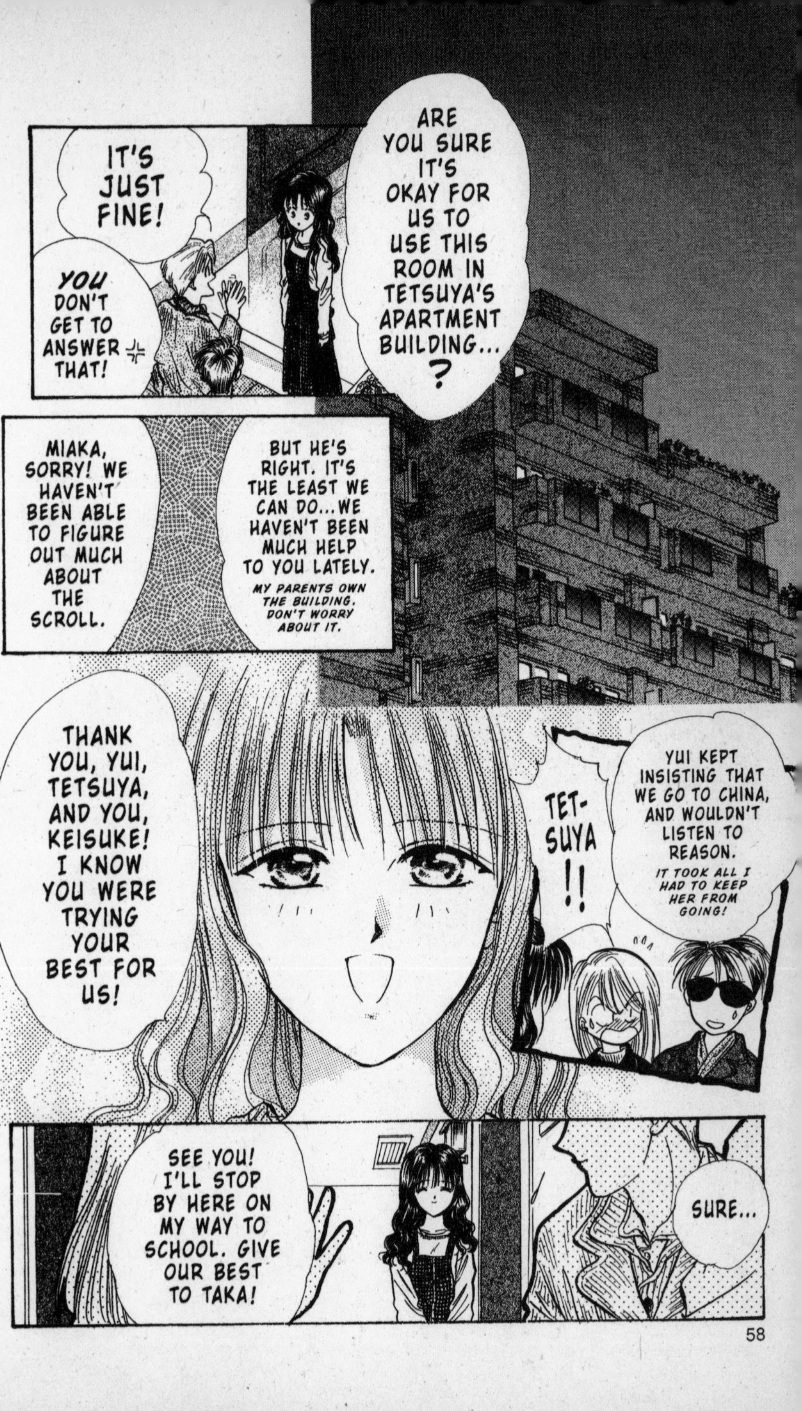
ARE YOU SURE IT'S OKAY FOR US TO USE THIS ROOM IN TETSUYA'S APARTMENT BUILDING...?
IT'S JUST FINE!
YOU DON'T GET TO ANSWER THAT!
BUT HE'S RIGHT. IT'S THE LEAST WE CAN DO...WE HAVEN'T BEEN MUCH HELP TO YOU LATELY.
MY PARENTS OWN THE BUILDING. DON'T WORRY ABOUT IT.
MIAKA, SORRY! WE HAVEN'T BEEN ABLE TO FIGURE OUT MUCH ABOUT THE SCROLL.
YUI KEPT INSISTING THAT WE GO TO CHINA, AND WOULDN'T LISTEN TO REASON.
IT TOOK ALL I HAD TO KEEP HER FROM GOING!
TET-SUYA!!
THANK YOU, YUI, TETSUYA, AND YOU, KEISUKE! I KNOW YOU WERE TRYING YOUR BEST FOR US!
SURE...
SEE YOU! I'LL STOP BY HERE ON MY WAY TO SCHOOL. GIVE OUR BEST TO TAKA!

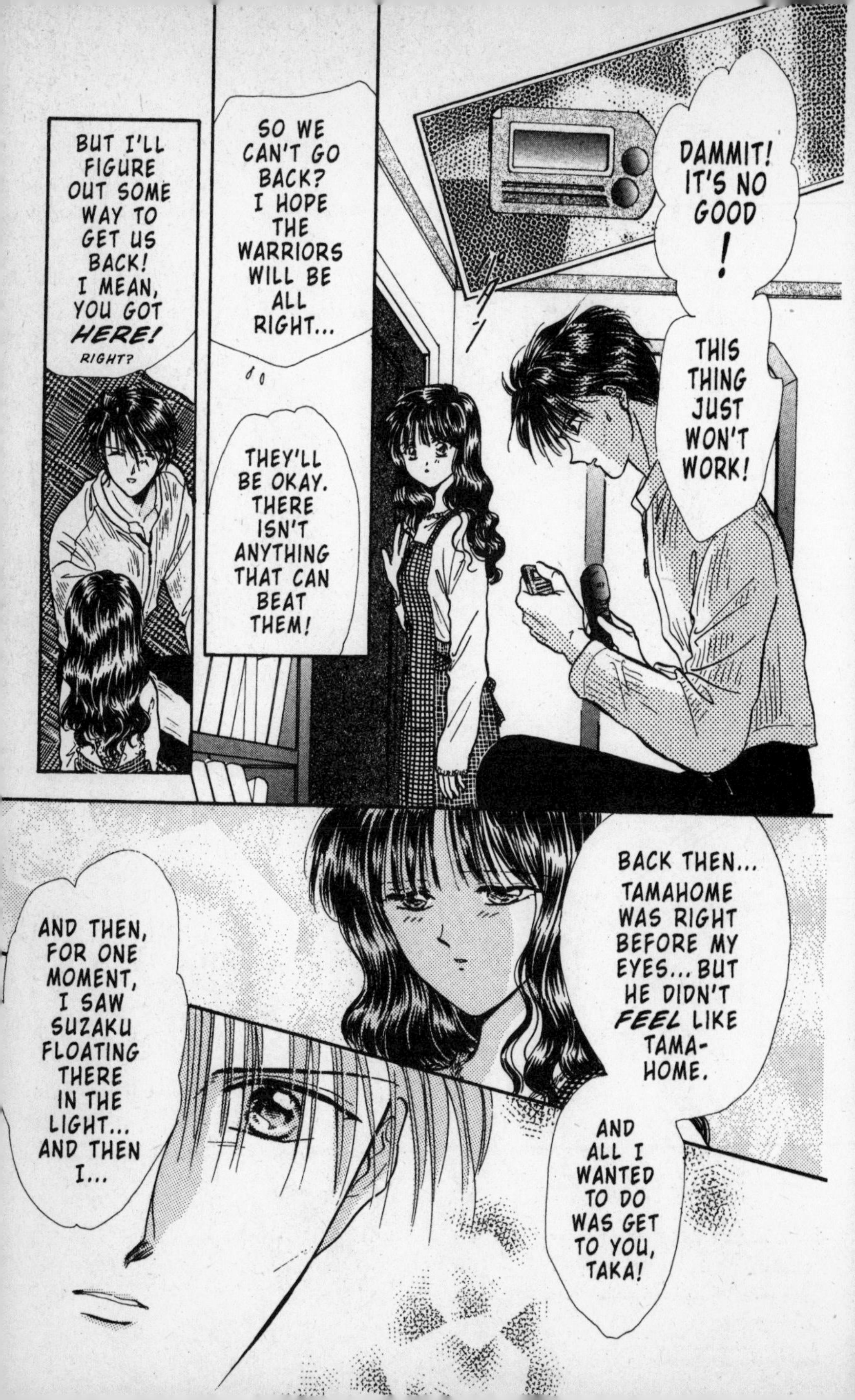
DAMMIT! IT'S NO GOOD!
THIS THING JUST WON'T WORK!
SO WE CAN'T GO BACK? I HOPE THE WARRIORS WILL BE ALL RIGHT...
THEY'LL BE OKAY. THERE ISN'T ANYTHING THAT CAN BEAT THEM!
BUT I'LL FIGURE OUT SOME WAY TO GET US BACK! I MEAN, YOU GOT *HERE!* RIGHT?
BACK THEN... TAMAHOME WAS RIGHT BEFORE MY EYES... BUT HE DIDN'T *FEEL* LIKE TAMA-HOME.
AND THEN, FOR ONE MOMENT, I SAW SUZAKU FLOATING THERE IN THE LIGHT... AND THEN I...
AND ALL I WANTED TO DO WAS GET TO YOU, TAKA!

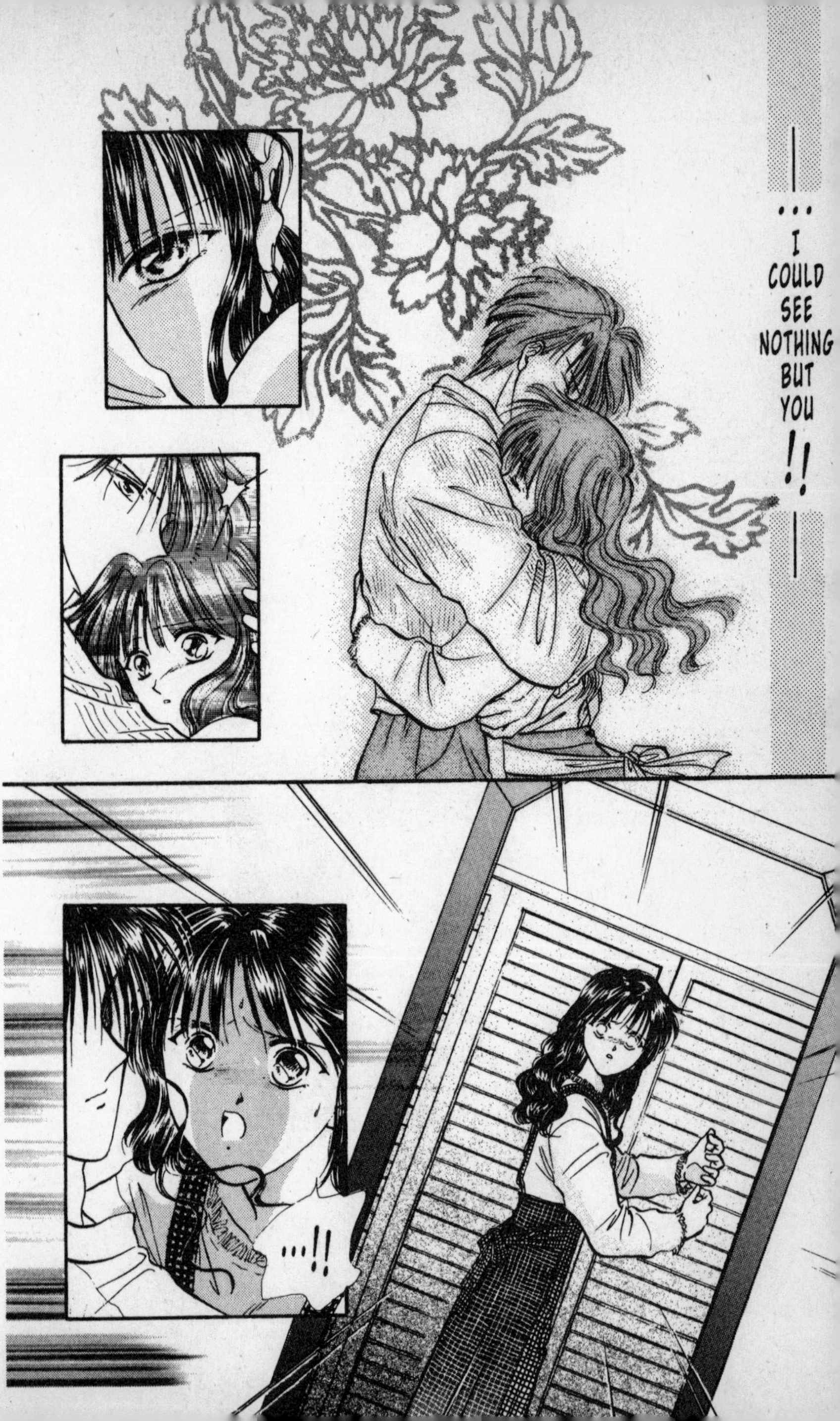
...I COULD SEE NOTHING BUT YOU!!
...!!

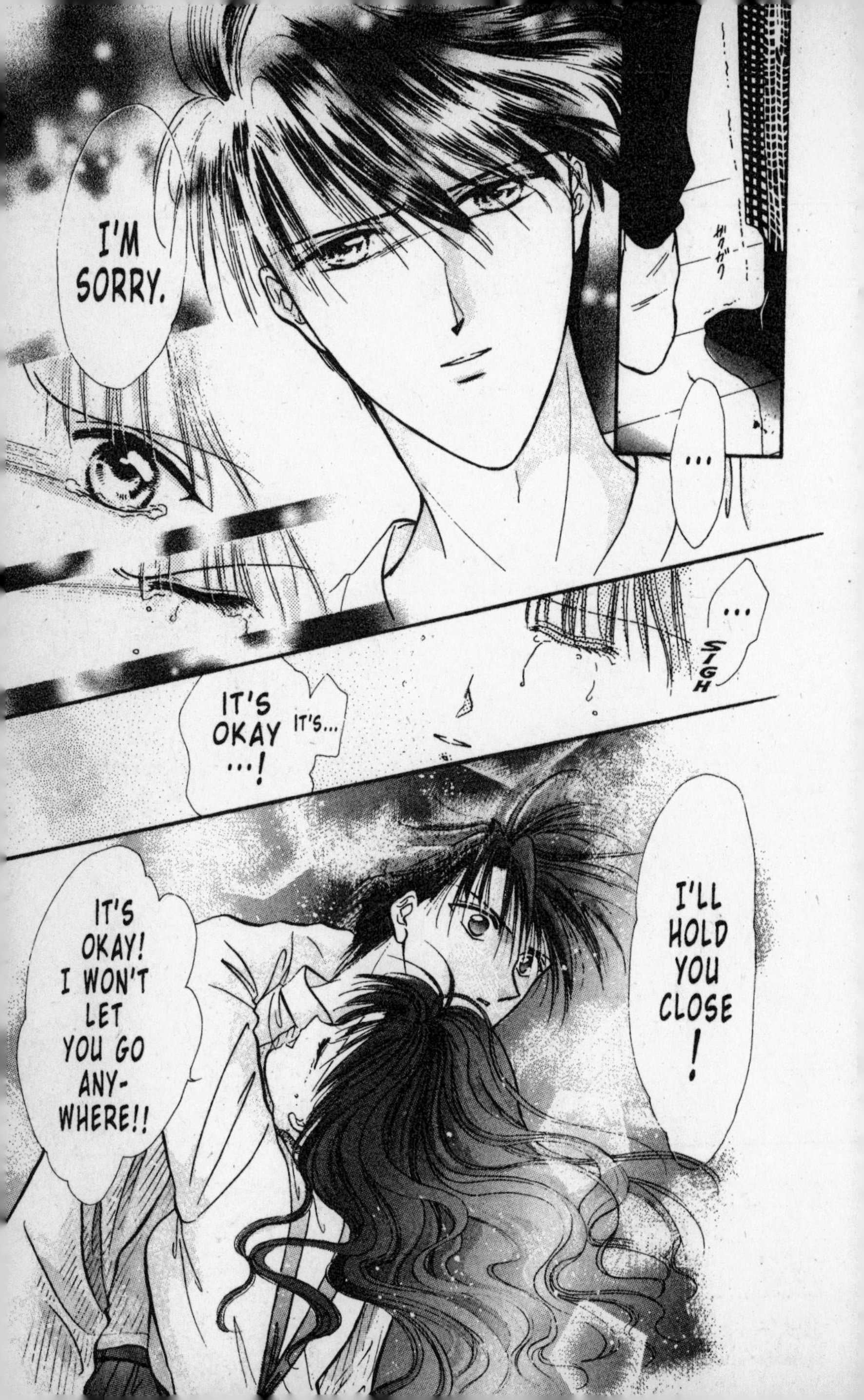
ガクガク
...
I'M SORRY.
...
SIGH
IT'S OKAY ...!
IT'S...
I'LL HOLD YOU CLOSE!
IT'S OKAY! I WON'T LET YOU GO ANY-WHERE!!

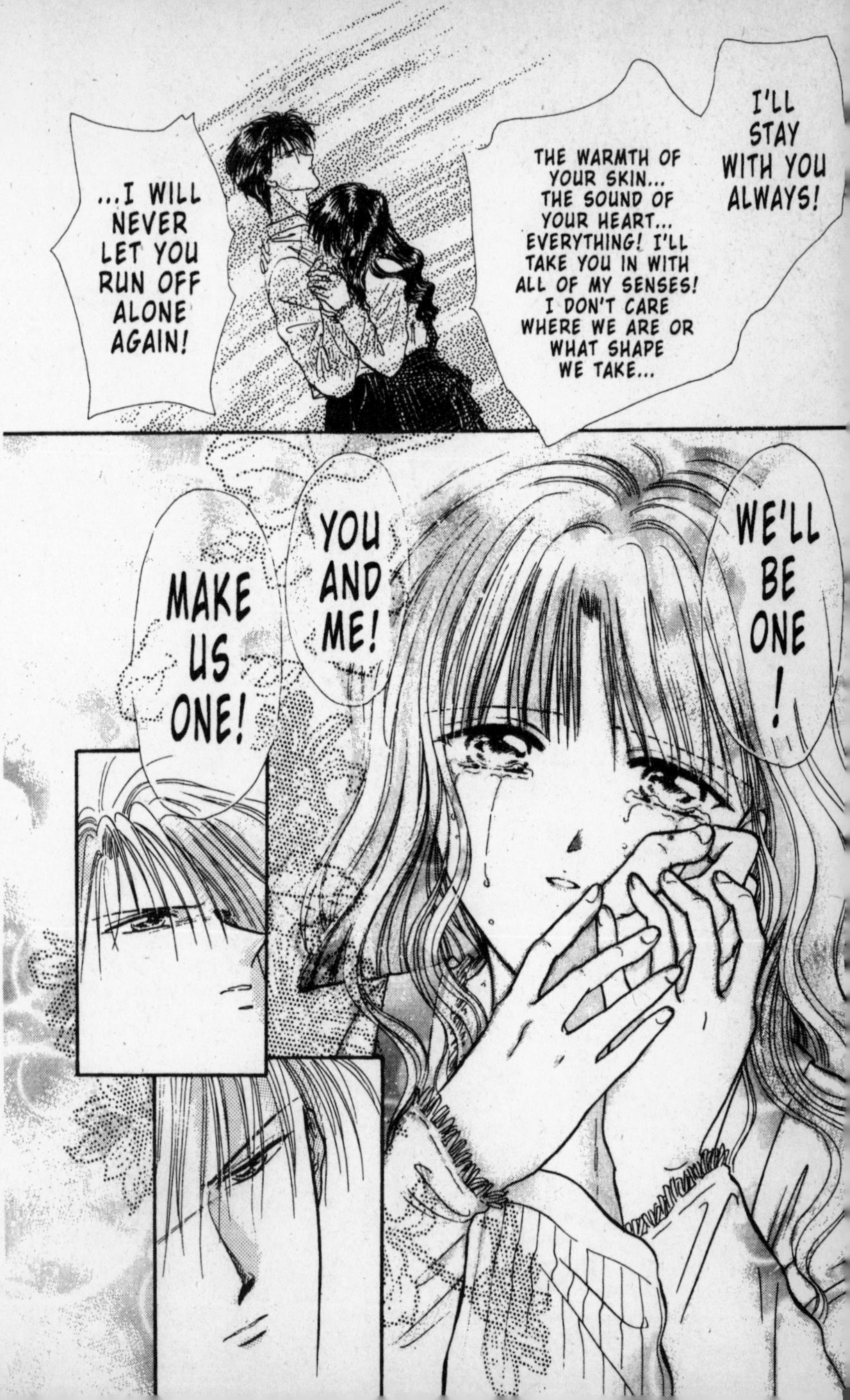
I'LL STAY WITH YOU ALWAYS!
THE WARMTH OF YOUR SKIN... THE SOUND OF YOUR HEART... EVERYTHING! I'LL TAKE YOU IN WITH ALL OF MY SENSES! I DON'T CARE WHERE WE ARE OR WHAT SHAPE WE TAKE...
...I WILL NEVER LET YOU RUN OFF ALONE AGAIN!
WE'LL BE ONE!
YOU AND ME!
MAKE US ONE!

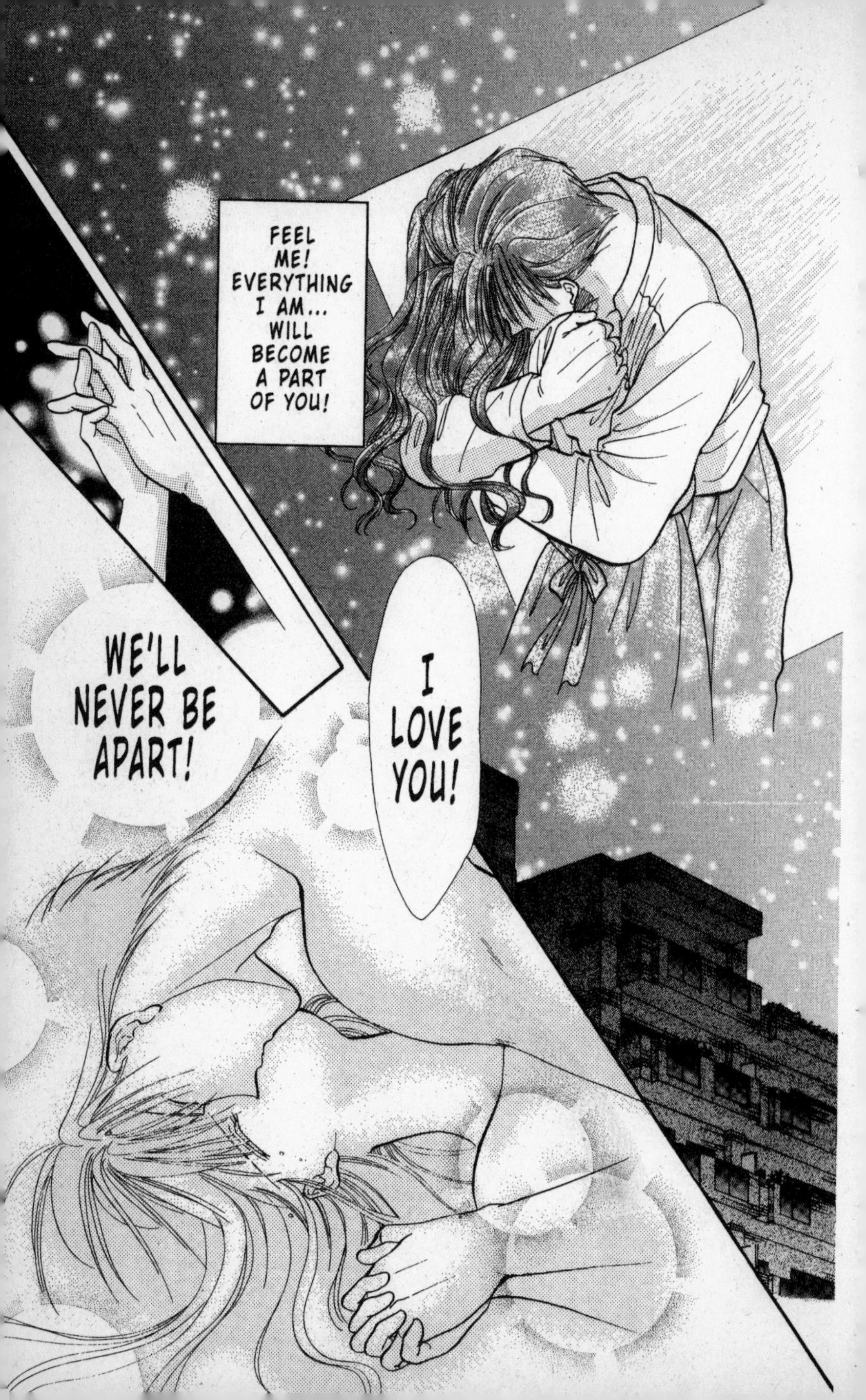
FEEL ME! EVERYTHING I AM... WILL BECOME A PART OF YOU!
I LOVE YOU!
WE'LL NEVER BE APART!

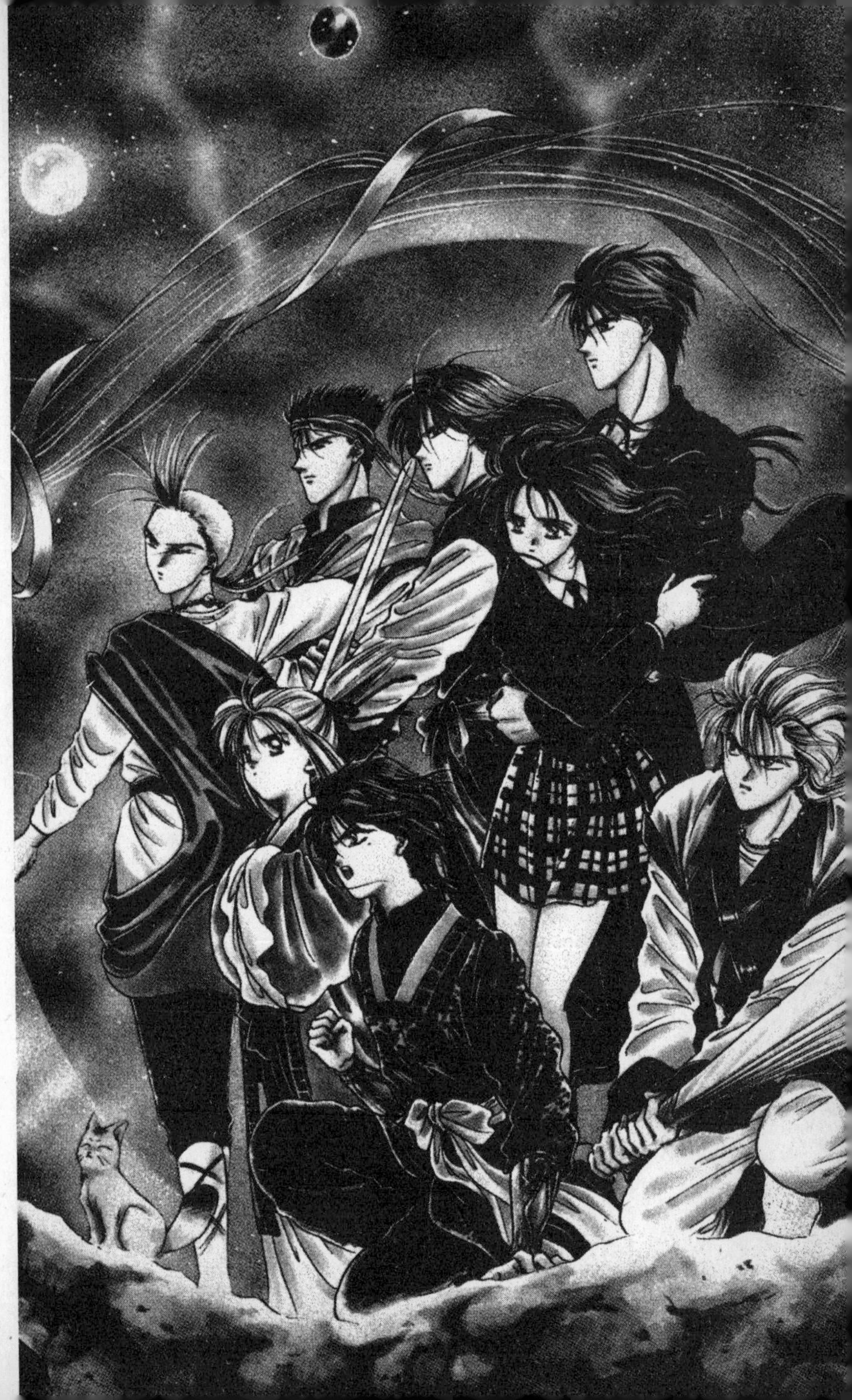

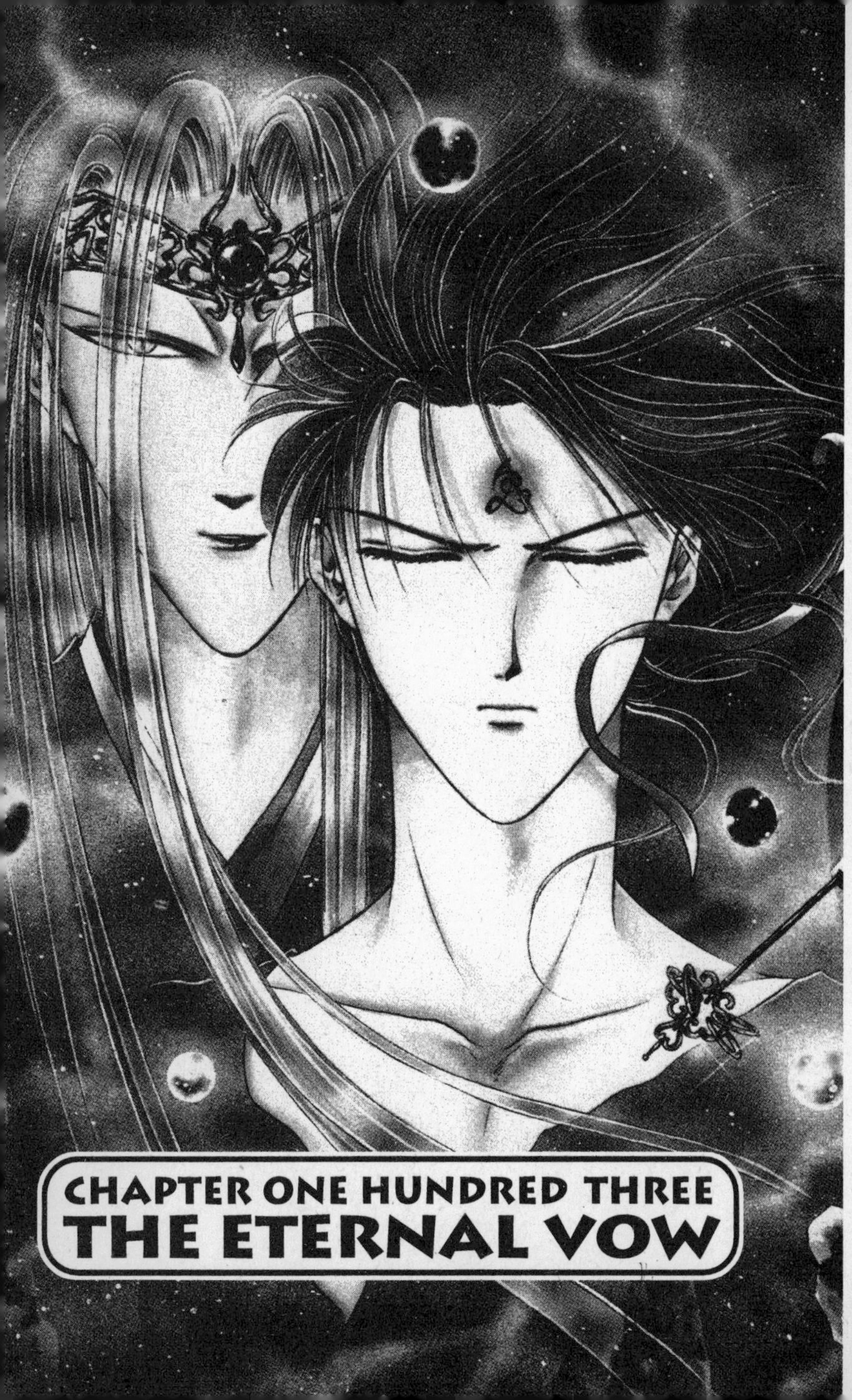

CHAPTER ONE HUNDRED THREE
THE ETERNAL VOW

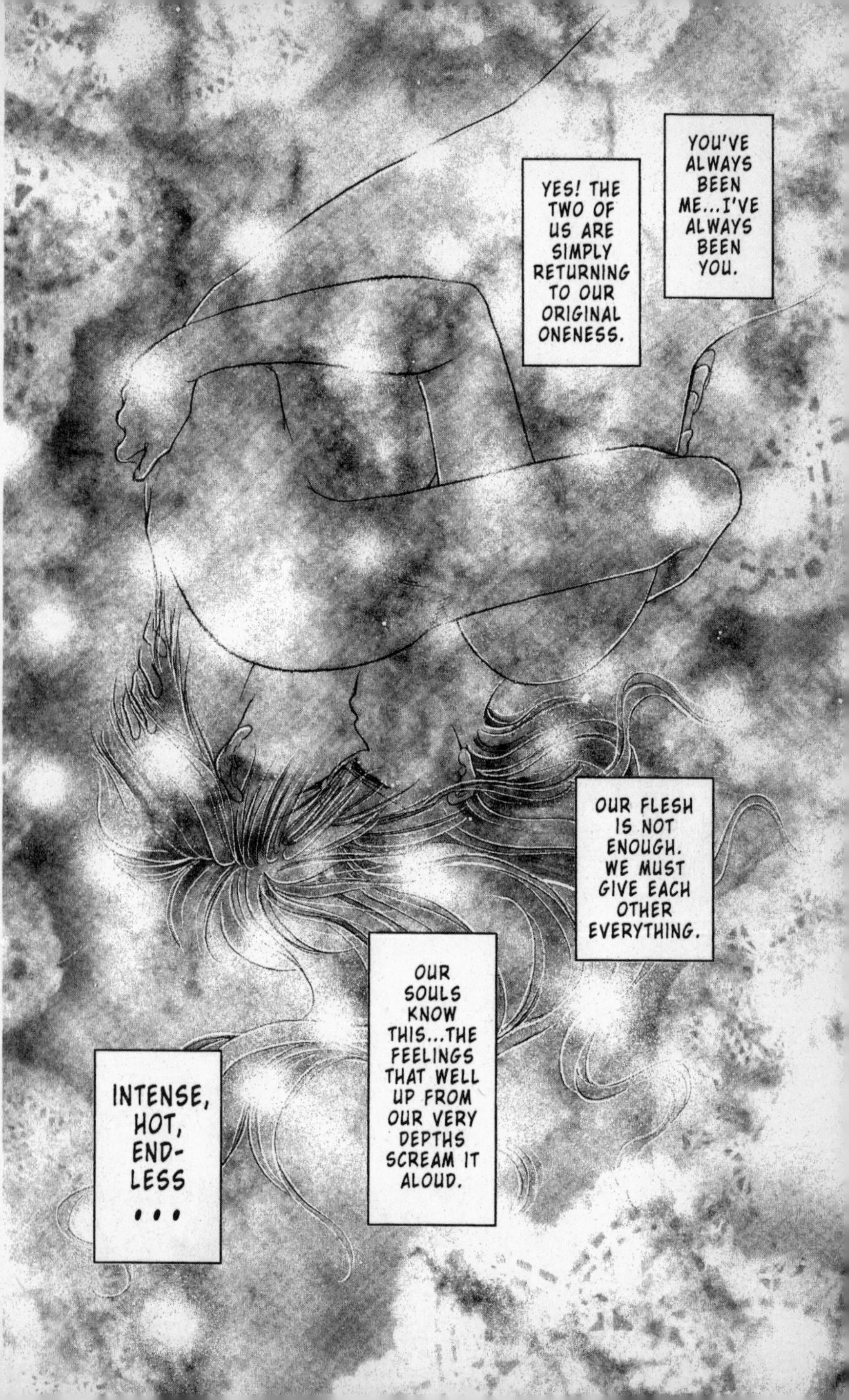
YOU'VE ALWAYS BEEN ME...I'VE ALWAYS BEEN YOU.
YES! THE TWO OF US ARE SIMPLY RETURNING TO OUR ORIGINAL ONENESS.
OUR FLESH IS NOT ENOUGH. WE MUST GIVE EACH OTHER EVERYTHING.
OUR SOULS KNOW THIS...THE FEELINGS THAT WELL UP FROM OUR VERY DEPTHS SCREAM IT ALOUD.
INTENSE, HOT, END-LESS...

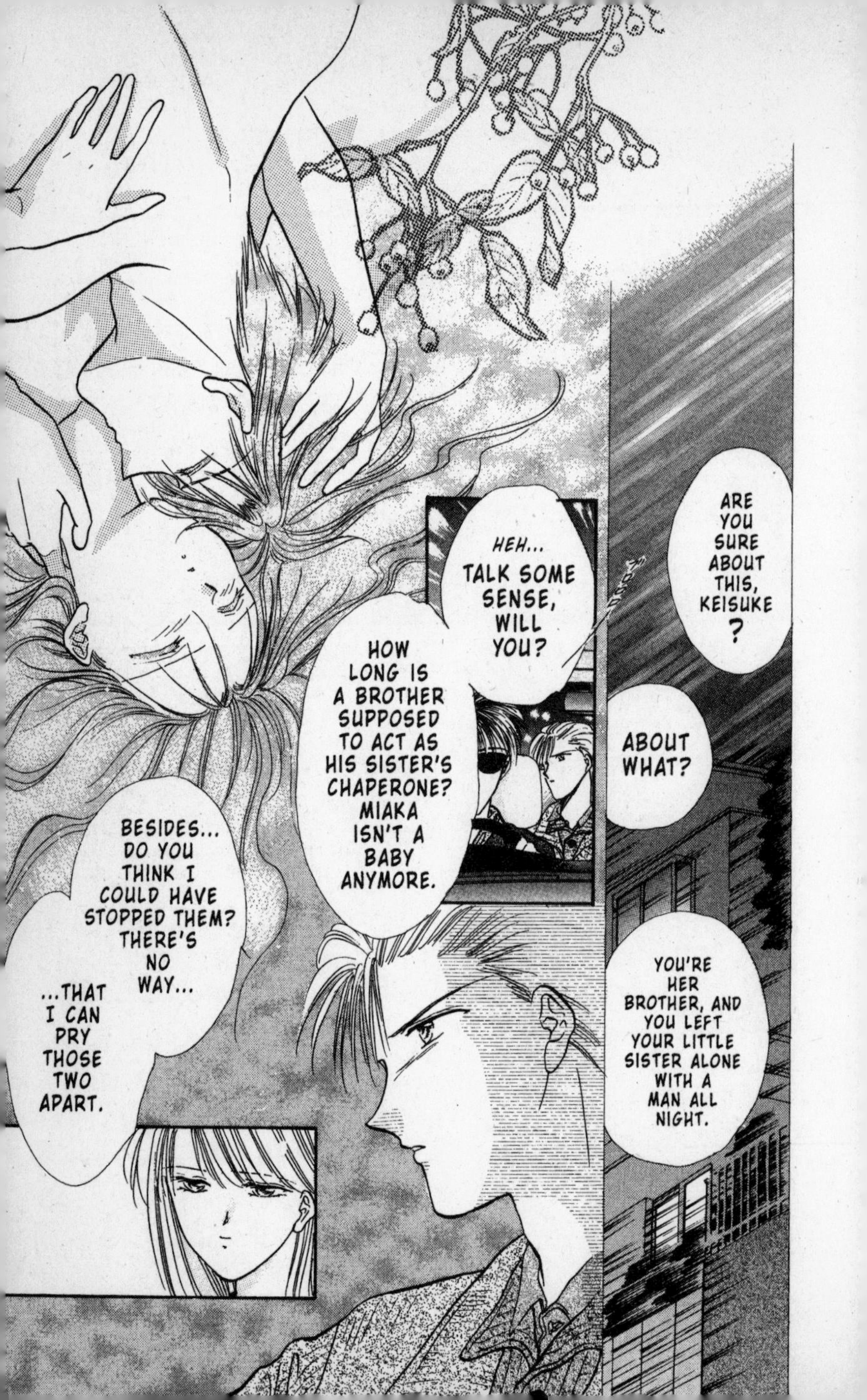
ARE YOU SURE ABOUT THIS, KEISUKE?
ABOUT WHAT?
YOU'RE HER BROTHER, AND YOU LEFT YOUR LITTLE SISTER ALONE WITH A MAN ALL NIGHT.
HEH... TALK SOME SENSE, WILL YOU?
HOW LONG IS A BROTHER SUPPOSED TO ACT AS HIS SISTER'S CHAPERONE? MIAKA ISN'T A BABY ANYMORE.
BESIDES... DO YOU THINK I COULD HAVE STOPPED THEM? THERE'S NO WAY...
...THAT I CAN PRY THOSE TWO APART.

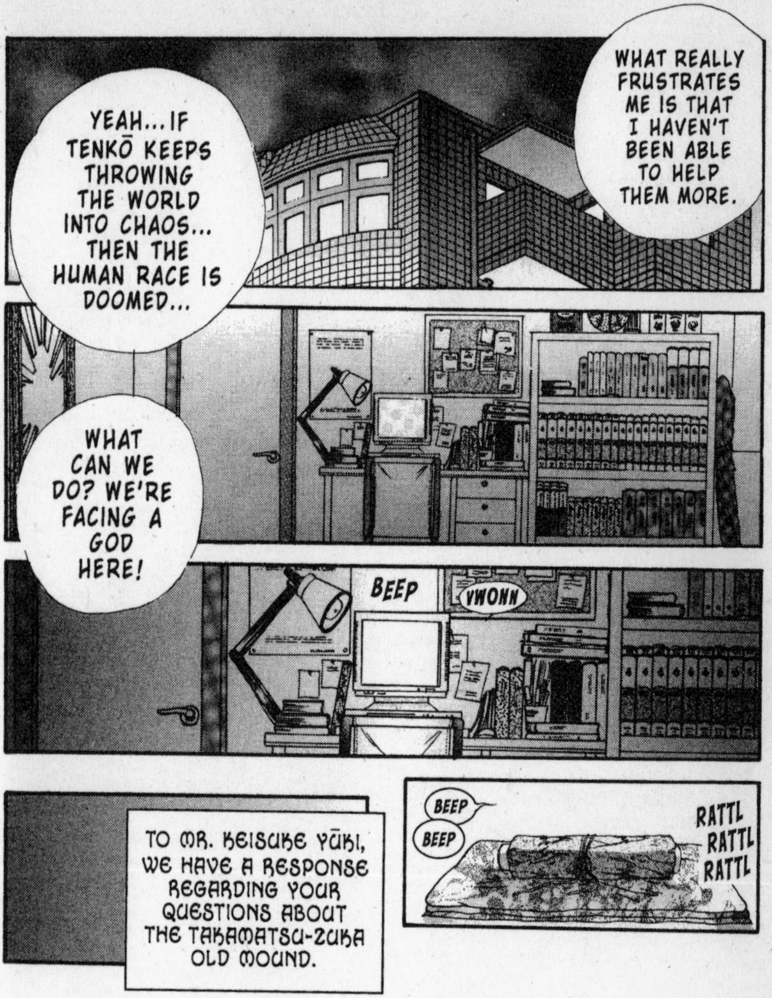
WHAT REALLY FRUSTRATES ME IS THAT I HAVEN'T BEEN ABLE TO HELP THEM MORE.
YEAH...IF TENKŌ KEEPS THROWING THE WORLD INTO CHAOS... THEN THE HUMAN RACE IS DOOMED...
WHAT CAN WE DO? WE'RE FACING A GOD HERE!
VWONN
BEEP
BEEP
BEEP
RATTL
RATTL
RATTL
TO MR. KEISUKE YŪKI, WE HAVE A RESPONSE REGARDING YOUR QUESTIONS ABOUT THE TAKAMATSU-ZUKA OLD MOUND.

TENKŌ IS NO GOD.

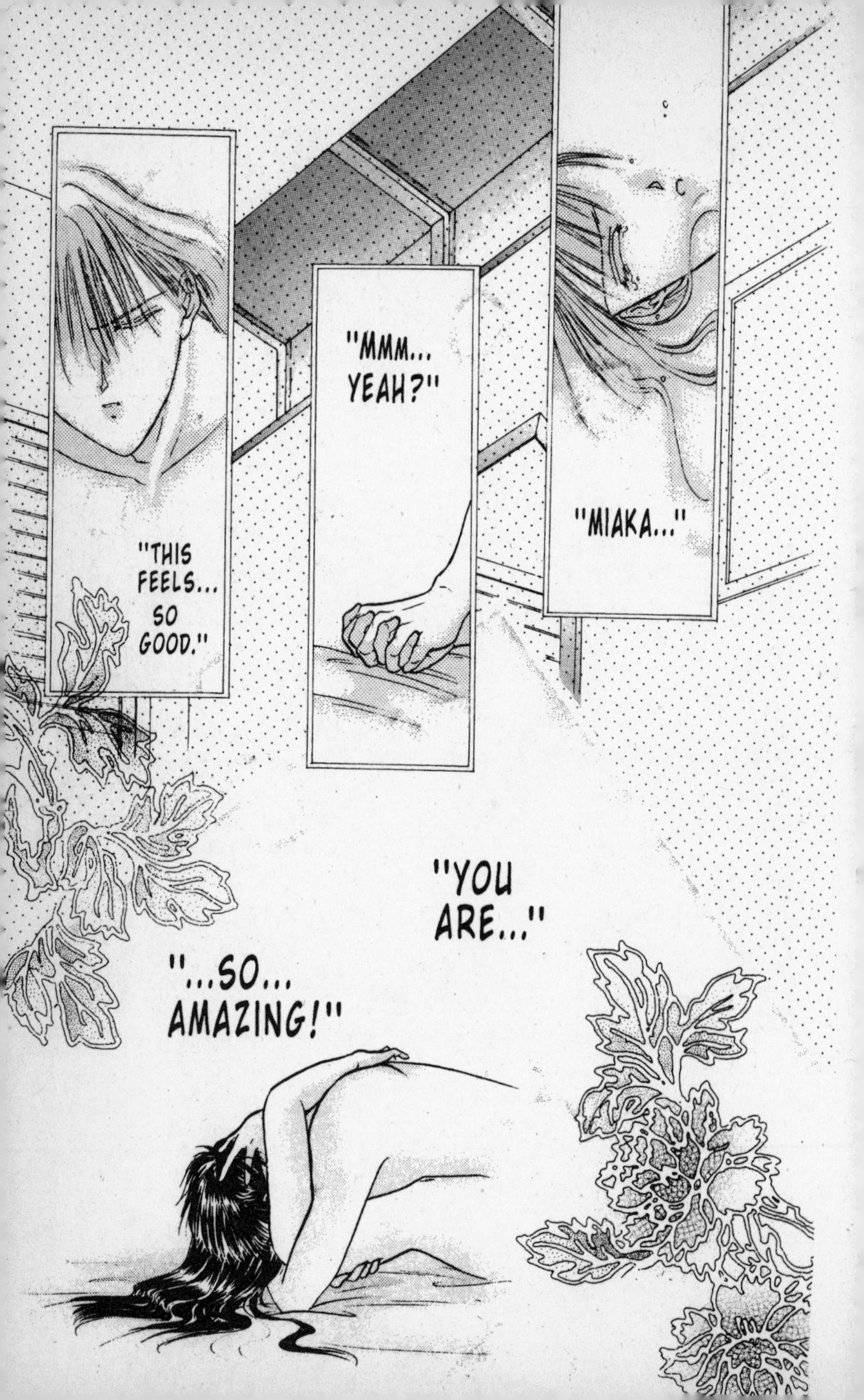
"MIAKA..."
"MMM... YEAH?"
"THIS FEELS... SO GOOD."
"YOU ARE..."
"...SO... AMAZING!"

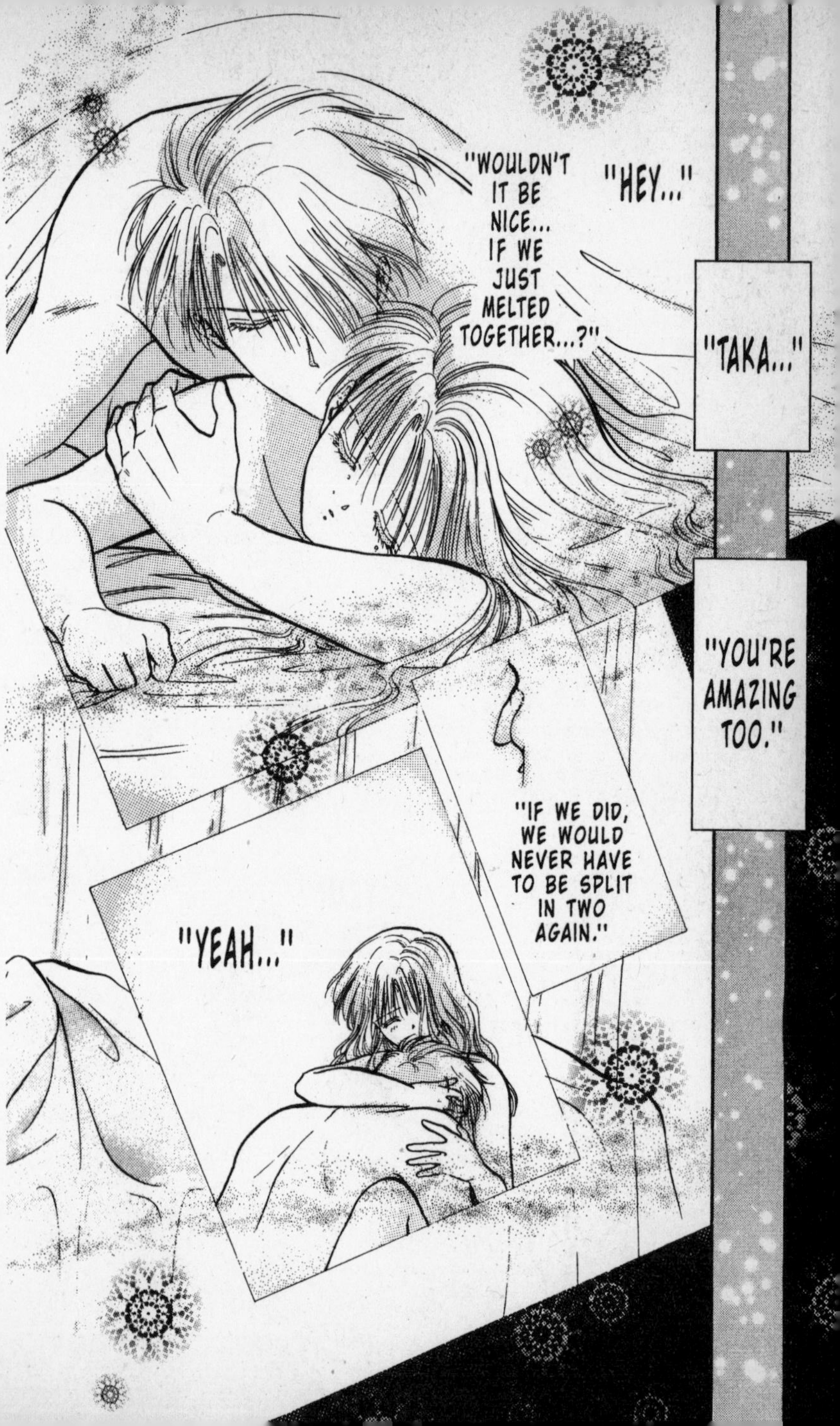
"TAKA..."
"YOU'RE AMAZING TOO."
"HEY..."
"WOULDN'T IT BE NICE... IF WE JUST MELTED TOGETHER...?"
"IF WE DID, WE WOULD NEVER HAVE TO BE SPLIT IN TWO AGAIN."
"YEAH..."

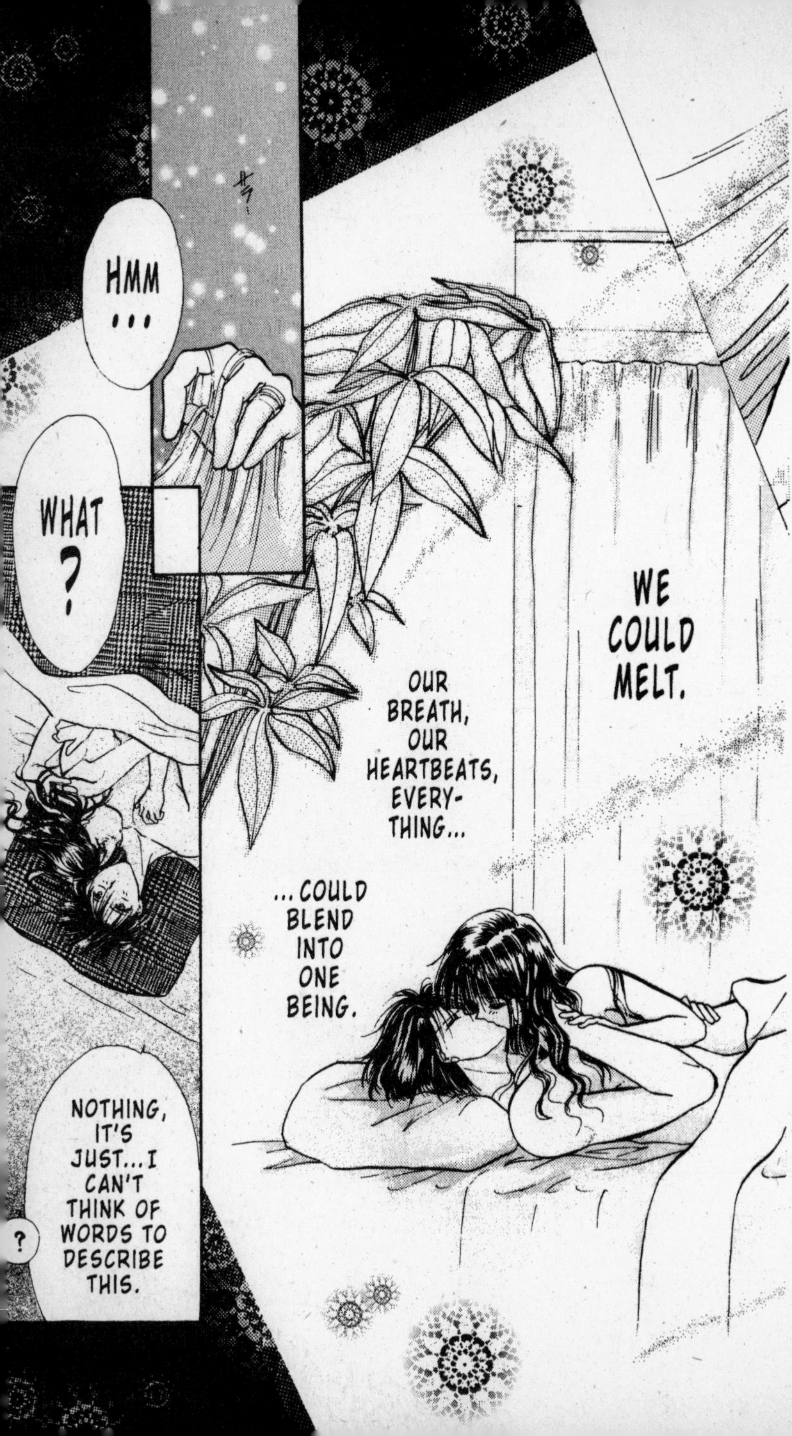
WE COULD MELT.
OUR BREATH, OUR HEARTBEATS, EVERY-THING...
...COULD BLEND INTO ONE BEING.
HMM...
WHAT?
NOTHING, IT'S JUST...I CAN'T THINK OF WORDS TO DESCRIBE THIS.
?

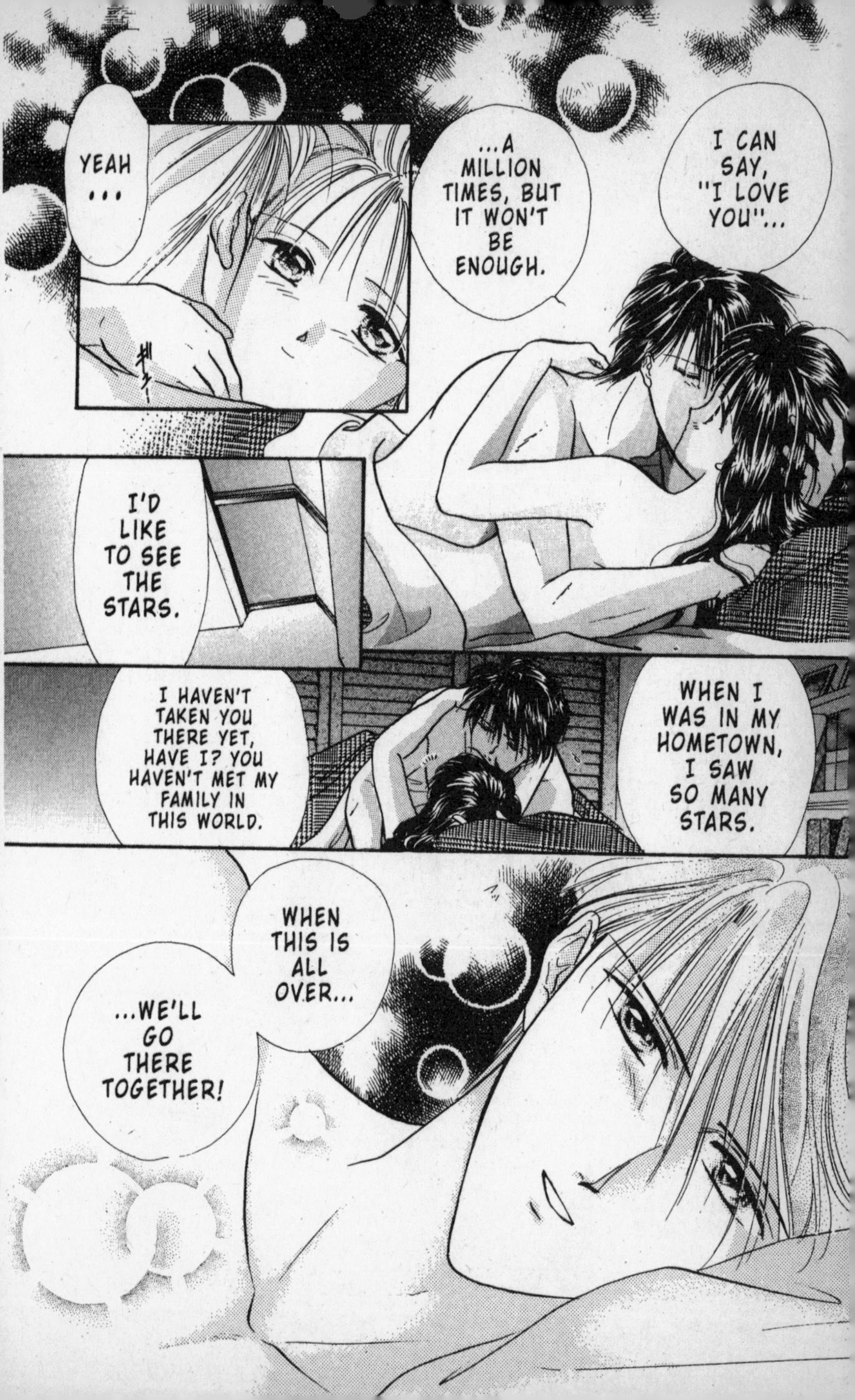
I CAN SAY, "I LOVE YOU"...
...A MILLION TIMES, BUT IT WON'T BE ENOUGH.
YEAH...
I'D LIKE TO SEE THE STARS.
WHEN I WAS IN MY HOMETOWN, I SAW SO MANY STARS.
I HAVEN'T TAKEN YOU THERE YET, HAVE I? YOU HAVEN'T MET MY FAMILY IN THIS WORLD.
WHEN THIS IS ALL OVER...
...WE'LL GO THERE TOGETHER!

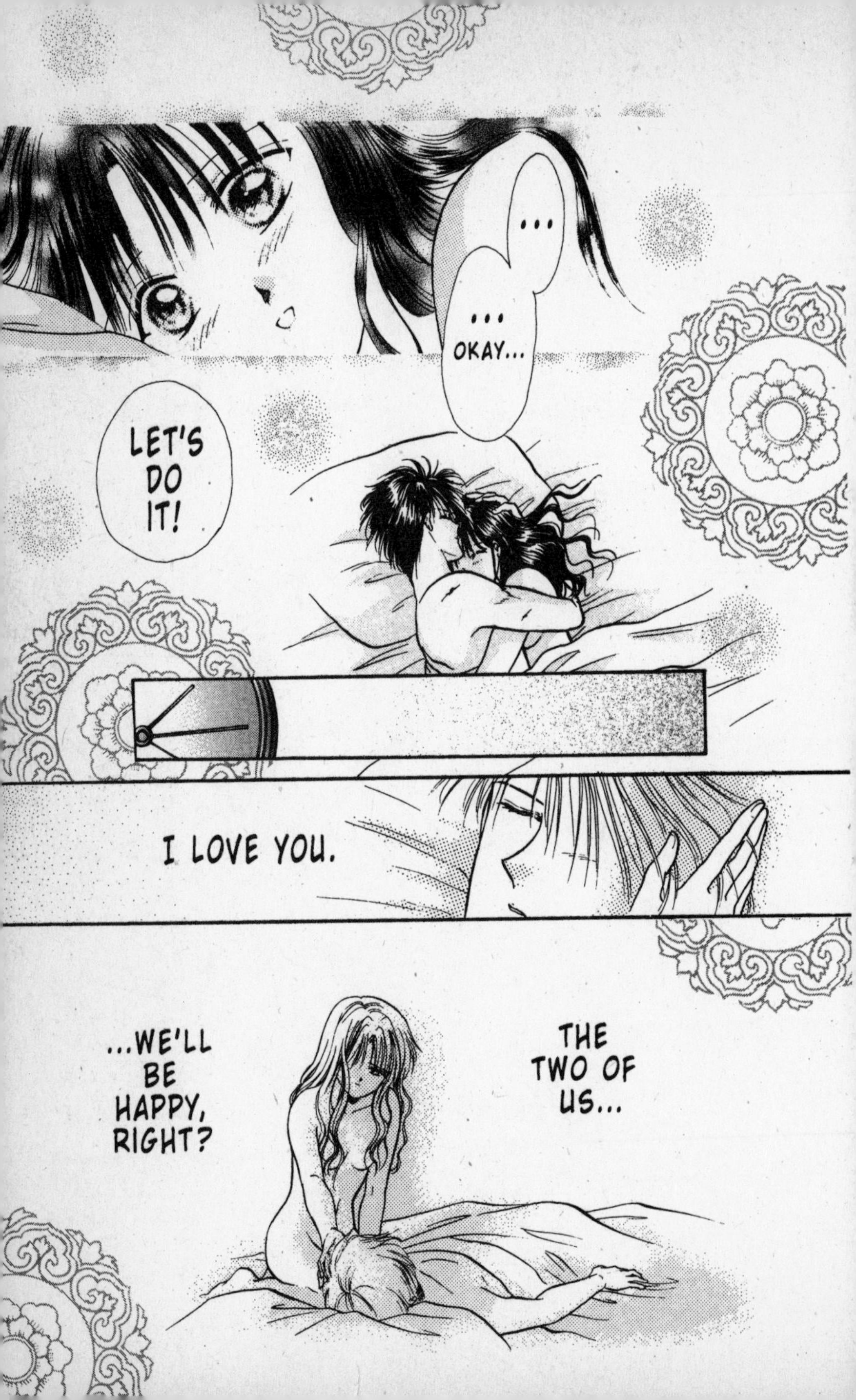
...
...OKAY...
LET'S DO IT!
I LOVE YOU.
THE TWO OF US...
...WE'LL BE HAPPY, RIGHT?

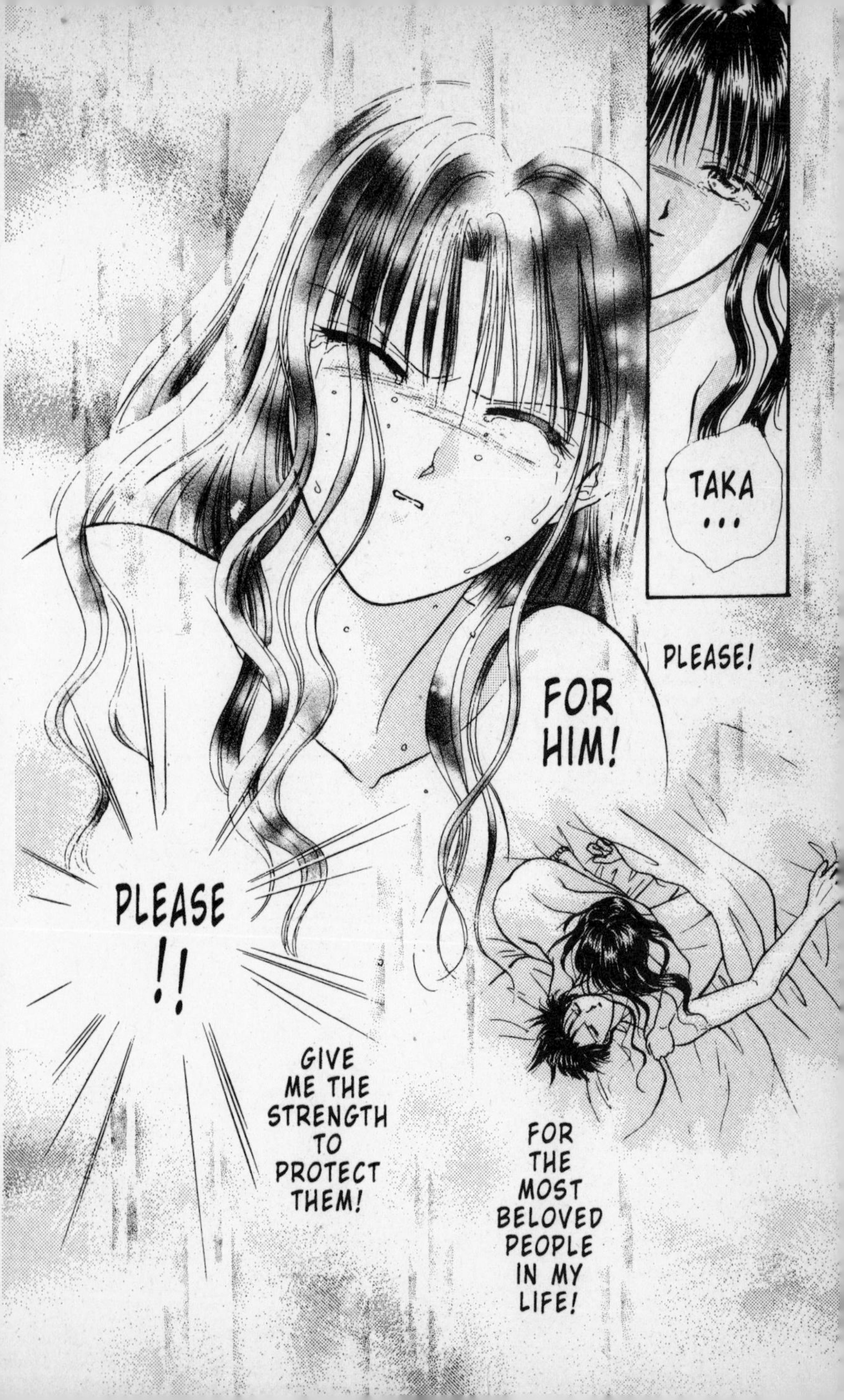
TAKA...
PLEASE!
FOR HIM!
PLEASE!!
FOR THE MOST BELOVED PEOPLE IN MY LIFE!
GIVE ME THE STRENGTH TO PROTECT THEM!

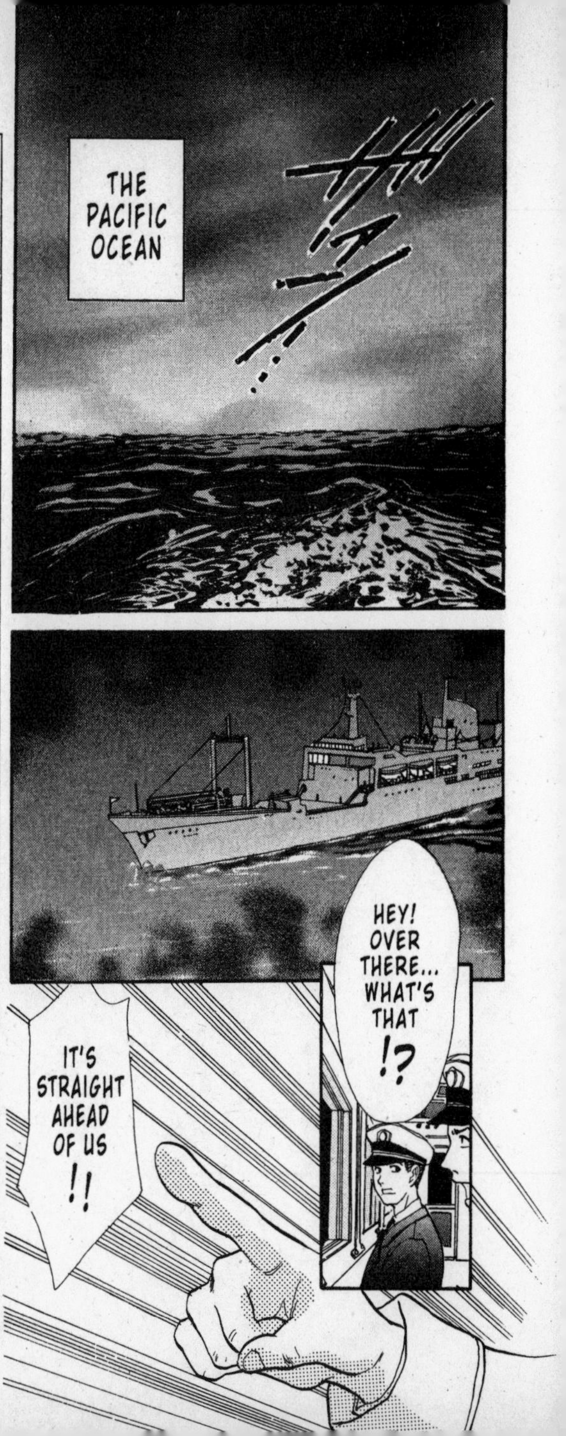
THE PACIFIC OCEAN
HEY! OVER THERE... WHAT'S THAT!?
IT'S STRAIGHT AHEAD OF US!!

I heard this from a whole bunch of people: "I thought the artist who drew this story was older!" Do I seem like such an old lady to you!? Or at least that was my first reaction...but I guess that wasn't what they meant. ☺ If you wonder why I'm commenting on this, I've heard from a bunch of people who say that Part 2 was a very adult story, or that children shouldn't be allowed to read it. *Oh, no! People may take that comment as being all about sex! (But the people who go on about sex... they DO know it's a 22.3-year-old woman writing this, right? It's what was in my heart at the time, and... um, I'll just end it there!)* There's the possibility of a book coming out that delves into the meanings of *Fushigi Yūgi* Parts 1 and 2, the dialog, and installments (really?). If they really did a thorough scrutiny, I could imagine it filling two or three books! ☺ The number of people who write letters analyzing my intentions for the story are very few, but... I think that after all the volumes are out, if my readers set the story aside and, after gaining more life experience or maturing into adulthood, they go back and read it one more time, they may get something different out of the story. Although I think it would be interesting to see a book written that explains the story from volume 1 to the end (a player's guide?), I think it's an impossible task. ☺ It just wouldn't fit in one book. I'm sure of that. And would it really serve the readers? You don't have to understand **everything!** Some of the stuff is just me being fanatical about the work. I planned out the story from the beginning of the series to the last scene of volume 13 in one go. And I followed that plan, so I never got off track, but there were times when my calculations were off or when a character started developing on his/her own. ☺ *Sometimes I just can't control them!* Wasn't Chiriko supposed to live until the big war? And wasn't Mitsukake supposed to die in a much flashier fashion, in his previous town? And wasn't Hotohori supposed to capture Tamahome's loving gaze... and leave Miaka stranded in the world of the book? ☺ *Now that would have been a problem!* About the villains... Certainly the installments with Lian made me say, "That's it!" According to my assistants, they were "hard" and "shadowy." ☺ The Seiryu Warriors were pretty straightforward and a little cute. The villains for Part 2 really attack your insides! From Lian to Miiru to Fei-Gao to Yong-Shua... You can see the emphasis move from the exterior to the interior as you read from start to finish. *But I'm still not very good at this. ὃὃ I guess it's not a big deal...*

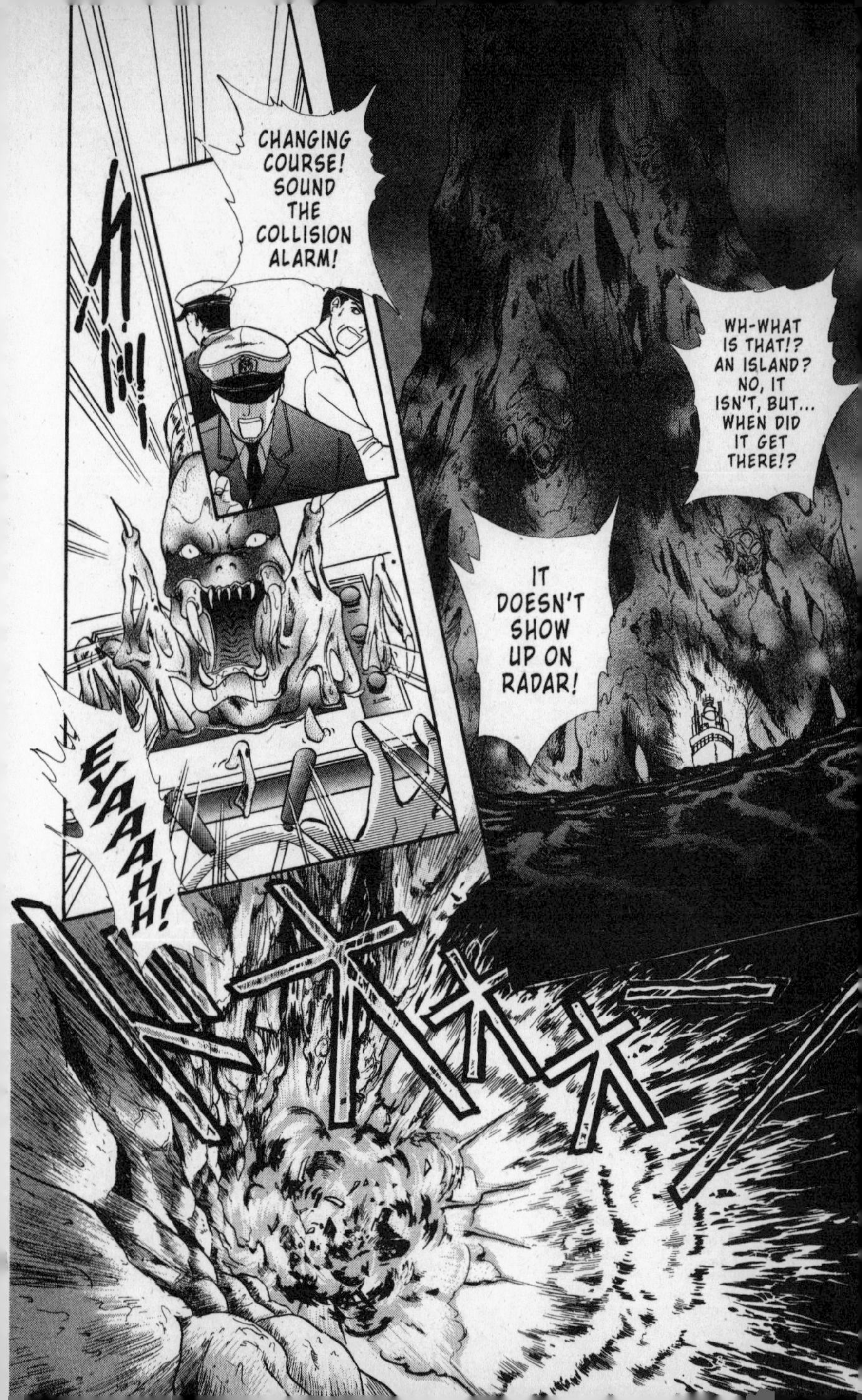
WH-WHAT IS THAT!? AN ISLAND? NO, IT ISN'T, BUT... WHEN DID IT GET THERE!?
IT DOESN'T SHOW UP ON RADAR!
CHANGING COURSE! SOUND THE COLLISION ALARM!
EYAAAH!

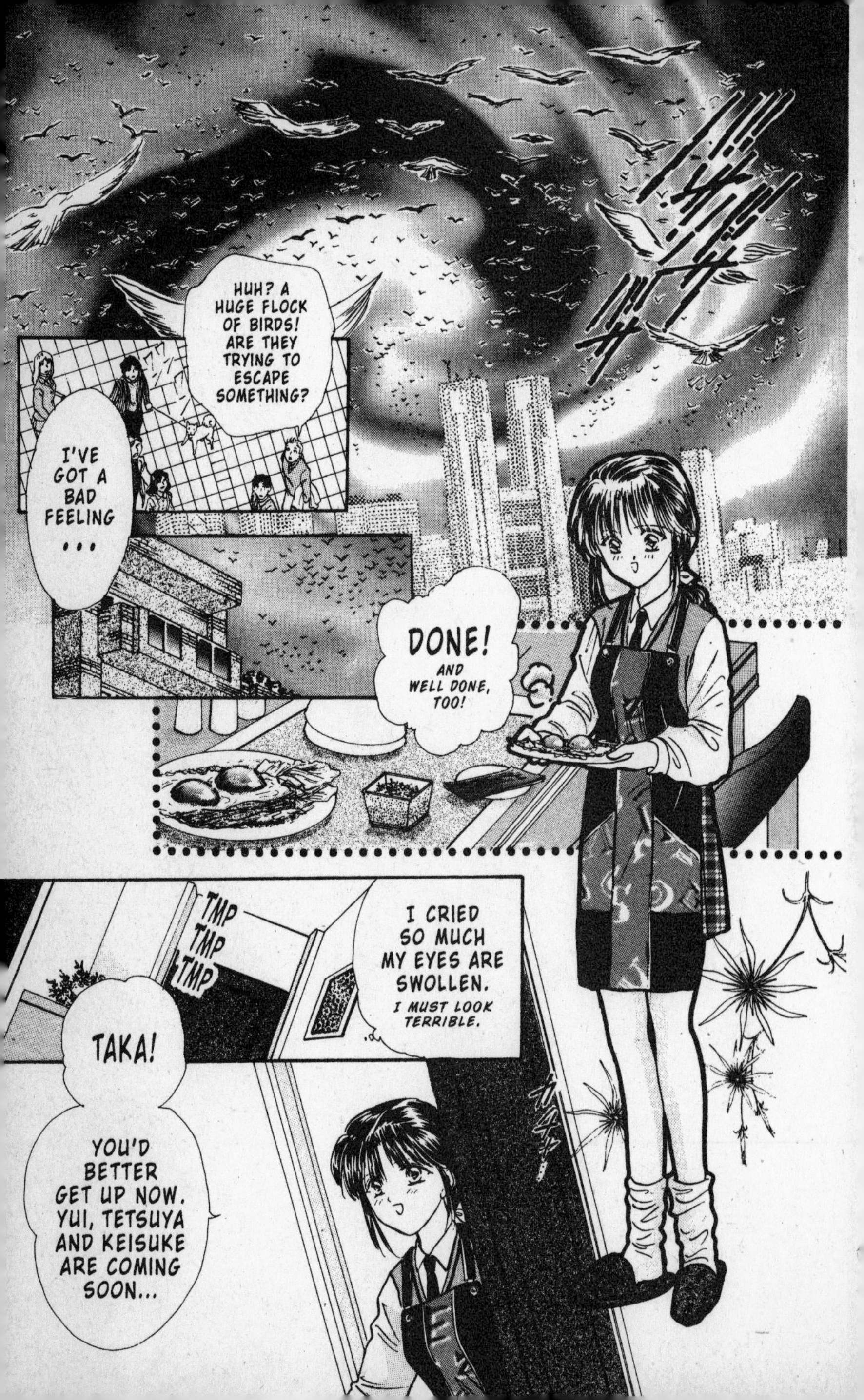

HUH? A HUGE FLOCK OF BIRDS! ARE THEY TRYING TO ESCAPE SOMETHING?
I'VE GOT A BAD FEELING...
DONE! AND WELL DONE, TOO!
TMP TMP TMP
I CRIED SO MUCH MY EYES ARE SWOLLEN. I MUST LOOK TERRIBLE.
TAKA!
YOU'D BETTER GET UP NOW. YUI, TETSUYA AND KEISUKE ARE COMING SOON...

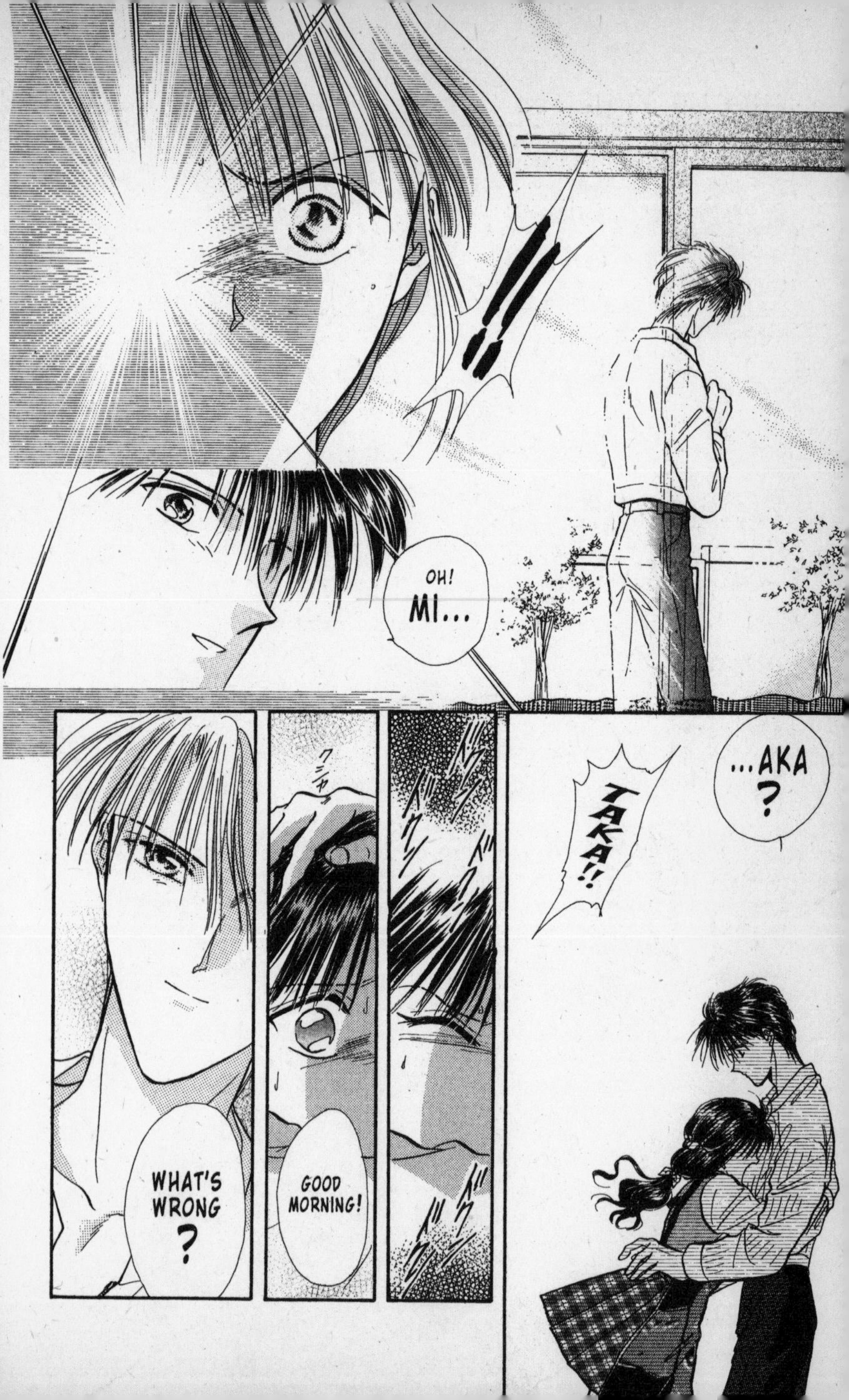
OH! MI...
...AKA ?
TAKA!!
GOOD MORNING!
WHAT'S WRONG ?

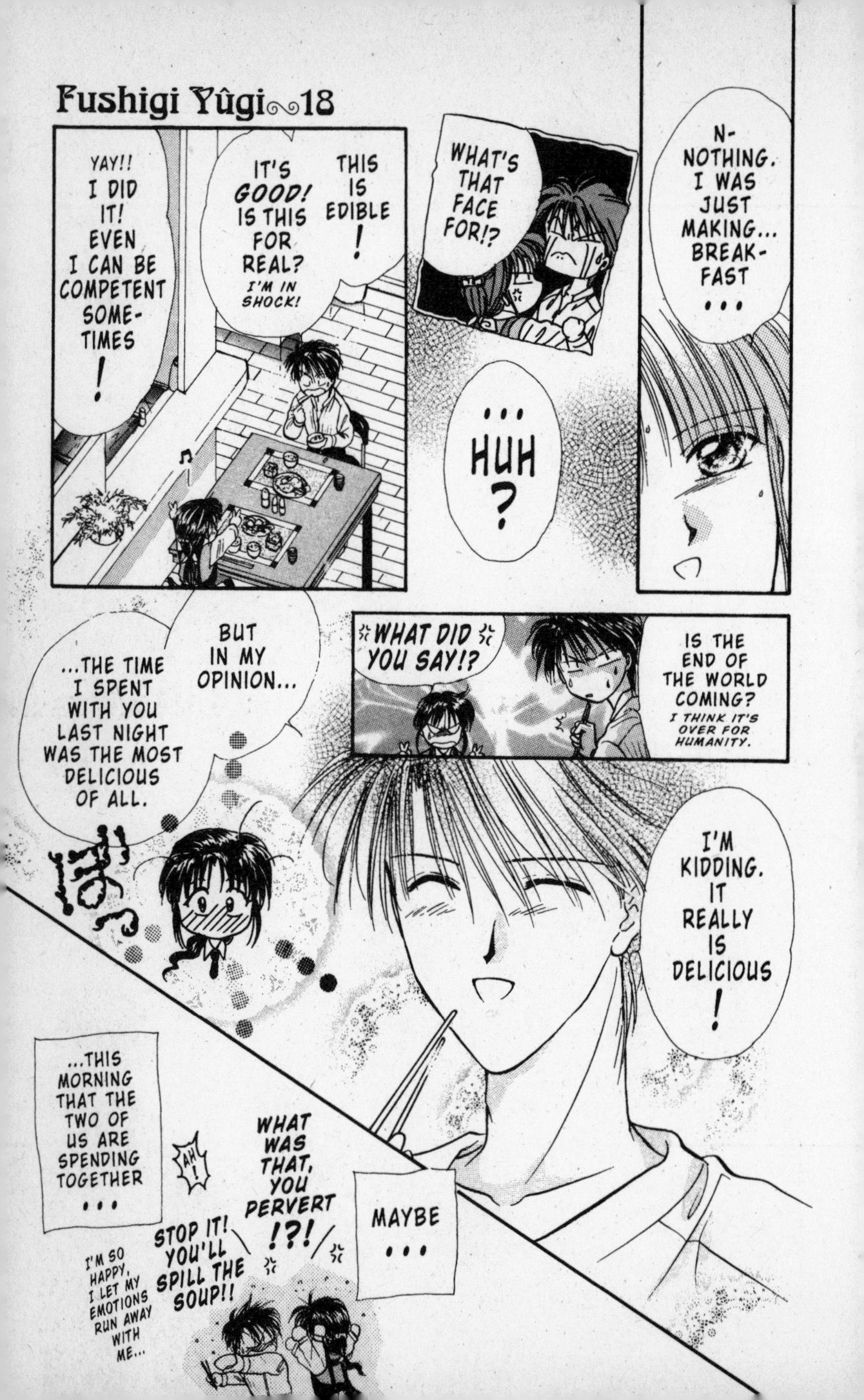
N-NOTHING. I WAS JUST MAKING... BREAK-FAST...
WHAT'S THAT FACE FOR!?
...HUH?
THIS IS EDIBLE!
IT'S GOOD! IS THIS FOR REAL? I'M IN SHOCK!
YAY!! I DID IT! EVEN I CAN BE COMPETENT SOME-TIMES!
IS THE END OF THE WORLD COMING? I THINK IT'S OVER FOR HUMANITY.
WHAT DID YOU SAY!?
I'M KIDDING. IT REALLY IS DELICIOUS!
BUT IN MY OPINION...
...THE TIME I SPENT WITH YOU LAST NIGHT WAS THE MOST DELICIOUS OF ALL.
MAYBE...
WHAT WAS THAT, YOU PERVERT!?!
STOP IT! YOU'LL SPILL THE SOUP!!
AH!
...THIS MORNING THAT THE TWO OF US ARE SPENDING TOGETHER...
I'M SO HAPPY, I LET MY EMOTIONS RUN AWAY WITH ME...

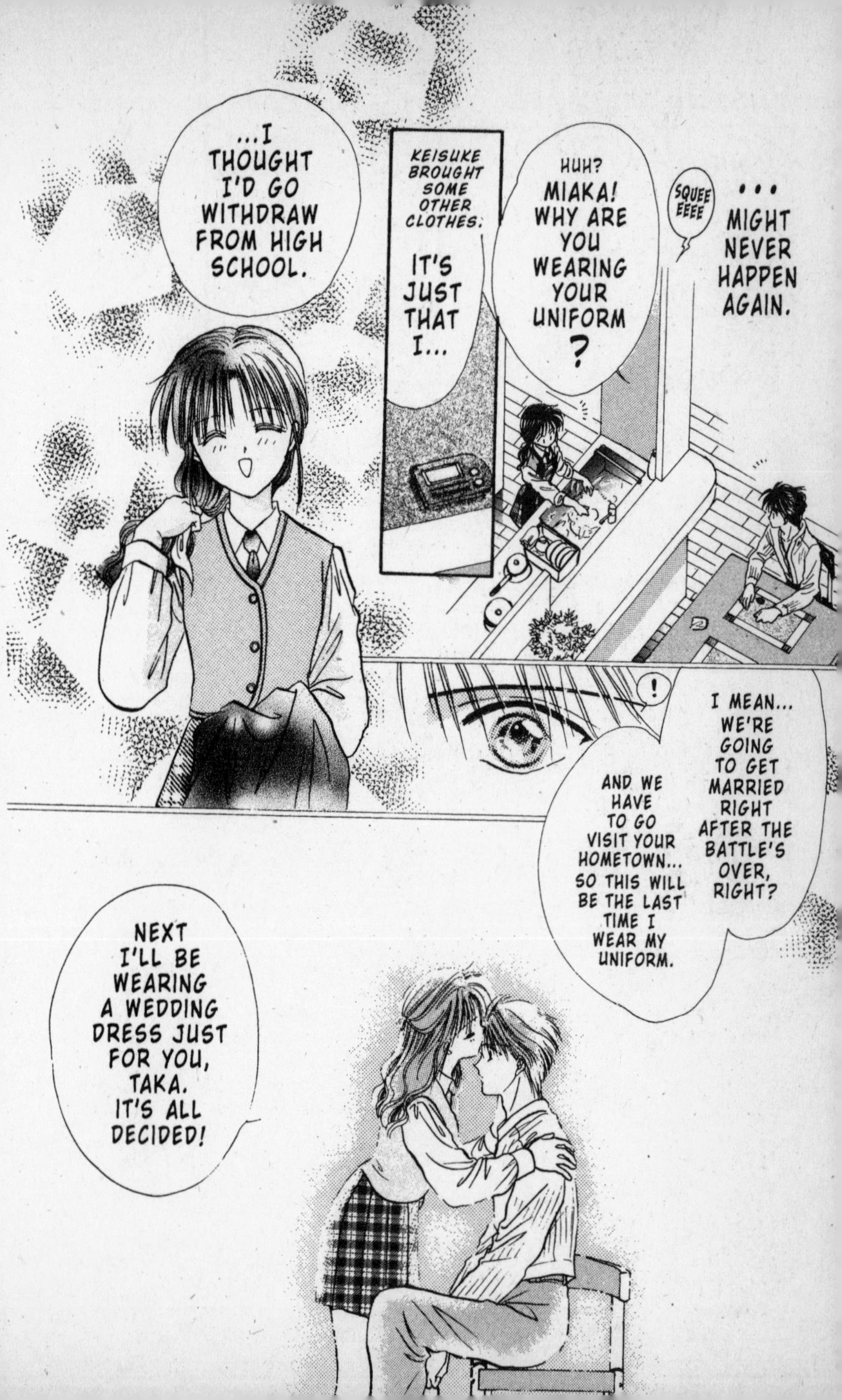

... MIGHT NEVER HAPPEN AGAIN.
SQUEEE EEEE
HUH? MIAKA! WHY ARE YOU WEARING YOUR UNIFORM?
KEISUKE BROUGHT SOME OTHER CLOTHES.
IT'S JUST THAT I...
...I THOUGHT I'D GO WITHDRAW FROM HIGH SCHOOL.
!
I MEAN... WE'RE GOING TO GET MARRIED RIGHT AFTER THE BATTLE'S OVER, RIGHT?
AND WE HAVE TO GO VISIT YOUR HOMETOWN... SO THIS WILL BE THE LAST TIME I WEAR MY UNIFORM.
NEXT I'LL BE WEARING A WEDDING DRESS JUST FOR YOU, TAKA. IT'S ALL DECIDED!

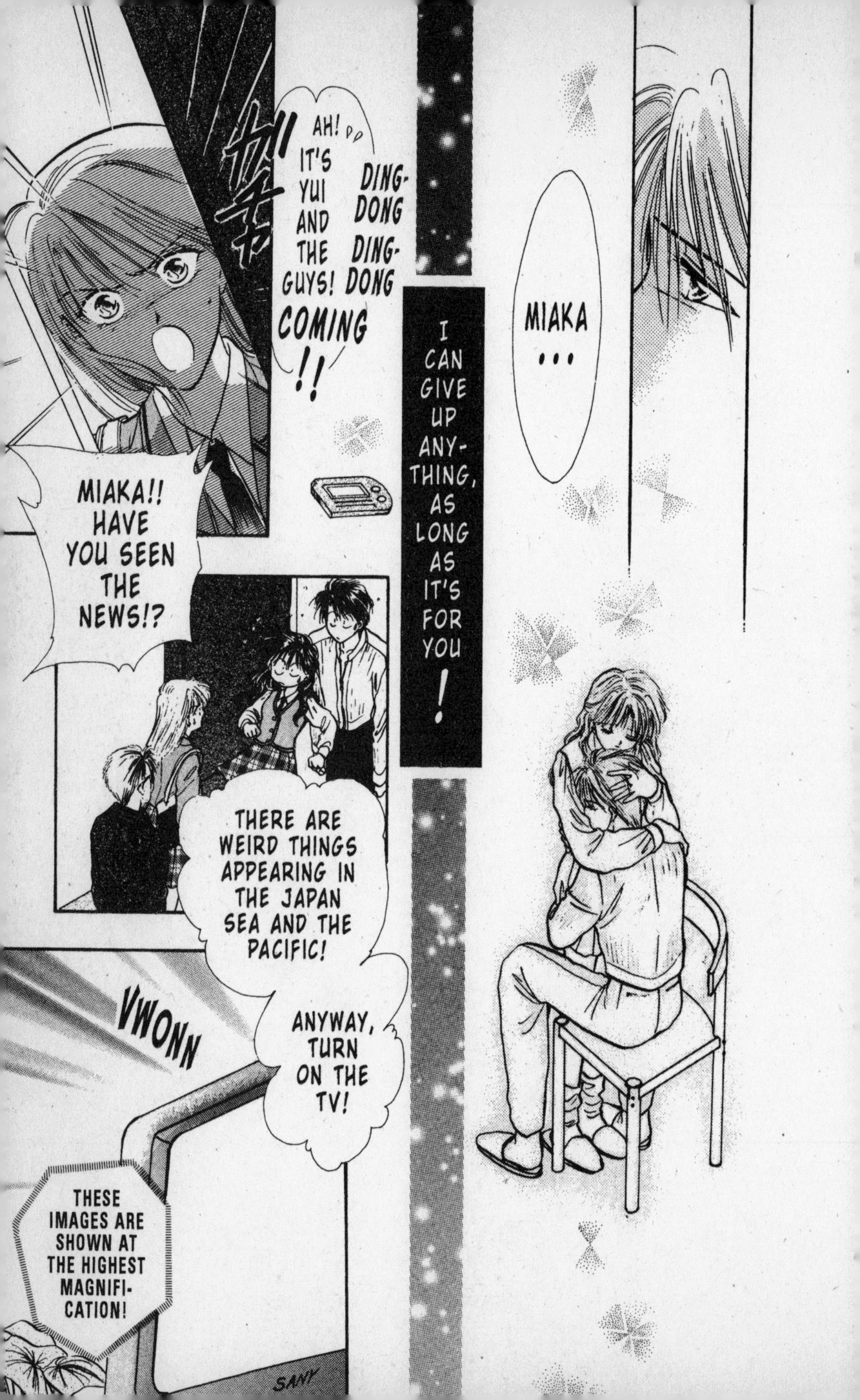

MIAKA...
I CAN GIVE UP ANYTHING, AS LONG AS IT'S FOR YOU!
DING-DONG DING-DONG
AH! IT'S YUI AND THE GUYS!
COMING!!
MIAKA!! HAVE YOU SEEN THE NEWS!?
THERE ARE WEIRD THINGS APPEARING IN THE JAPAN SEA AND THE PACIFIC!
ANYWAY, TURN ON THE TV!
VWONN
THESE IMAGES ARE SHOWN AT THE HIGHEST MAGNIFICATION!
SANY

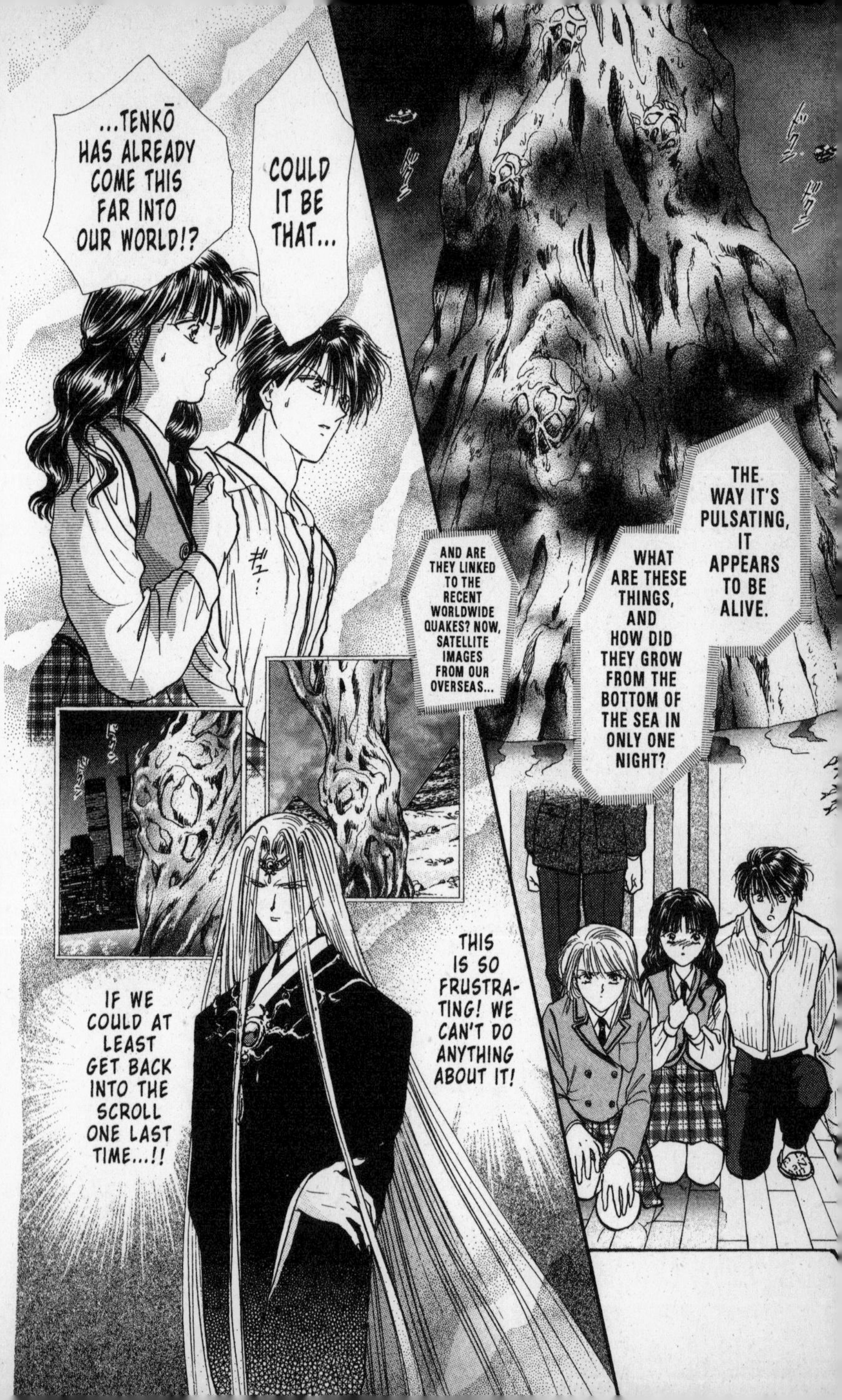
THE WAY IT'S PULSATING, IT APPEARS TO BE ALIVE.
WHAT ARE THESE THINGS, AND HOW DID THEY GROW FROM THE BOTTOM OF THE SEA IN ONLY ONE NIGHT?
AND ARE THEY LINKED TO THE RECENT WORLDWIDE QUAKES? NOW, SATELLITE IMAGES FROM OUR OVERSEAS...
THIS IS SO FRUSTRA-TING! WE CAN'T DO ANYTHING ABOUT IT!
COULD IT BE THAT...
...TENKŌ HAS ALREADY COME THIS FAR INTO OUR WORLD!?
IF WE COULD AT LEAST GET BACK INTO THE SCROLL ONE LAST TIME...!!

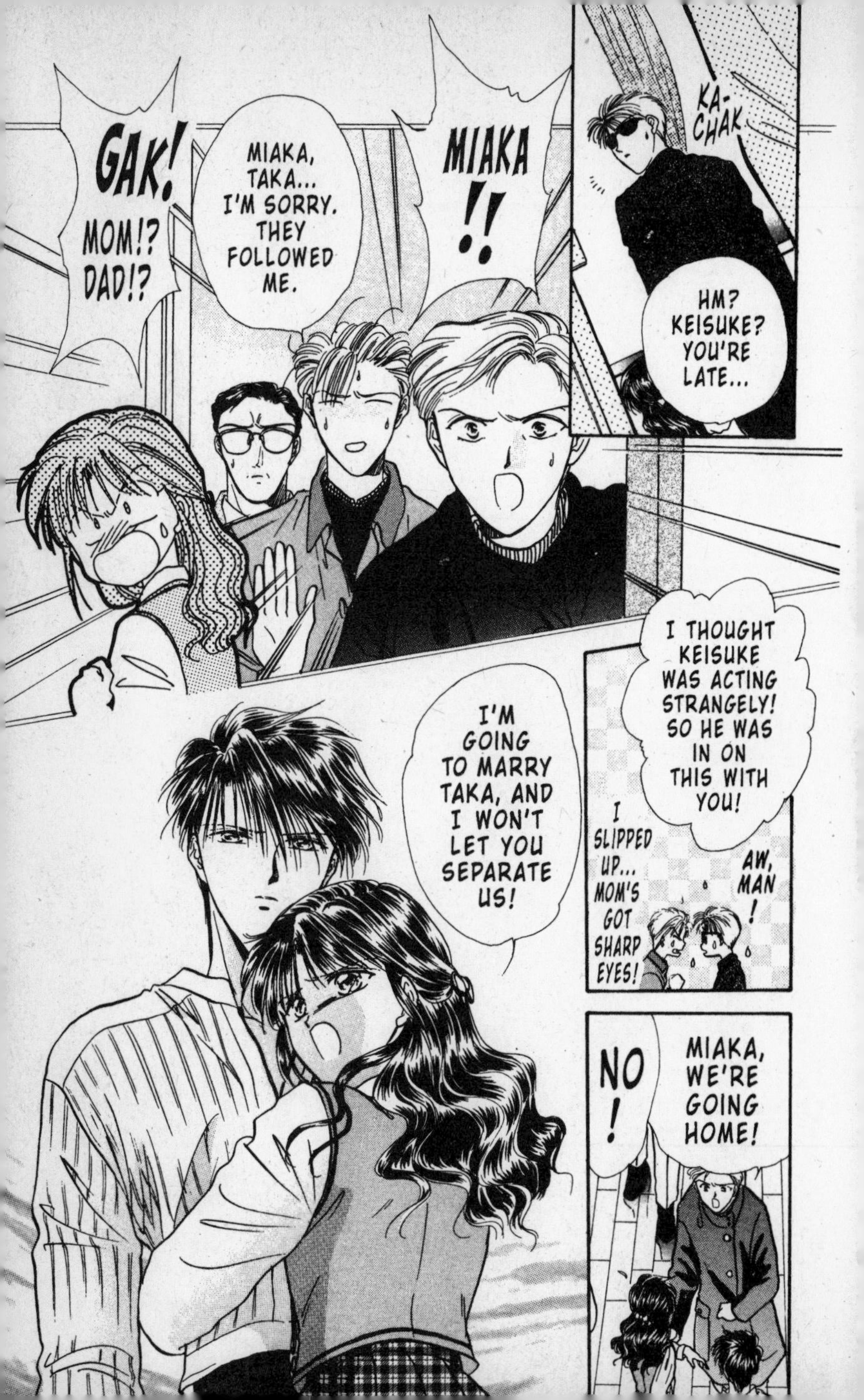
KA-CHAK
HM? KEISUKE? YOU'RE LATE...
MIAKA !!
MIAKA, TAKA... I'M SORRY. THEY FOLLOWED ME.
GAK!
MOM!? DAD!?
I THOUGHT KEISUKE WAS ACTING STRANGELY! SO HE WAS IN ON THIS WITH YOU!
AW, MAN!
I SLIPPED UP... MOM'S GOT SHARP EYES!
MIAKA, WE'RE GOING HOME!
NO!
I'M GOING TO MARRY TAKA, AND I WON'T LET YOU SEPARATE US!

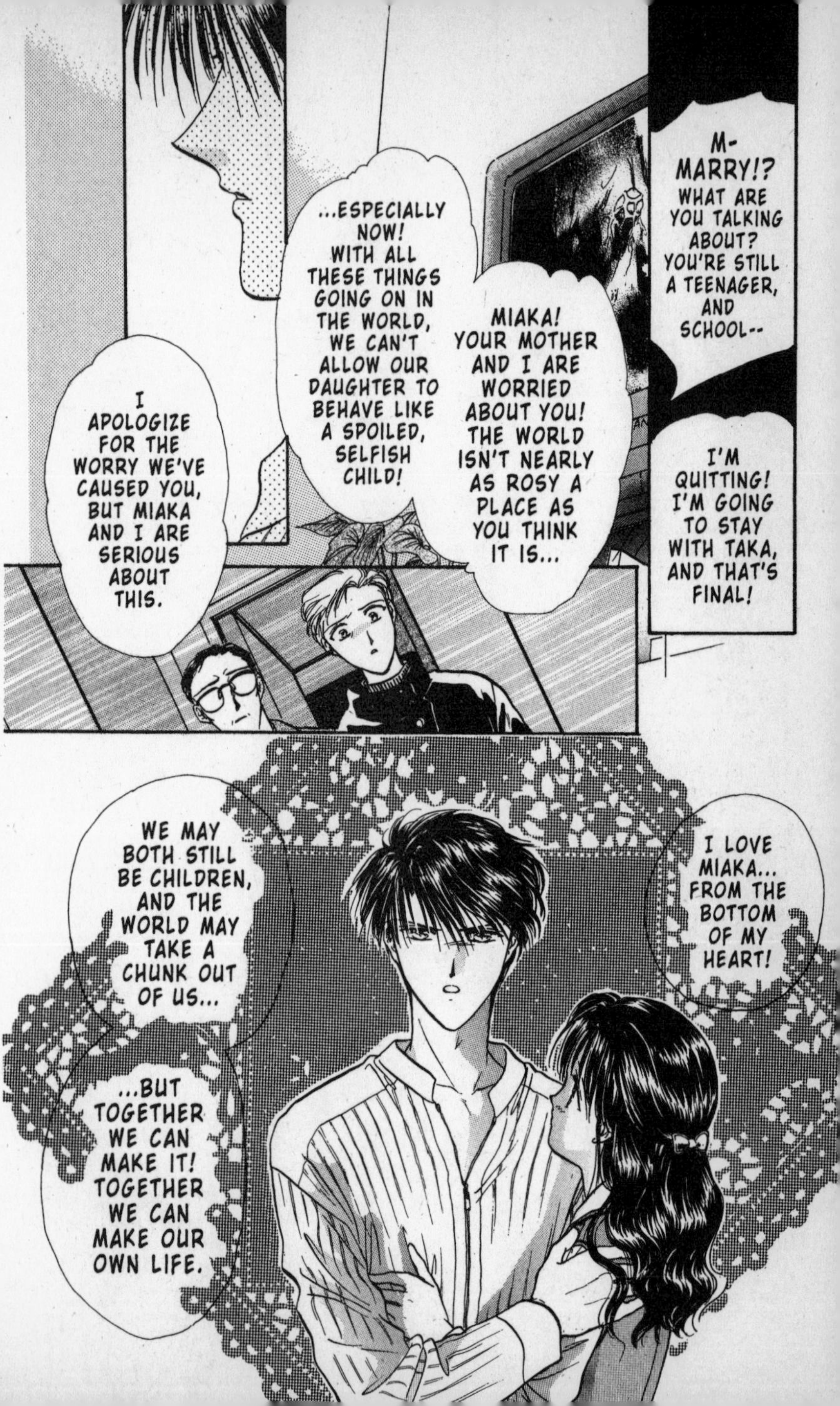
M-MARRY!? WHAT ARE YOU TALKING ABOUT? YOU'RE STILL A TEENAGER, AND SCHOOL--
I'M QUITTING! I'M GOING TO STAY WITH TAKA, AND THAT'S FINAL!
MIAKA! YOUR MOTHER AND I ARE WORRIED ABOUT YOU! THE WORLD ISN'T NEARLY AS ROSY A PLACE AS YOU THINK IT IS...
...ESPECIALLY NOW! WITH ALL THESE THINGS GOING ON IN THE WORLD, WE CAN'T ALLOW OUR DAUGHTER TO BEHAVE LIKE A SPOILED, SELFISH CHILD!
I APOLOGIZE FOR THE WORRY WE'VE CAUSED YOU, BUT MIAKA AND I ARE SERIOUS ABOUT THIS.
I LOVE MIAKA... FROM THE BOTTOM OF MY HEART!
WE MAY BOTH STILL BE CHILDREN, AND THE WORLD MAY TAKE A CHUNK OUT OF US...
...BUT TOGETHER WE CAN MAKE IT! TOGETHER WE CAN MAKE OUR OWN LIFE.

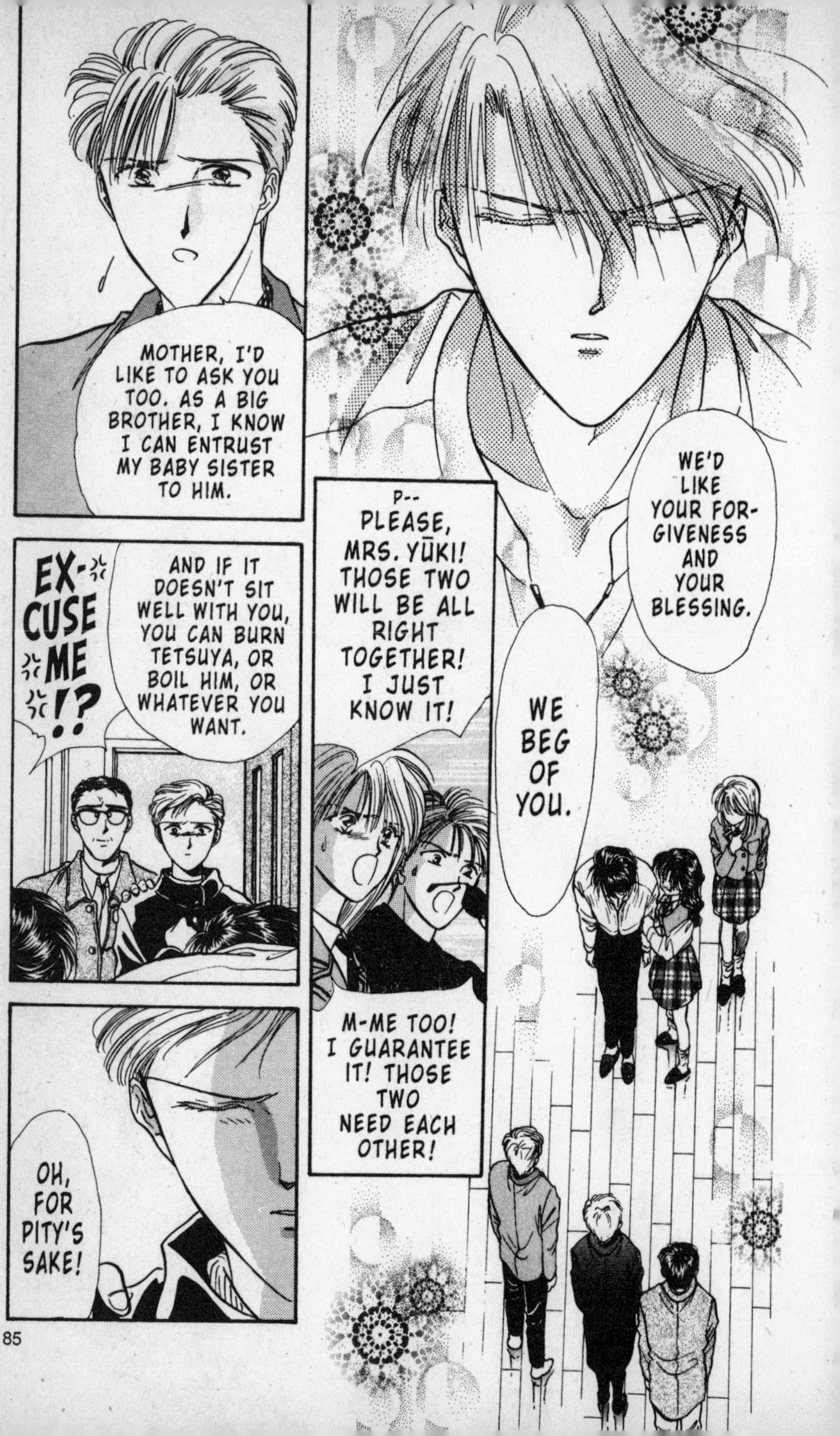
WE'D LIKE YOUR FORGIVENESS AND YOUR BLESSING.
WE BEG OF YOU.
MOTHER, I'D LIKE TO ASK YOU TOO. AS A BIG BROTHER, I KNOW I CAN ENTRUST MY BABY SISTER TO HIM.
P-- PLEASE, MRS. YŪKI! THOSE TWO WILL BE ALL RIGHT TOGETHER! I JUST KNOW IT!
M-ME TOO! I GUARANTEE IT! THOSE TWO NEED EACH OTHER!
AND IF IT DOESN'T SIT WELL WITH YOU, YOU CAN BURN TETSUYA, OR BOIL HIM, OR WHATEVER YOU WANT.
EX-CUSE ME!?
OH, FOR PITY'S SAKE!

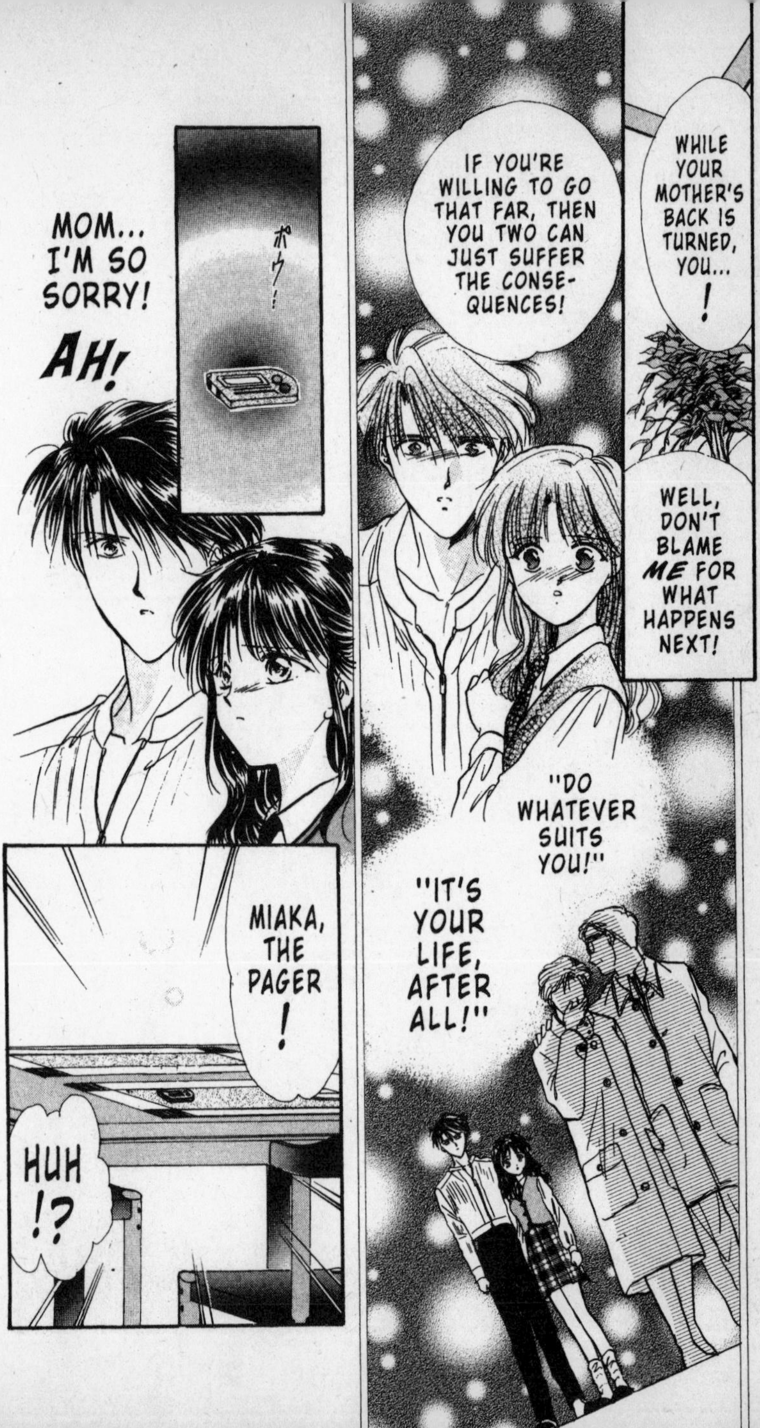

WHILE YOUR MOTHER'S BACK IS TURNED, YOU...!
IF YOU'RE WILLING TO GO THAT FAR, THEN YOU TWO CAN JUST SUFFER THE CONSEQUENCES!
WELL, DON'T BLAME *ME* FOR WHAT HAPPENS NEXT!
"DO WHATEVER SUITS YOU!"
"IT'S YOUR LIFE, AFTER ALL!"
ポウ！
MOM... I'M SO SORRY!
AH!
MIAKA, THE PAGER!
HUH!?

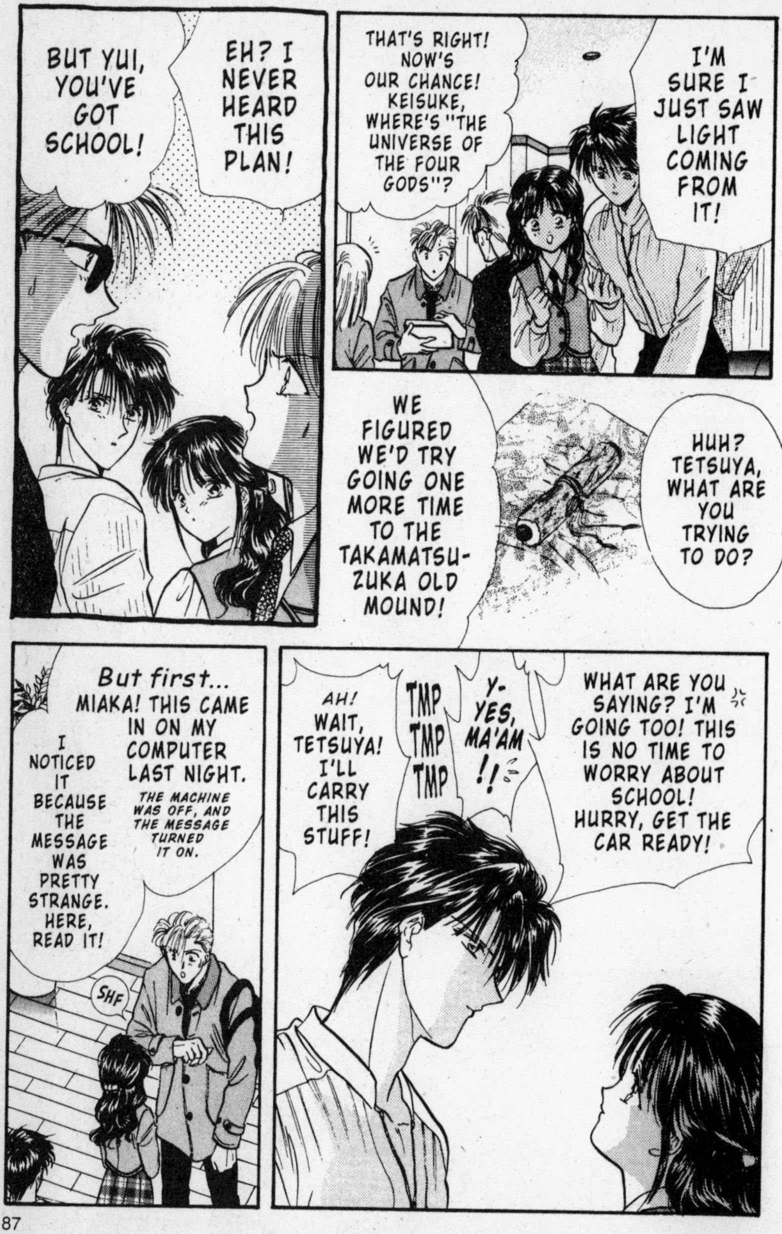
I'M SURE I JUST SAW LIGHT COMING FROM IT!
THAT'S RIGHT! NOW'S OUR CHANCE! KEISUKE, WHERE'S "THE UNIVERSE OF THE FOUR GODS"?
HUH? TETSUYA, WHAT ARE YOU TRYING TO DO?
WE FIGURED WE'D TRY GOING ONE MORE TIME TO THE TAKAMATSU-ZUKA OLD MOUND!
EH? I NEVER HEARD THIS PLAN!
BUT YUI, YOU'VE GOT SCHOOL!
WHAT ARE YOU SAYING? I'M GOING TOO! THIS IS NO TIME TO WORRY ABOUT SCHOOL! HURRY, GET THE CAR READY!
Y-YES, MA'AM!!
TMP TMP TMP
AH! WAIT, TETSUYA! I'LL CARRY THIS STUFF!
But first... MIAKA! THIS CAME IN ON MY COMPUTER LAST NIGHT.
THE MACHINE WAS OFF, AND THE MESSAGE TURNED IT ON.
I NOTICED IT BECAUSE THE MESSAGE WAS PRETTY STRANGE. HERE, READ IT!
SHF

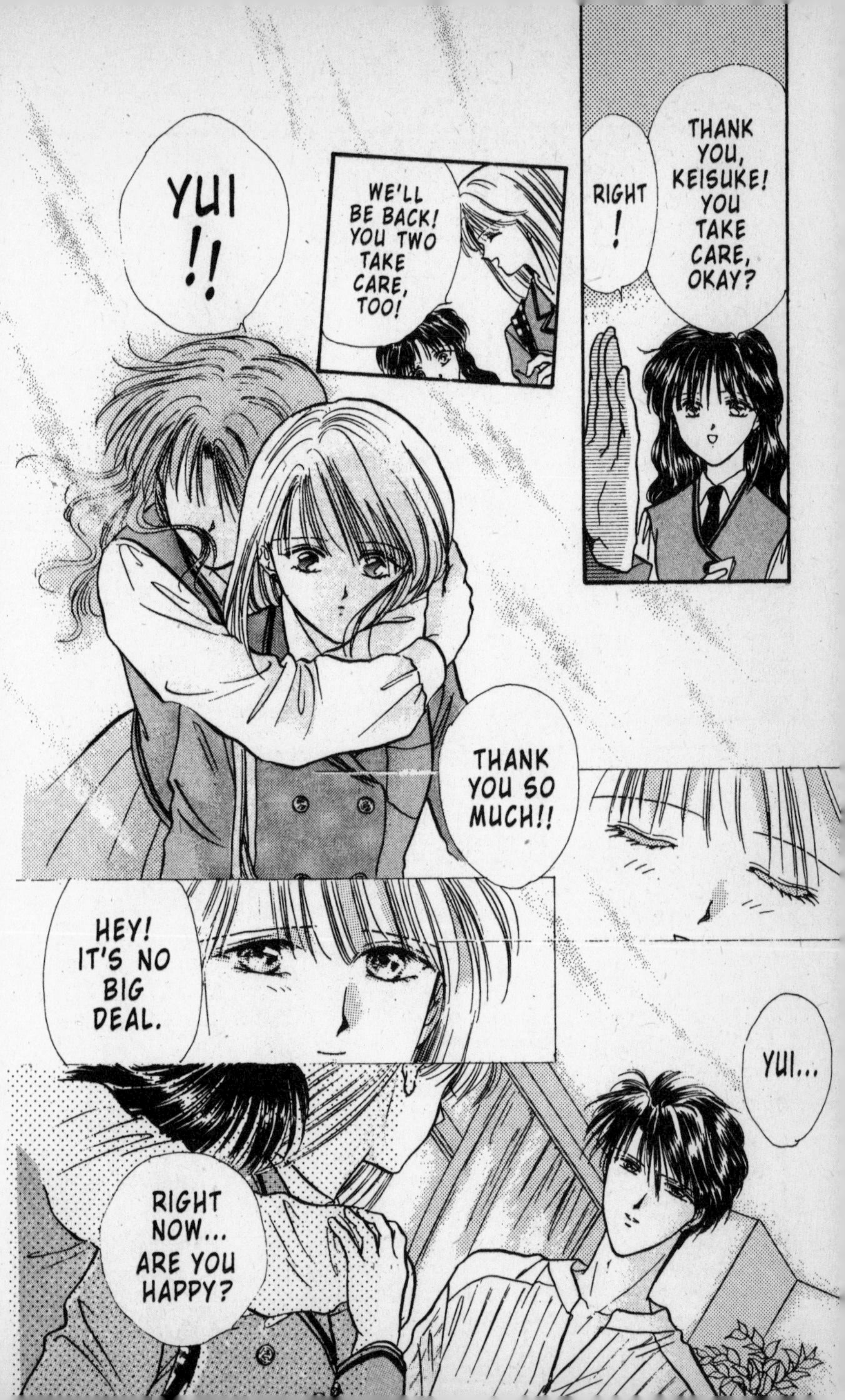
THANK YOU, KEISUKE! YOU TAKE CARE, OKAY?
RIGHT!
WE'LL BE BACK! YOU TWO TAKE CARE, TOO!
YUI!!
THANK YOU SO MUCH!!
HEY! IT'S NO BIG DEAL.
YUI...
RIGHT NOW... ARE YOU HAPPY?

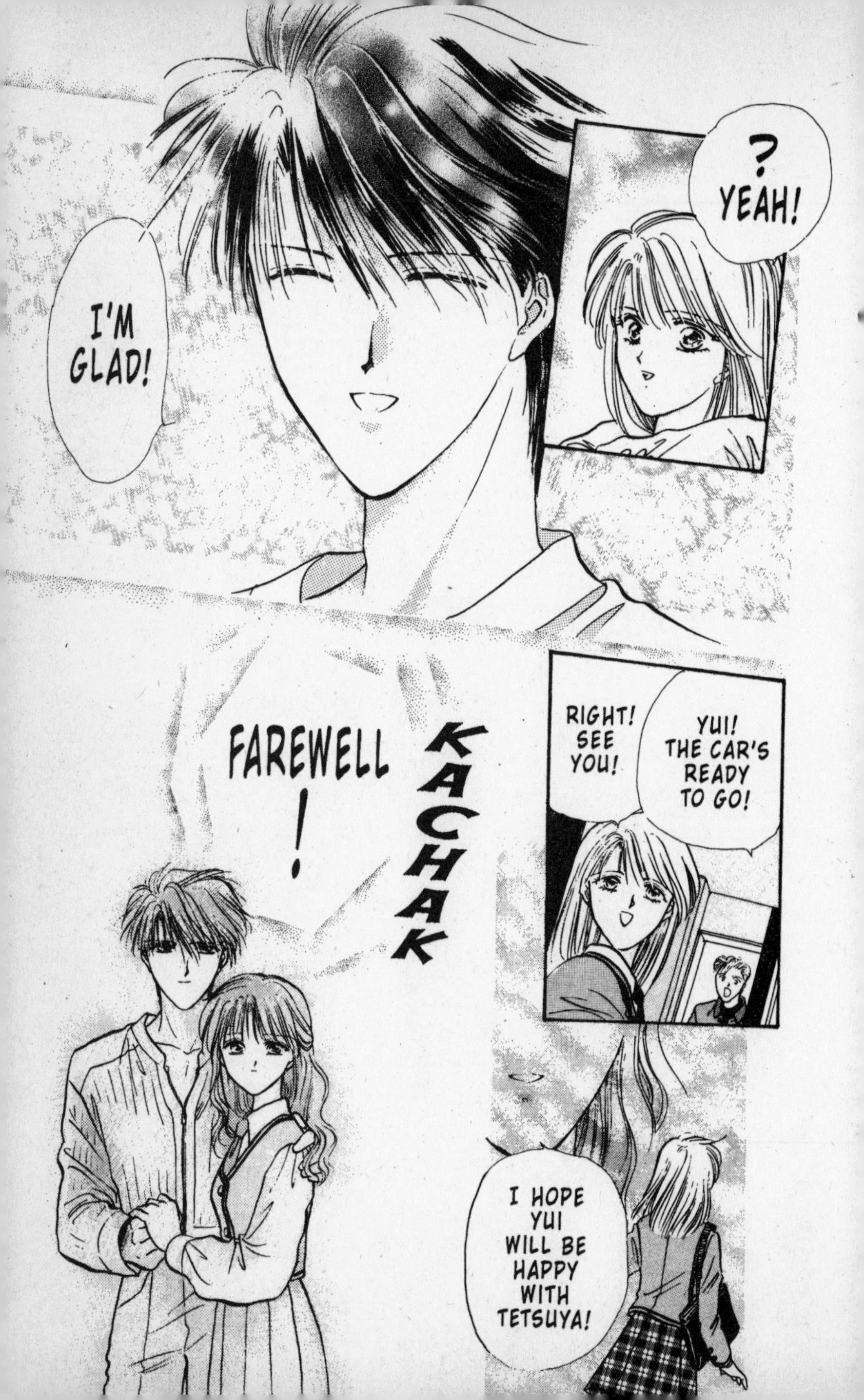
? YEAH!
I'M GLAD!
YUI! THE CAR'S READY TO GO!
RIGHT! SEE YOU!
KACHAK
FAREWELL!
I HOPE YUI WILL BE HAPPY WITH TETSUYA!

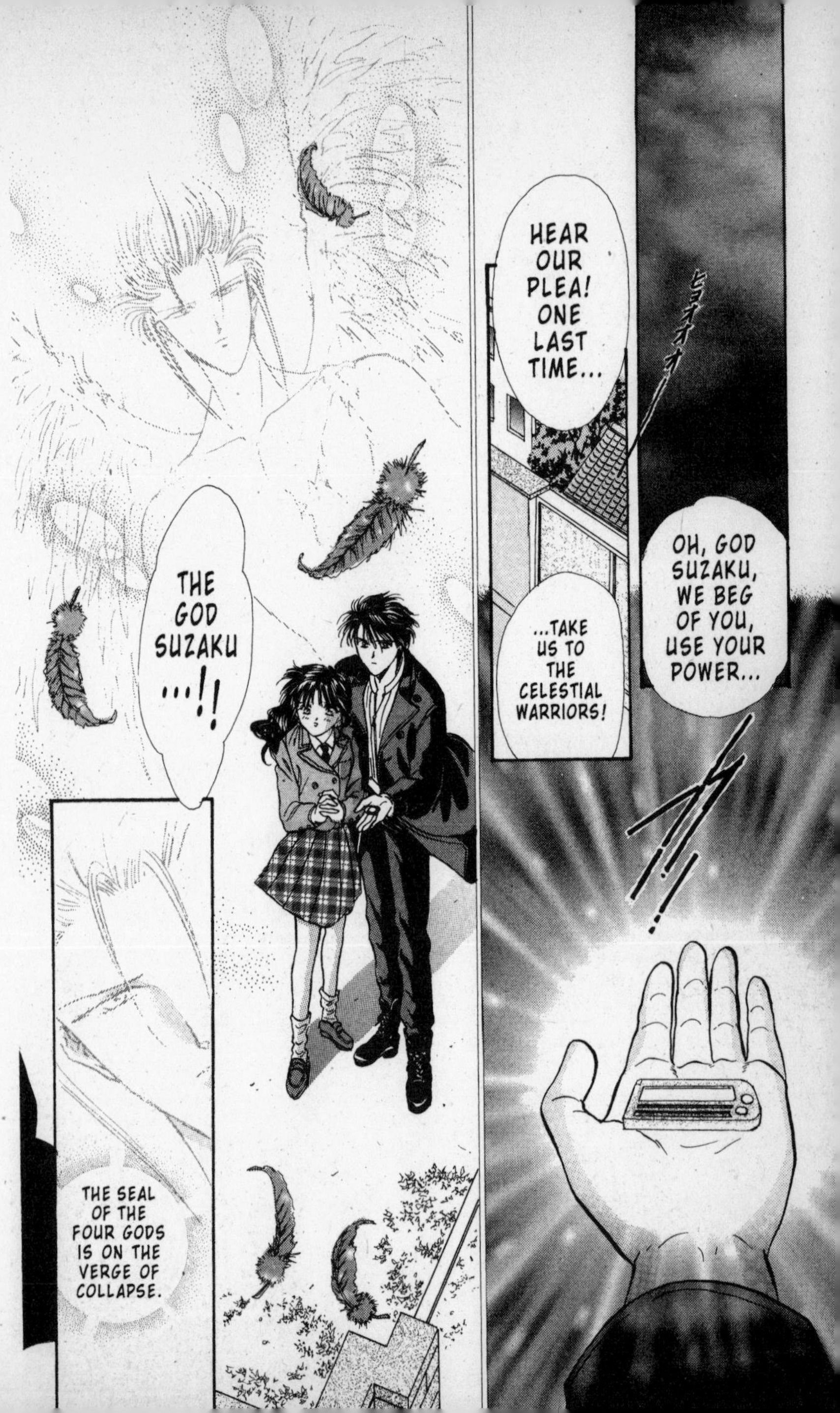
ヒョオオオー
OH, GOD SUZAKU, WE BEG OF YOU, USE YOUR POWER...
HEAR OUR PLEA! ONE LAST TIME...
...TAKE US TO THE CELESTIAL WARRIORS!
THE GOD SUZAKU...!!
THE SEAL OF THE FOUR GODS IS ON THE VERGE OF COLLAPSE.

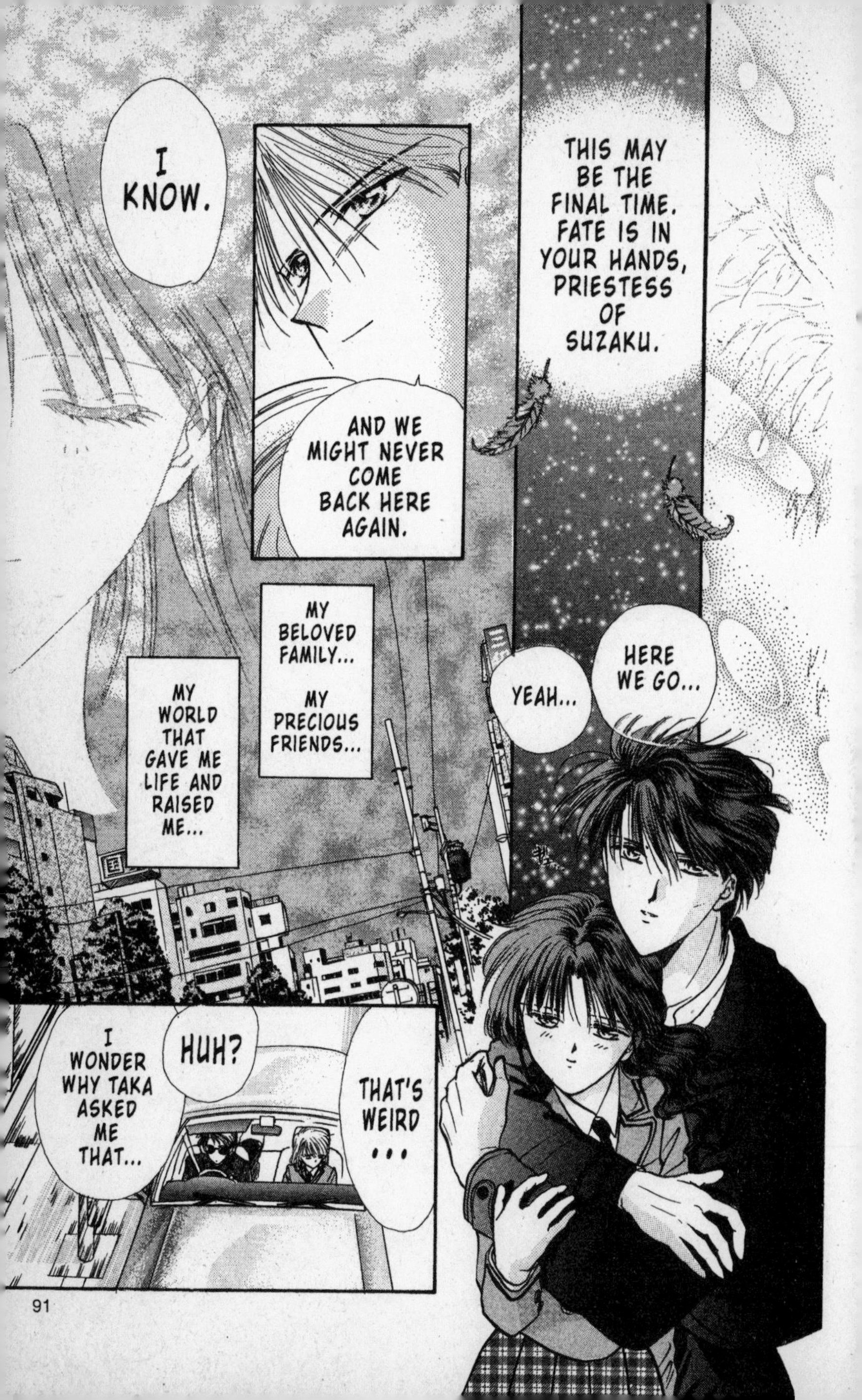
THIS MAY BE THE FINAL TIME. FATE IS IN YOUR HANDS, PRIESTESS OF SUZAKU.
AND WE MIGHT NEVER COME BACK HERE AGAIN.
I KNOW.
HERE WE GO...
YEAH...
MY BELOVED FAMILY...
MY PRECIOUS FRIENDS...
MY WORLD THAT GAVE ME LIFE AND RAISED ME...
THAT'S WEIRD...
HUH?
I WONDER WHY TAKA ASKED ME THAT...

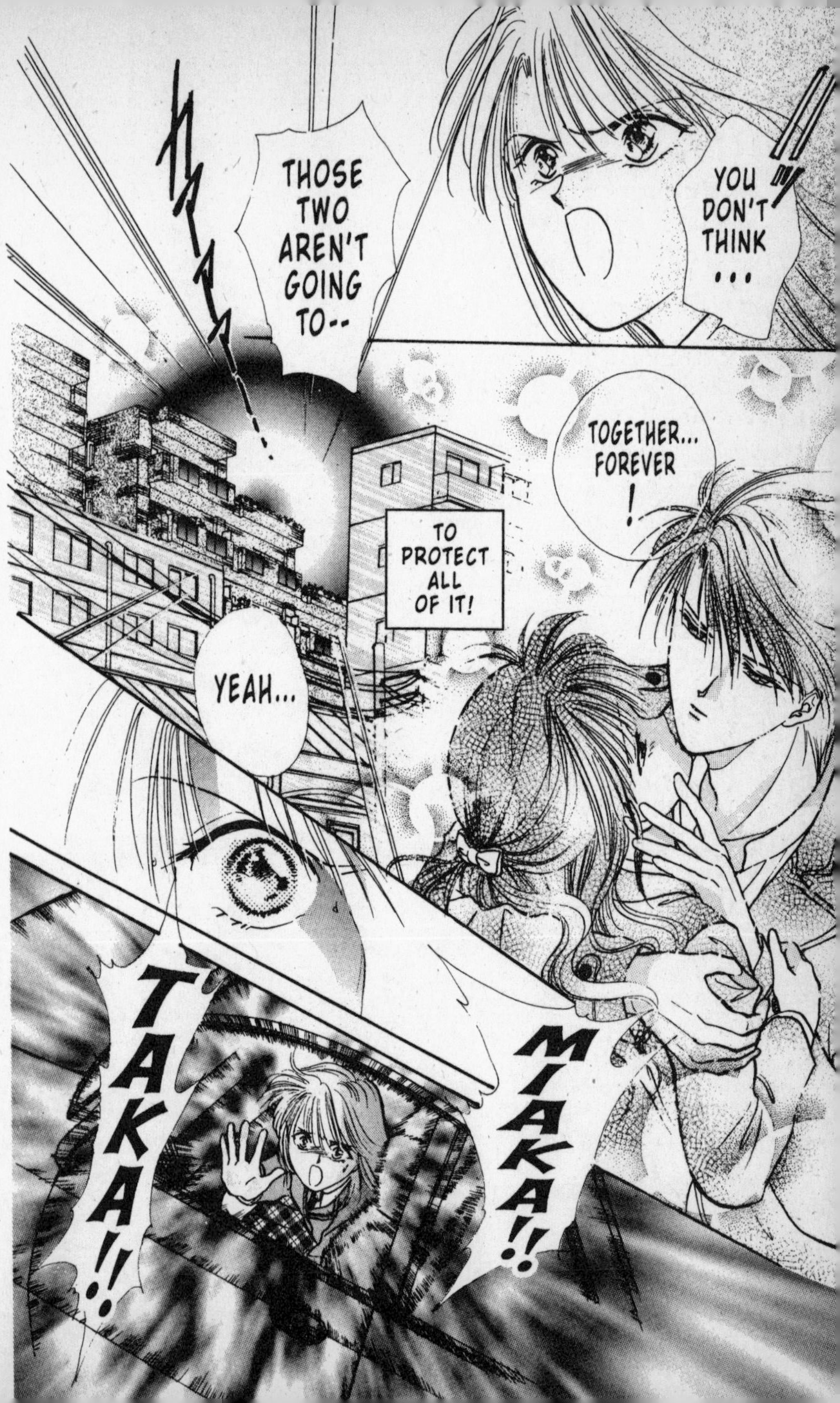
YOU DON'T THINK...
THOSE TWO AREN'T GOING TO--
TOGETHER... FOREVER!
TO PROTECT ALL OF IT!
YEAH...
MIAKA!!
TAKA!!

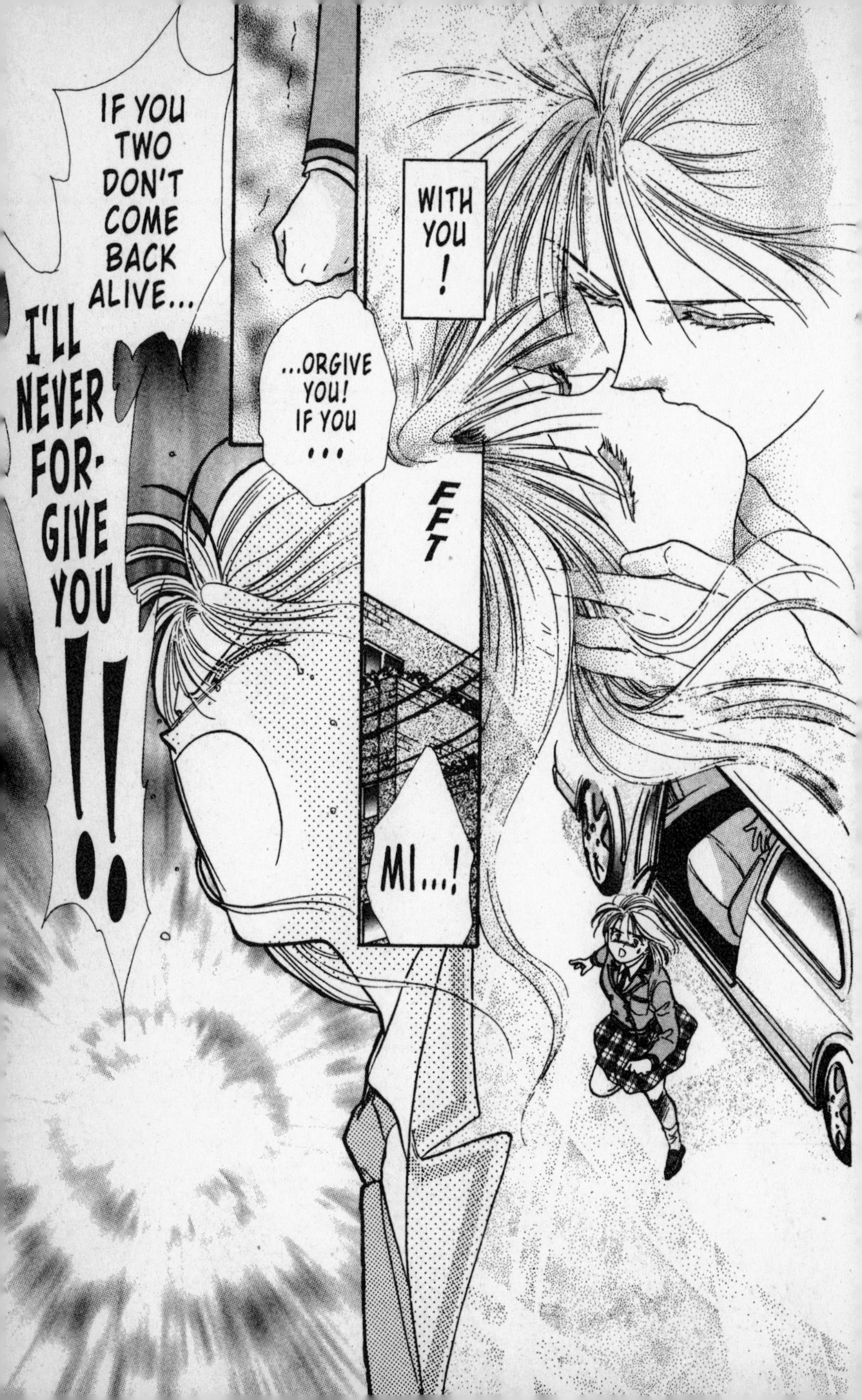
WITH YOU !
MI...!
FFT
...ORGIVE YOU! IF YOU ...
IF YOU TWO DON'T COME BACK ALIVE...
I'LL NEVER FOR-GIVE YOU!!

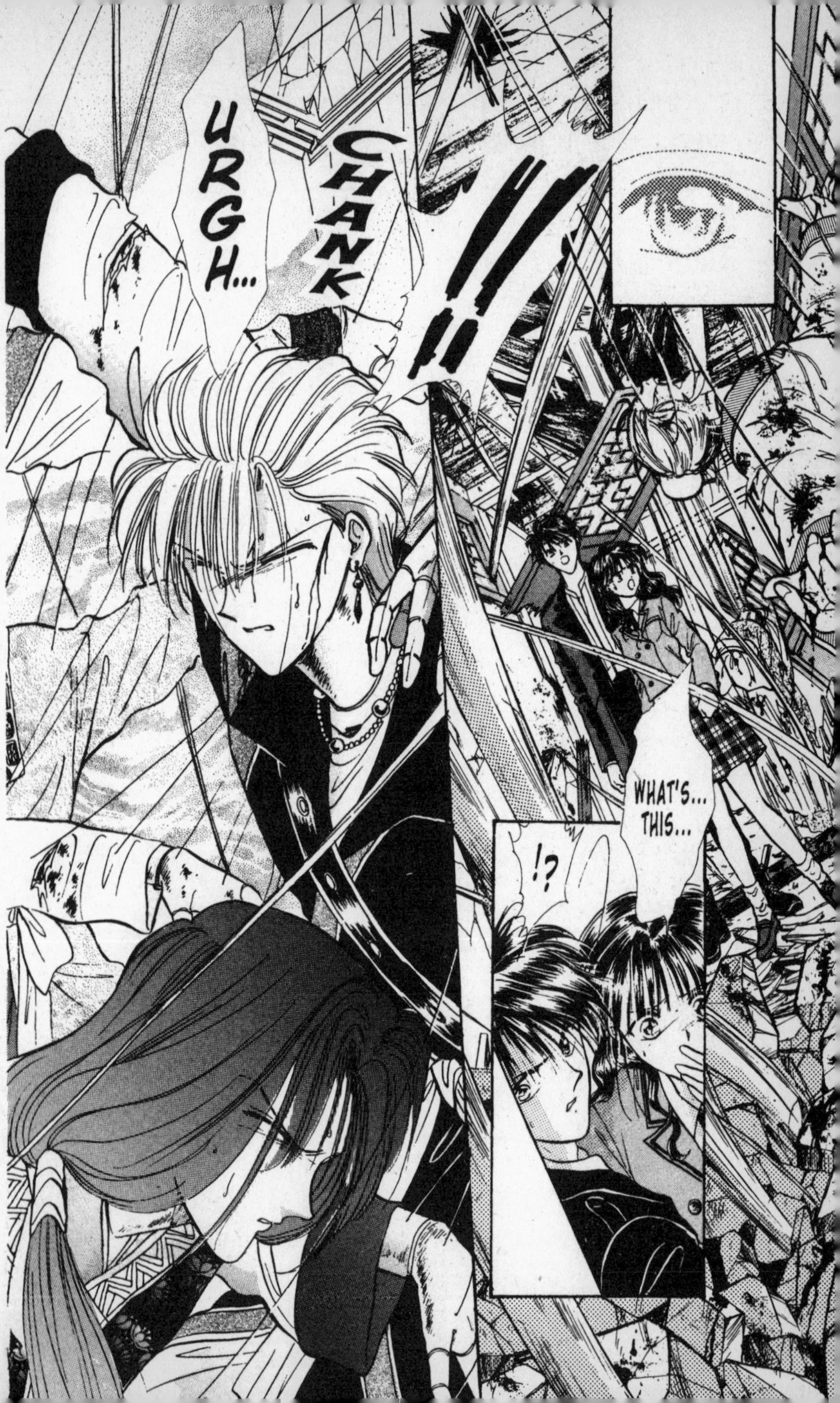
WHAT'S... THIS...
!?
CHANK
URGH...

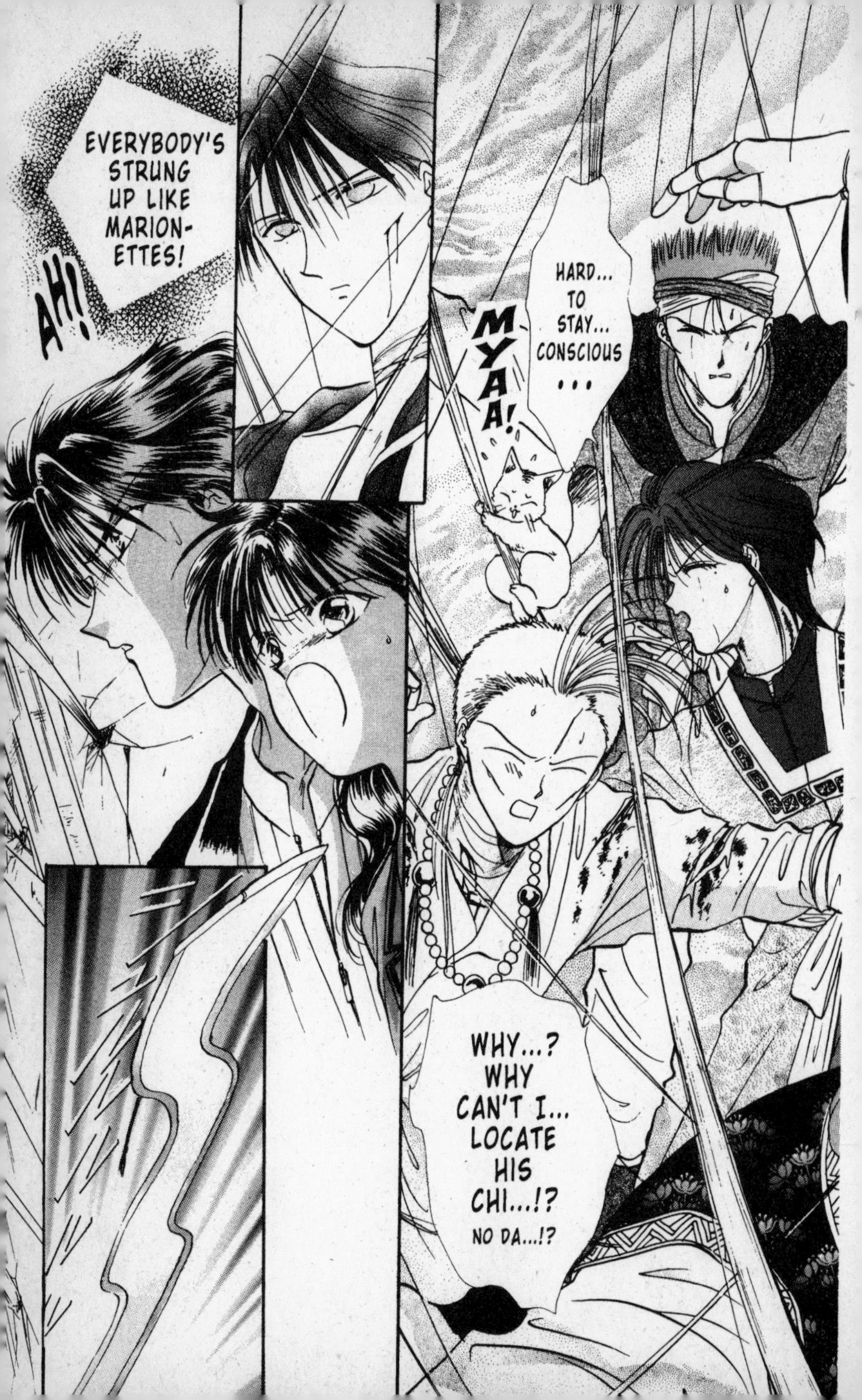
HARD... TO STAY... CONSCIOUS...
MYAA!
WHY...? WHY CAN'T I... LOCATE HIS CHI...!? NO DA...!?
EVERYBODY'S STRUNG UP LIKE MARION-ETTES!
AH!!

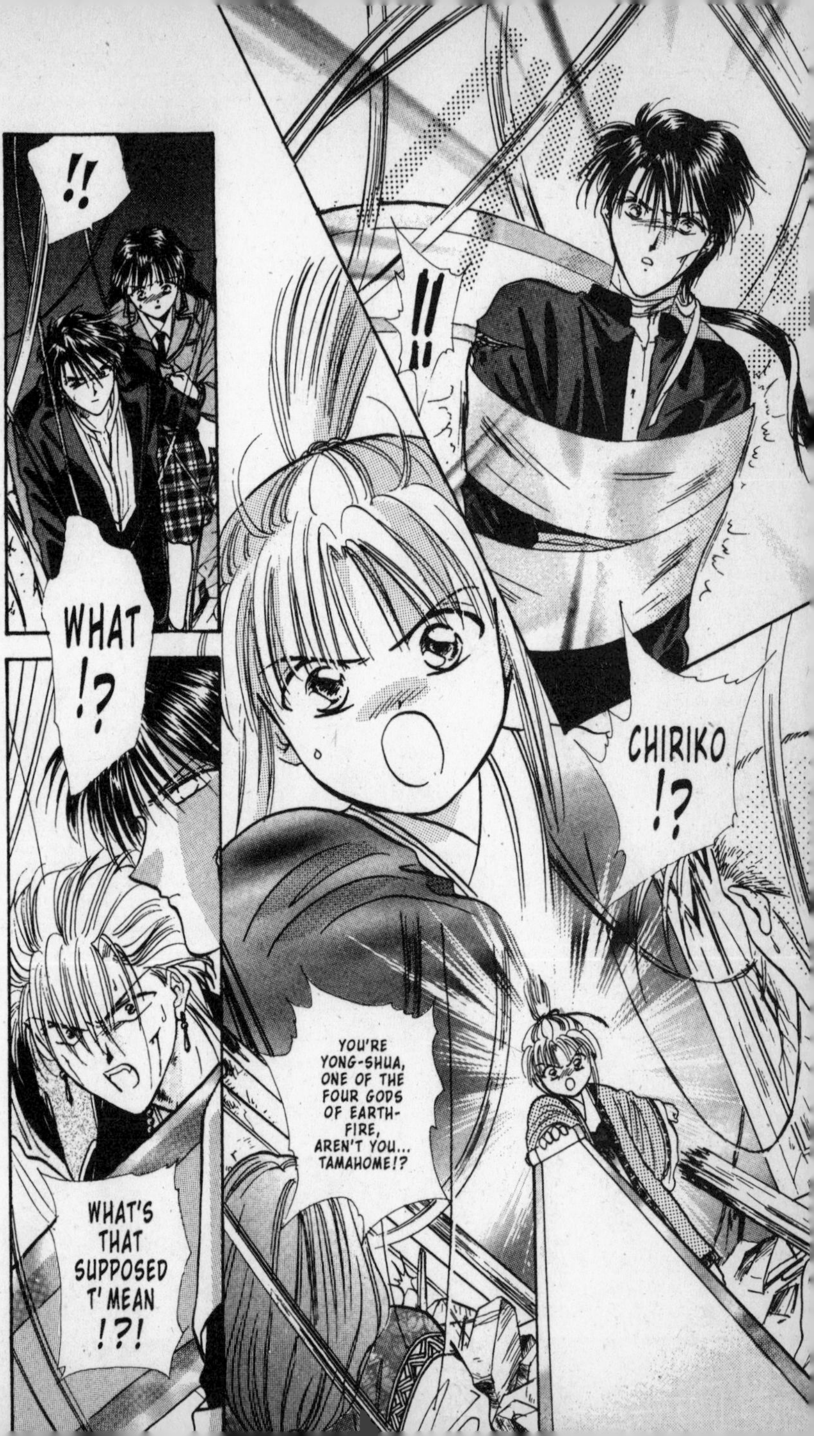
!!
CHIRIKO !?
YOU'RE YONG-SHUA, ONE OF THE FOUR GODS OF EARTH-FIRE, AREN'T YOU... TAMAHOME!?
!!
WHAT !?
WHAT'S THAT SUPPOSED T' MEAN !?!

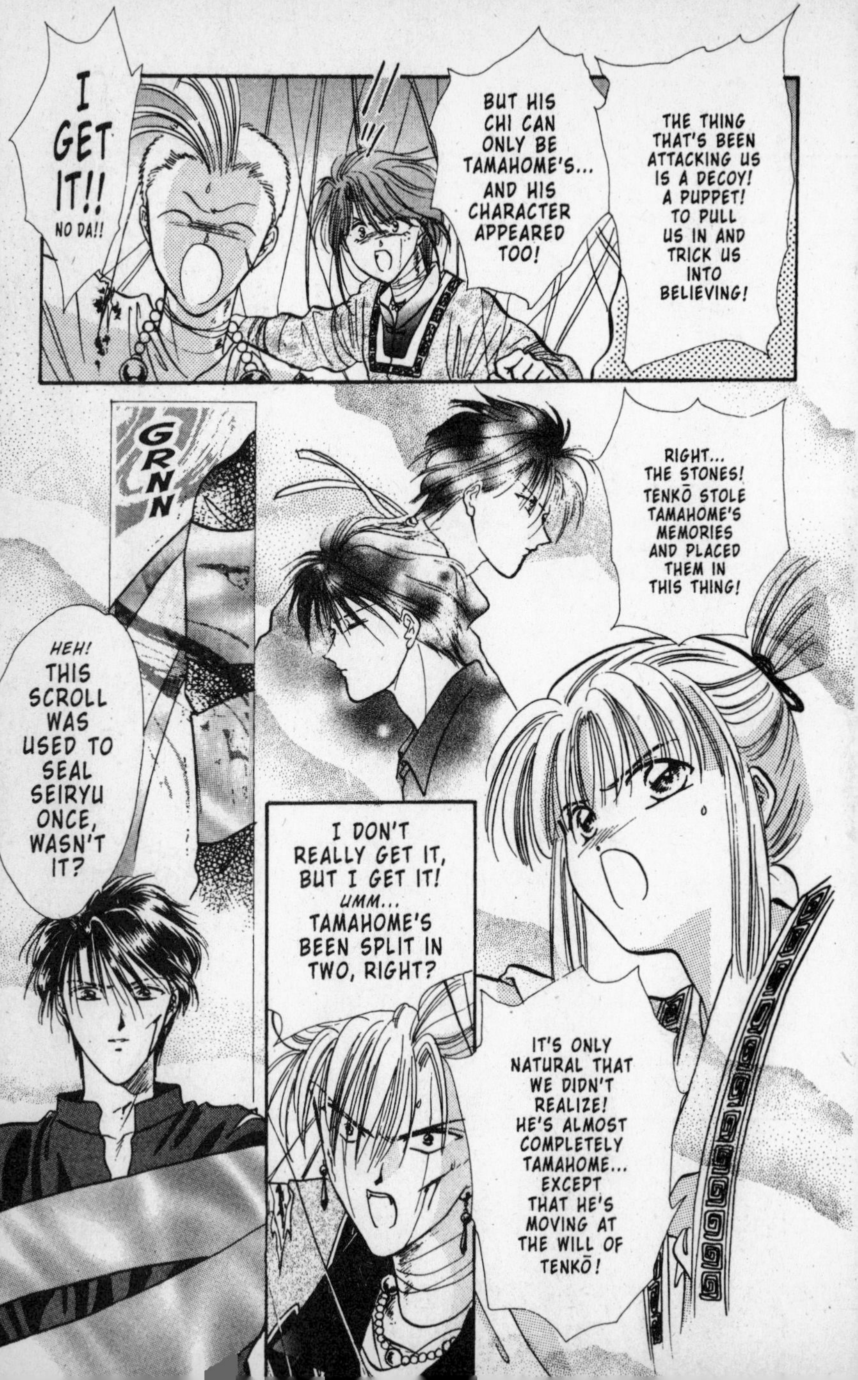
THE THING THAT'S BEEN ATTACKING US IS A DECOY! A PUPPET! TO PULL US IN AND TRICK US INTO BELIEVING!
BUT HIS CHI CAN ONLY BE TAMAHOME'S... AND HIS CHARACTER APPEARED TOO!
I GET IT!! NO DA!!
RIGHT... THE STONES! TENKŌ STOLE TAMAHOME'S MEMORIES AND PLACED THEM IN THIS THING!
GRNN
HEH! THIS SCROLL WAS USED TO SEAL SEIRYU ONCE, WASN'T IT?
I DON'T REALLY GET IT, BUT I GET IT! UMM... TAMAHOME'S BEEN SPLIT IN TWO, RIGHT?
IT'S ONLY NATURAL THAT WE DIDN'T REALIZE! HE'S ALMOST COMPLETELY TAMAHOME... EXCEPT THAT HE'S MOVING AT THE WILL OF TENKŌ!

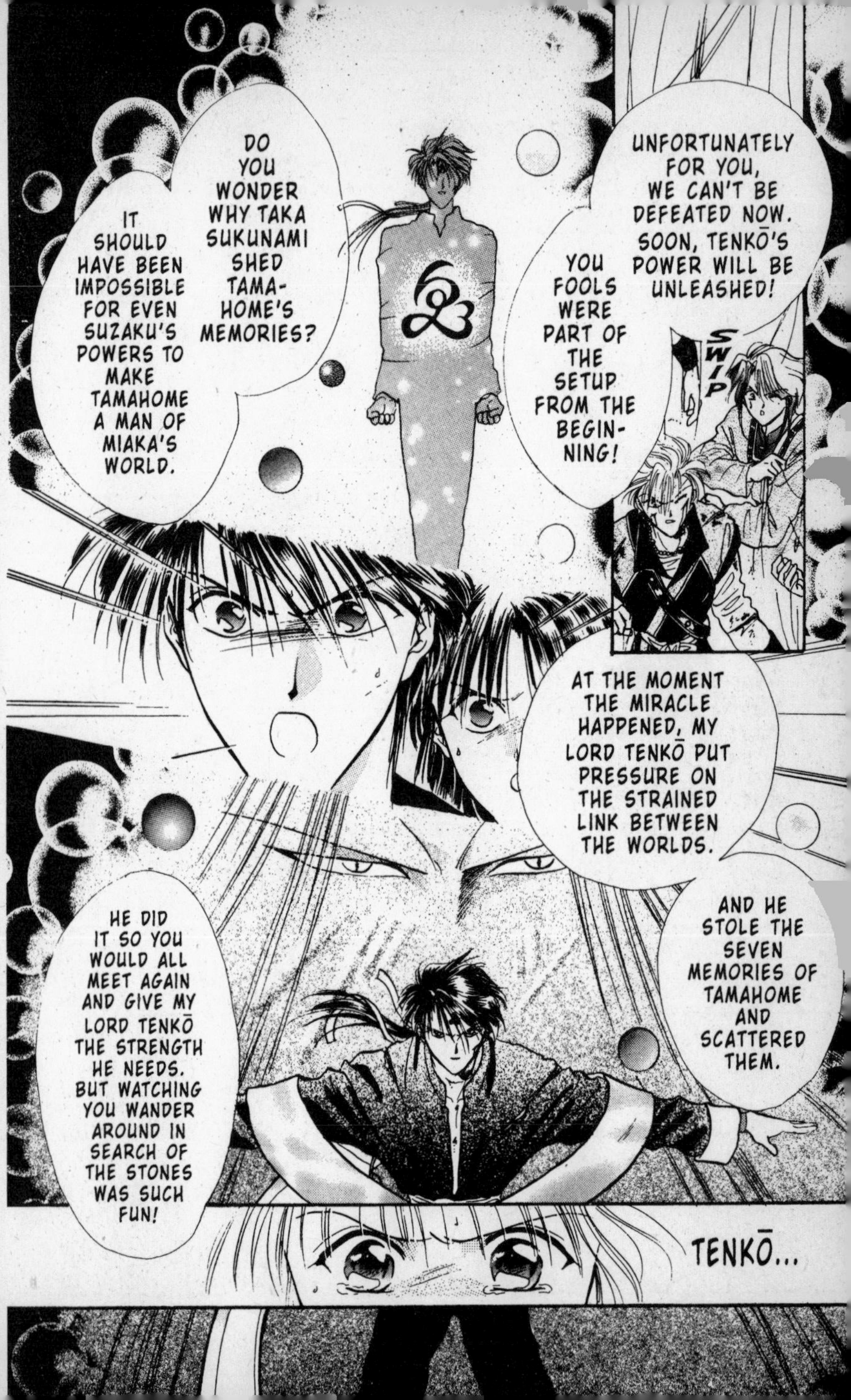
UNFORTUNATELY FOR YOU, WE CAN'T BE DEFEATED NOW. SOON, TENKŌ'S POWER WILL BE UNLEASHED!
YOU FOOLS WERE PART OF THE SETUP FROM THE BEGIN-NING!
SWIP
DO YOU WONDER WHY TAKA SUKUNAMI SHED TAMA-HOME'S MEMORIES?
IT SHOULD HAVE BEEN IMPOSSIBLE FOR EVEN SUZAKU'S POWERS TO MAKE TAMAHOME A MAN OF MIAKA'S WORLD.
AT THE MOMENT THE MIRACLE HAPPENED, MY LORD TENKŌ PUT PRESSURE ON THE STRAINED LINK BETWEEN THE WORLDS.
AND HE STOLE THE SEVEN MEMORIES OF TAMAHOME AND SCATTERED THEM.
HE DID IT SO YOU WOULD ALL MEET AGAIN AND GIVE MY LORD TENKŌ THE STRENGTH HE NEEDS. BUT WATCHING YOU WANDER AROUND IN SEARCH OF THE STONES WAS SUCH FUN!
TENKŌ...

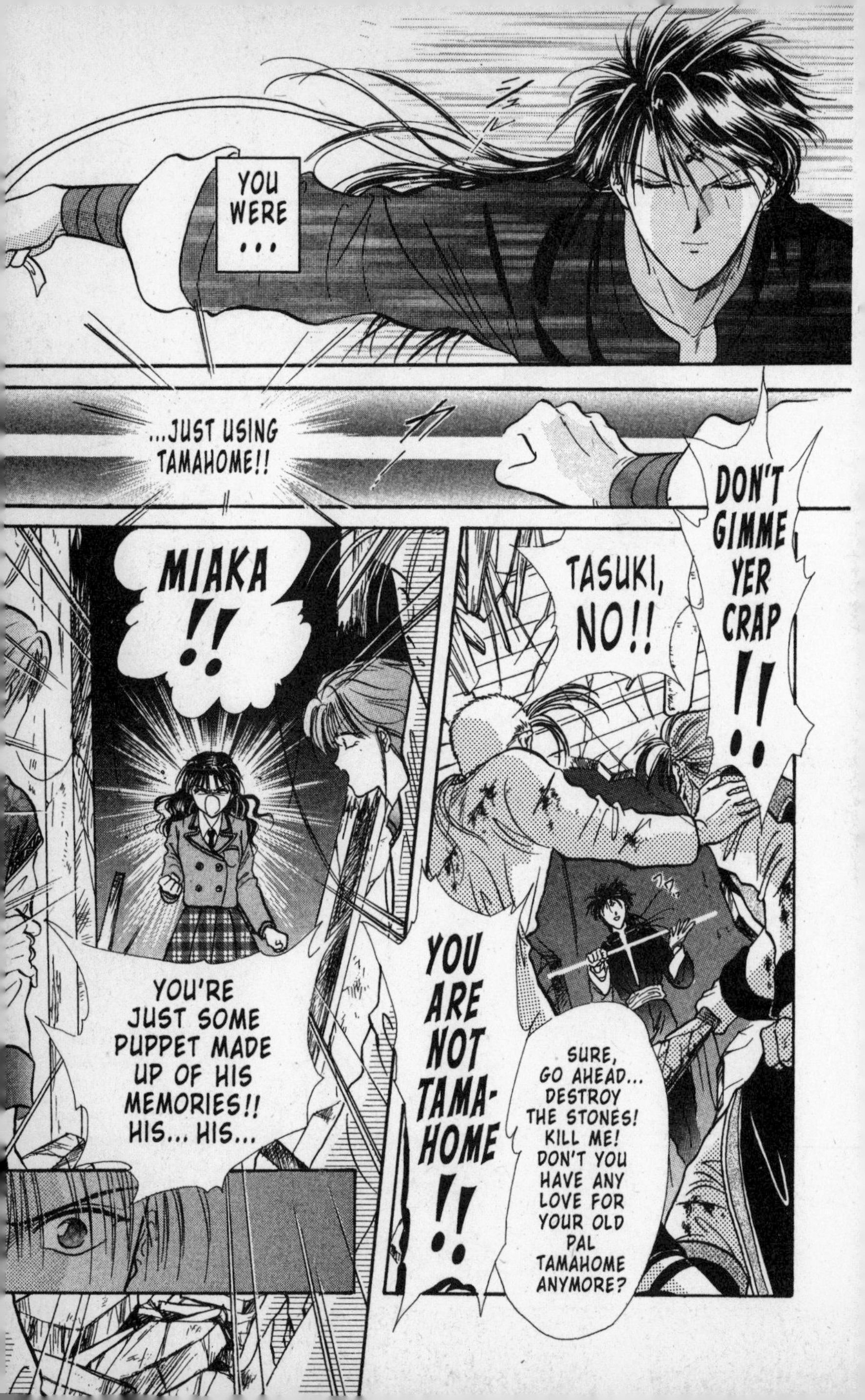
YOU WERE...
...JUST USING TAMAHOME!!
DON'T GIMME YER CRAP!!
TASUKI, NO!!
SURE, GO AHEAD... DESTROY THE STONES! KILL ME! DON'T YOU HAVE ANY LOVE FOR YOUR OLD PAL TAMAHOME ANYMORE?
YOU ARE NOT TAMAHOME!!
MIAKA!!
YOU'RE JUST SOME PUPPET MADE UP OF HIS MEMORIES!! HIS... HIS...

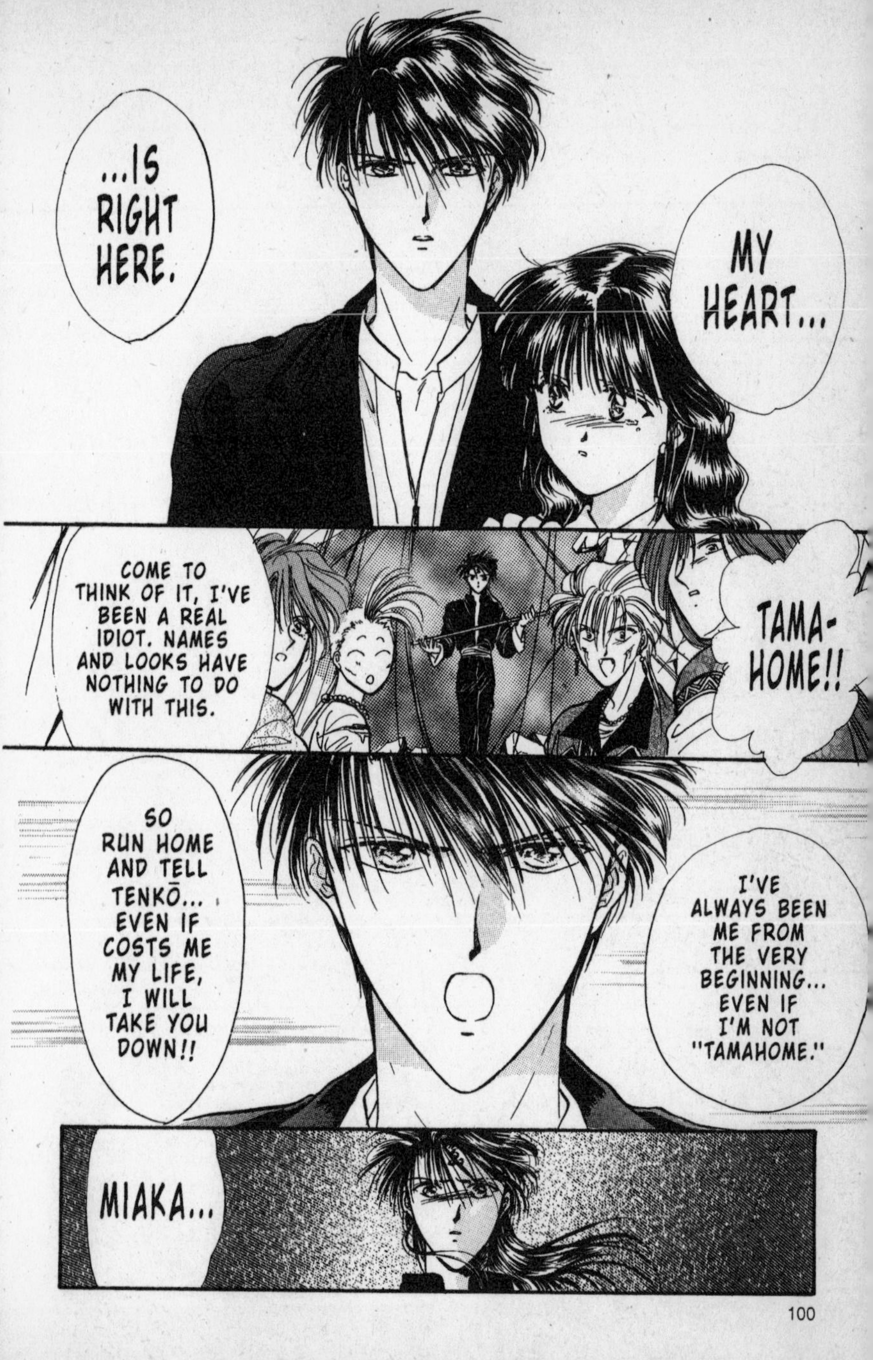
MY HEART...
...IS RIGHT HERE.
TAMA-HOME!!
COME TO THINK OF IT, I'VE BEEN A REAL IDIOT. NAMES AND LOOKS HAVE NOTHING TO DO WITH THIS.
I'VE ALWAYS BEEN ME FROM THE VERY BEGINNING... EVEN IF I'M NOT "TAMAHOME."
SO RUN HOME AND TELL TENKŌ... EVEN IF COSTS ME MY LIFE, I WILL TAKE YOU DOWN!!
MIAKA...

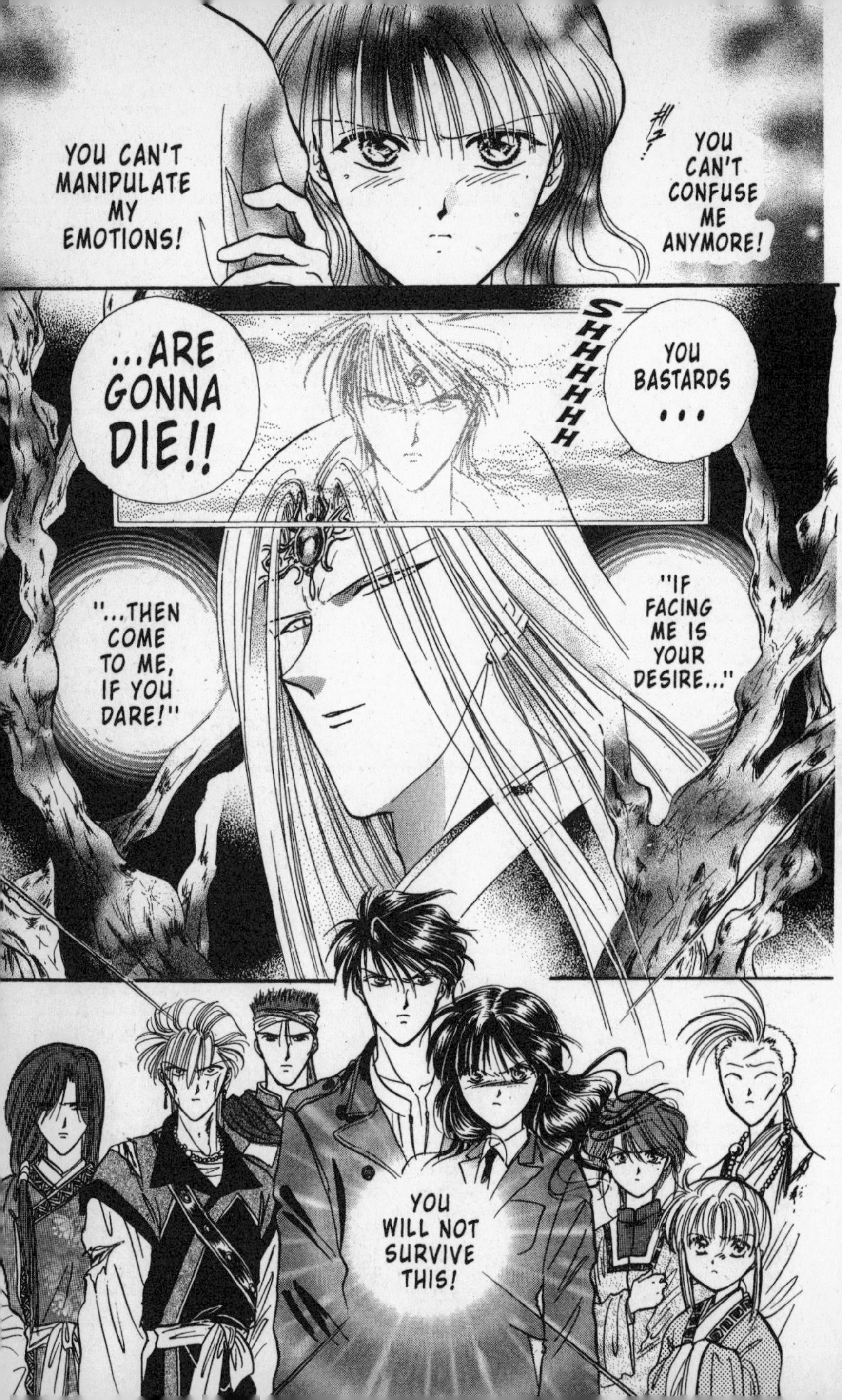
YOU CAN'T CONFUSE ME ANYMORE!
YOU CAN'T MANIPULATE MY EMOTIONS!
YOU BASTARDS ...
SHHHHHH
...ARE GONNA DIE!!
"IF FACING ME IS YOUR DESIRE..."
"...THEN COME TO ME, IF YOU DARE!"
YOU WILL NOT SURVIVE THIS!

GEE, IT'S BEEN SO LONG! THE SECRETS OF "FUSHIGI YŪGI"

Number...Um... what number is this again?

Q1. How come Chichiri's mask can do all those things?
A. Actually, it's one of Chichiri's techniques -- a special power. He can make it rigid or flexible. But to put an expression on it or make it move like a real face, he has to actually wear the mask. But at other times, when he's using other powers or techniques, he takes it off. If another person were to try to use it, that person would need Chichiri's cooperation to make the mask work.

Q2. Can anybody use Tasuki's harisen (metal fan)?
A. From the time when Tai Yi-Jun gave everyone their powered-up equipment, the only person able to use the harisen was Tasuki. (He's able to use the harisen for some other powers too.) When he uses it, he has to concentrate really hard if he wants to limit the flames to only the thing he wants to burn, so it's very difficult. Especially when he shouts, "Dammit, Tama!!" and pulls it out to toast somebody. *But those are just jokes.*

Q3. Why can the dead Celestial Warriors still use their powers?
A. Because their powers are not tied to their bodies, but to their life forces.

Q4. I understood that in Part 1, Miaka could understand everybody because she was sucked into a Japanese translation of the original book, but Part 2 uses the Chinese version. How does she communicate?
A. In Part 2, Miaka is sent to the world of the book directly by the god Suzaku, and since Suzaku can speak both Chinese and Japanese, it only stands to reason that he can give Miaka and Taka his power to communicate as well. (But it's the thought that counts.)
Also, about Tasuki's Kansai accent (let it go, folks. If you're too picky about detail, manga will never be fun!) ...anyway, think of Hong-Nan as Japan. The capital is Tokyo, and Ko Prefecture (where Tasuki was born) would be near the Kansai area where Osaka and Kobe are.

Q5. What about Taka's real-world family?
A. He has both his parents, a younger brother and a younger sister, and he is the eldest son of a farm family surrounded by a natural setting in the country. They're never short of food. Isn't that great, Miaka? I'm sure Taka's family is very much like Tamahome's family.

Q6. When you use names like Taiitsukun (Tai Yi-Jun) and Suzaku-seikun (The God Suzaku), why do you put "-kun" at the end?
A. This is completely different than when you call a boy "Yamada-kun" in Japan today. Ages ago when you really wanted to show respect for someone who was much higher in status than yourself, you added "no kimi" to their names, and the "kimi" uses the same kanji as "kun."

Q7. So why did you decide to use the name "Taka"?
A. I wanted to use the "demon" character, and a long time ago in China there was a country name that used Taka's character (pronounced "Gi"). In ancient times in what was called The Third Year of Seiryu, the Japanese Queen Himiko was given the "Four Gods Mirror" by the country of Gi.

Q8. The biggest question!! How does Miaka eat so much and never get fat!?
A. She moves around a lot. She also has a lot of worries and nervous energy.

• LONELY GUY •

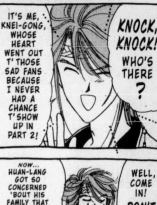

KNOCK, KNOCK! WHO'S THERE?
IT'S ME, KNEI-GONG, WHOSE HEART WENT OUT T' THOSE SAD FANS BECAUSE I NEVER HAD A CHANCE T' SHOW UP IN PART 2!
WELL, COME IN!
DON'T MIND IF I DO!
NOW... HUAN-LANG GOT SO CONCERNED 'BOUT HIS FAMILY THAT HE LEFT THE MOUNTAIN, AND TH' LAST FEW MONTHS HAVE BEEN SO BORING!
WHO'S HE TALKIN' TO?
BEATS ME!
BUT EVERY-THING'S OKAY!
I GOT MY ROOM! SEE?
A COLLECTION OF HUAN-LANG IMAGES DRAWN BY THE BANDITS!
1ST PRIZE
NOW I'M NEVER LONELY, EVEN AT NIGHT!
KNEI-GONG, IF YOU DON'T SHAPE UP, I AIN'T NEVER COMIN' BACK!!
TRMBL TRMBL

WHAT IF KNEI-GONG SAYS, "SO WHAT?" WHAT'LL YOU DO THEN!?

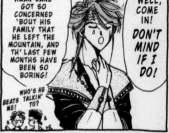

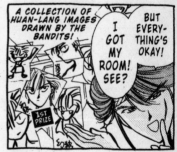

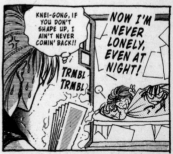

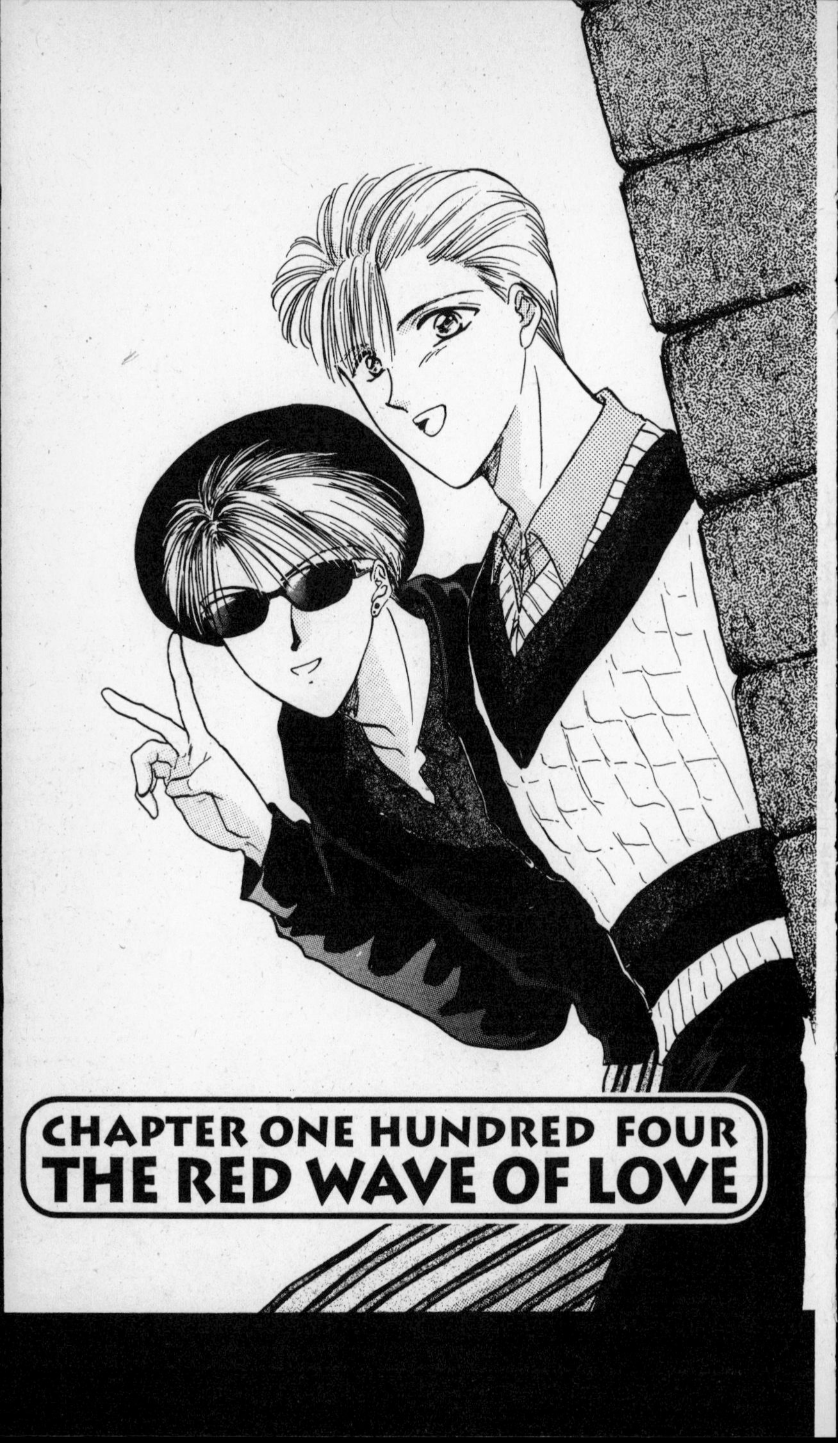
CHAPTER ONE HUNDRED FOUR
THE RED WAVE OF LOVE

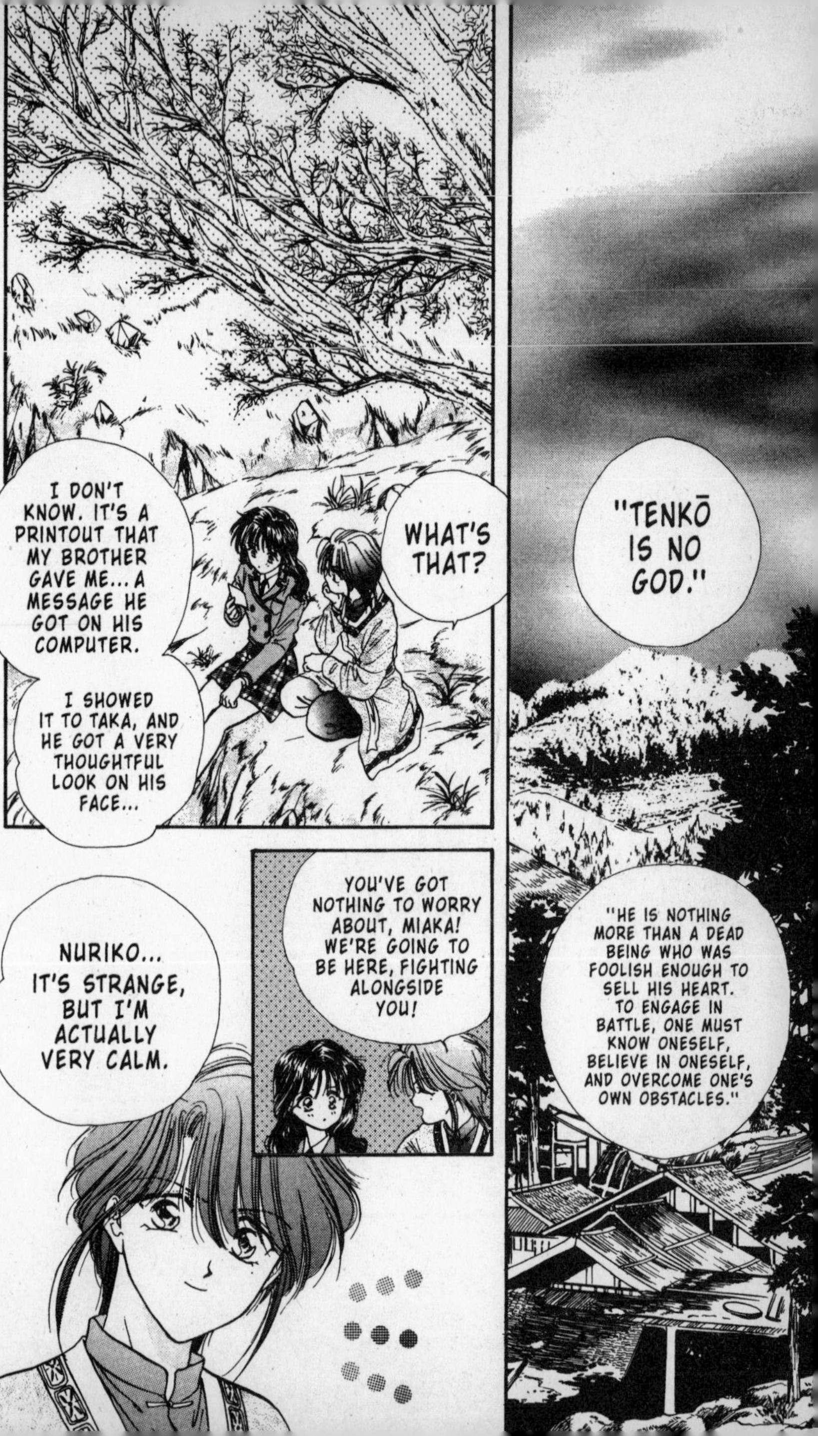
"TENKŌ IS NO GOD."
"HE IS NOTHING MORE THAN A DEAD BEING WHO WAS FOOLISH ENOUGH TO SELL HIS HEART. TO ENGAGE IN BATTLE, ONE MUST KNOW ONESELF, BELIEVE IN ONESELF, AND OVERCOME ONE'S OWN OBSTACLES."
WHAT'S THAT?
I DON'T KNOW. IT'S A PRINTOUT THAT MY BROTHER GAVE ME... A MESSAGE HE GOT ON HIS COMPUTER.
I SHOWED IT TO TAKA, AND HE GOT A VERY THOUGHTFUL LOOK ON HIS FACE...
YOU'VE GOT NOTHING TO WORRY ABOUT, MIAKA! WE'RE GOING TO BE HERE, FIGHTING ALONGSIDE YOU!
NURIKO... IT'S STRANGE, BUT I'M ACTUALLY VERY CALM.

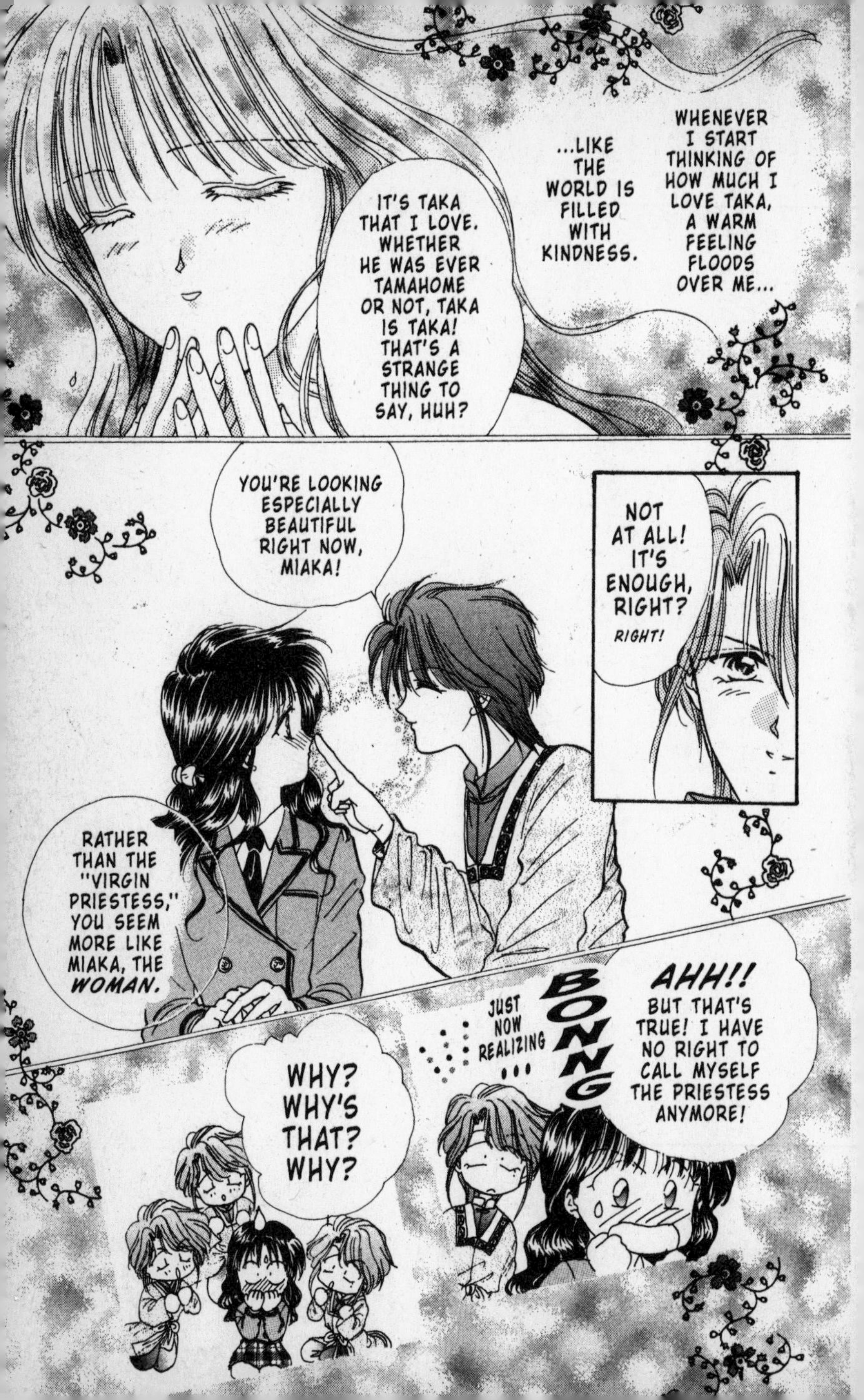
WHENEVER I START THINKING OF HOW MUCH I LOVE TAKA, A WARM FEELING FLOODS OVER ME...
...LIKE THE WORLD IS FILLED WITH KINDNESS.
IT'S TAKA THAT I LOVE. WHETHER HE WAS EVER TAMAHOME OR NOT, TAKA IS TAKA! THAT'S A STRANGE THING TO SAY, HUH?
NOT AT ALL! IT'S ENOUGH, RIGHT?
RIGHT!
YOU'RE LOOKING ESPECIALLY BEAUTIFUL RIGHT NOW, MIAKA!
RATHER THAN THE "VIRGIN PRIESTESS," YOU SEEM MORE LIKE MIAKA, THE *WOMAN*.
AHH!! BUT THAT'S TRUE! I HAVE NO RIGHT TO CALL MYSELF THE PRIESTESS ANYMORE!
BONNG
JUST NOW REALIZING ...
WHY? WHY'S THAT? WHY?

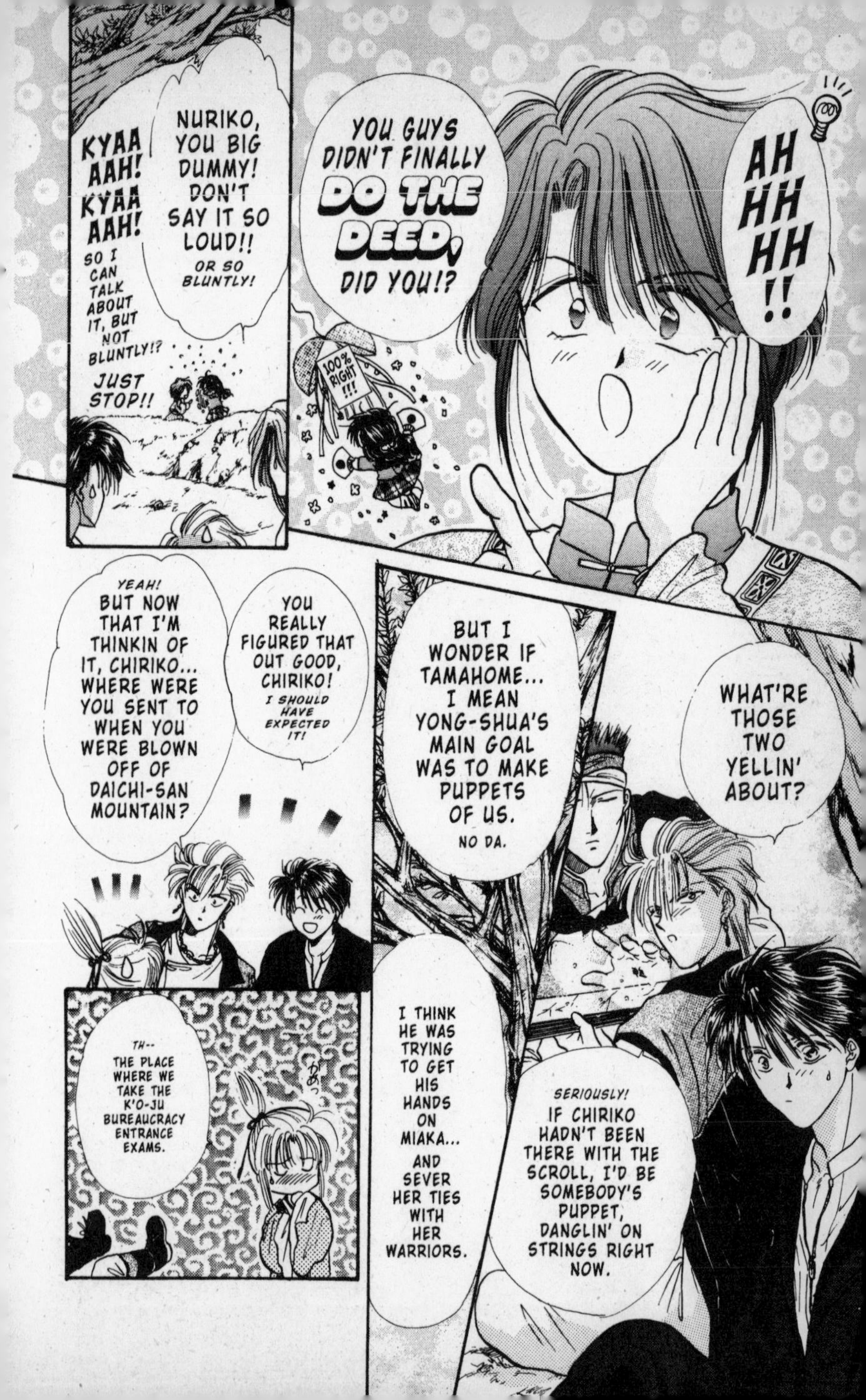
AHHHHH!!
YOU GUYS DIDN'T FINALLY DO THE DEED, DID YOU!?
100% RIGHT!!!
NURIKO, YOU BIG DUMMY! DON'T SAY IT SO LOUD!! OR SO BLUNTLY!
KYAA AAH! KYAA AAH! SO I CAN TALK ABOUT IT, BUT NOT BLUNTLY!? JUST STOP!!
WHAT'RE THOSE TWO YELLIN' ABOUT?
BUT I WONDER IF TAMAHOME... I MEAN YONG-SHUA'S MAIN GOAL WAS TO MAKE PUPPETS OF US. NO DA.
I THINK HE WAS TRYING TO GET HIS HANDS ON MIAKA... AND SEVER HER TIES WITH HER WARRIORS.
SERIOUSLY! IF CHIRIKO HADN'T BEEN THERE WITH THE SCROLL, I'D BE SOMEBODY'S PUPPET, DANGLIN' ON STRINGS RIGHT NOW.
YOU REALLY FIGURED THAT OUT GOOD, CHIRIKO! I SHOULD HAVE EXPECTED IT!
YEAH! BUT NOW THAT I'M THINKIN OF IT, CHIRIKO... WHERE WERE YOU SENT TO WHEN YOU WERE BLOWN OFF OF DAICHI-SAN MOUNTAIN?
TH-- THE PLACE WHERE WE TAKE THE K'O-JU BUREAUCRACY ENTRANCE EXAMS.

I don't have the right to ask, but...
Don't read this until you finish the story!

There are people out there who are just like Lian. Um... I mean, people with charisma...the type who naturally become leaders. Charismatic people falling from rooftops is getting a little into the dark areas, but... oh well. And Miiru... there are girls like her out there, too -- women who think of men as prey they can eat up. They're both self-destructive. For the men, unless they realize what they're doing, they can bring everyone else down with them (like their friends and family). Then there's Fei-gao and the love triangle. If you don't treat friendship well, you can destroy it. Then there's Yong-Shua... I mean Tamahome... I talked about dolls tied up with strings a little earlier, but if you think of the very earliest Taka in the story, he was a doll without strings... just the opposite of what was happening with Yong-Shua/Tamahome. Then, when Miaka gets hit with the strings, that's a way of symbolizing a man's jealousy. Still, that only happened because love was there... but if you handle jealousy wrong, you could lose the one you love forever. It's a tough thing to balance. Tenkō, this time, may seem like an extension of Nakago, done to a greater degree... but that isn't the case. He's a symbol. (By the way, in the original set-up, he possessed stones of much the same variety that Miaka and Taka had to deal with.) For Taka, the real enemy was actually HIMSELF in the form of Tamahome.
I'm sure that if Tenkō never existed, Taka would have been able to collect all of the parts of his heart and turn into the complete Taka, but... That wouldn't have allowed Taka to mature as Taka, and in the last scene where he is able to take Tamahome into himself, he wouldn't have come out as strong, right? What that scene shows is a man who is able to accept a part of himself, even though that part murdered his lover. I don't think strength is something a person can see. That's why I kept the scenes of Taka fighting to a bare minimum. There's nothing "pathetic" about a man worrying or crying. If tomorrow, you're stronger (even just a little), then I think that's good enough. An assistant said that she felt the most kindness emanating from Taka, and although he didn't talk of love nearly as much as Tamahome (did he lose interest during the story?) , one could really feel the depth of his emotions at times.

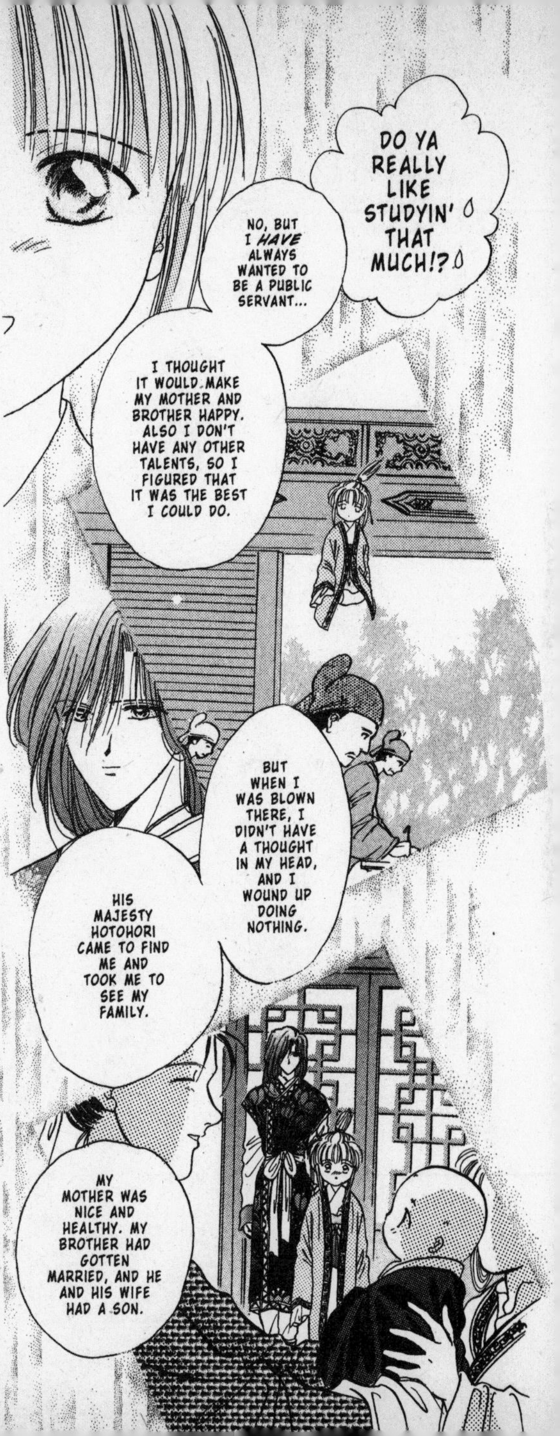
DO YA REALLY LIKE STUDYIN' THAT MUCH!?
NO, BUT I *HAVE* ALWAYS WANTED TO BE A PUBLIC SERVANT...
I THOUGHT IT WOULD MAKE MY MOTHER AND BROTHER HAPPY. ALSO I DON'T HAVE ANY OTHER TALENTS, SO I FIGURED THAT IT WAS THE BEST I COULD DO.
BUT WHEN I WAS BLOWN THERE, I DIDN'T HAVE A THOUGHT IN MY HEAD, AND I WOUND UP DOING NOTHING.
HIS MAJESTY HOTOHORI CAME TO FIND ME AND TOOK ME TO SEE MY FAMILY.
MY MOTHER WAS NICE AND HEALTHY. MY BROTHER HAD GOTTEN MARRIED, AND HE AND HIS WIFE HAD A SON.

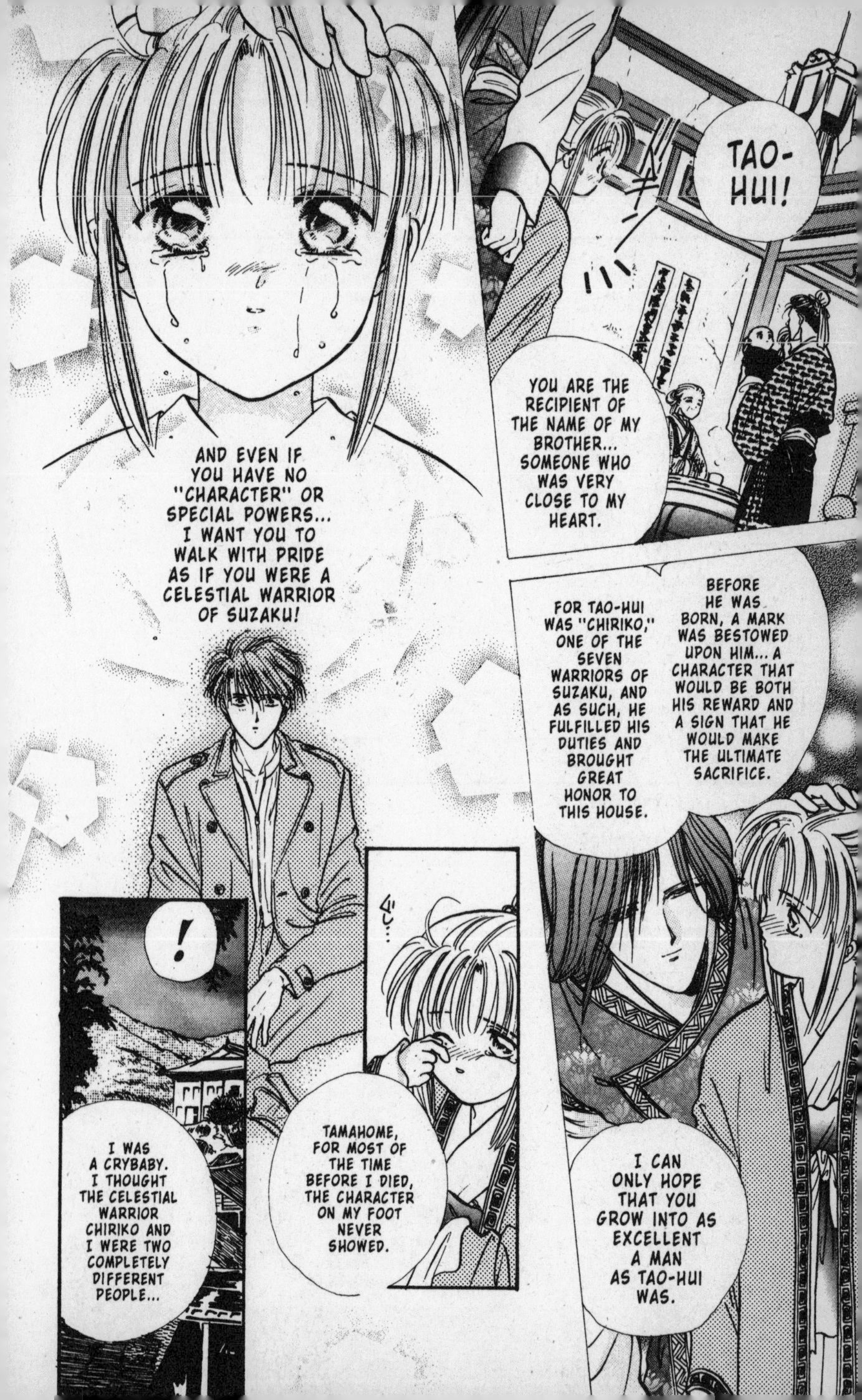
TAO-HUI!
YOU ARE THE RECIPIENT OF THE NAME OF MY BROTHER... SOMEONE WHO WAS VERY CLOSE TO MY HEART.
FOR TAO-HUI WAS "CHIRIKO," ONE OF THE SEVEN WARRIORS OF SUZAKU, AND AS SUCH, HE FULFILLED HIS DUTIES AND BROUGHT GREAT HONOR TO THIS HOUSE.
BEFORE HE WAS BORN, A MARK WAS BESTOWED UPON HIM... A CHARACTER THAT WOULD BE BOTH HIS REWARD AND A SIGN THAT HE WOULD MAKE THE ULTIMATE SACRIFICE.
I CAN ONLY HOPE THAT YOU GROW INTO AS EXCELLENT A MAN AS TAO-HUI WAS.
AND EVEN IF YOU HAVE NO "CHARACTER" OR SPECIAL POWERS... I WANT YOU TO WALK WITH PRIDE AS IF YOU WERE A CELESTIAL WARRIOR OF SUZAKU!
ぶ…
TAMAHOME, FOR MOST OF THE TIME BEFORE I DIED, THE CHARACTER ON MY FOOT NEVER SHOWED.
!
I WAS A CRYBABY. I THOUGHT THE CELESTIAL WARRIOR CHIRIKO AND I WERE TWO COMPLETELY DIFFERENT PEOPLE...

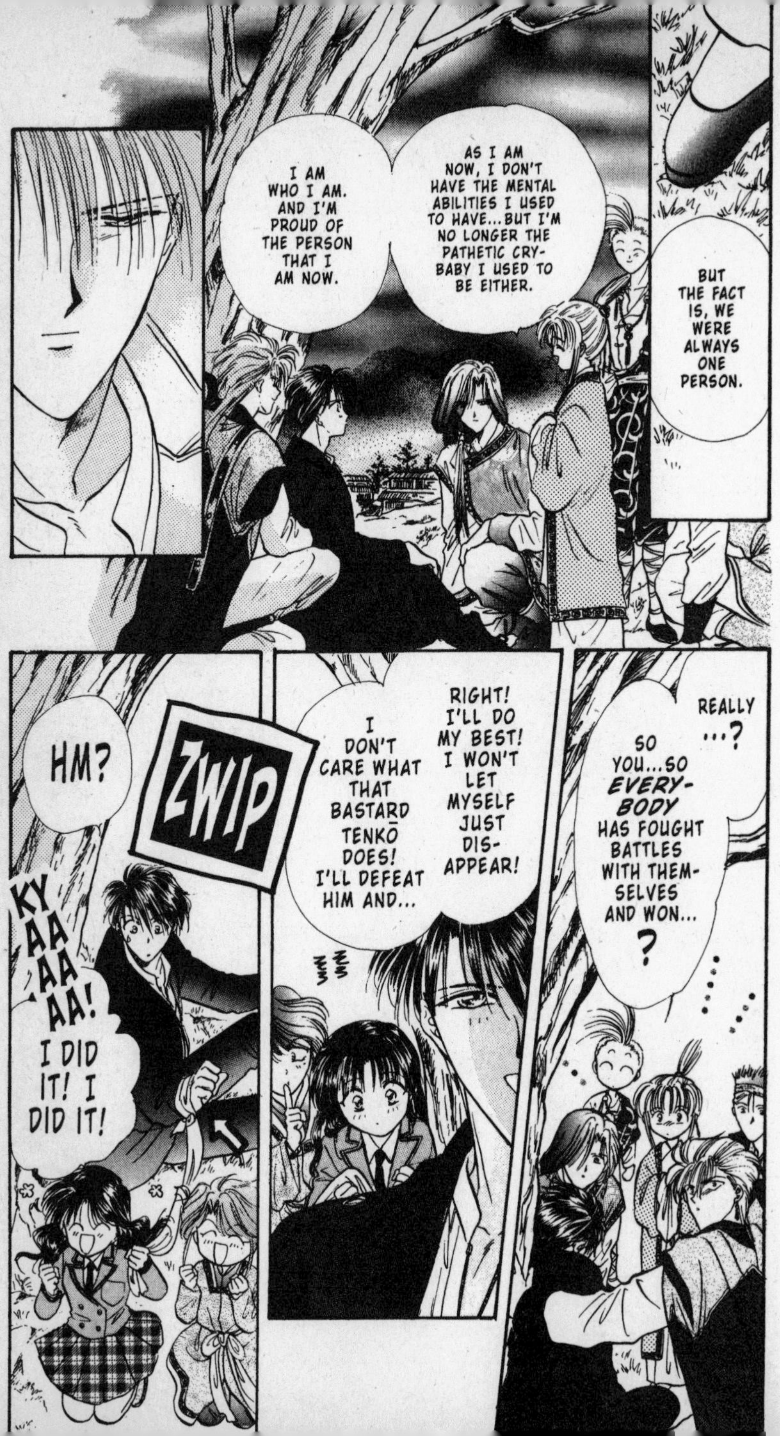
BUT THE FACT IS, WE WERE ALWAYS ONE PERSON.
AS I AM NOW, I DON'T HAVE THE MENTAL ABILITIES I USED TO HAVE...BUT I'M NO LONGER THE PATHETIC CRY-BABY I USED TO BE EITHER.
I AM WHO I AM. AND I'M PROUD OF THE PERSON THAT I AM NOW.
REALLY ...?
SO YOU...SO *EVERY-BODY* HAS FOUGHT BATTLES WITH THEM-SELVES AND WON...?
RIGHT! I'LL DO MY BEST! I WON'T LET MYSELF JUST DIS-APPEAR!
I DON'T CARE WHAT THAT BASTARD TENKŌ DOES! I'LL DEFEAT HIM AND...
ZWIP
HM?
KYAAAAAA!
I DID IT! I DID IT!

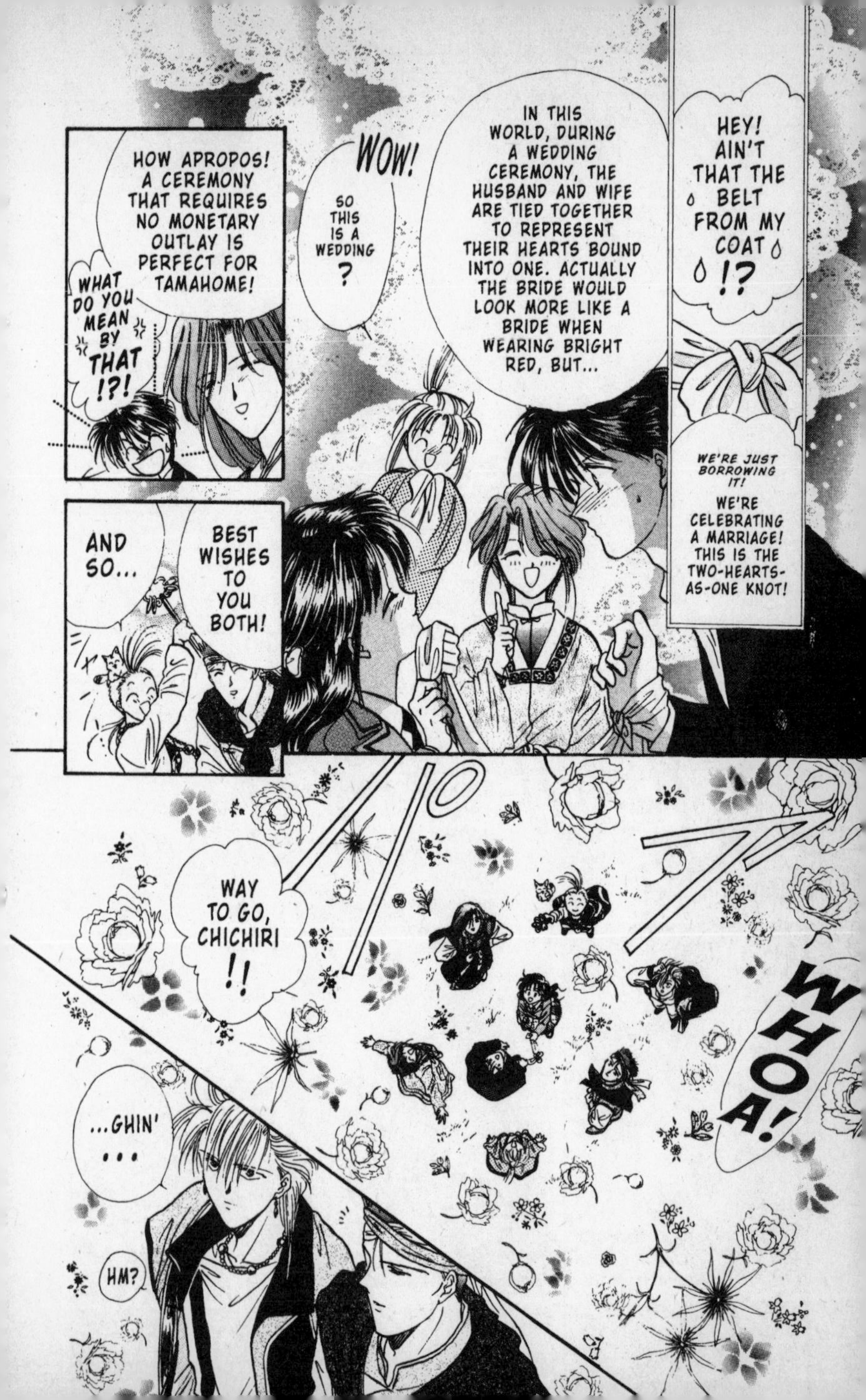
HEY! AIN'T THAT THE BELT FROM MY COAT !?
WE'RE JUST BORROWING IT!
WE'RE CELEBRATING A MARRIAGE! THIS IS THE TWO-HEARTS-AS-ONE KNOT!
IN THIS WORLD, DURING A WEDDING CEREMONY, THE HUSBAND AND WIFE ARE TIED TOGETHER TO REPRESENT THEIR HEARTS BOUND INTO ONE. ACTUALLY THE BRIDE WOULD LOOK MORE LIKE A BRIDE WHEN WEARING BRIGHT RED, BUT...
WOW!
SO THIS IS A WEDDING ?
HOW APROPOS! A CEREMONY THAT REQUIRES NO MONETARY OUTLAY IS PERFECT FOR TAMAHOME!
WHAT DO YOU MEAN BY THAT !?!
BEST WISHES TO YOU BOTH!
AND SO...
WHOA!
WAY TO GO, CHICHIRI !!
...GHIN' ...
HM?

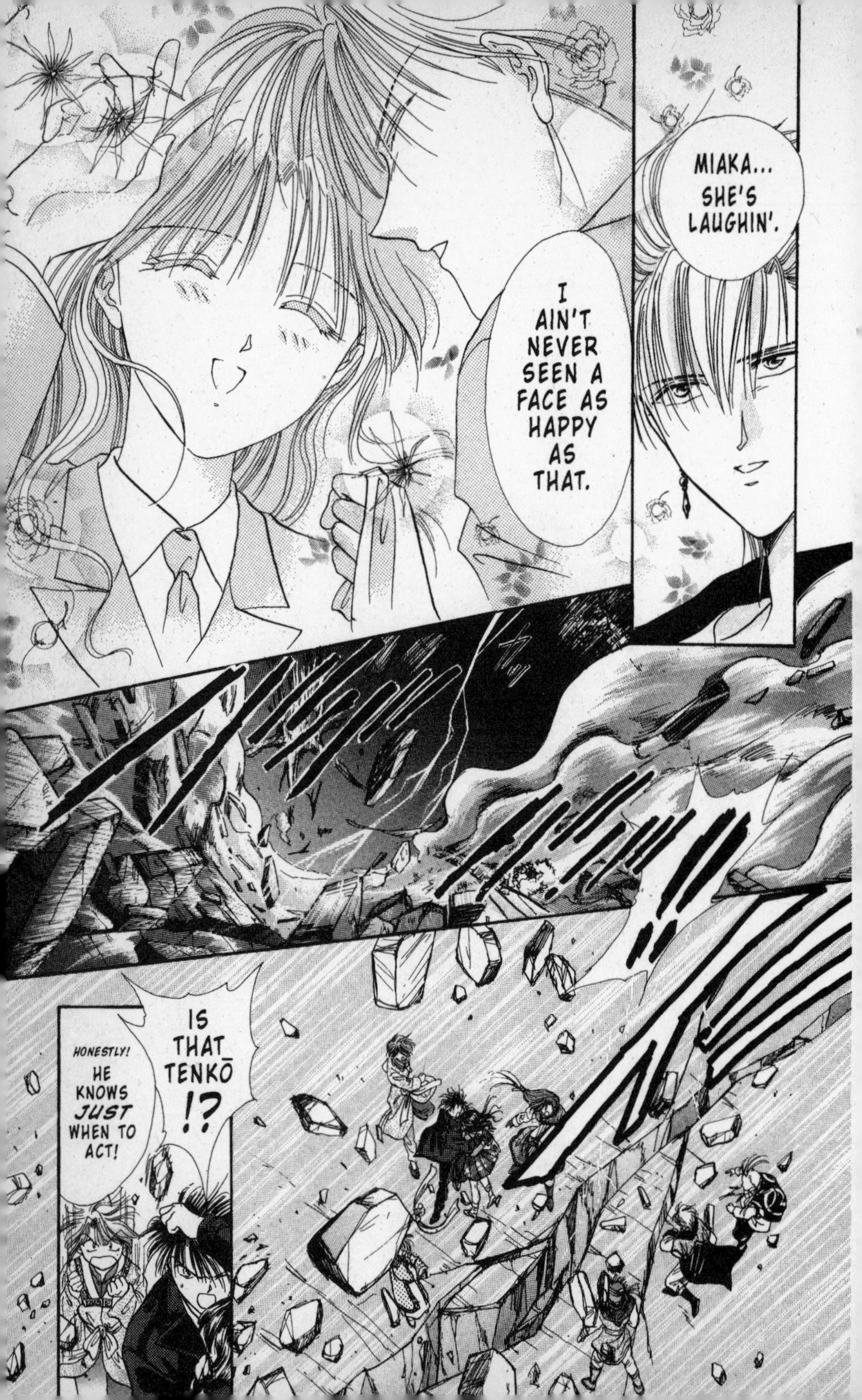
MIAKA... SHE'S LAUGHIN'.
I AIN'T NEVER SEEN A FACE AS HAPPY AS THAT.
IS THAT TENKŌ!?
HONESTLY! HE KNOWS JUST WHEN TO ACT!

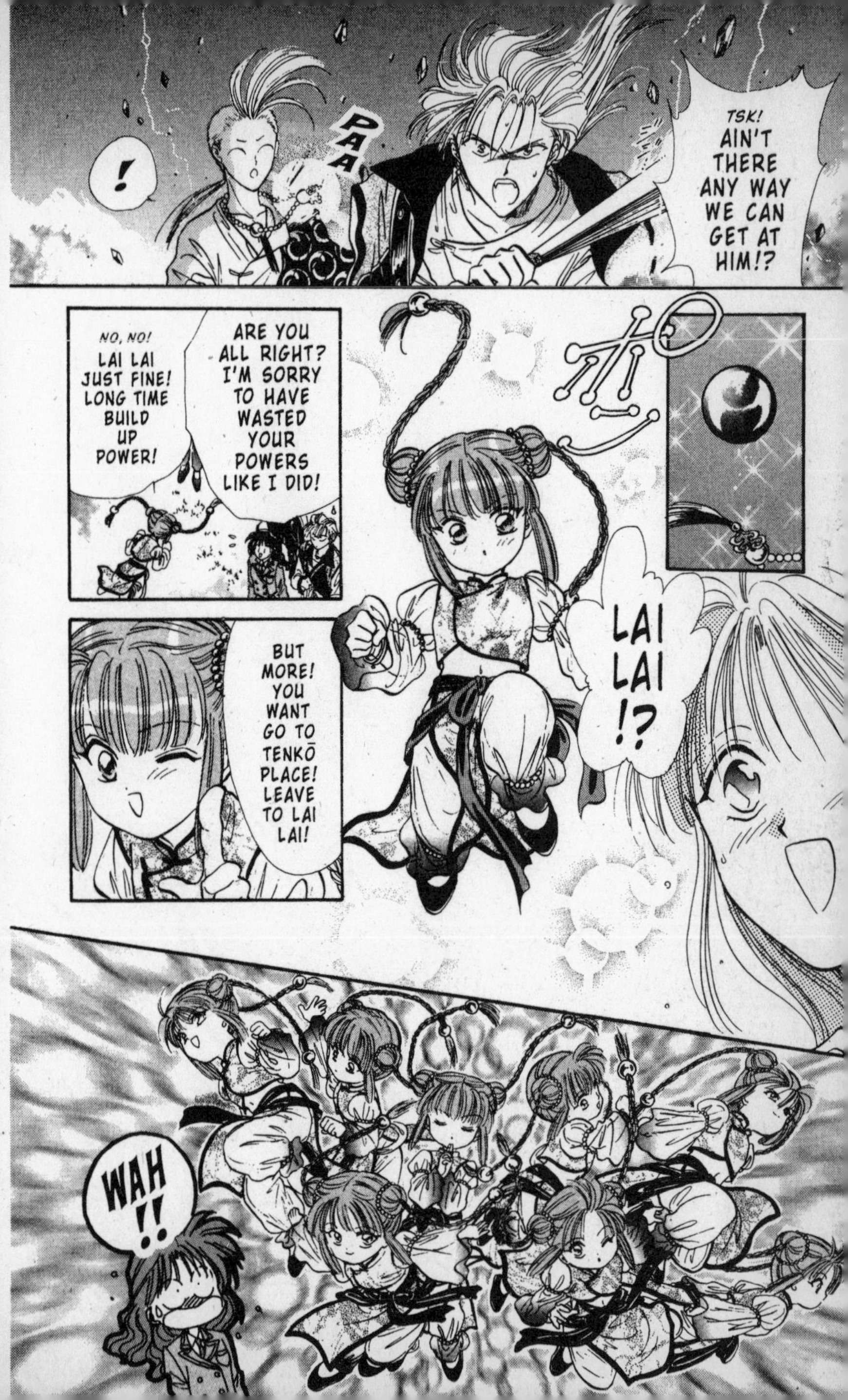
TSK! AIN'T THERE ANY WAY WE CAN GET AT HIM!?
PAA
!
LAI LAI!?
ARE YOU ALL RIGHT? I'M SORRY TO HAVE WASTED YOUR POWERS LIKE I DID!
NO, NO! LAI LAI JUST FINE! LONG TIME BUILD UP POWER!
BUT MORE! YOU WANT GO TO TENKŌ PLACE! LEAVE TO LAI LAI!
WAH!!

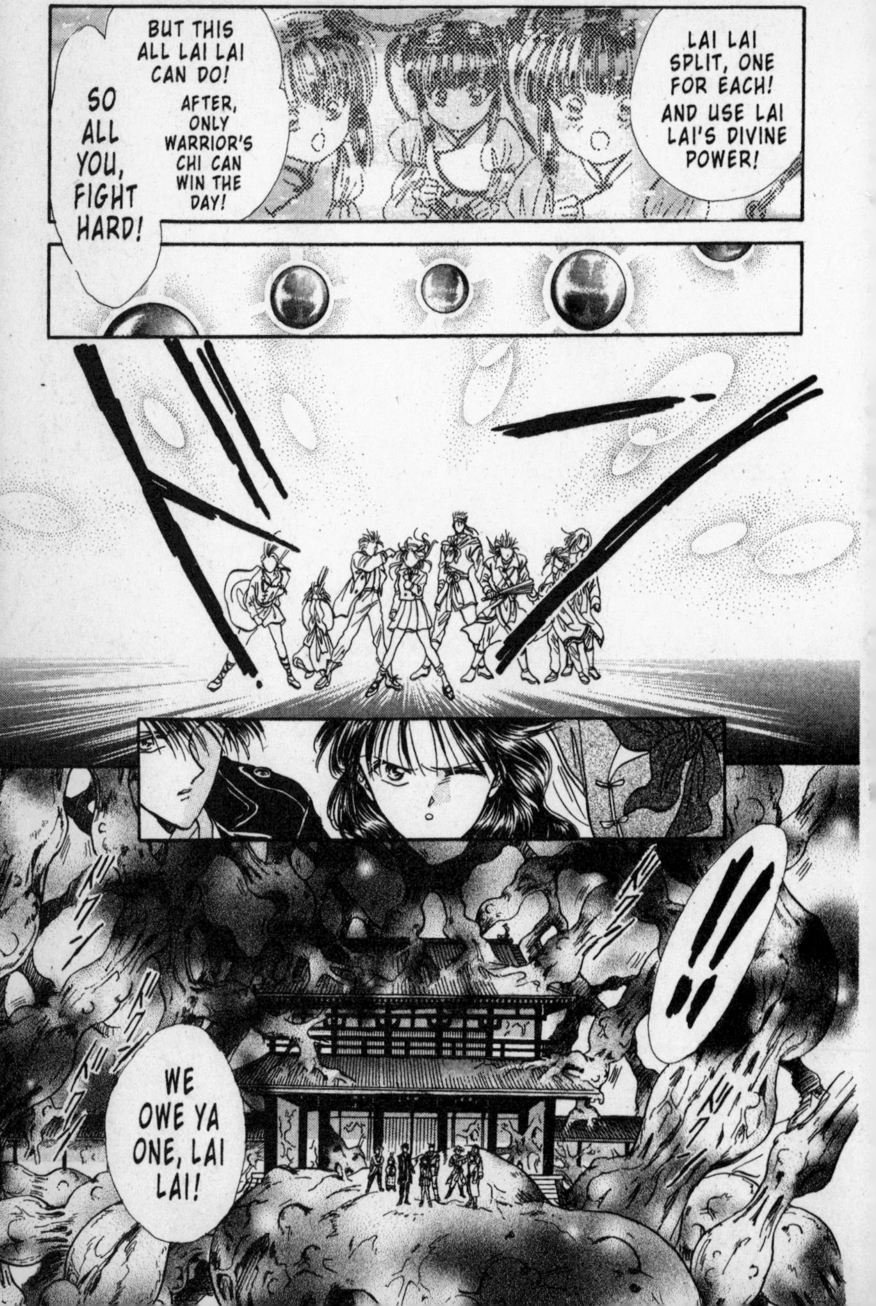
LAI LAI SPLIT, ONE FOR EACH! AND USE LAI LAI'S DIVINE POWER!
BUT THIS ALL LAI LAI CAN DO!
AFTER, ONLY WARRIOR'S CHI CAN WIN THE DAY!
SO ALL YOU, FIGHT HARD!
!!
WE OWE YA ONE, LAI LAI!

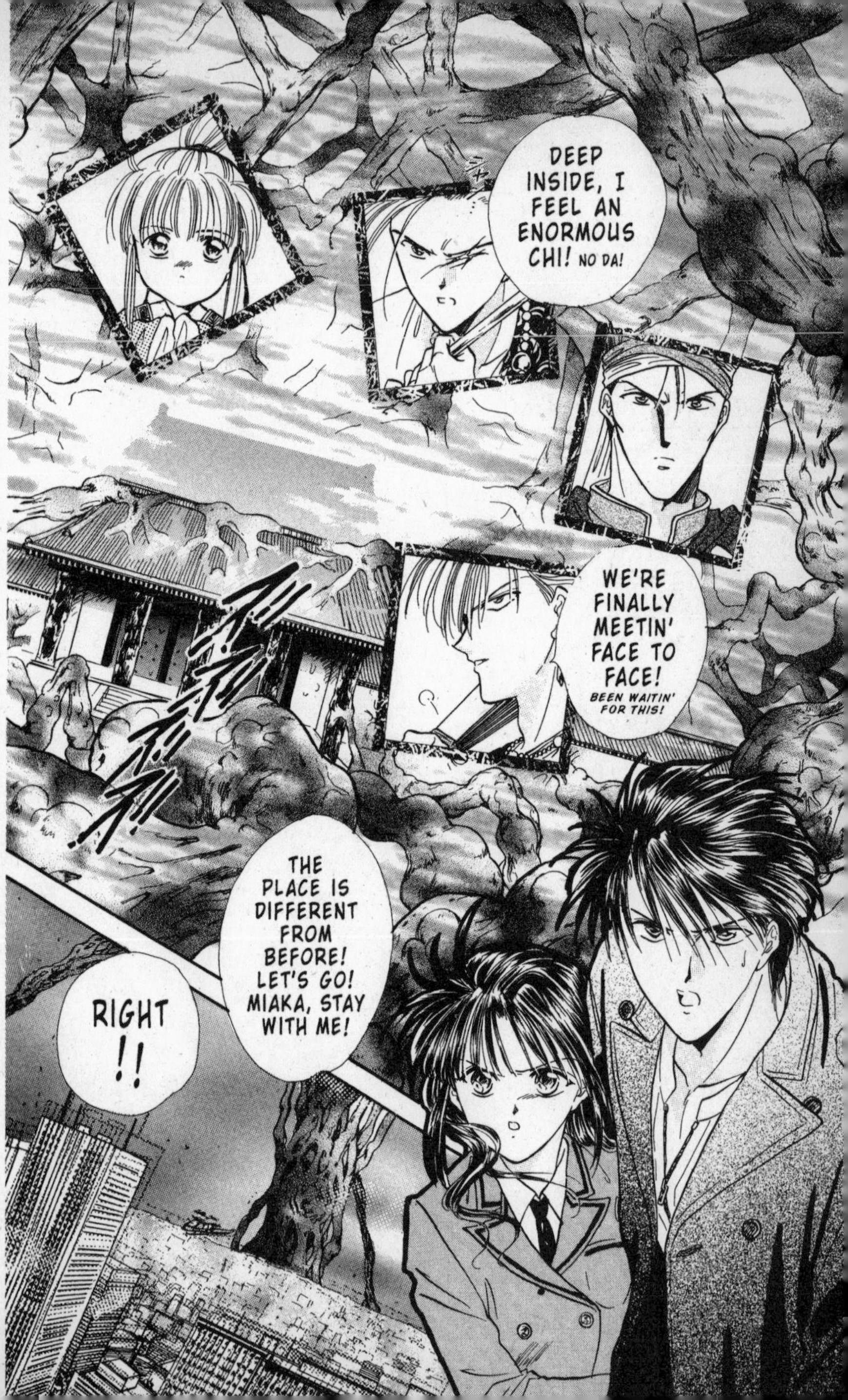
DEEP INSIDE, I FEEL AN ENORMOUS CHI! NO DA!
WE'RE FINALLY MEETIN' FACE TO FACE! BEEN WAITIN' FOR THIS!
THE PLACE IS DIFFERENT FROM BEFORE! LET'S GO! MIAKA, STAY WITH ME!
RIGHT !!

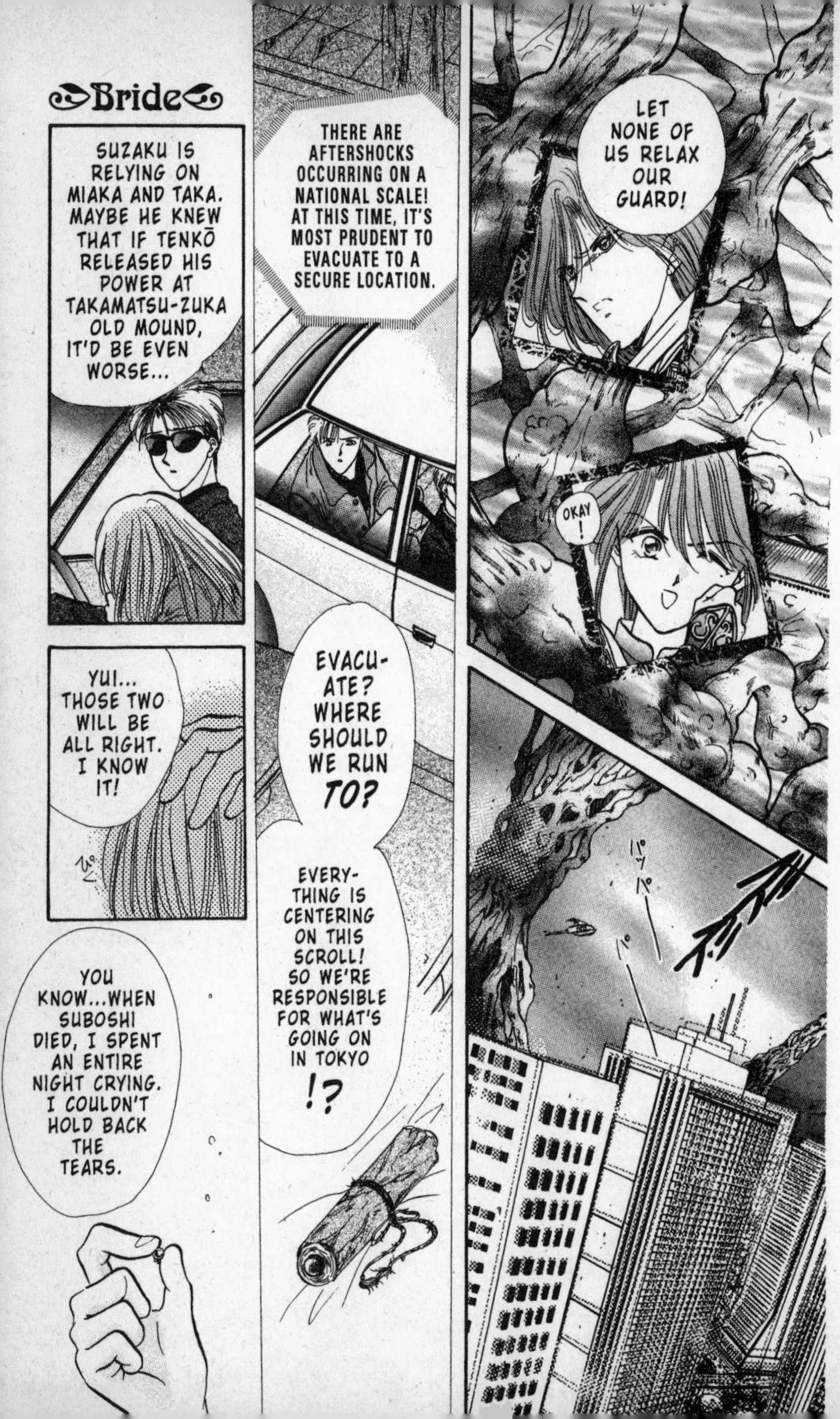
LET NONE OF US RELAX OUR GUARD!
OKAY!
THERE ARE AFTERSHOCKS OCCURRING ON A NATIONAL SCALE! AT THIS TIME, IT'S MOST PRUDENT TO EVACUATE TO A SECURE LOCATION.
EVACU-ATE? WHERE SHOULD WE RUN *TO?*
EVERY-THING IS CENTERING ON THIS SCROLL! SO WE'RE RESPONSIBLE FOR WHAT'S GOING ON IN TOKYO !?
SUZAKU IS RELYING ON MIAKA AND TAKA. MAYBE HE KNEW THAT IF TENKŌ RELEASED HIS POWER AT TAKAMATSU-ZUKA OLD MOUND, IT'D BE EVEN WORSE...
YUI... THOSE TWO WILL BE ALL RIGHT. I KNOW IT!
YOU KNOW...WHEN SUBOSHI DIED, I SPENT AN ENTIRE NIGHT CRYING. I COULDN'T HOLD BACK THE TEARS.

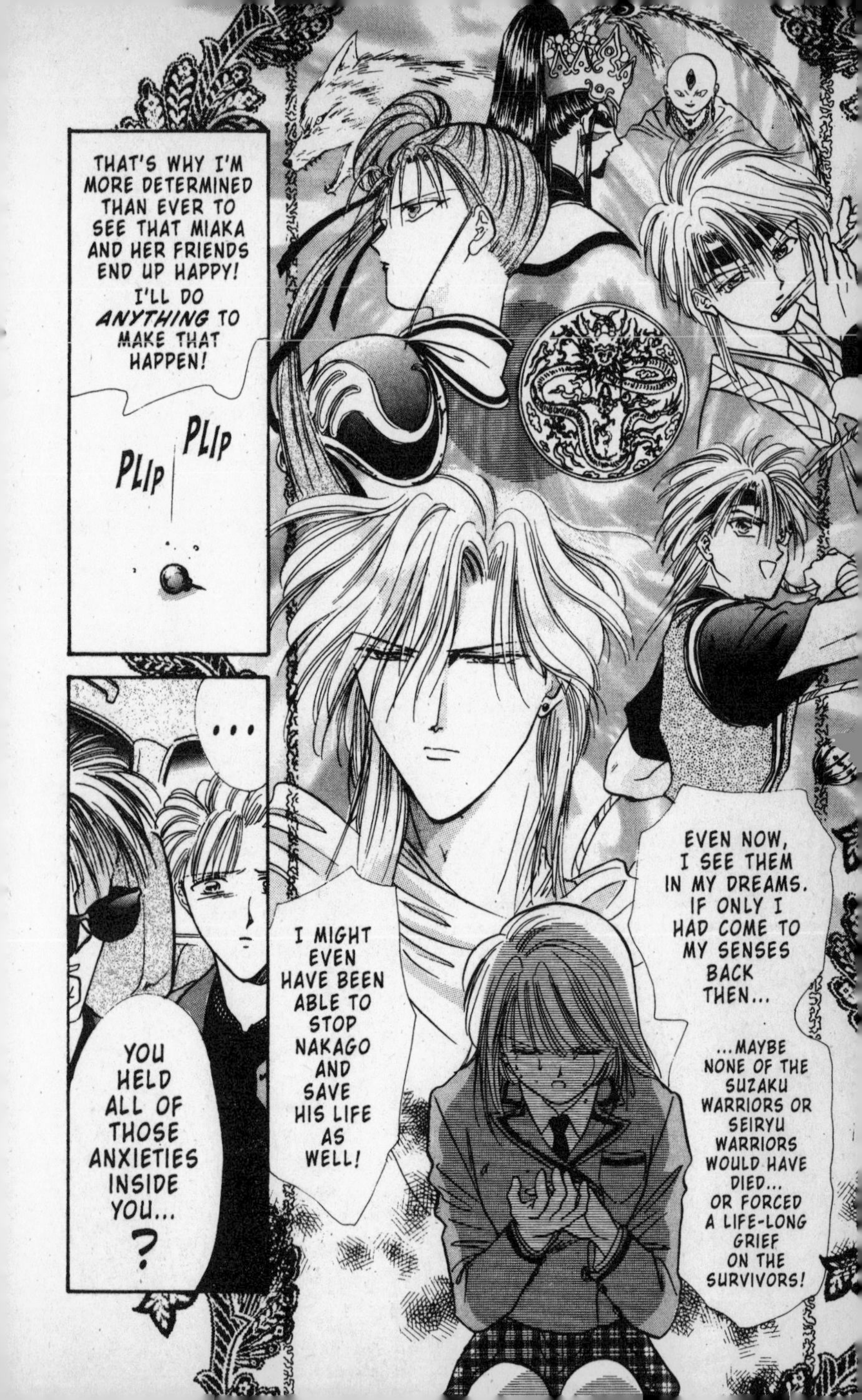

EVEN NOW, I SEE THEM IN MY DREAMS. IF ONLY I HAD COME TO MY SENSES BACK THEN...
...MAYBE NONE OF THE SUZAKU WARRIORS OR SEIRYU WARRIORS WOULD HAVE DIED... OR FORCED A LIFE-LONG GRIEF ON THE SURVIVORS!
I MIGHT EVEN HAVE BEEN ABLE TO STOP NAKAGO AND SAVE HIS LIFE AS WELL!
THAT'S WHY I'M MORE DETERMINED THAN EVER TO SEE THAT MIAKA AND HER FRIENDS END UP HAPPY! I'LL DO *ANYTHING* TO MAKE THAT HAPPEN!
PLIP
PLIP
...
YOU HELD ALL OF THOSE ANXIETIES INSIDE YOU...?

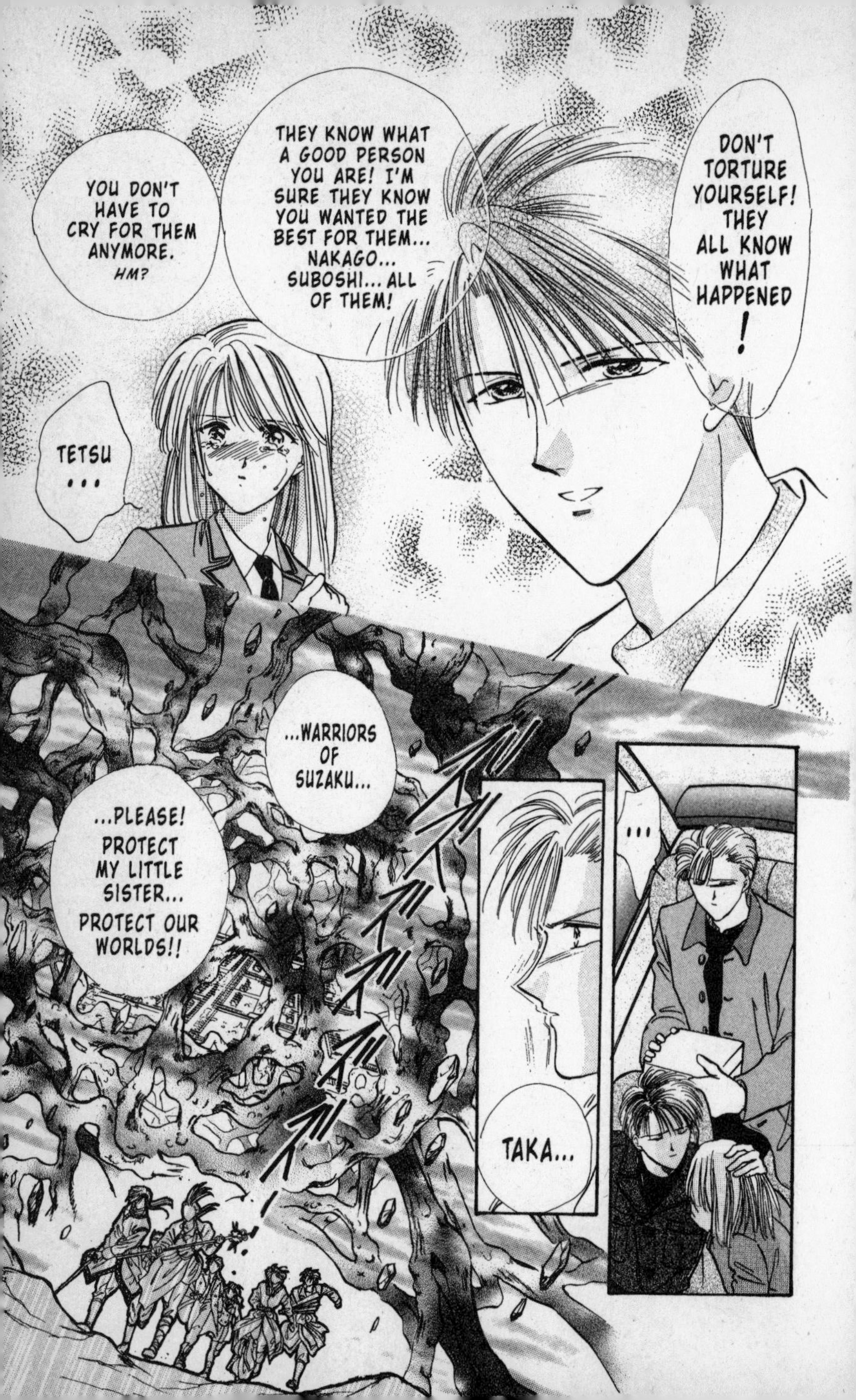
DON'T TORTURE YOURSELF! THEY ALL KNOW WHAT HAPPENED!
THEY KNOW WHAT A GOOD PERSON YOU ARE! I'M SURE THEY KNOW YOU WANTED THE BEST FOR THEM... NAKAGO... SUBOSHI... ALL OF THEM!
YOU DON'T HAVE TO CRY FOR THEM ANYMORE.
HM?
TETSU...
...
TAKA...
...WARRIORS OF SUZAKU...
...PLEASE! PROTECT MY LITTLE SISTER... PROTECT OUR WORLDS!!

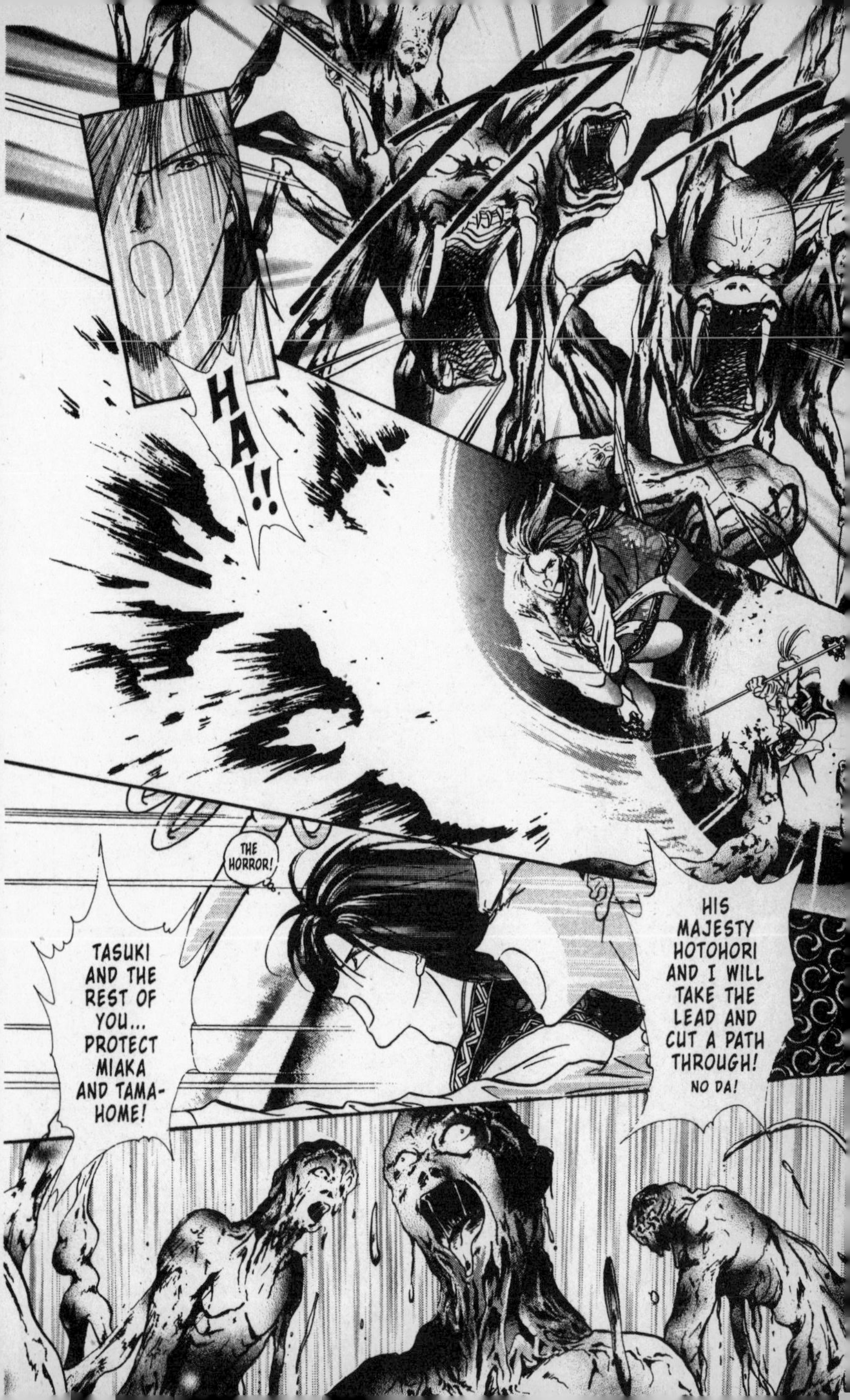
HA!!
HIS MAJESTY HOTOHORI AND I WILL TAKE THE LEAD AND CUT A PATH THROUGH! NO DA!
THE HORROR!
TASUKI AND THE REST OF YOU... PROTECT MIAKA AND TAMA-HOME!

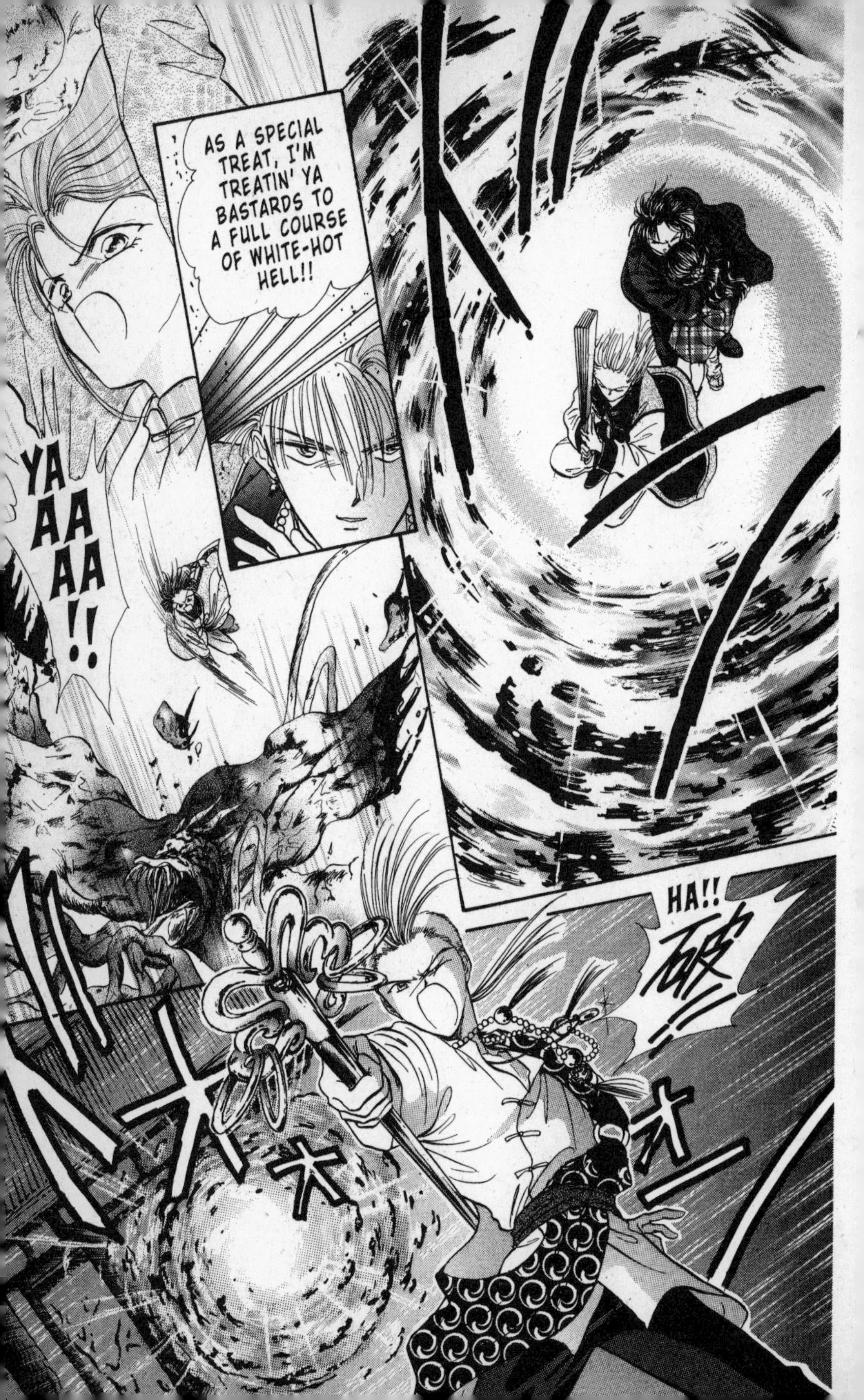
AS A SPECIAL TREAT, I'M TREATIN' YA BASTARDS TO A FULL COURSE OF WHITE-HOT HELL!!
YAAAAAA!!
HA!!

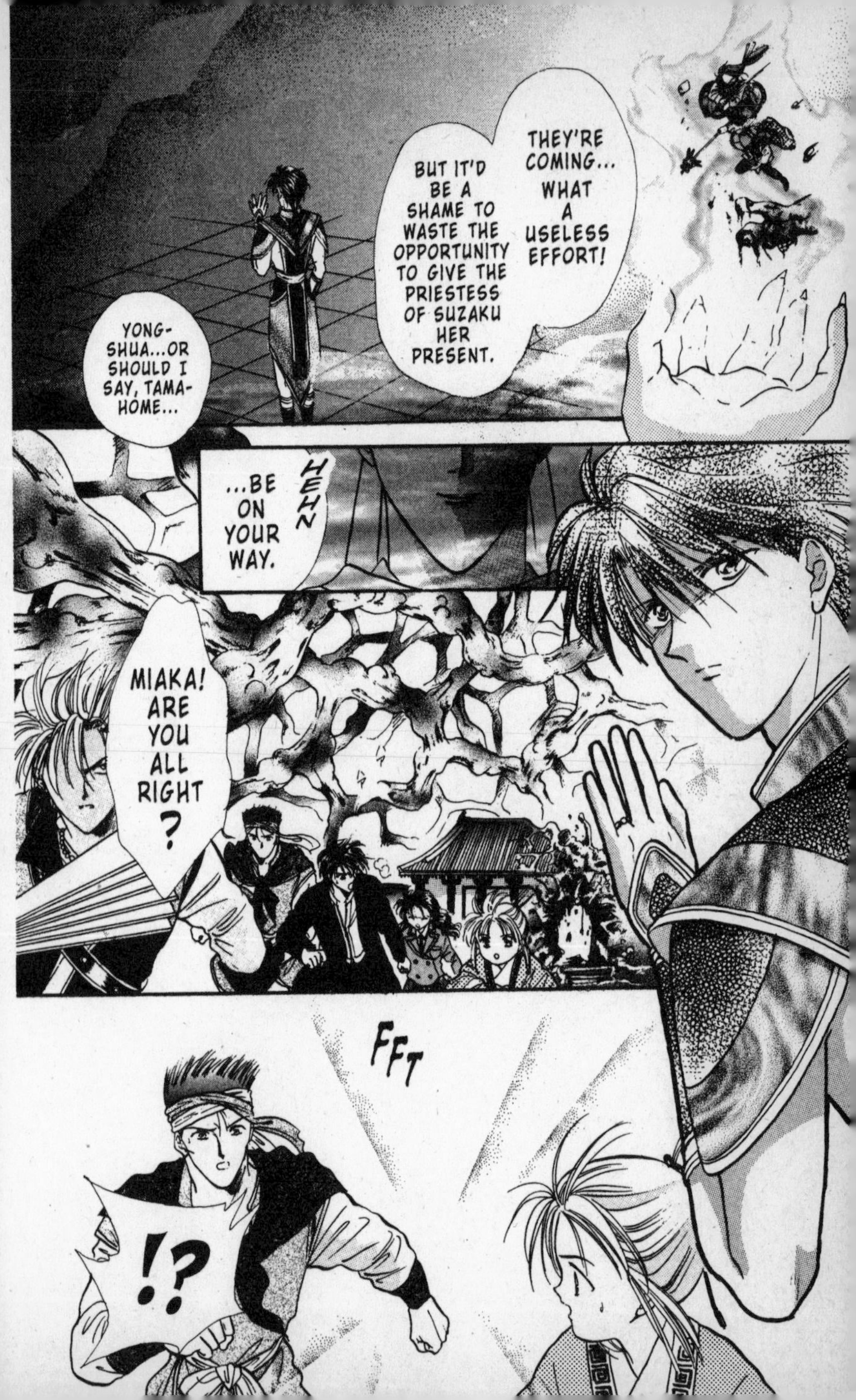
THEY'RE COMING... WHAT A USELESS EFFORT!
BUT IT'D BE A SHAME TO WASTE THE OPPORTUNITY TO GIVE THE PRIESTESS OF SUZAKU HER PRESENT.
YONG-SHUA...OR SHOULD I SAY, TAMA-HOME...
HEHN
...BE ON YOUR WAY.
MIAKA! ARE YOU ALL RIGHT?
FFT
!?

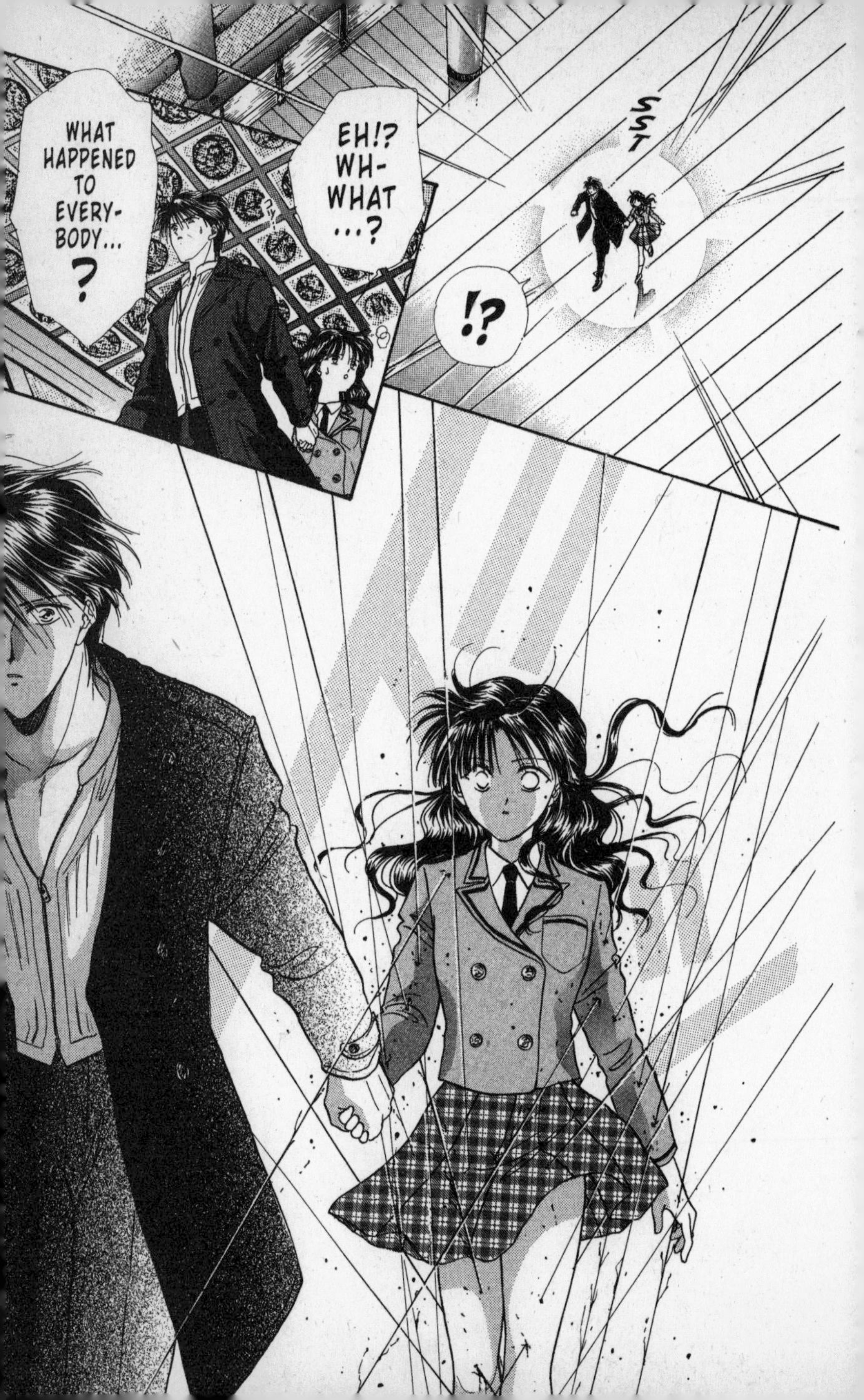
SST
!?
EH!? WH-WHAT...?
WHAT HAPPENED TO EVERY-BODY...?

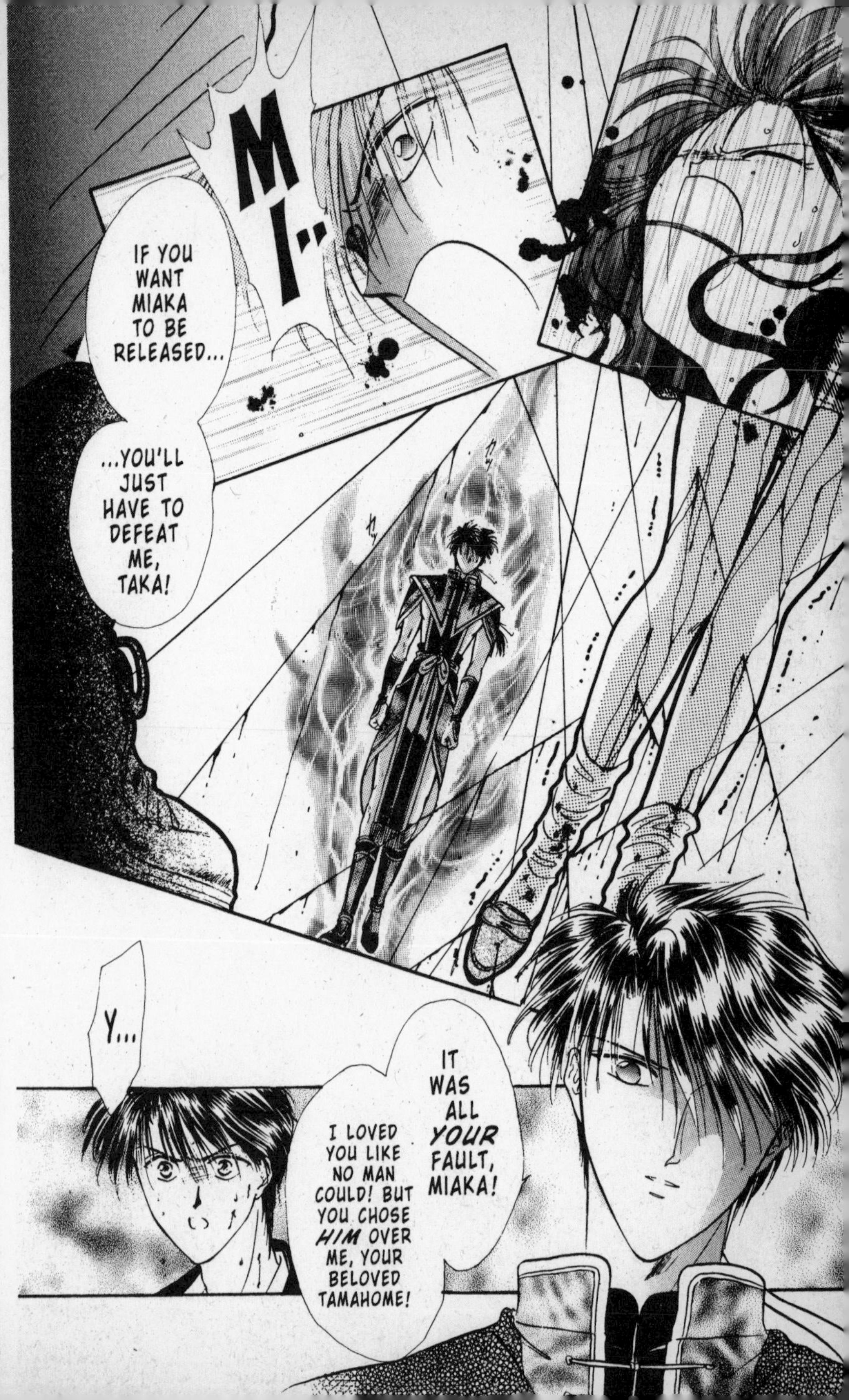
MI..
IF YOU WANT MIAKA TO BE RELEASED...
...YOU'LL JUST HAVE TO DEFEAT ME, TAKA!
IT WAS ALL *YOUR* FAULT, MIAKA!
I LOVED YOU LIKE NO MAN COULD! BUT YOU CHOSE *HIM* OVER ME, YOUR BELOVED TAMAHOME!
Y...

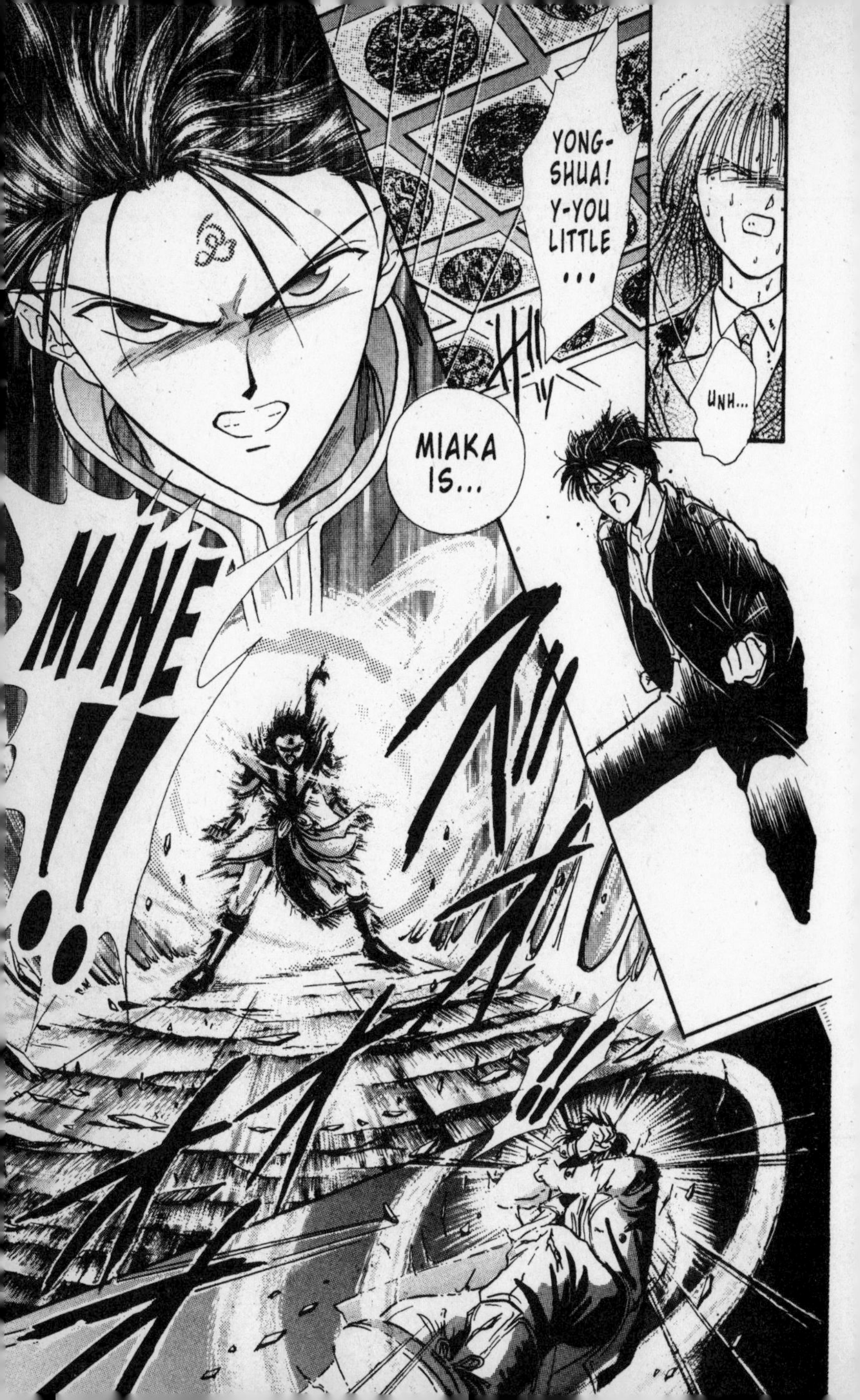
UNH...
YONG-SHUA! Y-YOU LITTLE ...
MIAKA IS...
MINE!!..

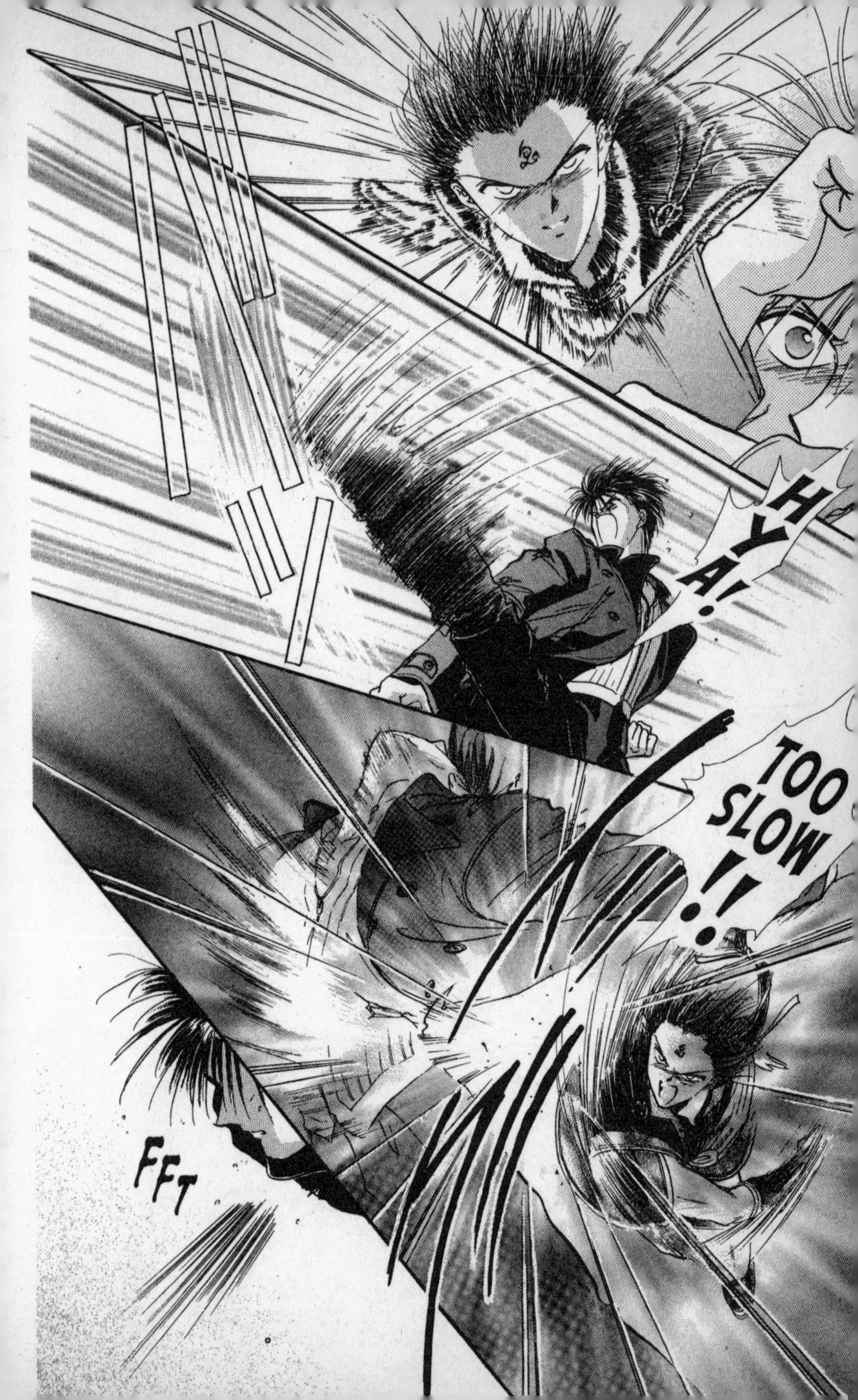
HYA!
TOO SLOW!!
FFT

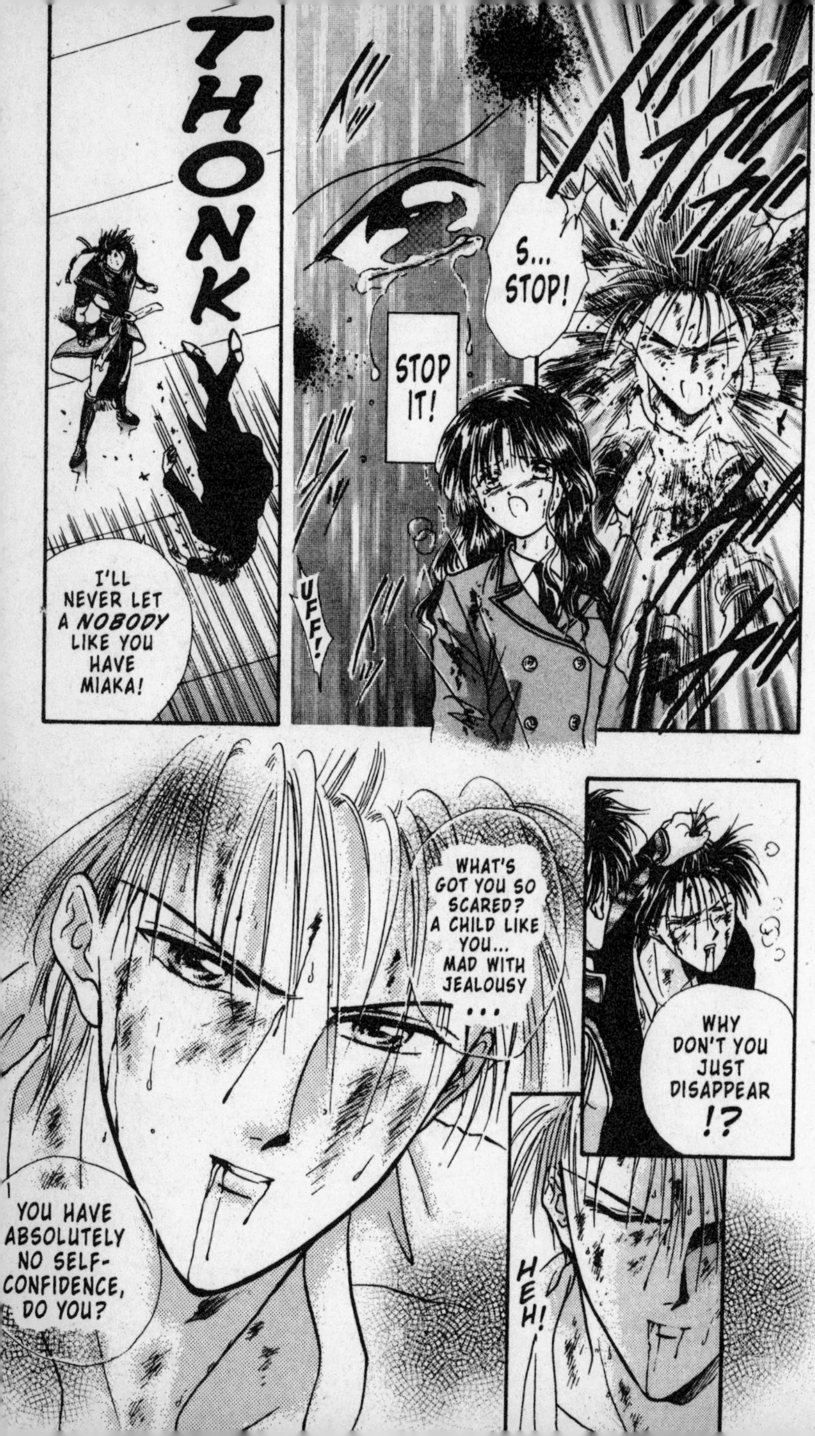
S... STOP!
STOP IT!
UFF!
THONK
I'LL NEVER LET A NOBODY LIKE YOU HAVE MIAKA!
WHY DON'T YOU JUST DISAPPEAR!?
HEH!
WHAT'S GOT YOU SO SCARED? A CHILD LIKE YOU... MAD WITH JEALOUSY...
YOU HAVE ABSOLUTELY NO SELF-CONFIDENCE, DO YOU?

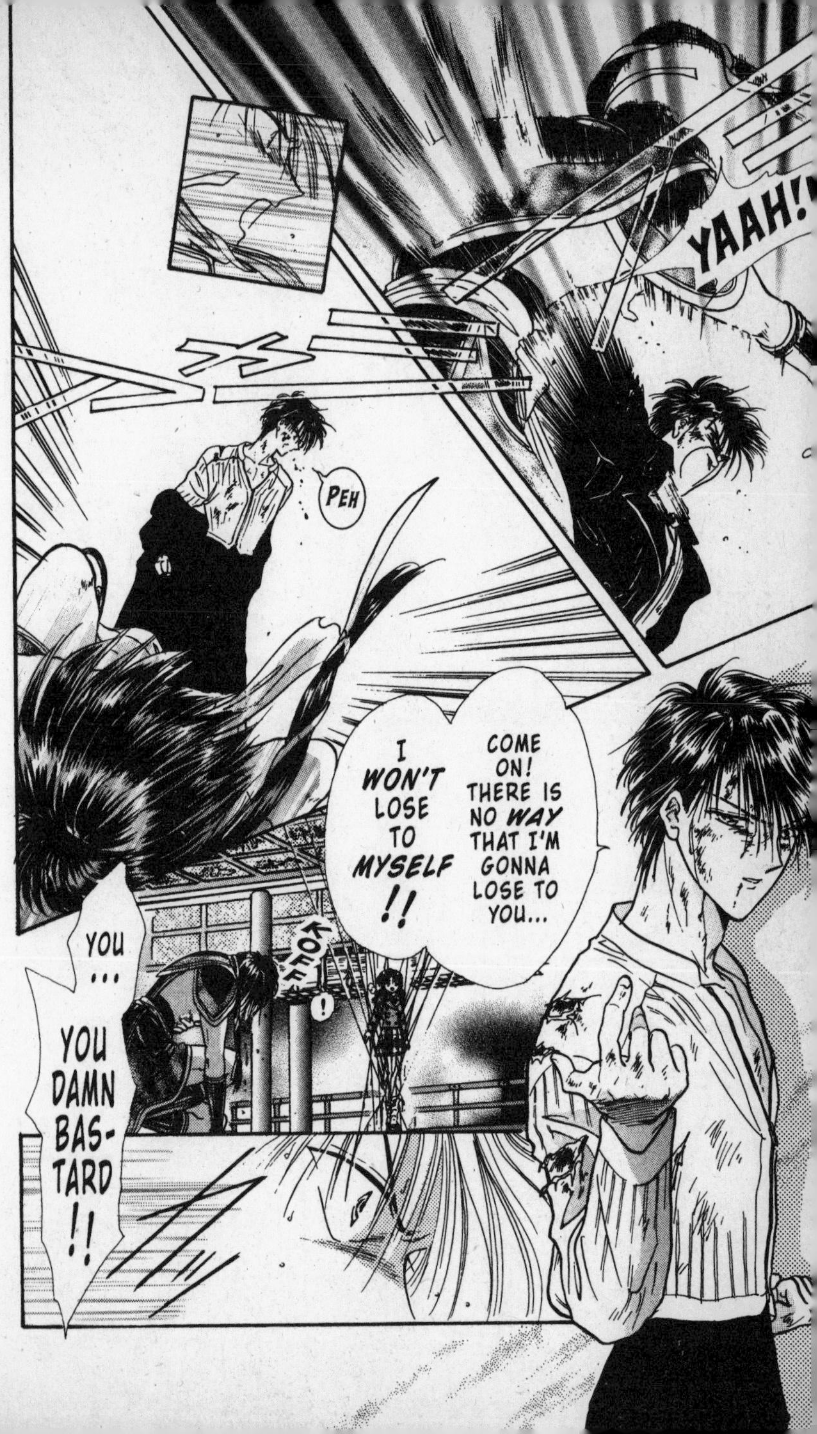
YAAH!!
PEH
COME ON! THERE IS NO WAY THAT I'M GONNA LOSE TO YOU...
I WON'T LOSE TO MYSELF !!
KOFF
!
YOU...
YOU DAMN BASTARD!!

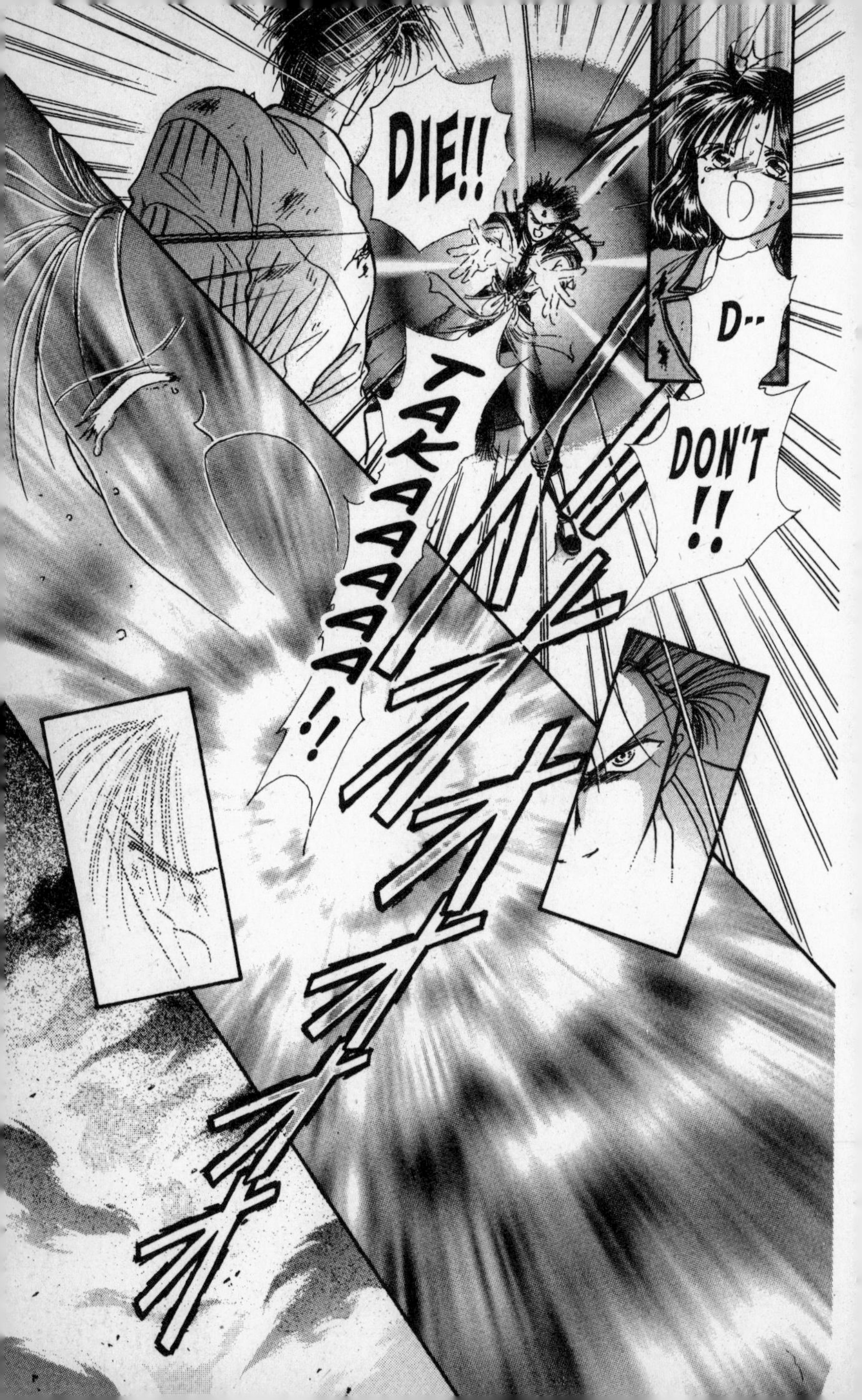
D--
DON'T !!
DIE!!
TAKAAAAAAA!!

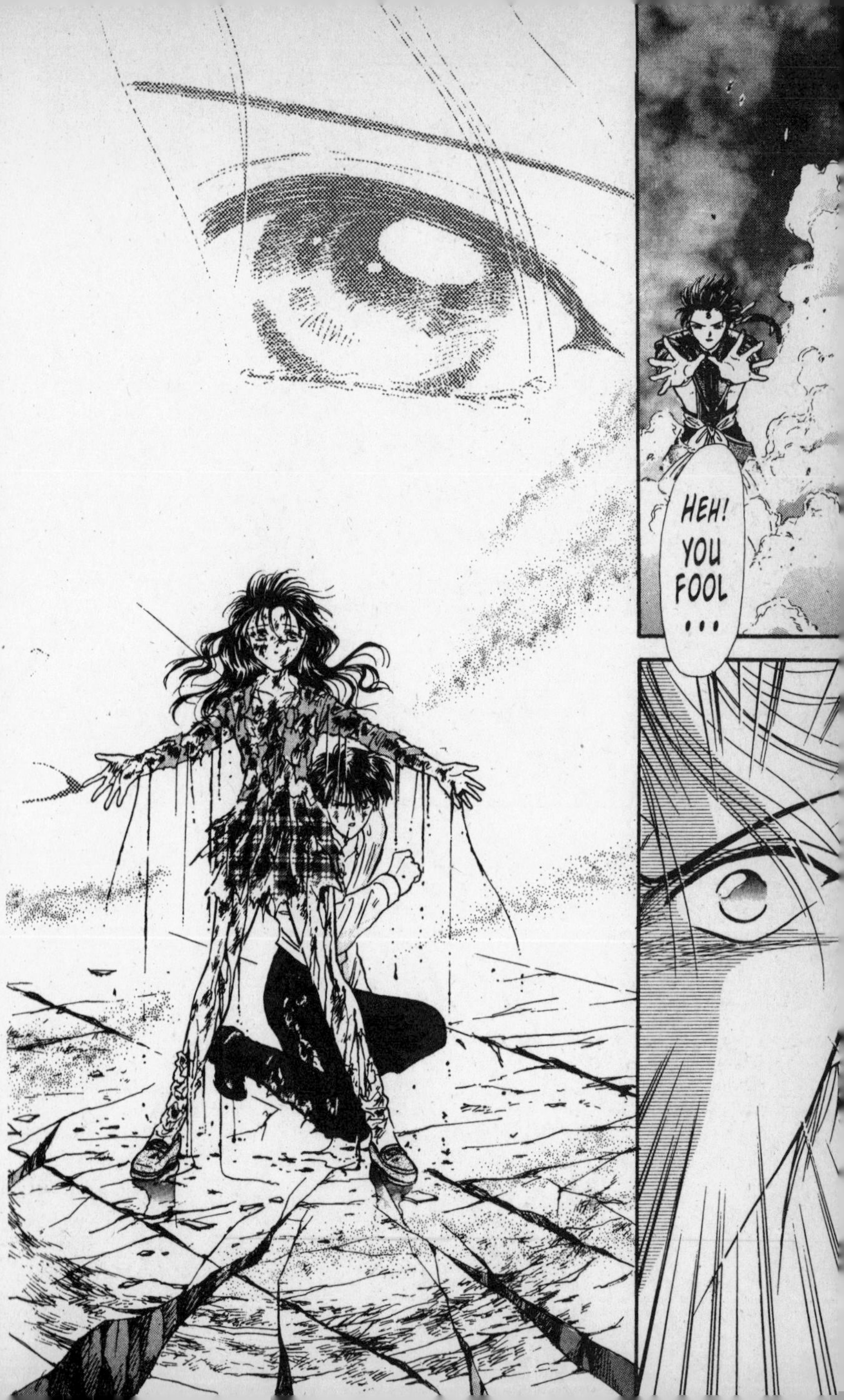
HEH! YOU FOOL ...

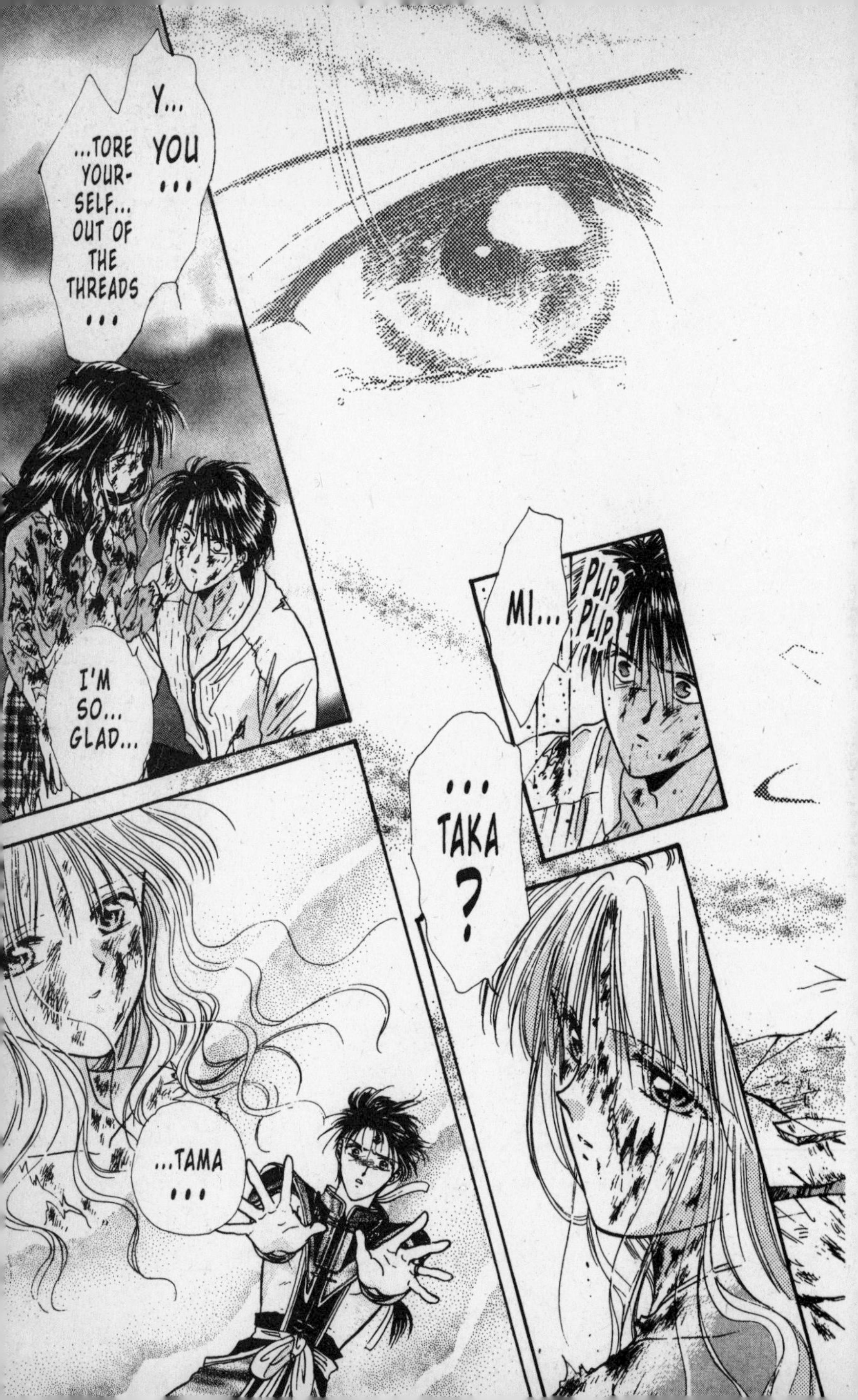
Y... YOU...
...TORE YOUR-SELF... OUT OF THE THREADS...
I'M SO... GLAD...
MI...
PLIP PLIP
...TAKA?
...TAMA...

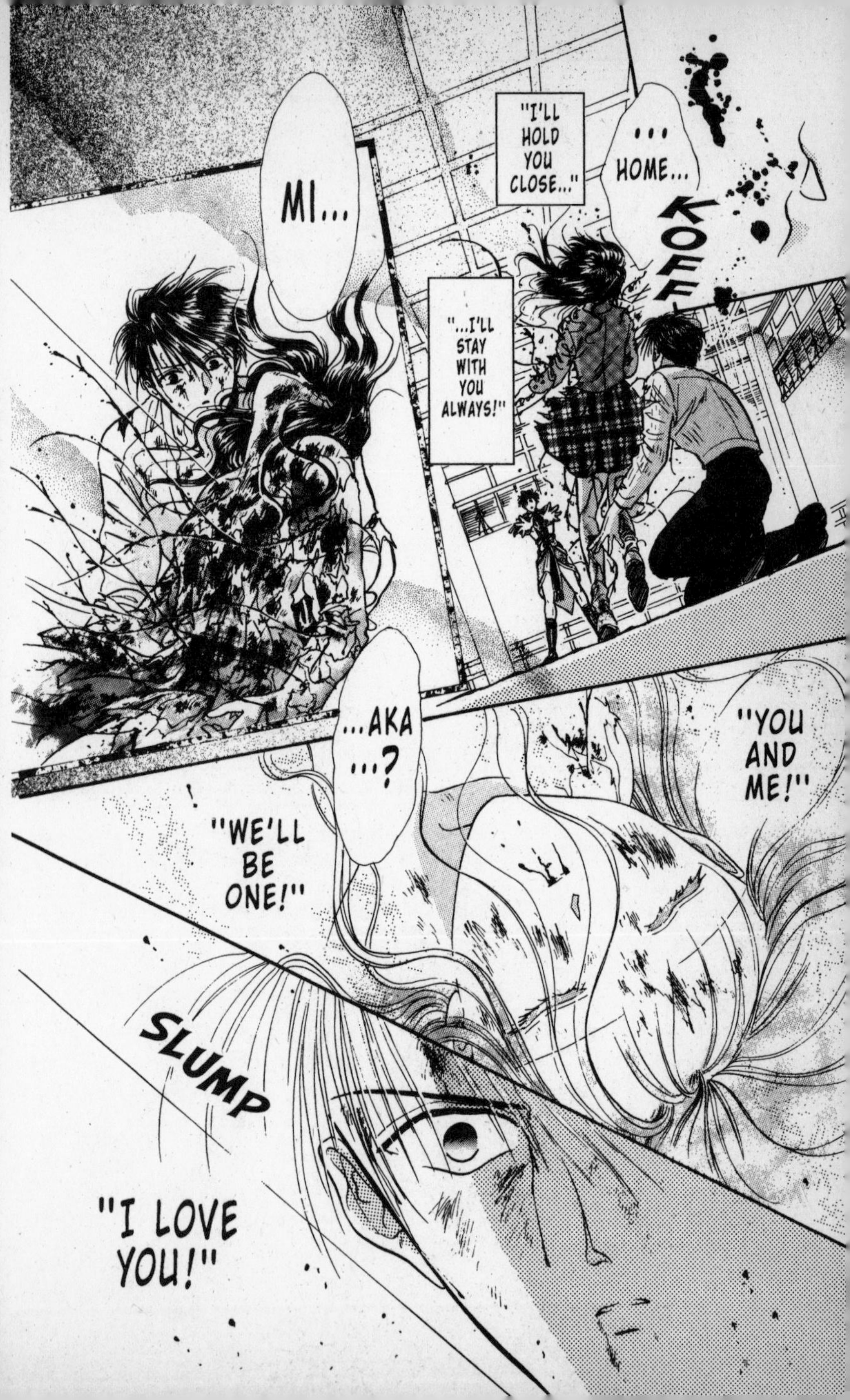
...HOME...
KOFF
"I'LL HOLD YOU CLOSE..."
"...I'LL STAY WITH YOU ALWAYS!"
MI...
"YOU AND ME!"
...AKA ...?
"WE'LL BE ONE!"
SLUMP
"I LOVE YOU!"

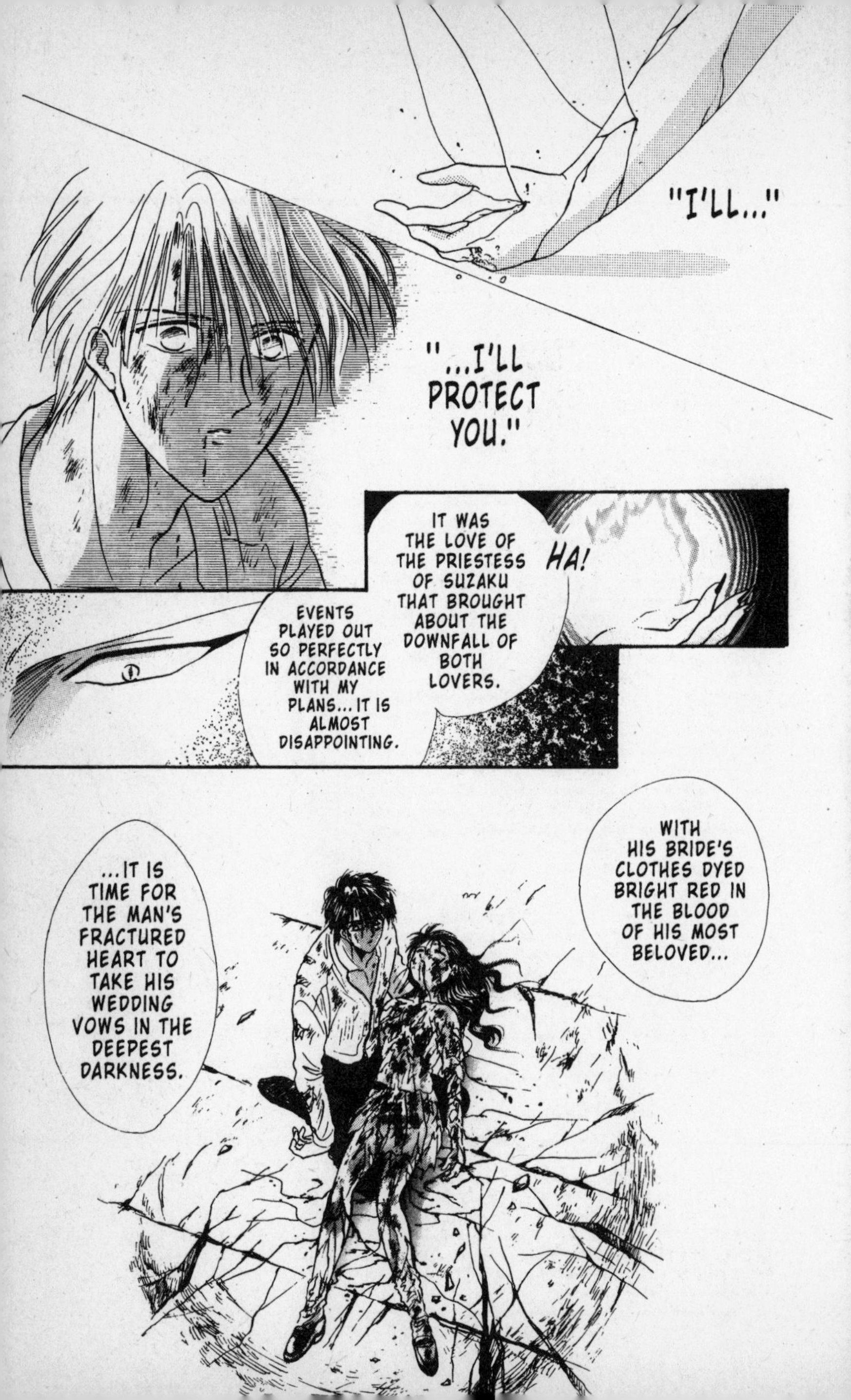
"I'LL..."
"...I'LL PROTECT YOU."
HA!
IT WAS THE LOVE OF THE PRIESTESS OF SUZAKU THAT BROUGHT ABOUT THE DOWNFALL OF BOTH LOVERS.
EVENTS PLAYED OUT SO PERFECTLY IN ACCORDANCE WITH MY PLANS... IT IS ALMOST DISAPPOINTING.
WITH HIS BRIDE'S CLOTHES DYED BRIGHT RED IN THE BLOOD OF HIS MOST BELOVED...
...IT IS TIME FOR THE MAN'S FRACTURED HEART TO TAKE HIS WEDDING VOWS IN THE DEEPEST DARKNESS.

NAKAGO...

At a meeting, I had decided that I would have him live until nearly the very end. I was determined for him to be the villain (it didn't quite work). Maybe that's the reason why he's the most controversial character among readers, with fans having so many different mental images of him. (I thought so!) Anyway, to me, Nakago is both sad and lonely. He's the fragile little boy who cries in the darkness. Others call him "a big bad guy," or "cool and strong"... actually, lots of different things. But Nakago is, even now, extremely popular (in Part 1, he was unstoppable!☺) It seems that there are a lot of people who, when reading what happened at the end, went, "Wow!"

Nakago said that he wants to "become a god," and that he wants to "control the world," but really, that was just him trying his hardest to figure out a purpose that would allow him to go on living. In reality, his heart was a complete void. Even if he wanted to die, he couldn't figure out a death where his mother would be on the other side waiting for him...so he couldn't die yet. It's very possible that he hated himself when he lost control of his power, and he even probably was glad his defeat came at the hands of Tamahome (a man who, unlike himself, had a heart that was straight and true). When Yui was questioning Nakago, he probably could easily have lied, but at the time, he just didn't care anymore. I think the scene of Ashitare's death was still playing out in his head. What Ashitare did broke a few centimeters through the armor that surrounds Nakago's heart.

A 12.3-year-old reader wrote a letter saying something to the effect of, "I once said that there was no other place for Nakago to go but hell, but now I don't think so. Hell is a place where not even one person loves you." As a woman, I can't help but believe that a woman's emotions and actions that are powerful enough to move the heart of a man are incredibly important to their relationship. Nakago has been said to have an enormous sadness... still, the image of Nakago that persists within me isn't of a strong person at all. That's why, even though he played the role of the bad guy, he wasn't a bad person. While I was drawing Part 2, I came to this realization about Part 1: The strong ones were the girls. They gave a love as strong as that fabled mother's love to their men. Now that's strong!

● INFORMATION! (CIRCA 1996)

- Speaking of Nakago... On July 25, the "Fushigi Yūgi Special" Parts 1 & 2 will come out on video!! (2900 yen.) This one will sell out quick! It covers a lot of ground, and it has a short animated segment for "Nakago Shikkari-shinasai!" ("Hang In There, Nakago!") Let's all watch how pathetic he can be!☺
- For October, they're planning a series of videos (bonus animation and funny stuff) with Suboshi and Amiboshi...? Tomo and Nakago and Tenkō and a super-sexy Tamahome... Everything you've been waiting for! The story is supposed to take place between Parts 1 & 2, and you might be surprised and shout out, "Huh? THAT happened!?"
- Be sure to pick up the very last CD Book, "Eien Wo Ai Ni" ("Eternal I Love You")! *It's a CD but it also comes with an old jewel case that came out during an "All That Sho-Comi" event at Animate.*
- Also, there are anime CDs, soundtracks, "Itōshii Hito no Tame ni" ("For the One I Love") off of a mini album by Akemi Satō, "Seiryu no Gyakushū-hen" ("Revenge of the Seiryu Warriors"), and songs, and drama disks... a huge number of really great CDs out there! Get them at your neighborhood CD shop. They say they're going to release soundtrack CDs for the OAVs! I'm really looking forward to them! ♫

One other thing. According to my assistants, the Fushigi Yūgi theme song for Part 1 is trf's "Boy Meets Girl" (Remix • 3). Take a listen!

I'm also hooked on "Access"!

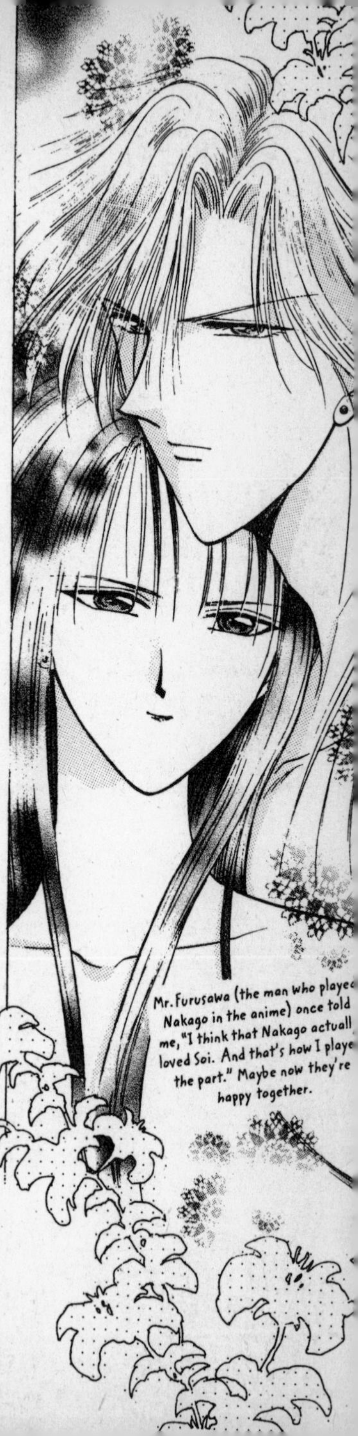
Mr. Furusawa (the man who playe
Nakago in the anime) once told
me, "I think that Nakago actuall
loved Soi. And that's how I playe
the part." Maybe now they're
happy together.

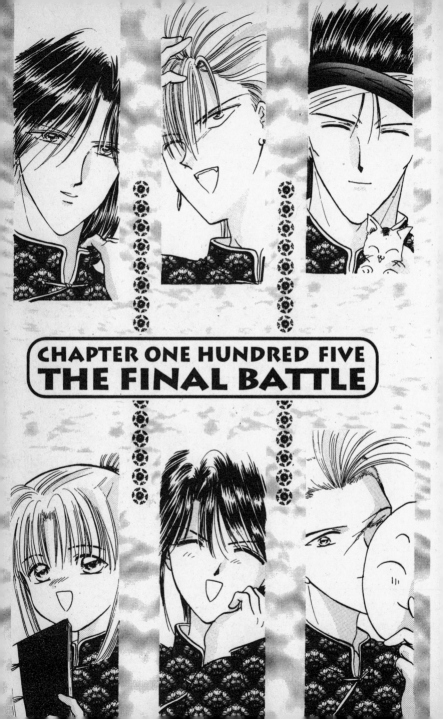

CHAPTER ONE HUNDRED FIVE
THE FINAL BATTLE

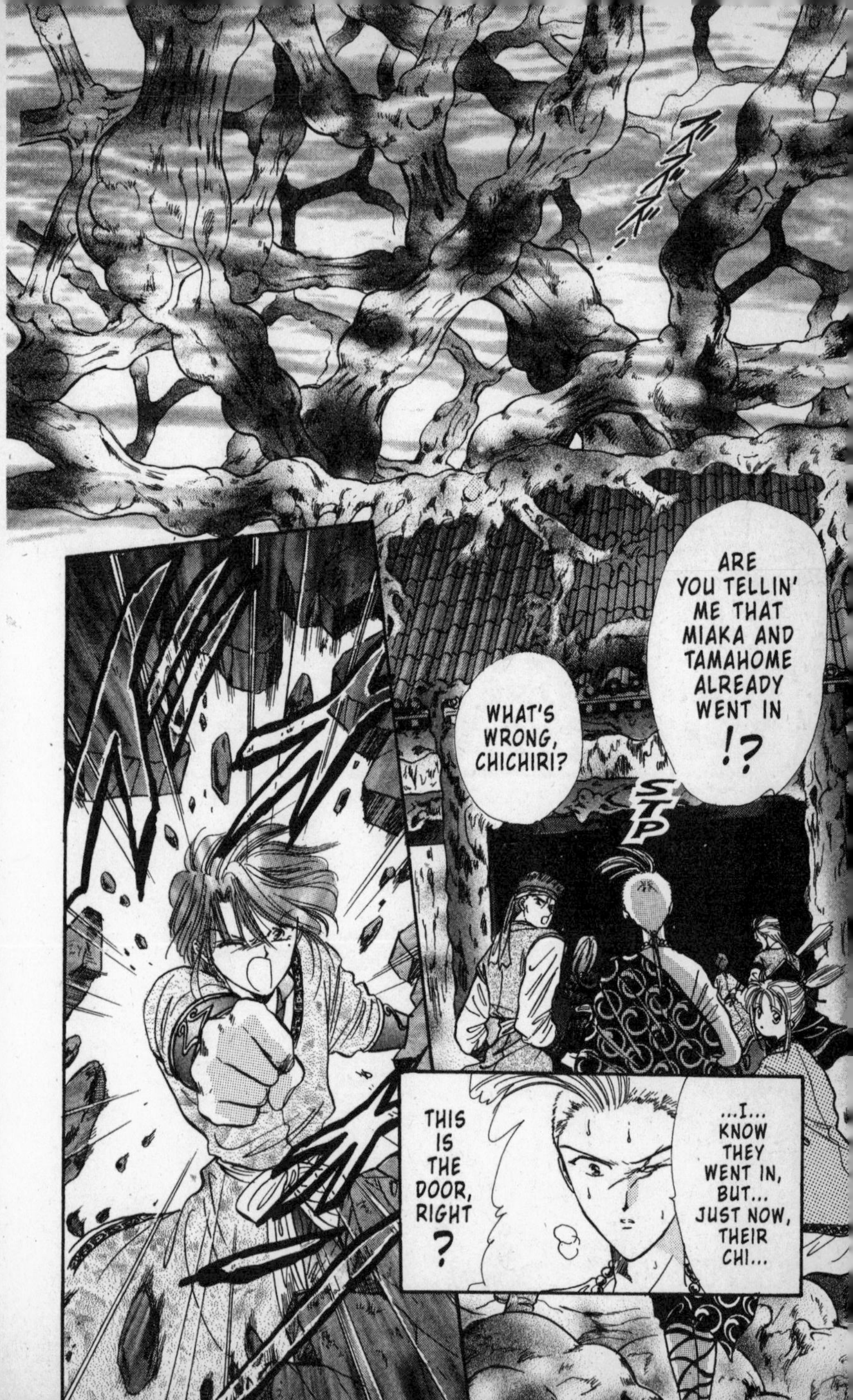
ARE YOU TELLIN' ME THAT MIAKA AND TAMAHOME ALREADY WENT IN !?
WHAT'S WRONG, CHICHIRI?
STP
...I... KNOW THEY WENT IN, BUT... JUST NOW, THEIR CHI...
THIS IS THE DOOR, RIGHT ?

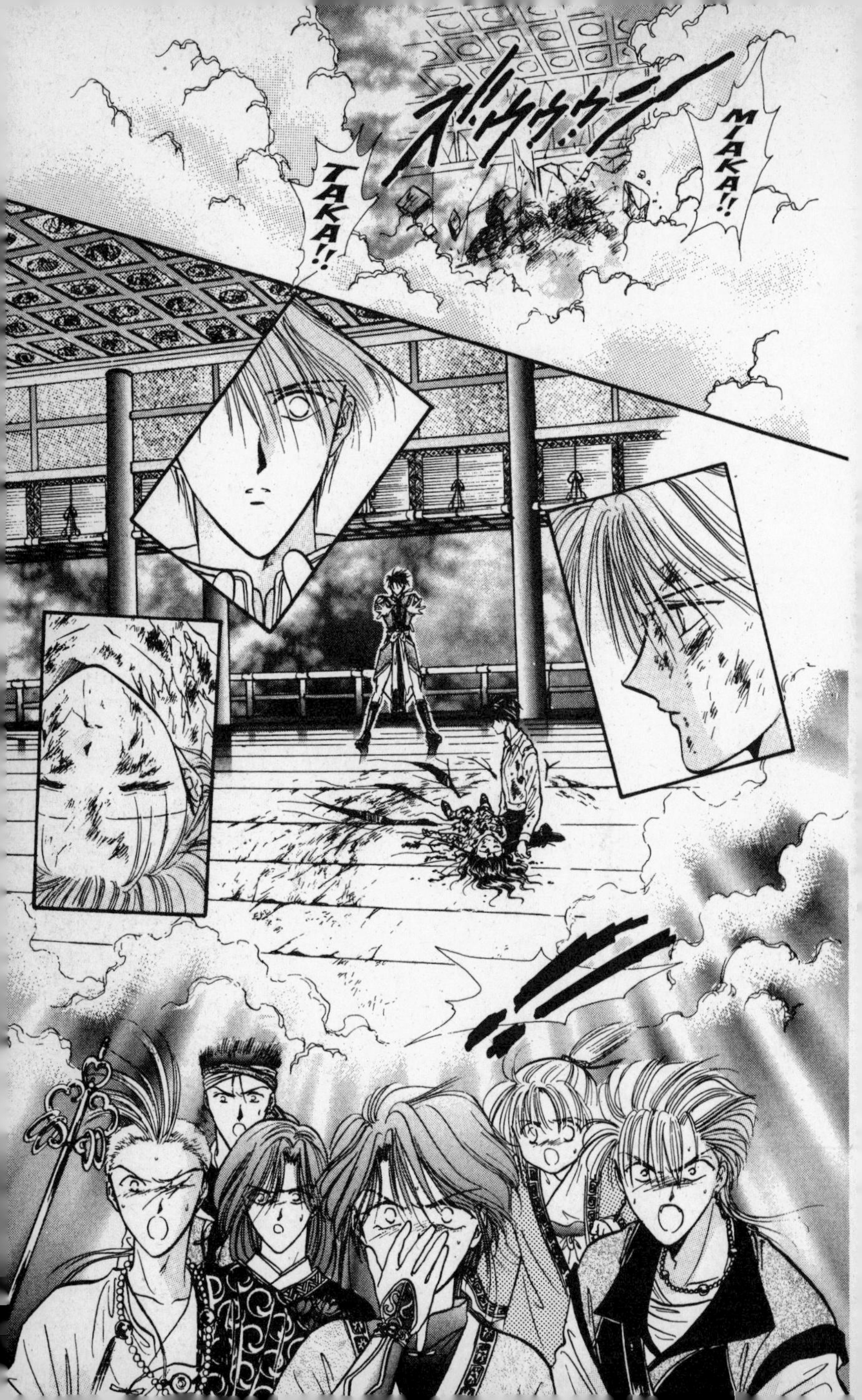
MIAKA!!
TAKA!!

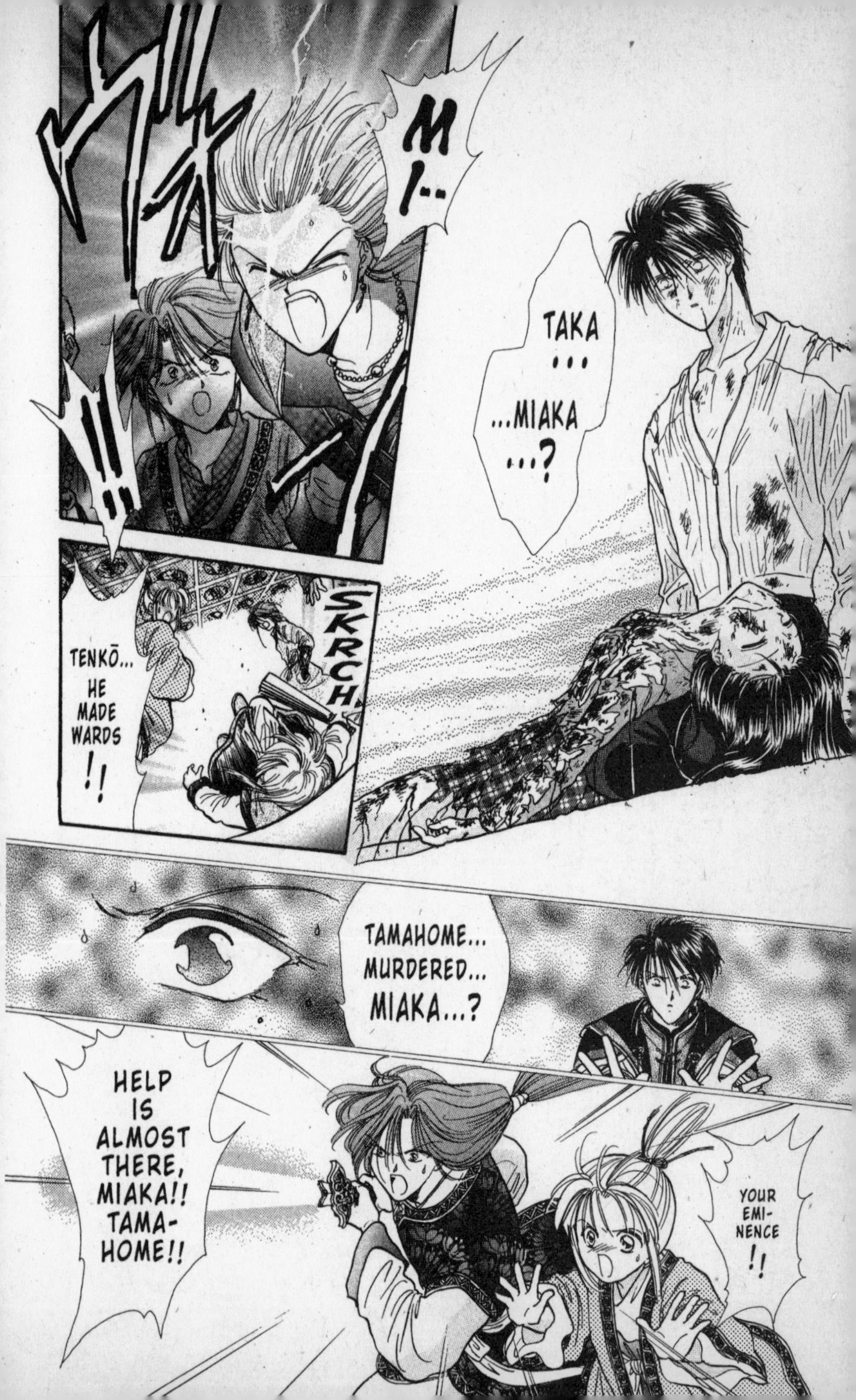
TAKA... ...MIAKA...?
MI...
!!
SKRCH
TENKŌ... HE MADE WARDS!!
TAMAHOME... MURDERED... MIAKA...?
YOUR EMINENCE!!
HELP IS ALMOST THERE, MIAKA!! TAMAHOME!!

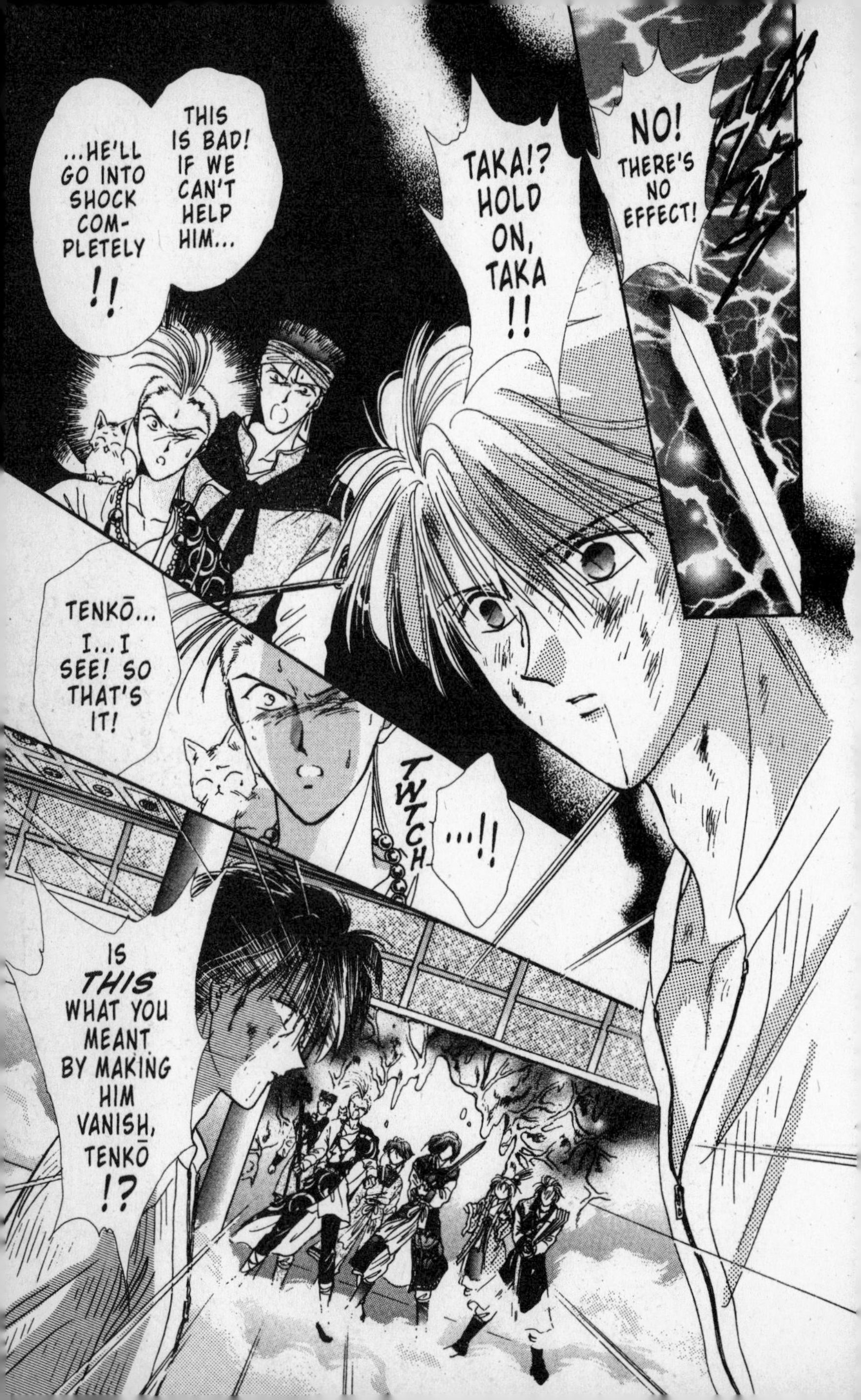
NO! THERE'S NO EFFECT!
TAKA!? HOLD ON, TAKA!!
THIS IS BAD! IF WE CAN'T HELP HIM...
...HE'LL GO INTO SHOCK COM-PLETELY!!
...!!
TWTCH
TENKŌ... I...I SEE! SO THAT'S IT!
IS *THIS* WHAT YOU MEANT BY MAKING HIM VANISH, TENKŌ!?

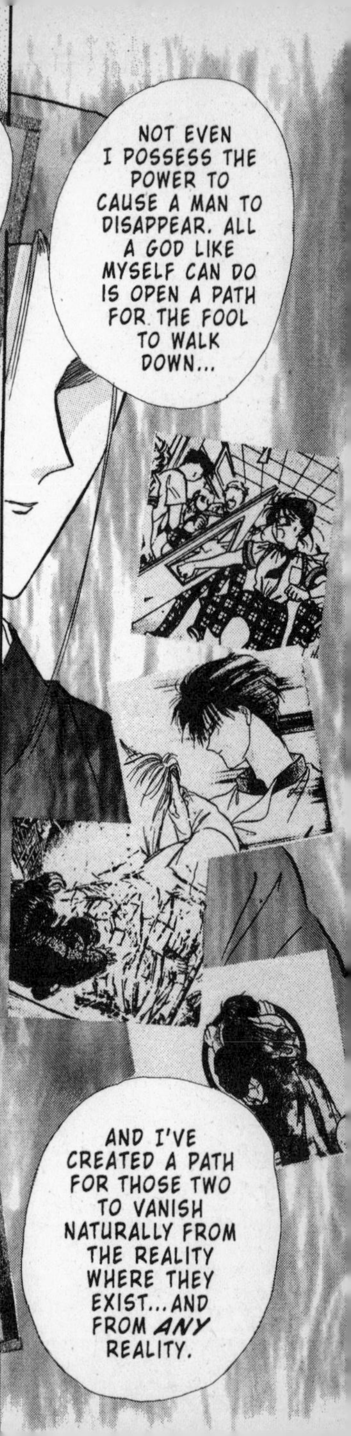
NOT EVEN I POSSESS THE POWER TO CAUSE A MAN TO DISAPPEAR. ALL A GOD LIKE MYSELF CAN DO IS OPEN A PATH FOR THE FOOL TO WALK DOWN...
AND I'VE CREATED A PATH FOR THOSE TWO TO VANISH NATURALLY FROM THE REALITY WHERE THEY EXIST...AND FROM *ANY* REALITY.

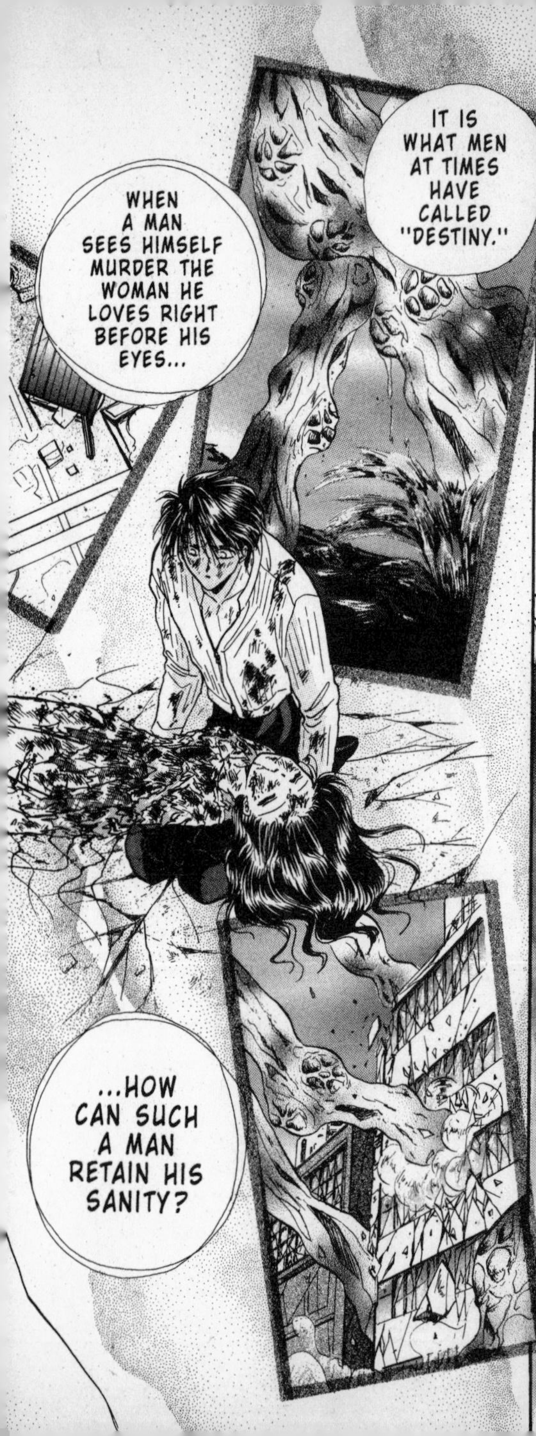
IT IS WHAT MEN AT TIMES HAVE CALLED "DESTINY."
WHEN A MAN SEES HIMSELF MURDER THE WOMAN HE LOVES RIGHT BEFORE HIS EYES...
...HOW CAN SUCH A MAN RETAIN HIS SANITY?

Tamahome is the kind of guy who runs flat-out, full speed ahead, and that's one way in which he and Taka are different. But Tamahome only exists because Taka exists... so the two really are one person. By the way... The coat that Taka always wears is the same as the coat Tamahome wore in volumes 12 and 13. *Did you notice?*

Since I thought of Tamahome as a "shōjo manga hero," I had him spout out some pretty clichéd lines. But he really meant them when he said them. There were some people who didn't like him because of his corny dialog, but he was sincere. It's just proof of how dumb some characters can be... just like Miaka! They're just so emotional. But with all his insecurities, he threw away the part of himself named Tamahome. "He" had vanished for Taka... by an act of Taka's will. Do you remember that drawing at the end with Tamahome in the clouds? The tears were streaming down while I was drawing that. I was thinking, "Wow, he was one incredible man!" Even my assistants said, "Before anybody says anything bad about him, just look at how far the guy goes to show his love! He made himself vanish for the woman he loves!" They were all worked up! ☺ And so, Taka was born. Those last words by the god Suzaku...! These are just the thoughts in my head, but Taka was reborn eighteen years ago... even before Miaka was born. That first time when Miaka went to the library and opened the book, Taka already existed. He had the ring, and he was waiting for the day when he would meet that girl. But it could be the opposite... that because Tamahome existed, Taka existed too. I leave that one to my readers' imaginations. But that may mean that the Seven Suzaku Celestial Warriors exist somewhere as well. ☺ Even though the world changes over the ages. ...Maybe some of you out there may meet them. *Ah... the romance of it! They may be close to you even now!*

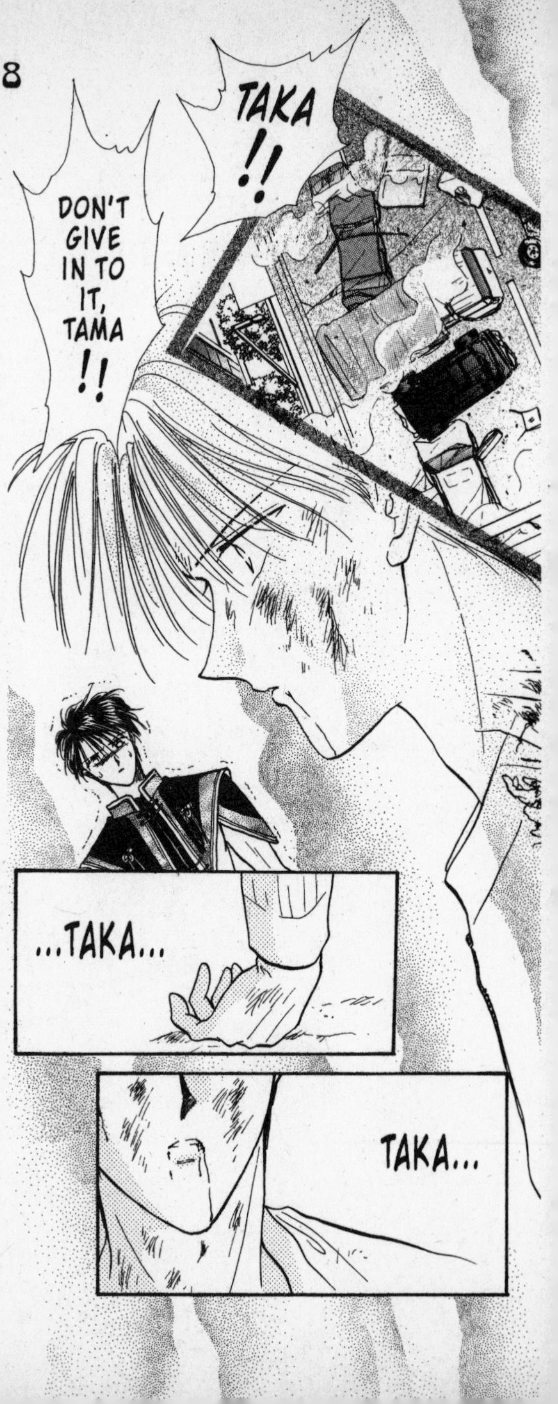
TAKA !!
DON'T GIVE IN TO IT, TAMA !!
...TAKA...
TAKA...

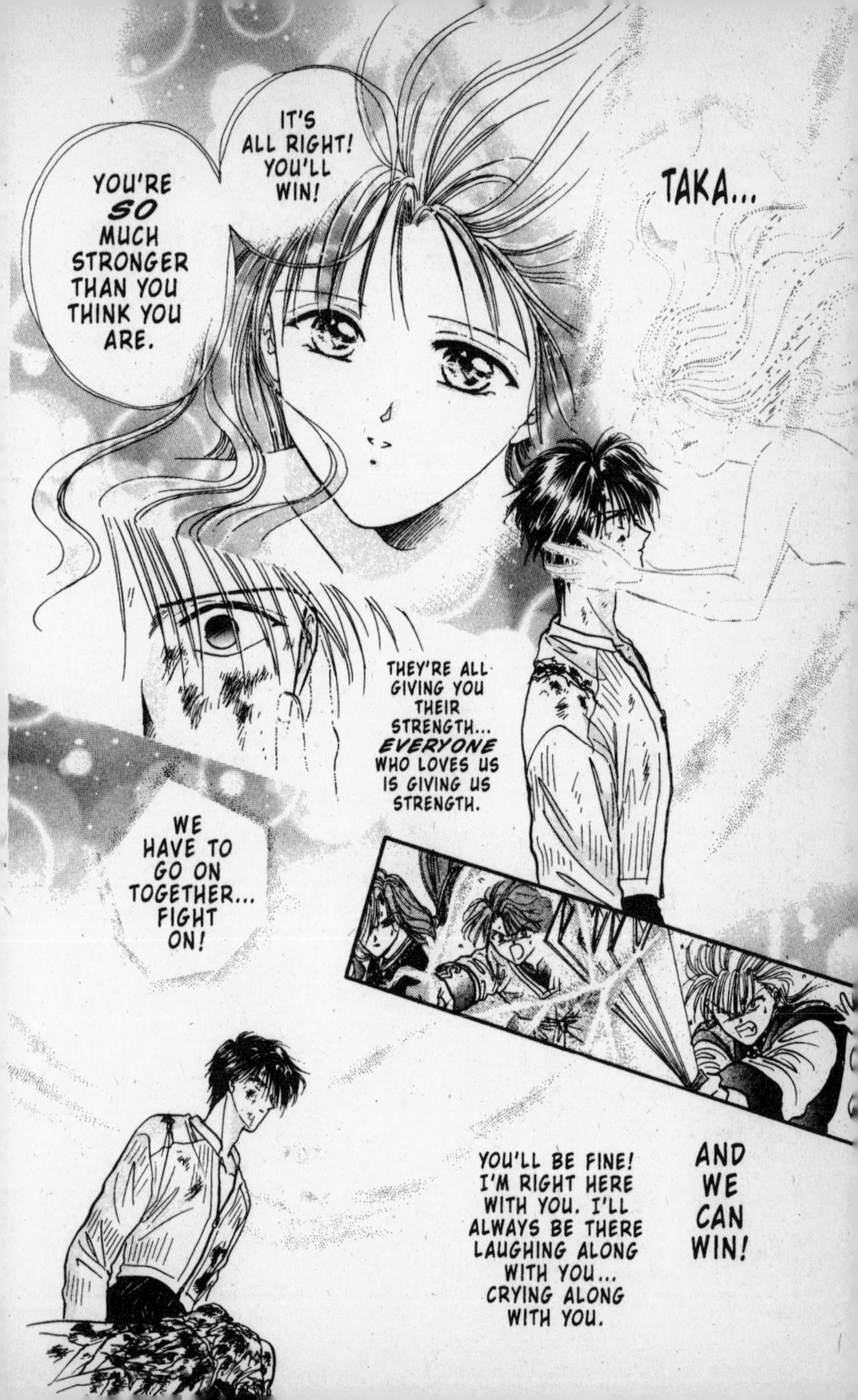
TAKA...
IT'S ALL RIGHT! YOU'LL WIN!
YOU'RE *SO* MUCH STRONGER THAN YOU THINK YOU ARE.
THEY'RE ALL GIVING YOU THEIR STRENGTH... *EVERYONE* WHO LOVES US IS GIVING US STRENGTH.
WE HAVE TO GO ON TOGETHER... FIGHT ON!
AND WE CAN WIN!
YOU'LL BE FINE! I'M RIGHT HERE WITH YOU. I'LL ALWAYS BE THERE LAUGHING ALONG WITH YOU... CRYING ALONG WITH YOU.

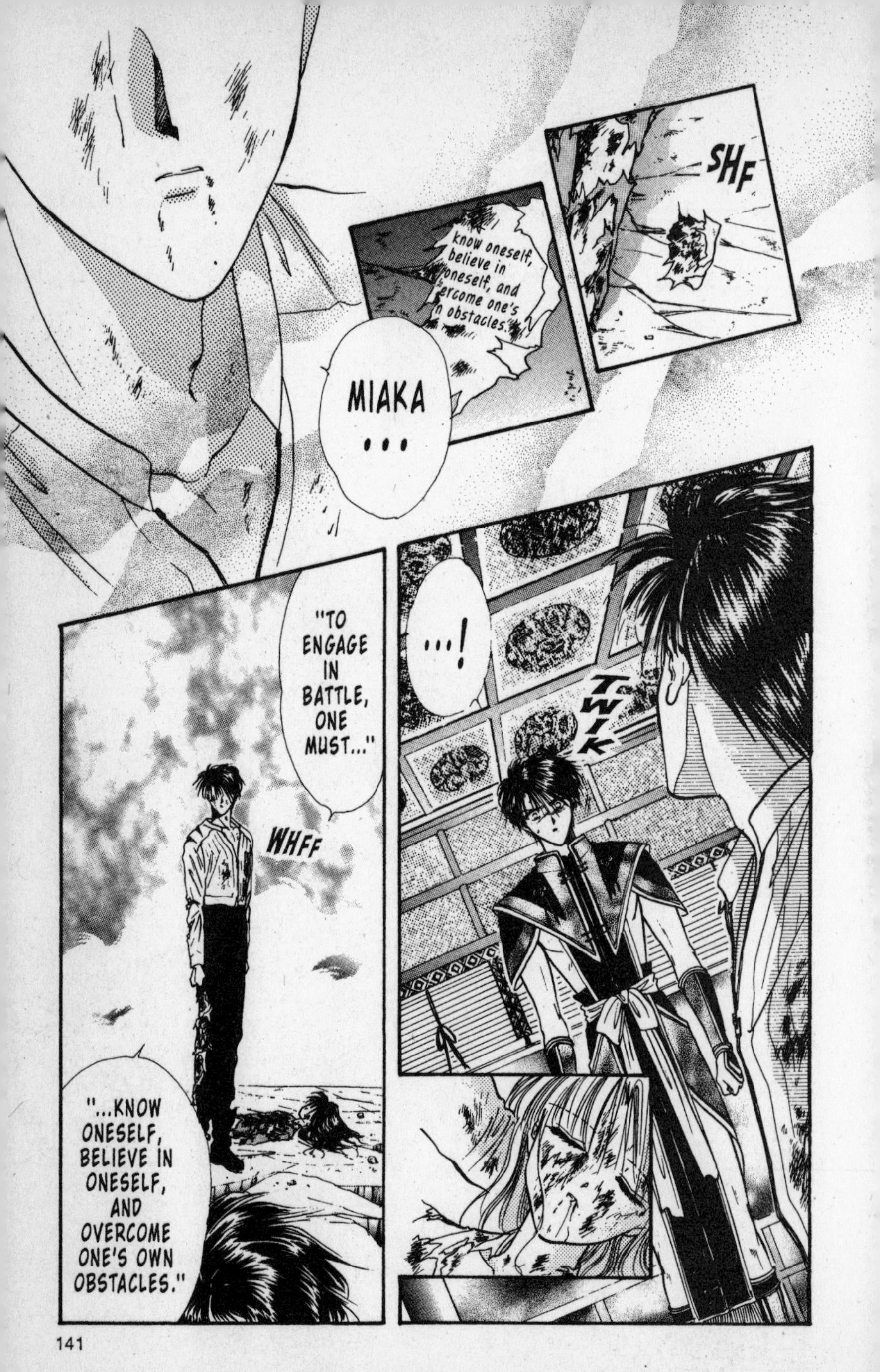
SHF
know oneself, believe in oneself, and overcome one's own obstacles.
MIAKA ...
...!
TWIK
"TO ENGAGE IN BATTLE, ONE MUST..."
WHFF
"...KNOW ONESELF, BELIEVE IN ONESELF, AND OVERCOME ONE'S OWN OBSTACLES."

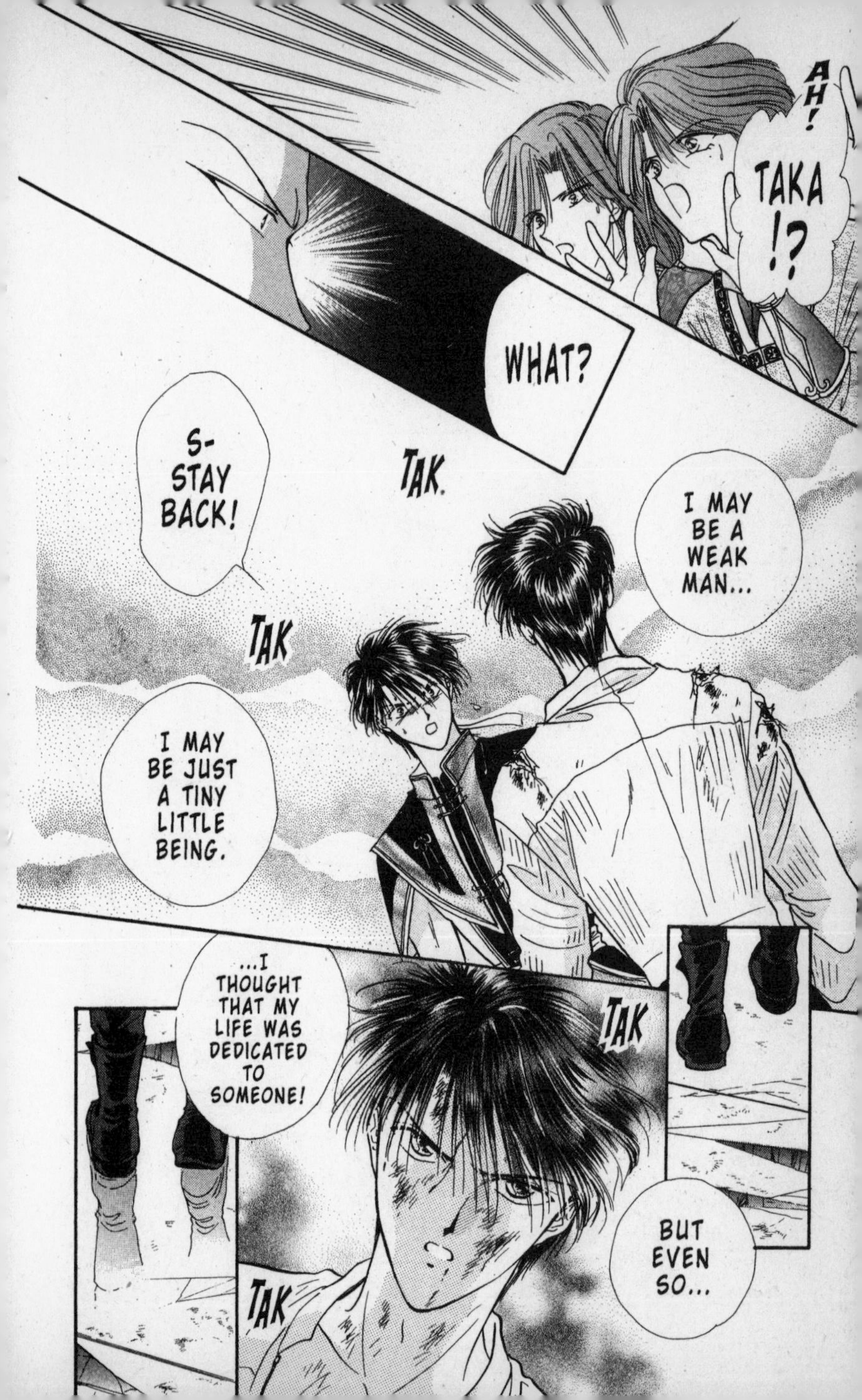
AH!
TAKA!?
WHAT?
S- STAY BACK!
TAK.
I MAY BE A WEAK MAN...
TAK
I MAY BE JUST A TINY LITTLE BEING.
TAK
BUT EVEN SO...
...I THOUGHT THAT MY LIFE WAS DEDICATED TO SOMEONE!
TAK

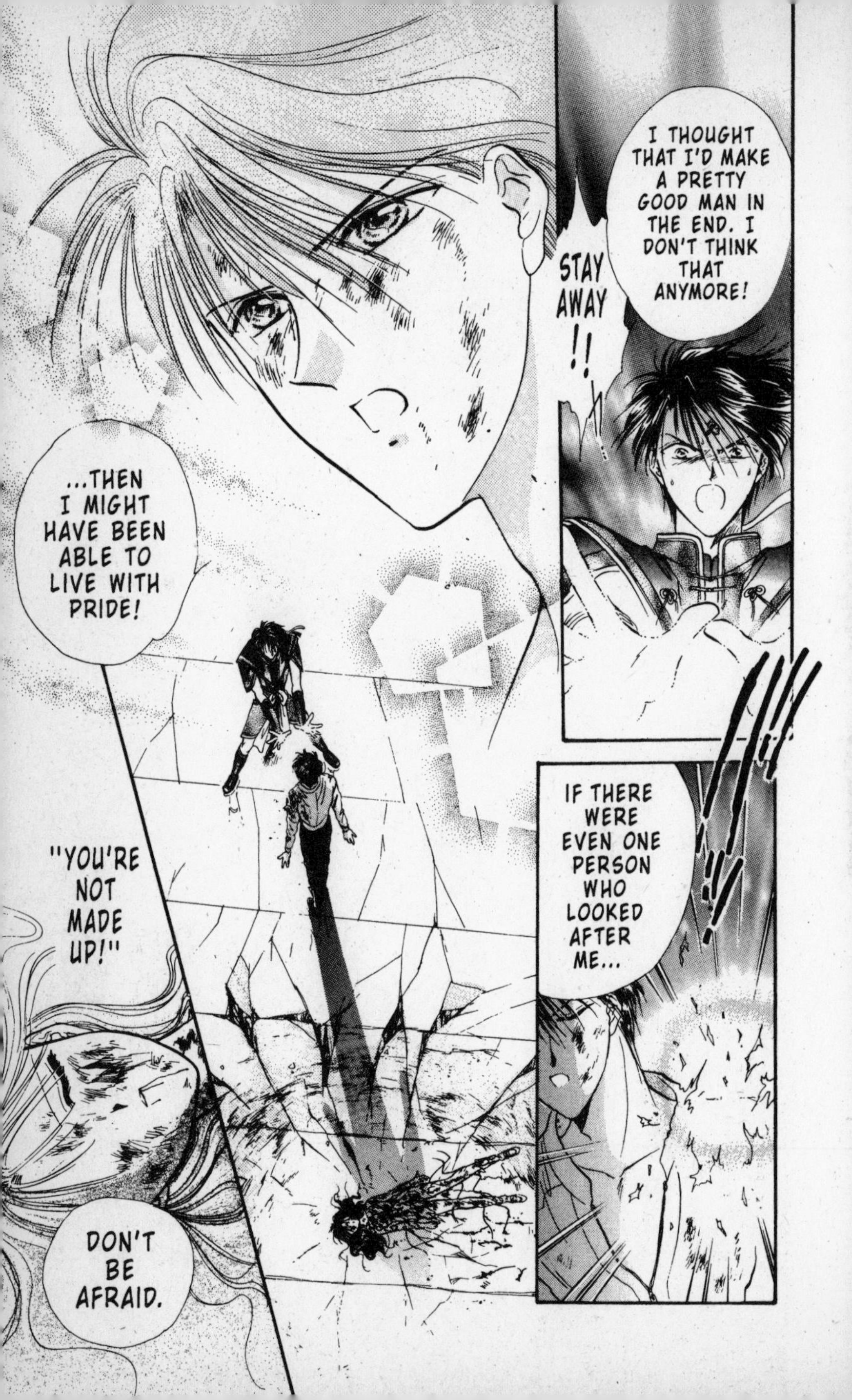
I THOUGHT THAT I'D MAKE A PRETTY GOOD MAN IN THE END. I DON'T THINK THAT ANYMORE!
STAY AWAY!!
IF THERE WERE EVEN ONE PERSON WHO LOOKED AFTER ME...
...THEN I MIGHT HAVE BEEN ABLE TO LIVE WITH PRIDE!
"YOU'RE NOT MADE UP!"
DON'T BE AFRAID.

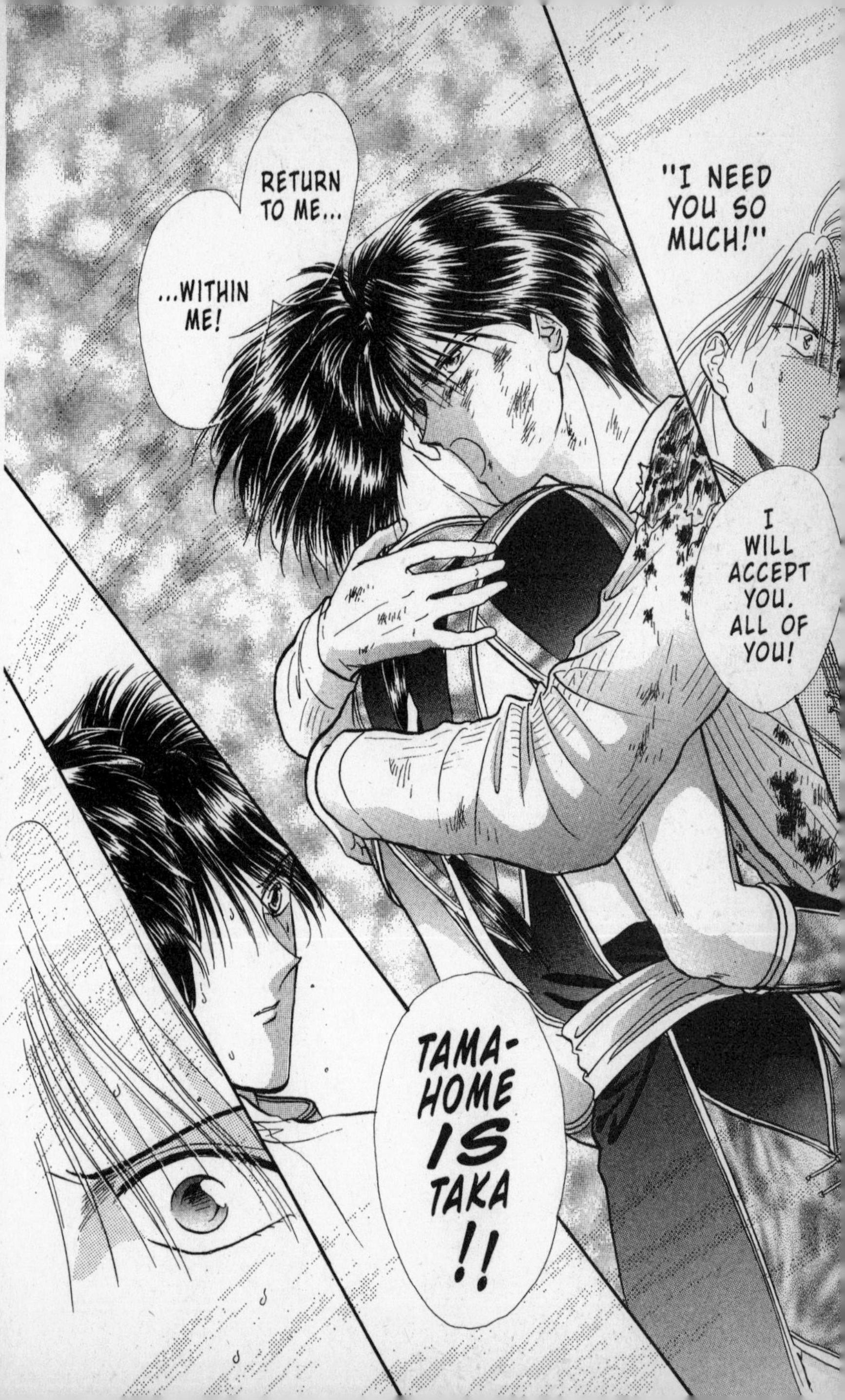
"I NEED YOU SO MUCH!"
RETURN TO ME...
...WITHIN ME!
I WILL ACCEPT YOU. ALL OF YOU!
TAMA-HOME IS TAKA!!

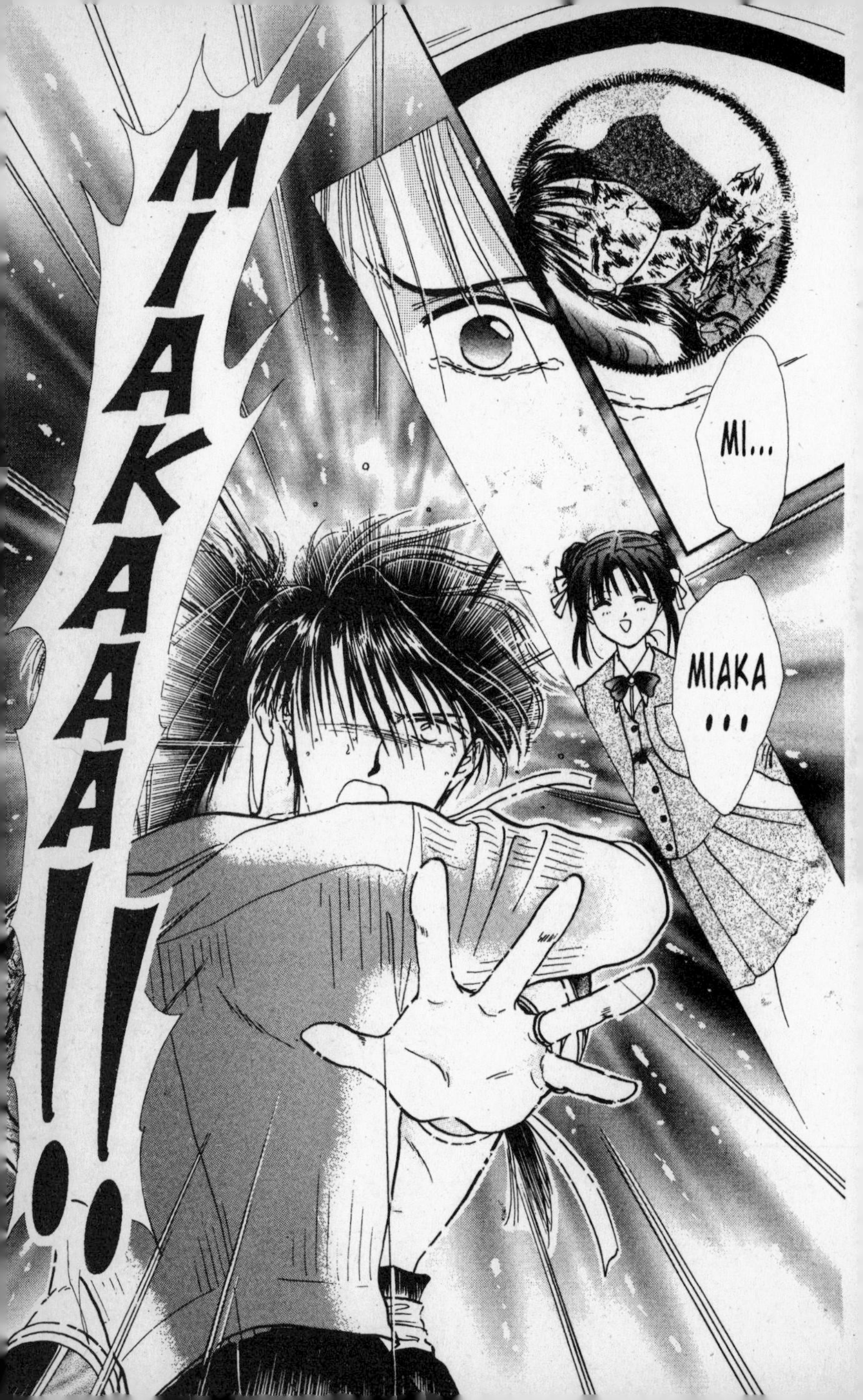
MI...
MIAKA ...
MIAKAAAA!!

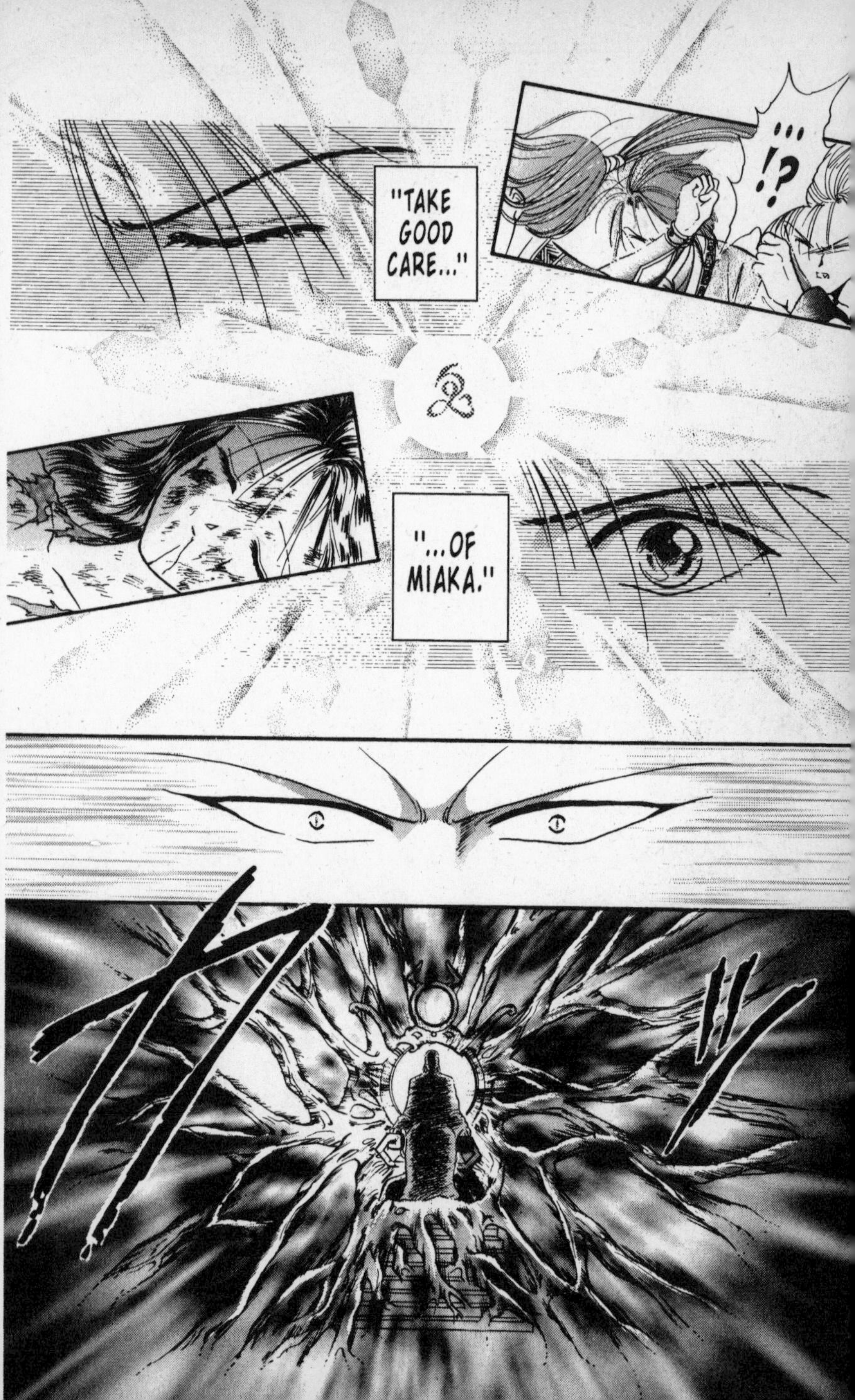
...!?
"TAKE GOOD CARE..."
"...OF MIAKA."

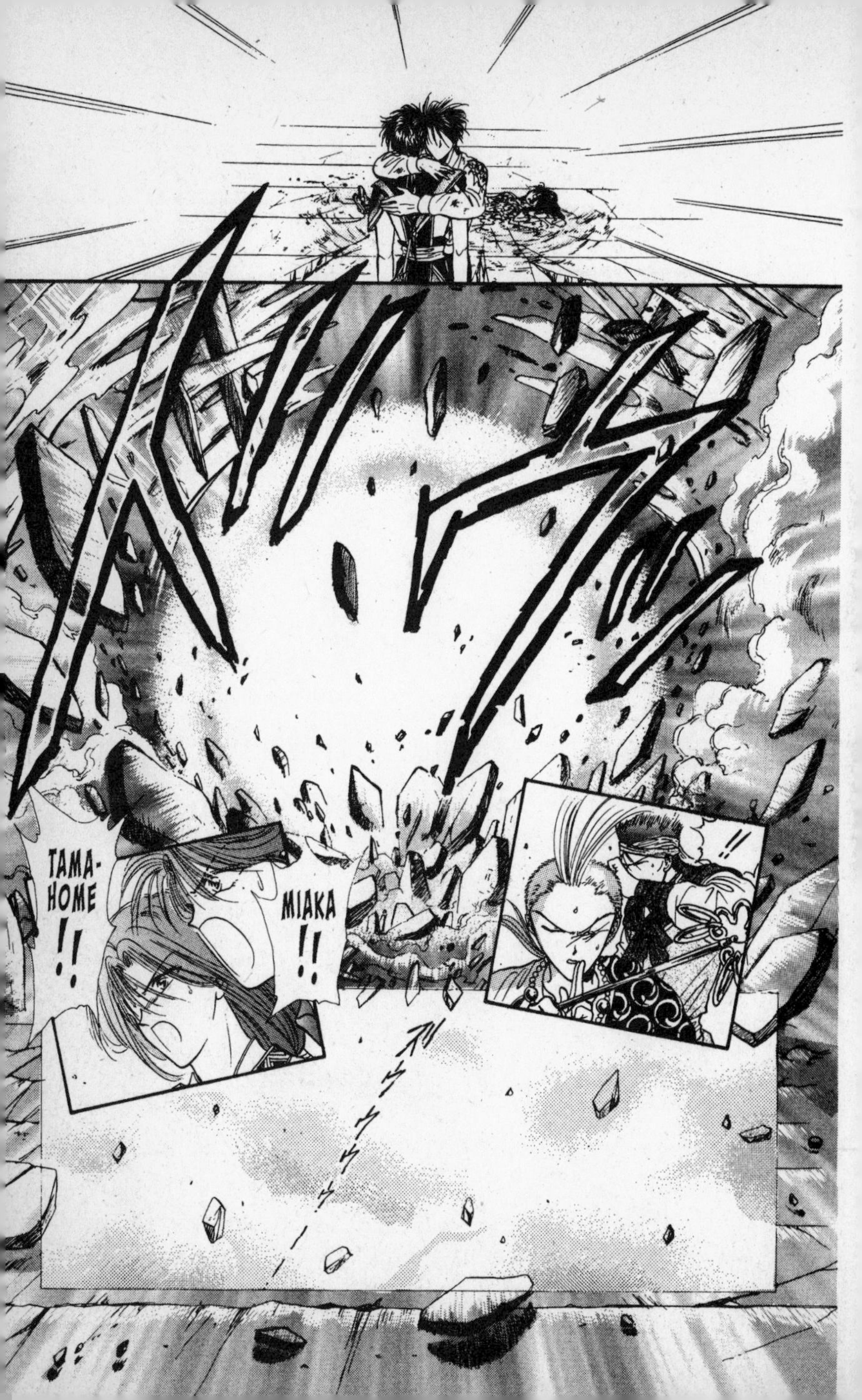
!!
MIAKA!!
TAMA-HOME!!

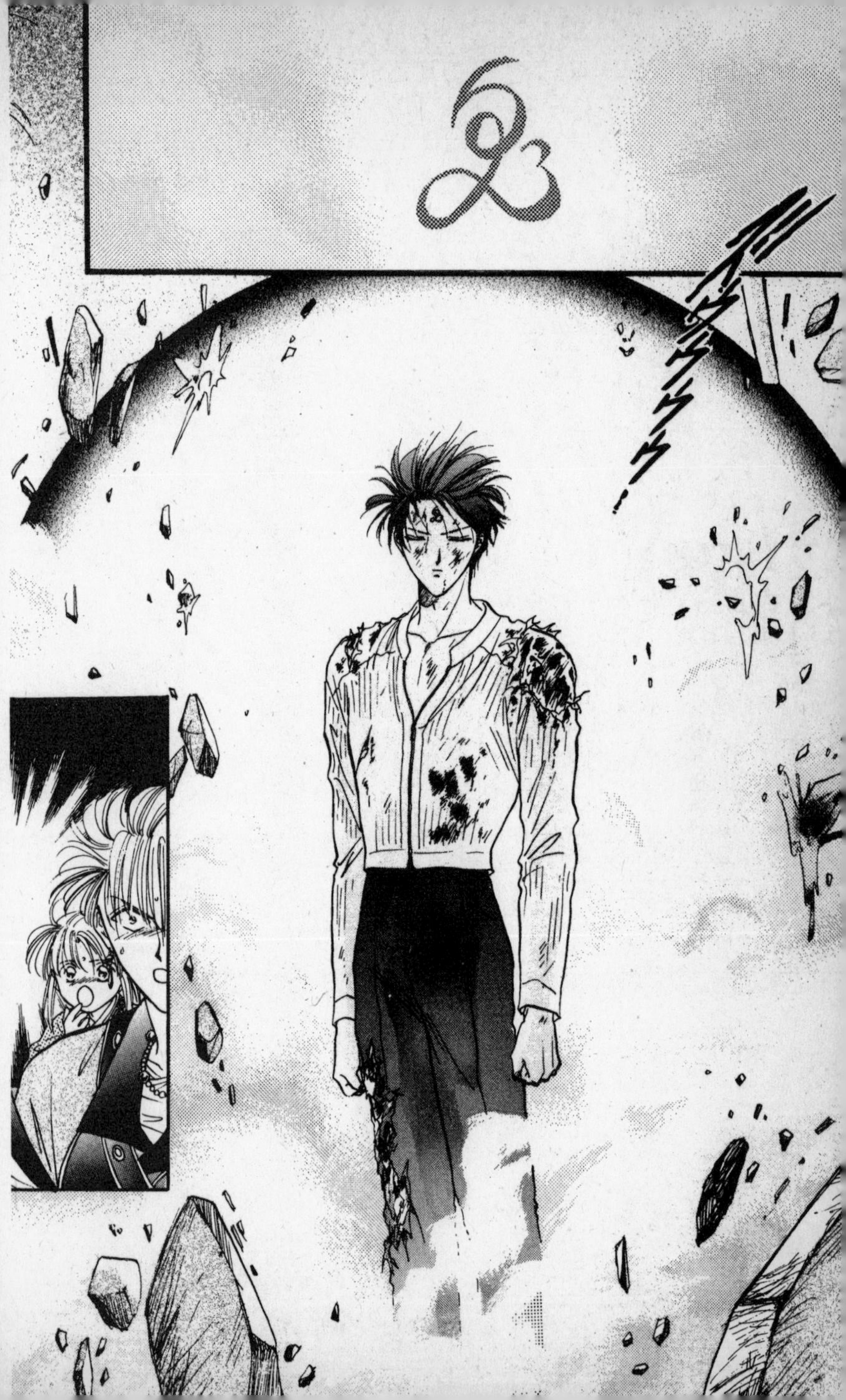

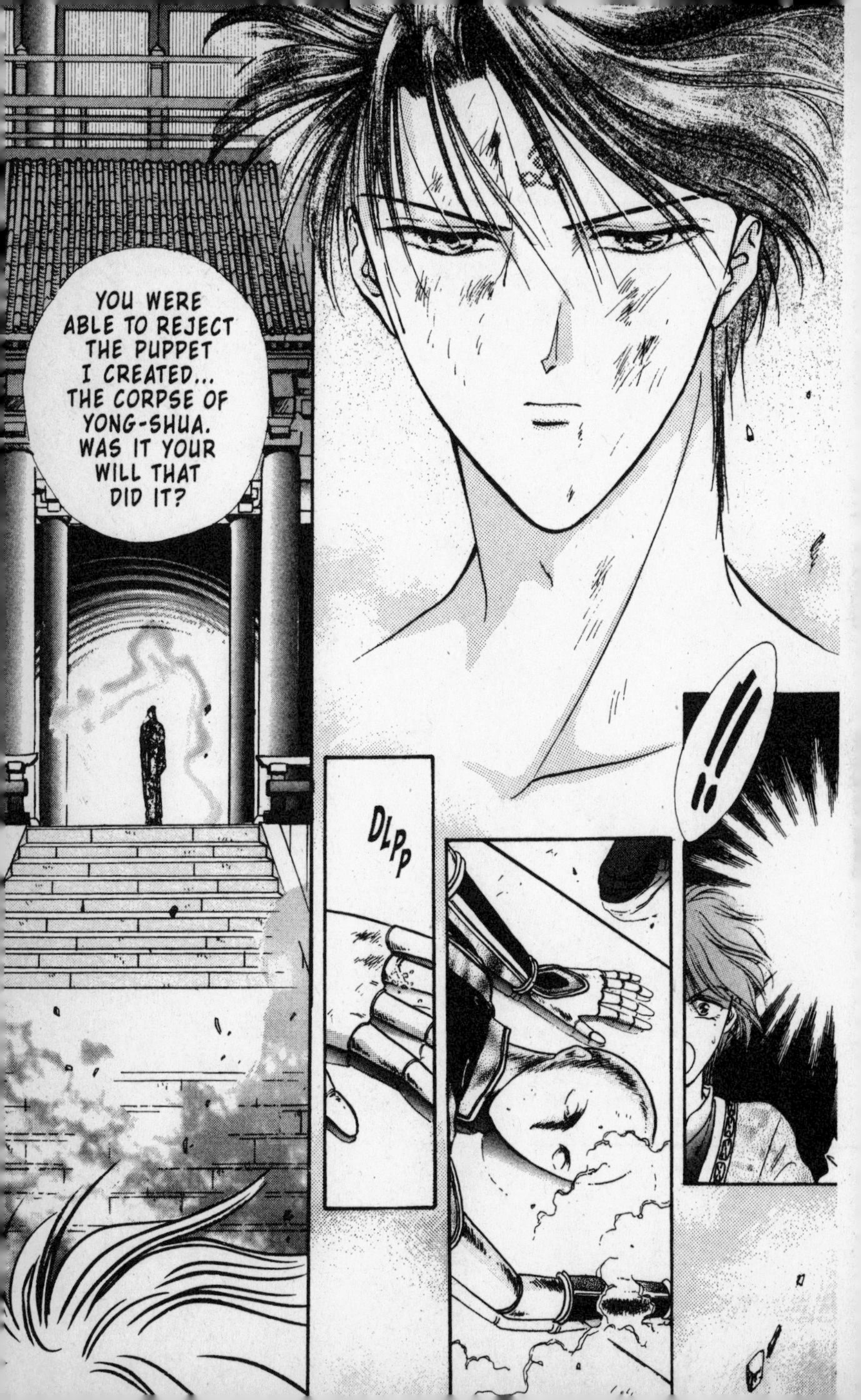
YOU WERE ABLE TO REJECT THE PUPPET I CREATED... THE CORPSE OF YONG-SHUA. WAS IT YOUR WILL THAT DID IT?
!!
DLPP

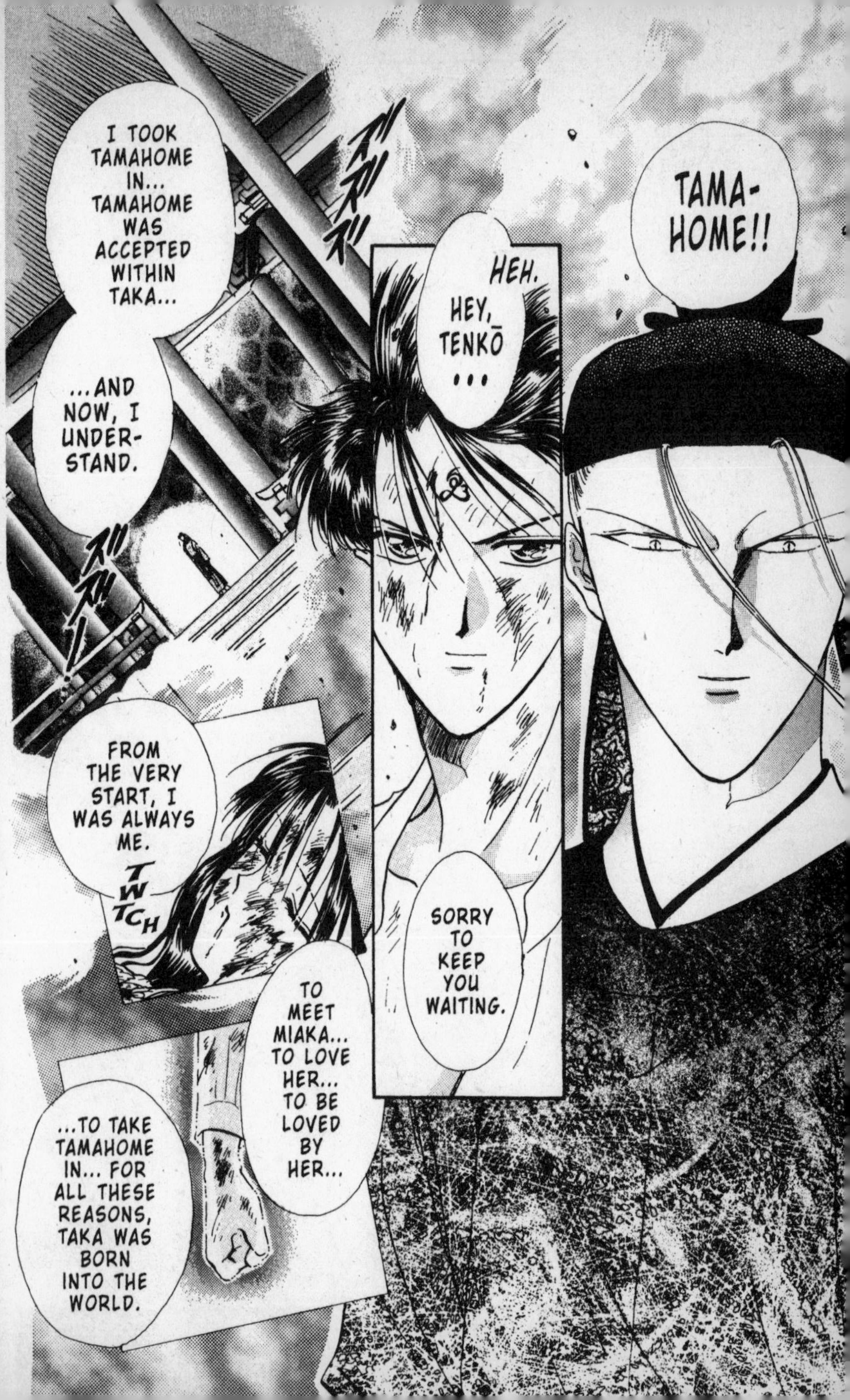
TAMA-HOME!!
HEH.
HEY, TENKŌ...
SORRY TO KEEP YOU WAITING.
I TOOK TAMAHOME IN... TAMAHOME WAS ACCEPTED WITHIN TAKA...
...AND NOW, I UNDERSTAND.
FROM THE VERY START, I WAS ALWAYS ME.
TWTCH
TO MEET MIAKA... TO LOVE HER... TO BE LOVED BY HER...
...TO TAKE TAMAHOME IN... FOR ALL THESE REASONS, TAKA WAS BORN INTO THE WORLD.

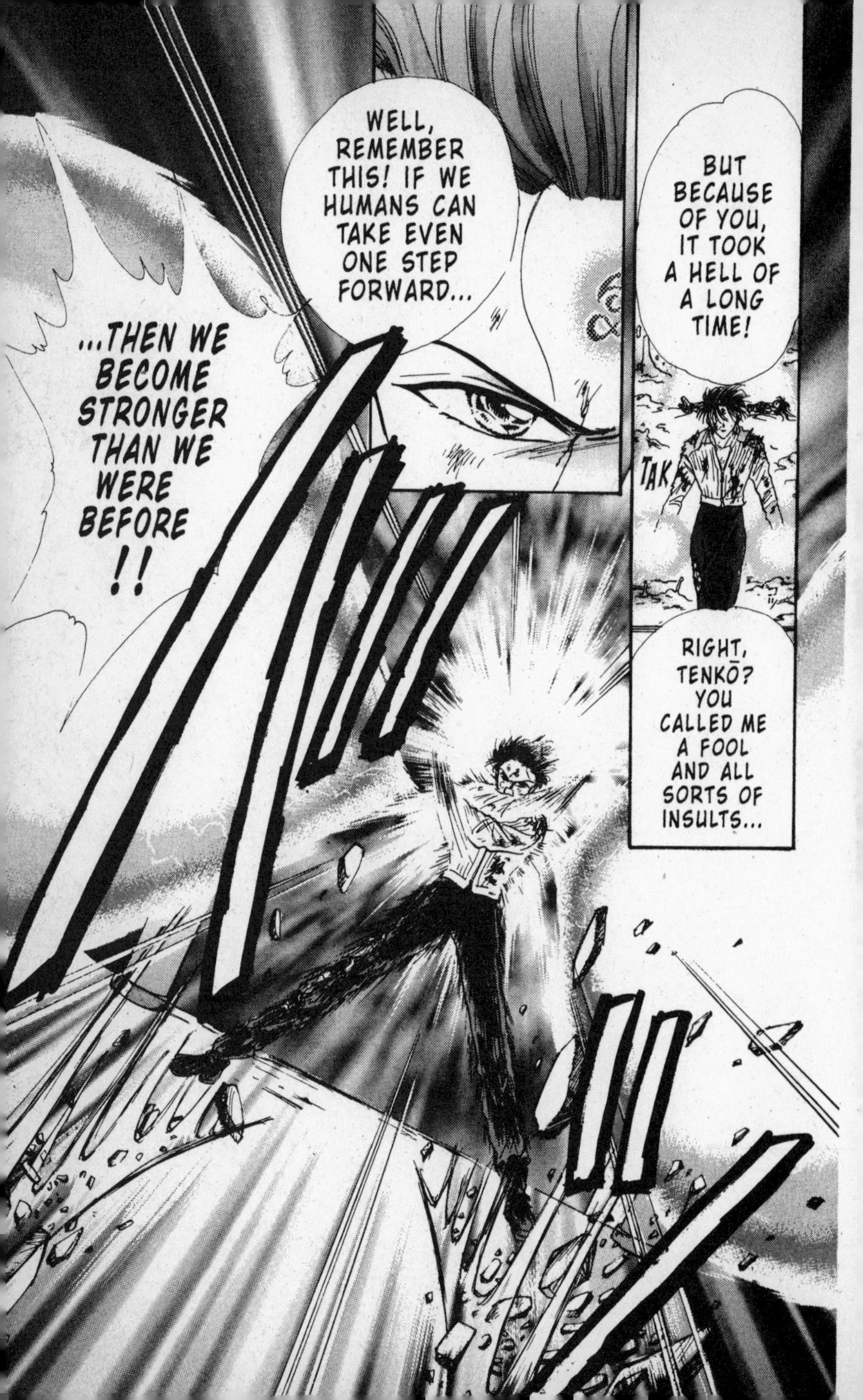
BUT BECAUSE OF YOU, IT TOOK A HELL OF A LONG TIME!
TAK
RIGHT, TENKŌ? YOU CALLED ME A FOOL AND ALL SORTS OF INSULTS...
WELL, REMEMBER THIS! IF WE HUMANS CAN TAKE EVEN ONE STEP FORWARD...
...THEN WE BECOME STRONGER THAN WE WERE BEFORE !!

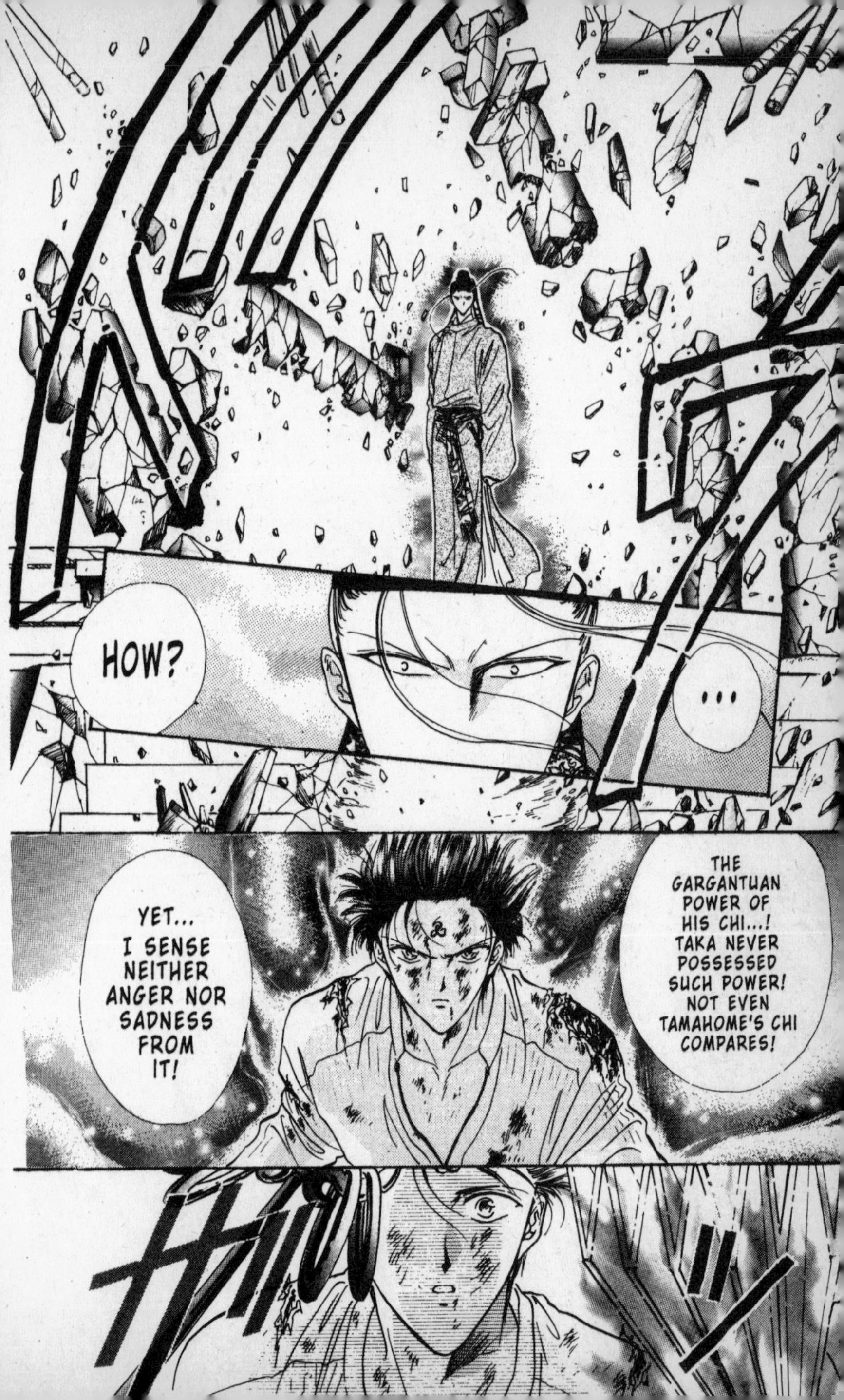
...
HOW?
THE GARGANTUAN POWER OF HIS CHI...! TAKA NEVER POSSESSED SUCH POWER! NOT EVEN TAMAHOME'S CHI COMPARES!
YET... I SENSE NEITHER ANGER NOR SADNESS FROM IT!

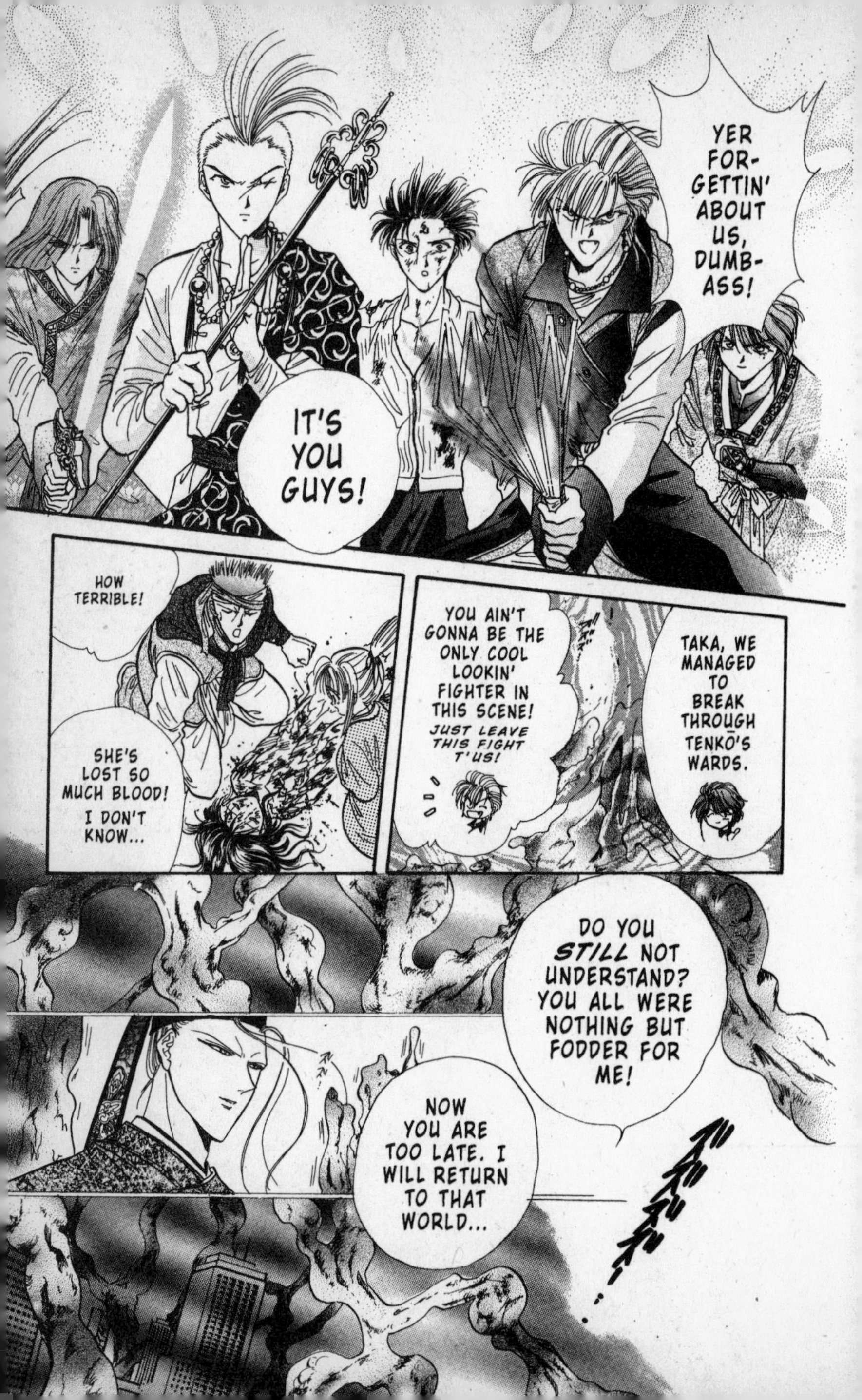
YER FOR-GETTIN' ABOUT US, DUMB-ASS!
IT'S YOU GUYS!
TAKA, WE MANAGED TO BREAK THROUGH TENKŌ'S WARDS.
YOU AIN'T GONNA BE THE ONLY COOL LOOKIN' FIGHTER IN THIS SCENE!
JUST LEAVE THIS FIGHT T'US!
HOW TERRIBLE!
SHE'S LOST SO MUCH BLOOD! I DON'T KNOW...
DO YOU *STILL* NOT UNDERSTAND? YOU ALL WERE NOTHING BUT FODDER FOR ME!
NOW YOU ARE TOO LATE. I WILL RETURN TO THAT WORLD...

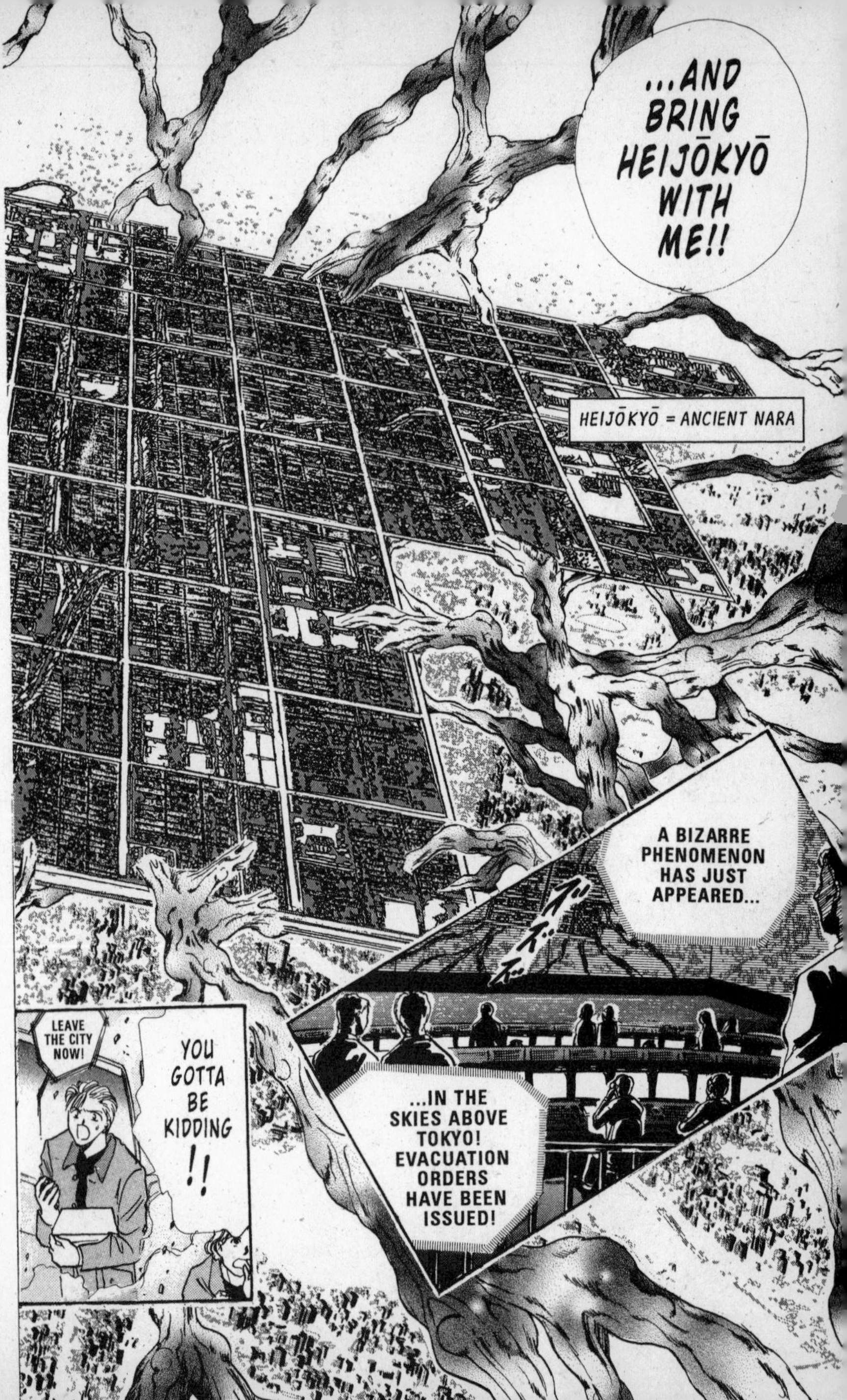
...AND BRING HEIJŌKYŌ WITH ME!!
HEIJŌKYŌ = ANCIENT NARA
A BIZARRE PHENOMENON HAS JUST APPEARED...
...IN THE SKIES ABOVE TOKYO! EVACUATION ORDERS HAVE BEEN ISSUED!
LEAVE THE CITY NOW!
YOU GOTTA BE KIDDING!!

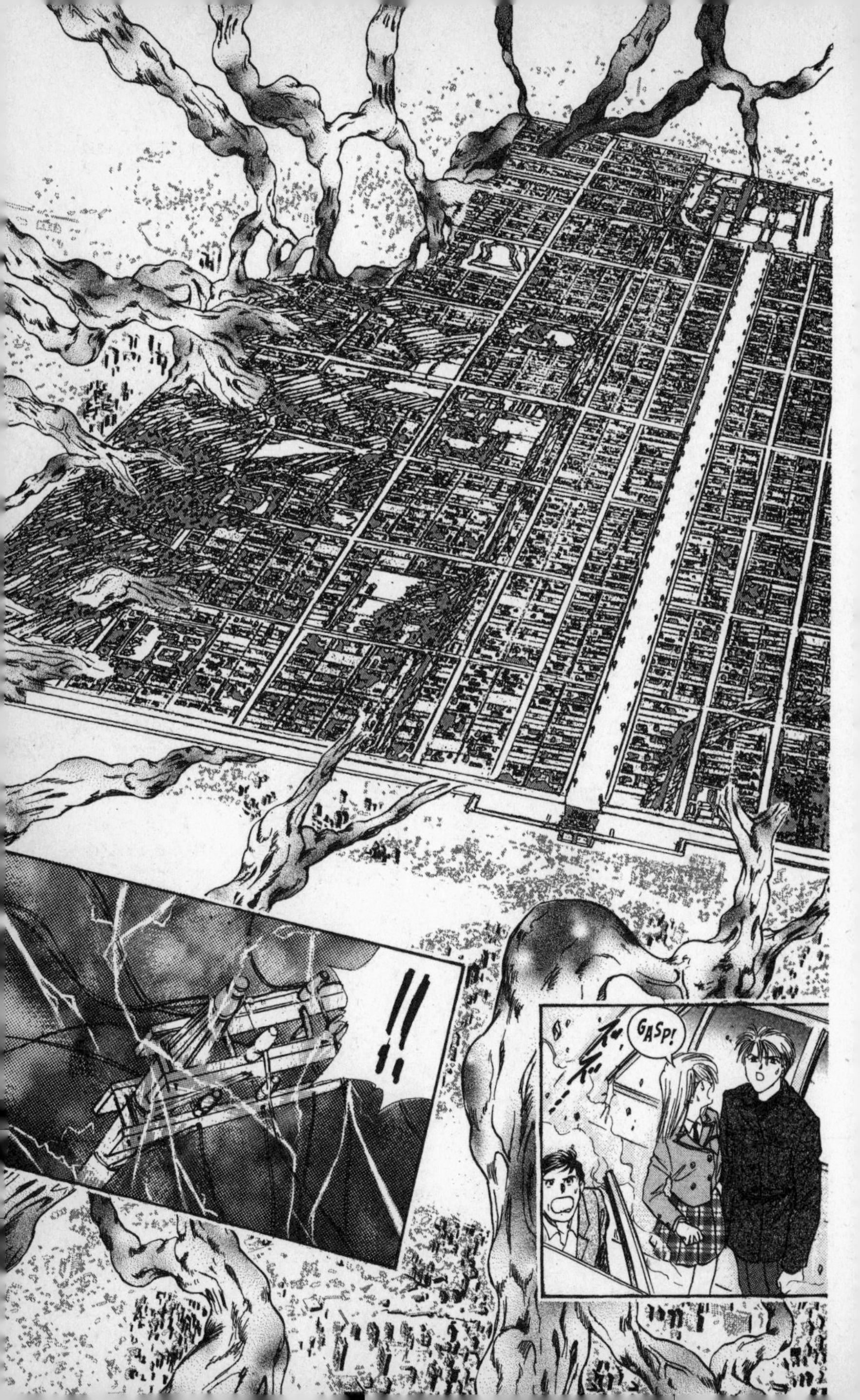
GASP!
!!

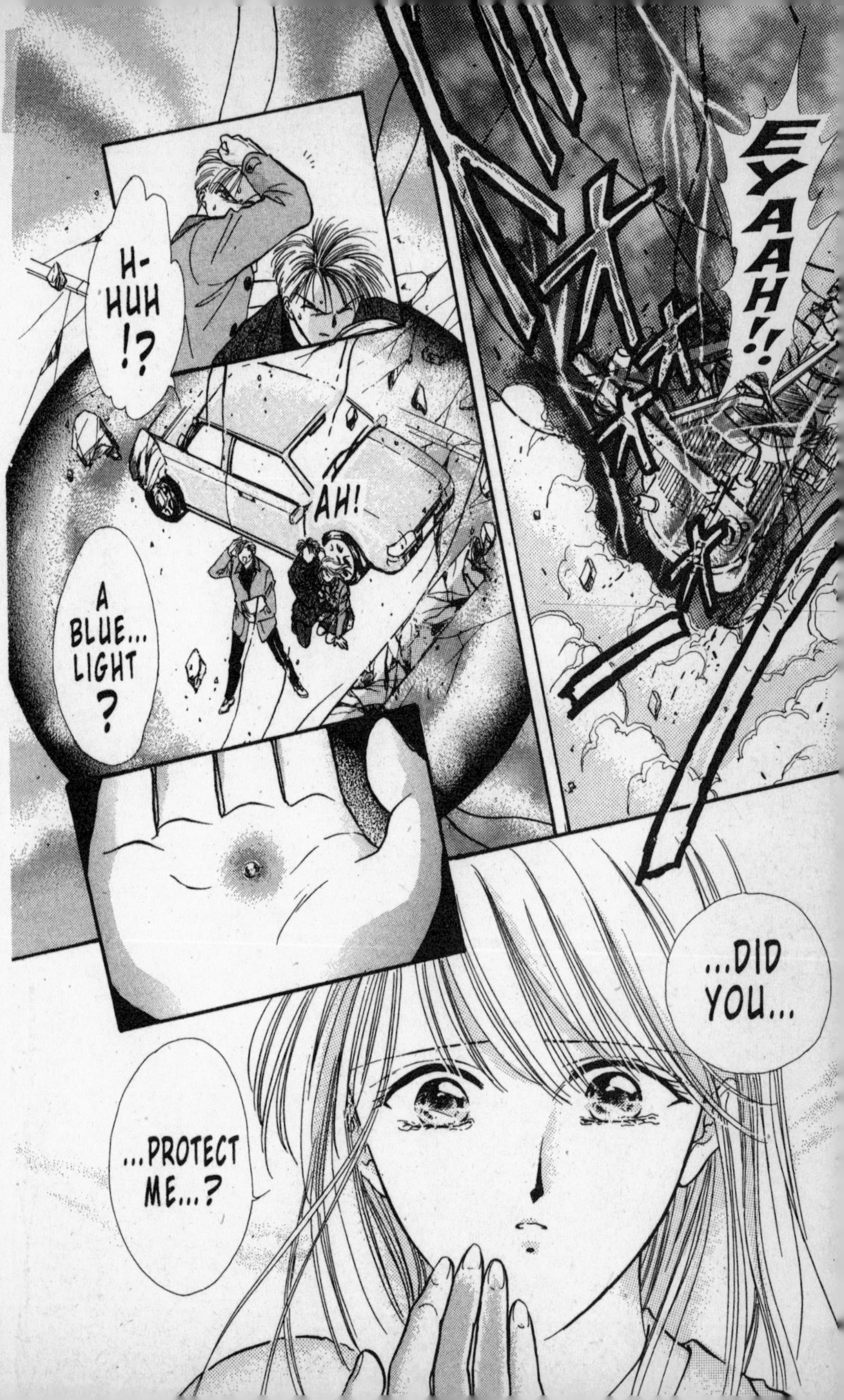
EYAAAH!!
H-HUH!?
AH!
A BLUE... LIGHT?
...DID YOU...
...PROTECT ME...?

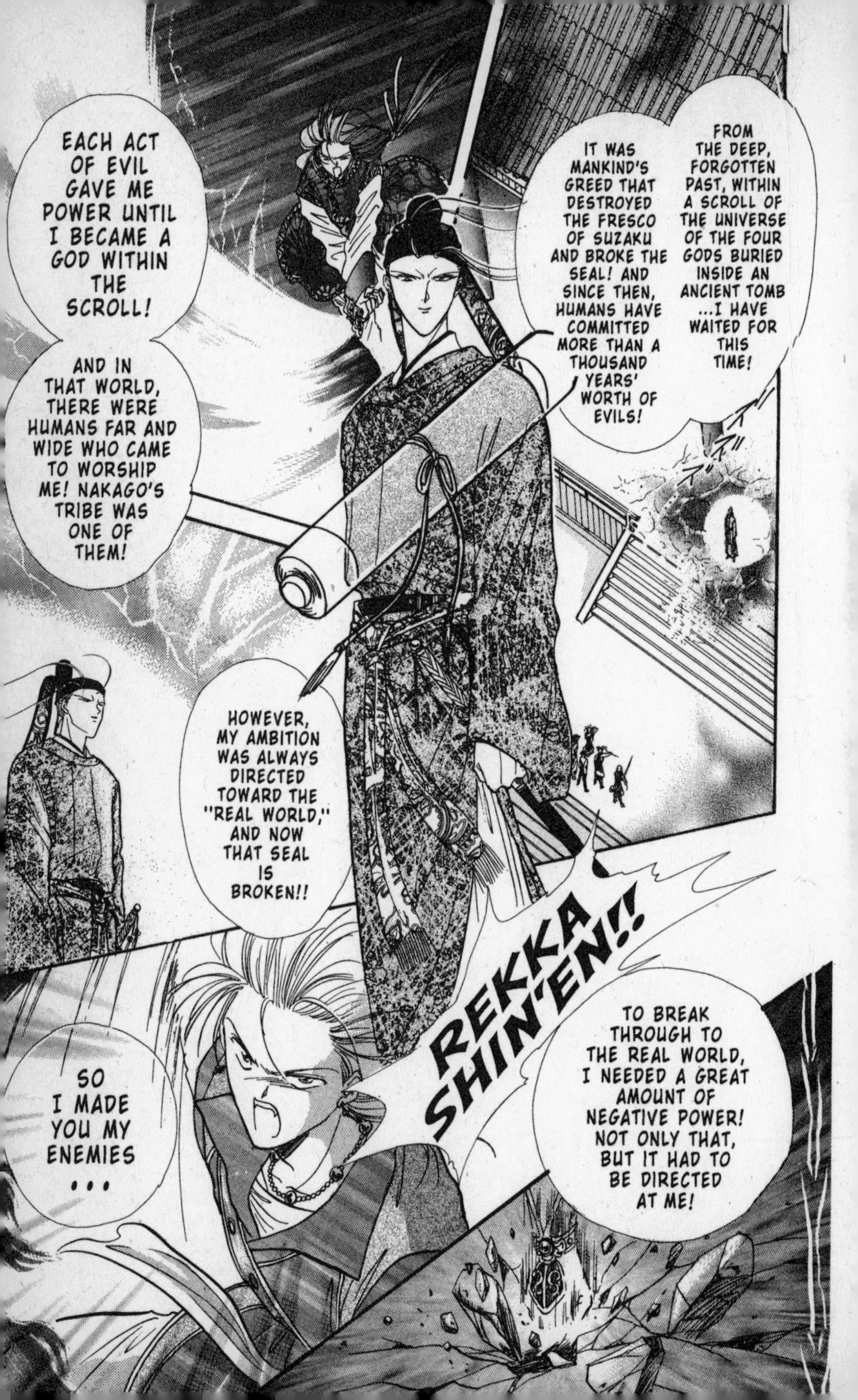
FROM THE DEEP, FORGOTTEN PAST, WITHIN A SCROLL OF THE UNIVERSE OF THE FOUR GODS BURIED INSIDE AN ANCIENT TOMB ...I HAVE WAITED FOR THIS TIME!
IT WAS MANKIND'S GREED THAT DESTROYED THE FRESCO OF SUZAKU AND BROKE THE SEAL! AND SINCE THEN, HUMANS HAVE COMMITTED MORE THAN A THOUSAND YEARS' WORTH OF EVILS!
EACH ACT OF EVIL GAVE ME POWER UNTIL I BECAME A GOD WITHIN THE SCROLL!
AND IN THAT WORLD, THERE WERE HUMANS FAR AND WIDE WHO CAME TO WORSHIP ME! NAKAGO'S TRIBE WAS ONE OF THEM!
HOWEVER, MY AMBITION WAS ALWAYS DIRECTED TOWARD THE "REAL WORLD," AND NOW THAT SEAL IS BROKEN!!
REKKA SHIN'EN!!
TO BREAK THROUGH TO THE REAL WORLD, I NEEDED A GREAT AMOUNT OF NEGATIVE POWER! NOT ONLY THAT, BUT IT HAD TO BE DIRECTED AT ME!
SO I MADE YOU MY ENEMIES ...

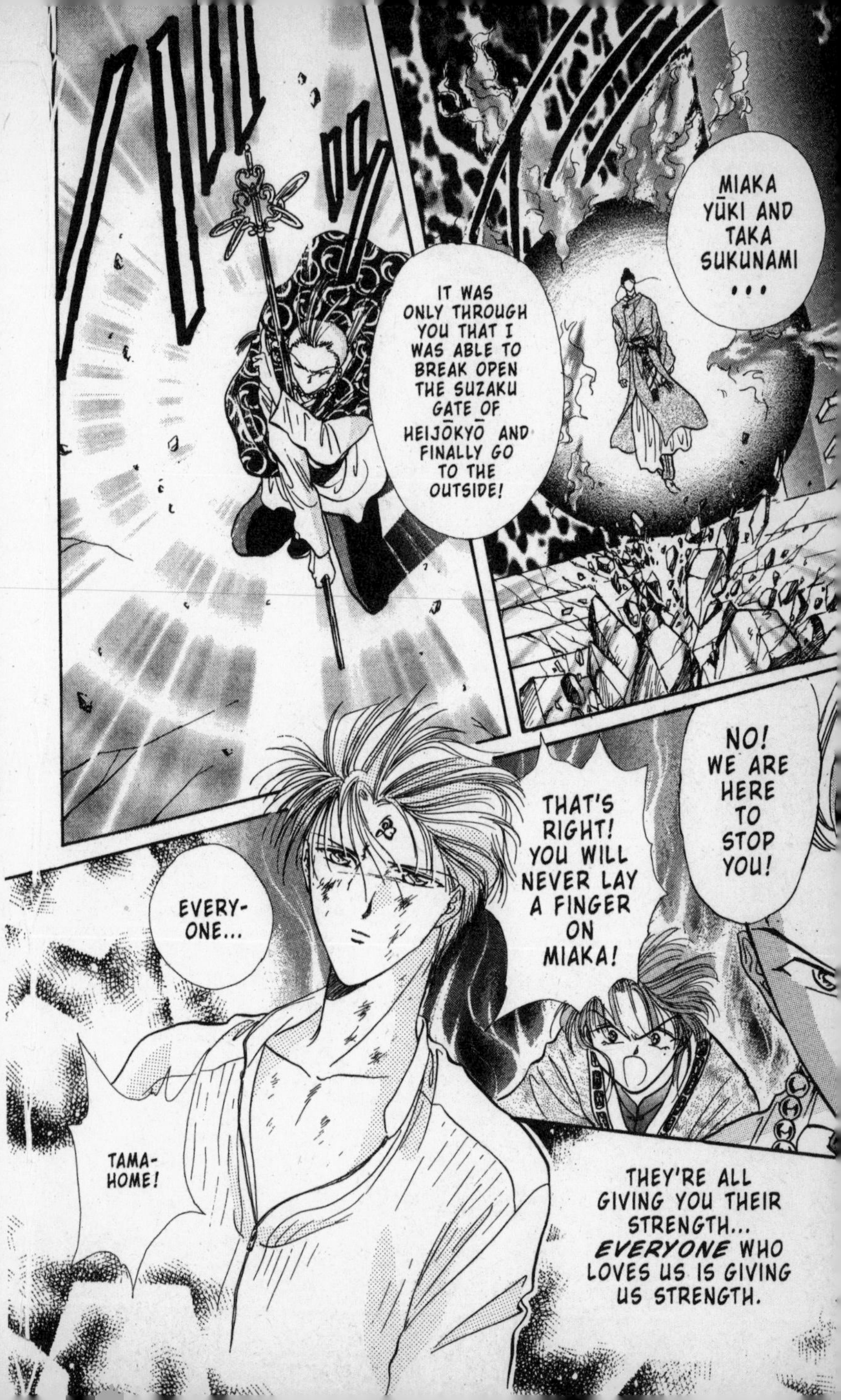

MIAKA YŪKI AND TAKA SUKUNAMI...
IT WAS ONLY THROUGH YOU THAT I WAS ABLE TO BREAK OPEN THE SUZAKU GATE OF HEIJŌKYŌ AND FINALLY GO TO THE OUTSIDE!
NO! WE ARE HERE TO STOP YOU!
THAT'S RIGHT! YOU WILL NEVER LAY A FINGER ON MIAKA!
EVERY-ONE...
TAMA-HOME!
THEY'RE ALL GIVING YOU THEIR STRENGTH... *EVERYONE* WHO LOVES US IS GIVING US STRENGTH.

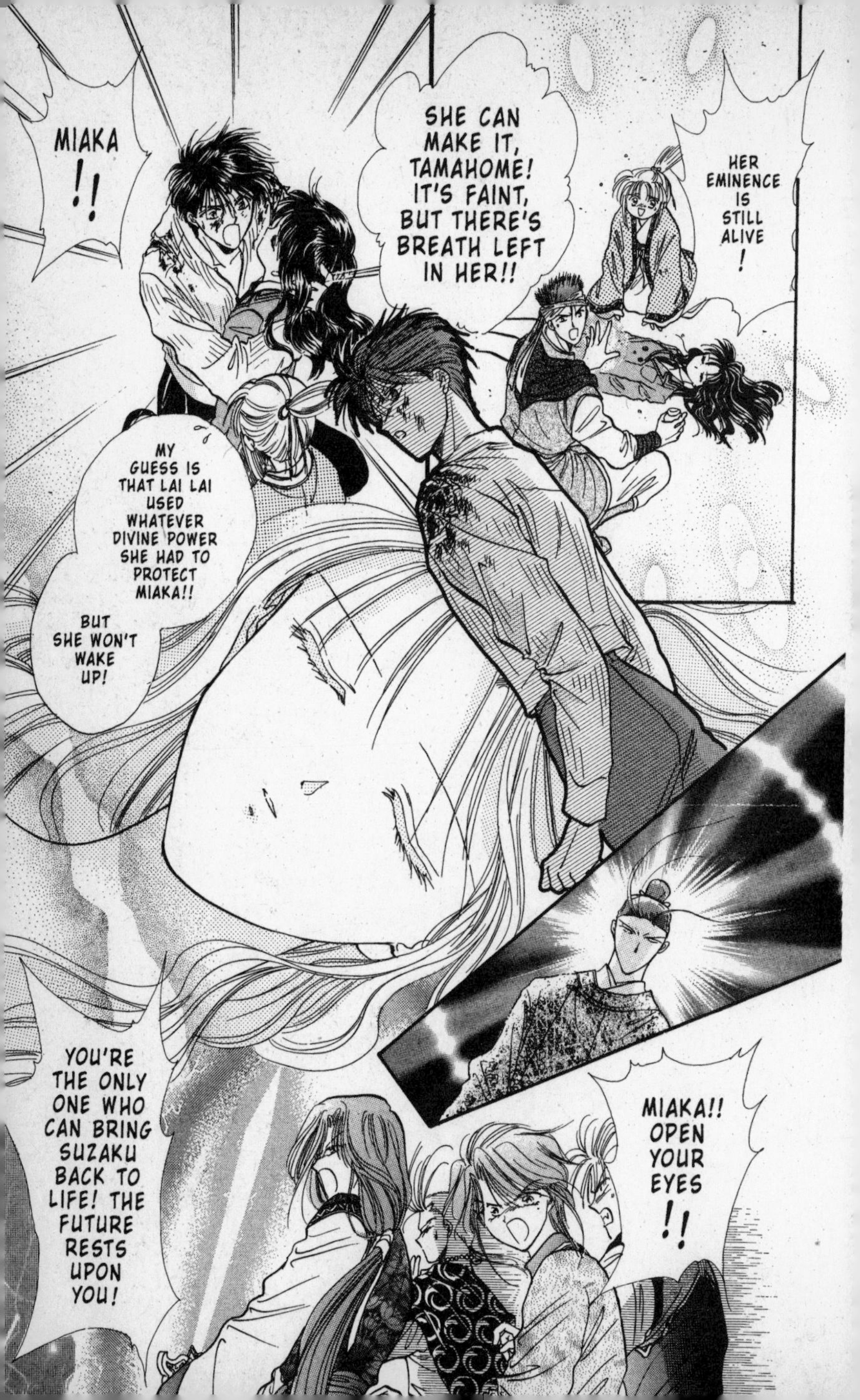
HER EMINENCE IS STILL ALIVE!
SHE CAN MAKE IT, TAMAHOME! IT'S FAINT, BUT THERE'S BREATH LEFT IN HER!!
MIAKA!!
MY GUESS IS THAT LAI LAI USED WHATEVER DIVINE POWER SHE HAD TO PROTECT MIAKA!!
BUT SHE WON'T WAKE UP!
MIAKA!! OPEN YOUR EYES!!
YOU'RE THE ONLY ONE WHO CAN BRING SUZAKU BACK TO LIFE! THE FUTURE RESTS UPON YOU!

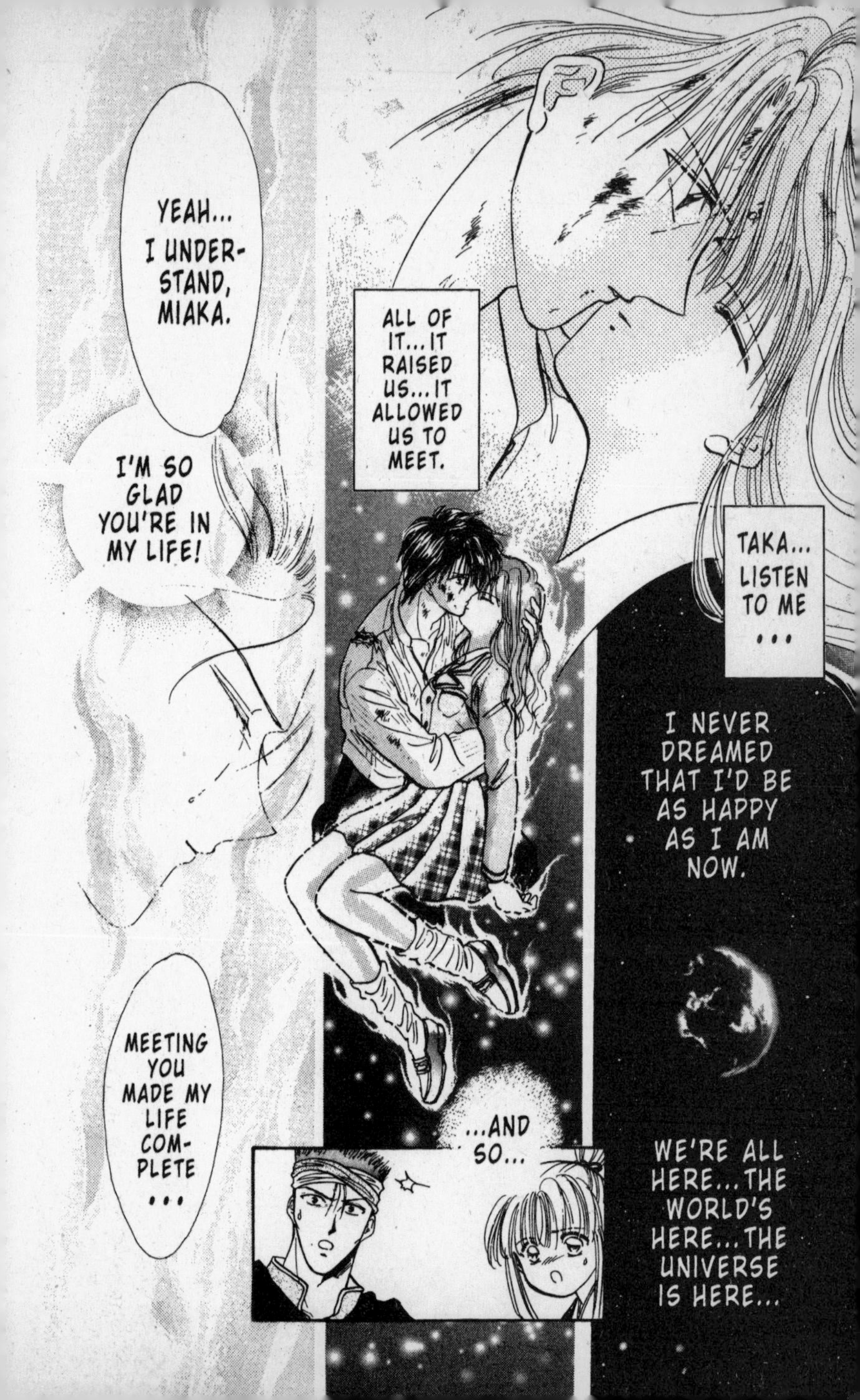

TAKA... LISTEN TO ME ...
I NEVER DREAMED THAT I'D BE AS HAPPY AS I AM NOW.
WE'RE ALL HERE... THE WORLD'S HERE... THE UNIVERSE IS HERE...
ALL OF IT... IT RAISED US... IT ALLOWED US TO MEET.
...AND SO...
YEAH... I UNDER-STAND, MIAKA.
I'M SO GLAD YOU'RE IN MY LIFE!
MEETING YOU MADE MY LIFE COM-PLETE ...

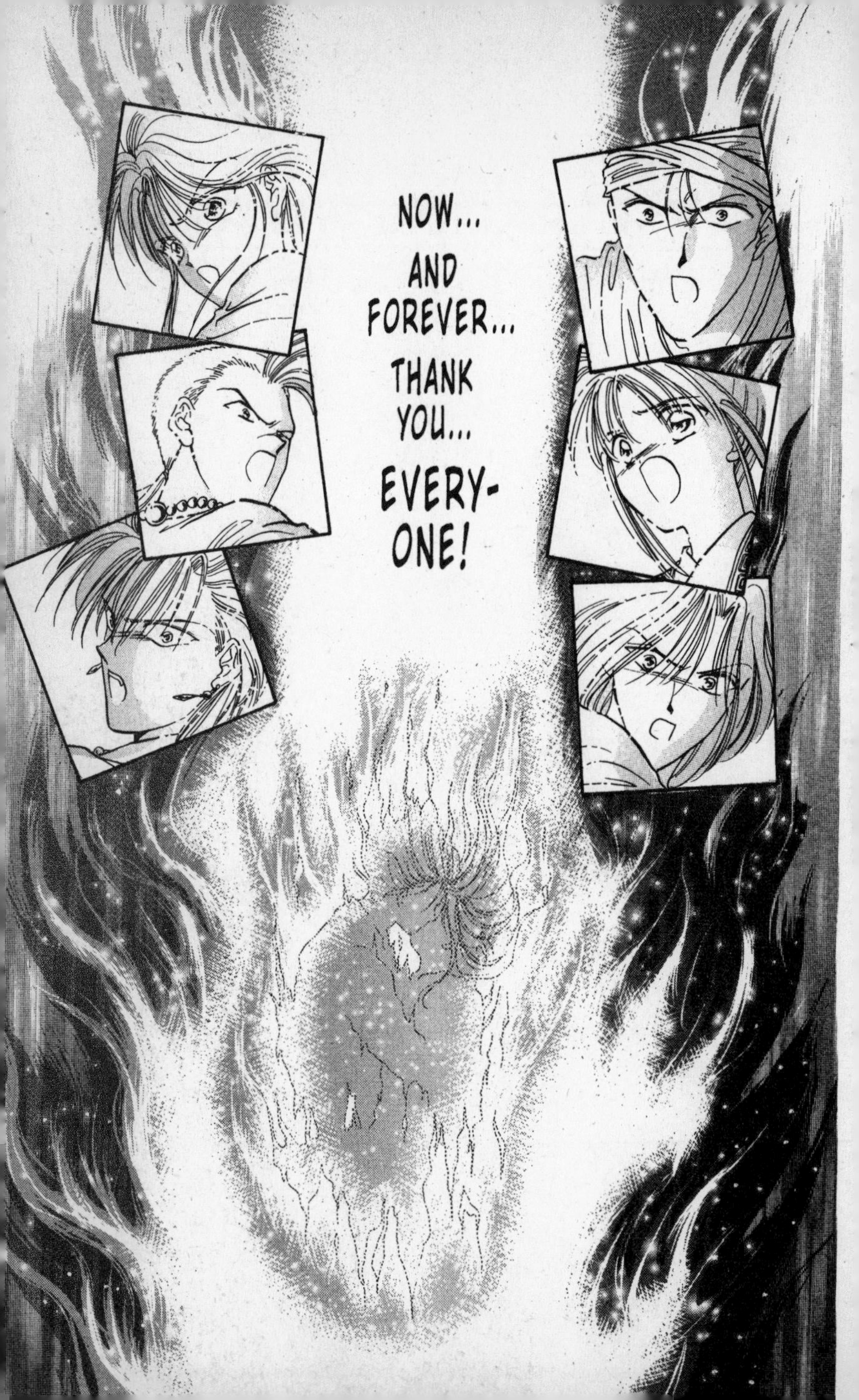
NOW... AND FOREVER... THANK YOU... EVERY-ONE!

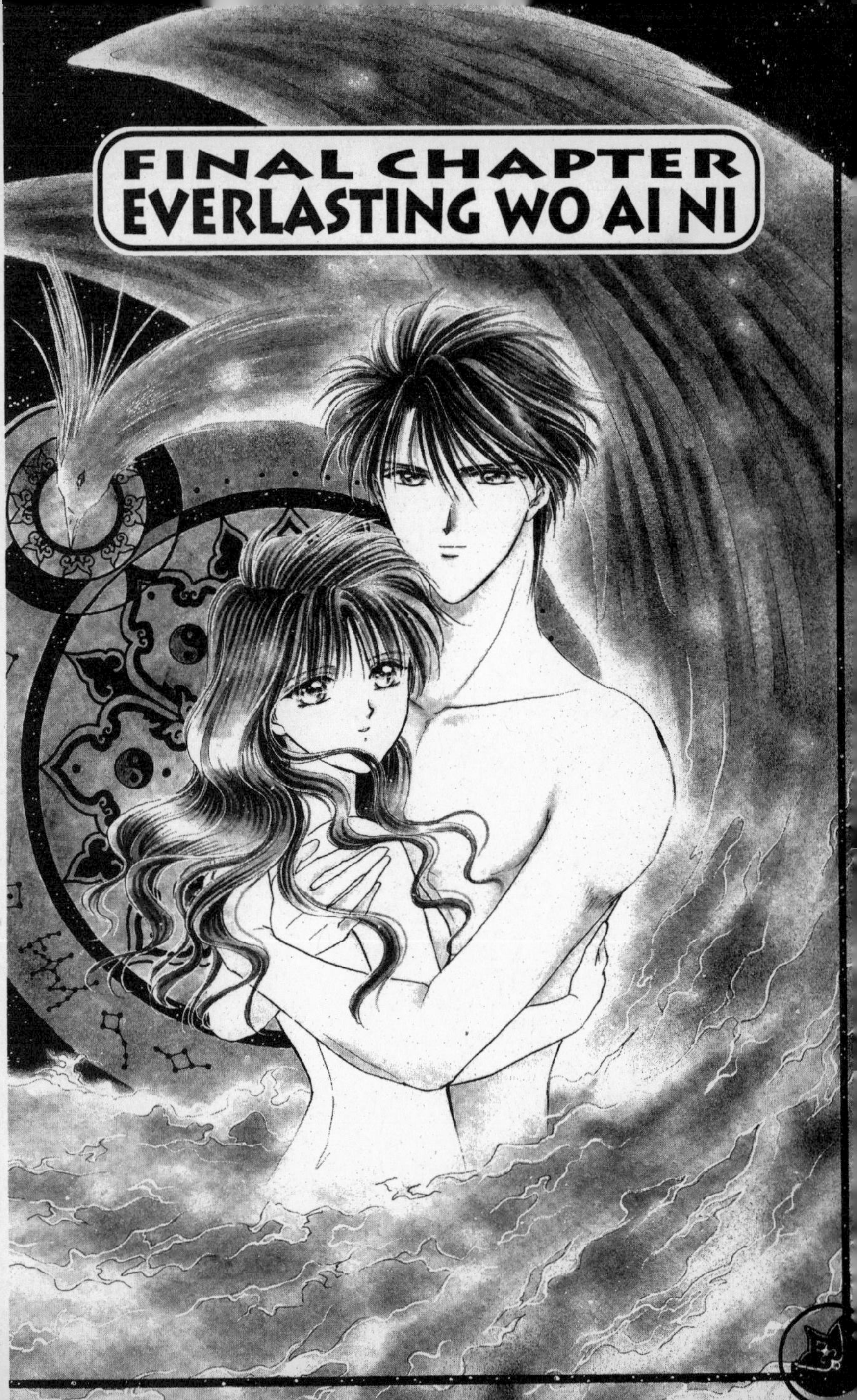
FINAL CHAPTER
EVERLASTING WO AI NI

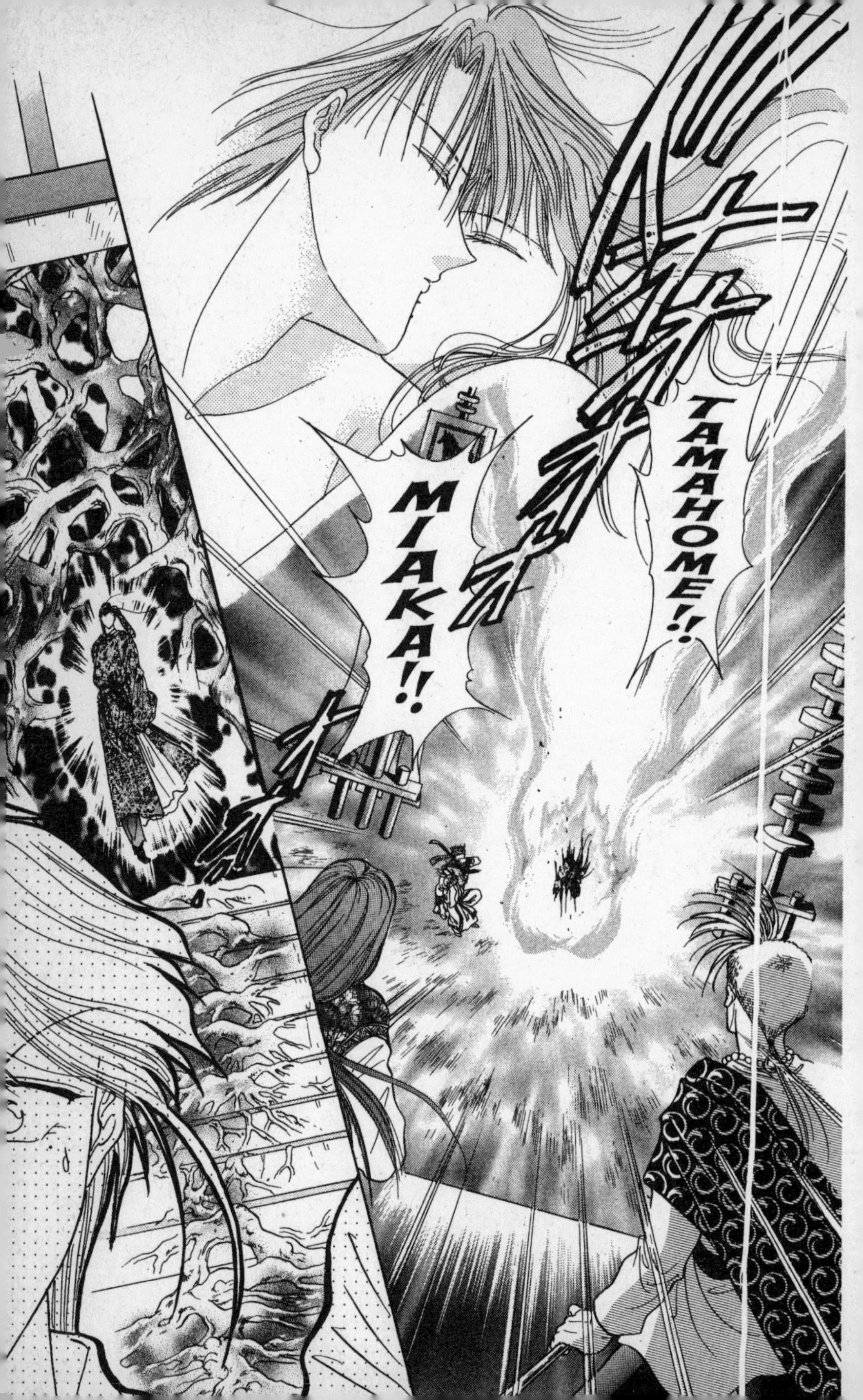
TAMAHOME!!
MIAKA!!

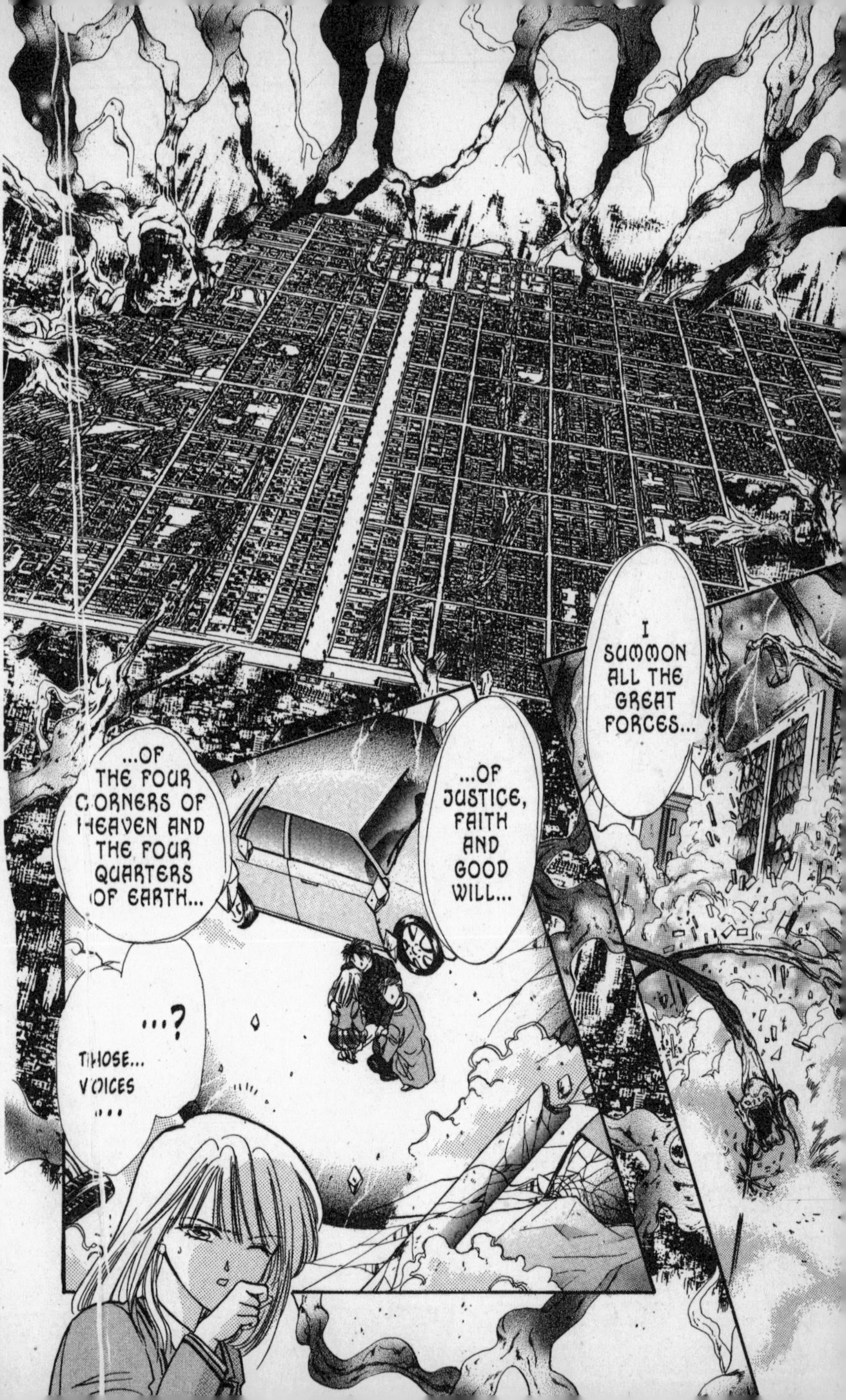
I SUMMON ALL THE GREAT FORCES...
...OF JUSTICE, FAITH AND GOOD WILL...
...OF THE FOUR CORNERS OF HEAVEN AND THE FOUR QUARTERS OF EARTH...
...?
THOSE... VOICES ...

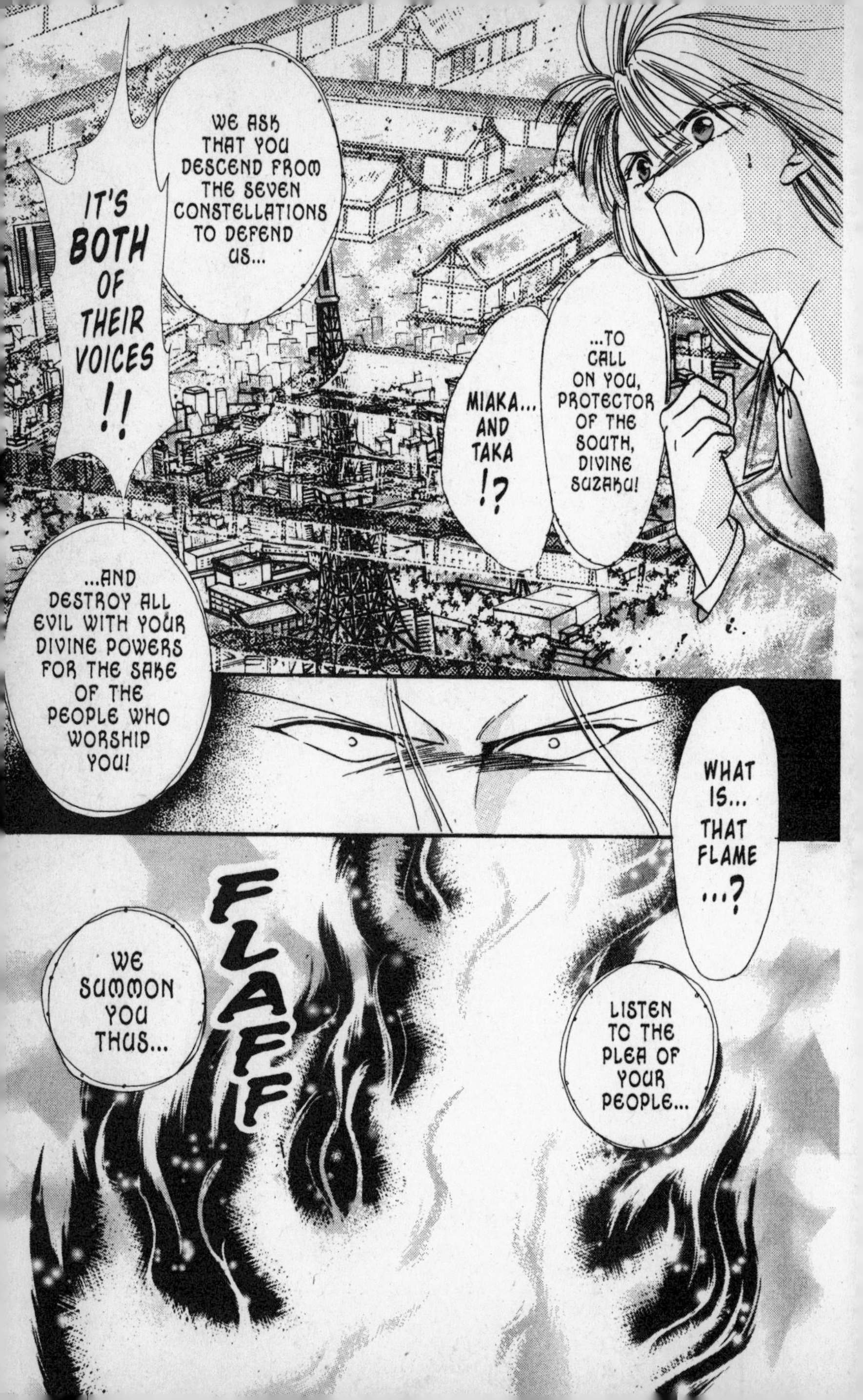
...TO CALL ON YOU, PROTECTOR OF THE SOUTH, DIVINE SUZAKU!
MIAKA... AND TAKA !?
WE ASK THAT YOU DESCEND FROM THE SEVEN CONSTELLATIONS TO DEFEND US...
IT'S BOTH OF THEIR VOICES !!
...AND DESTROY ALL EVIL WITH YOUR DIVINE POWERS FOR THE SAKE OF THE PEOPLE WHO WORSHIP YOU!
WHAT IS... THAT FLAME ...?
LISTEN TO THE PLEA OF YOUR PEOPLE...
FLAFF
WE SUMMON YOU THUS...

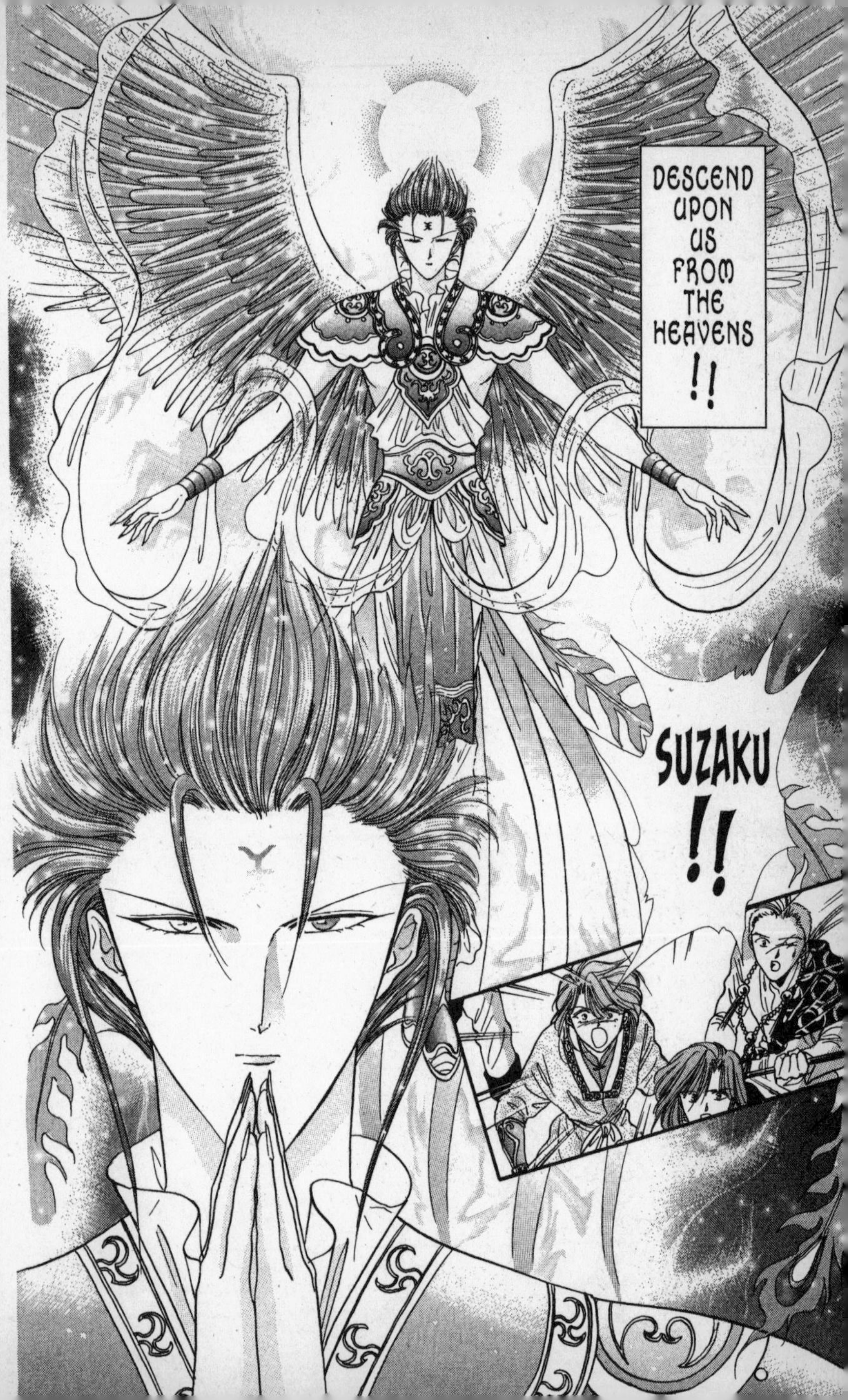
DESCEND UPON US FROM THE HEAVENS !!
SUZAKU !!

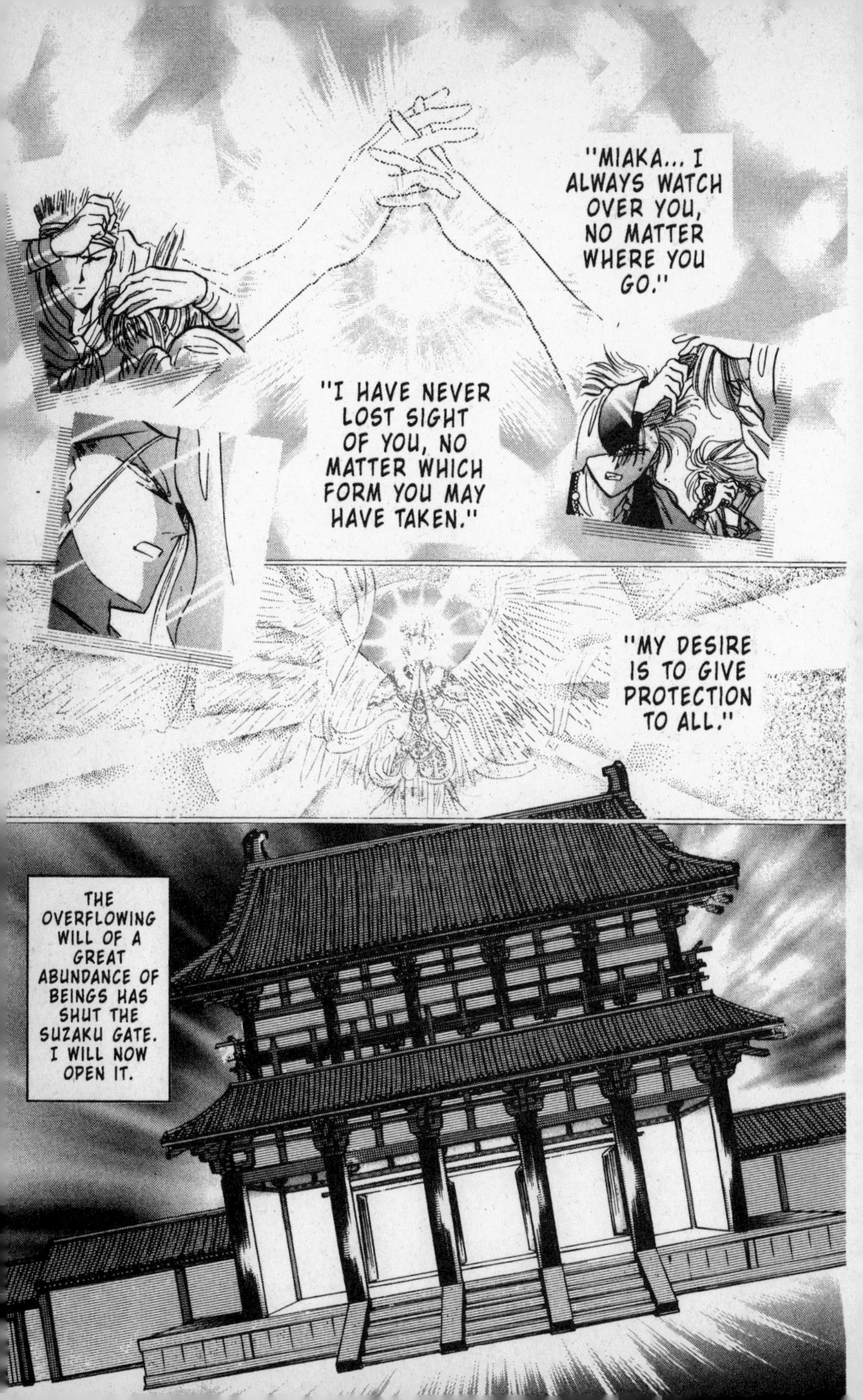
"MIAKA... I ALWAYS WATCH OVER YOU, NO MATTER WHERE YOU GO."
"I HAVE NEVER LOST SIGHT OF YOU, NO MATTER WHICH FORM YOU MAY HAVE TAKEN."
"MY DESIRE IS TO GIVE PROTECTION TO ALL."
THE OVERFLOWING WILL OF A GREAT ABUNDANCE OF BEINGS HAS SHUT THE SUZAKU GATE. I WILL NOW OPEN IT.

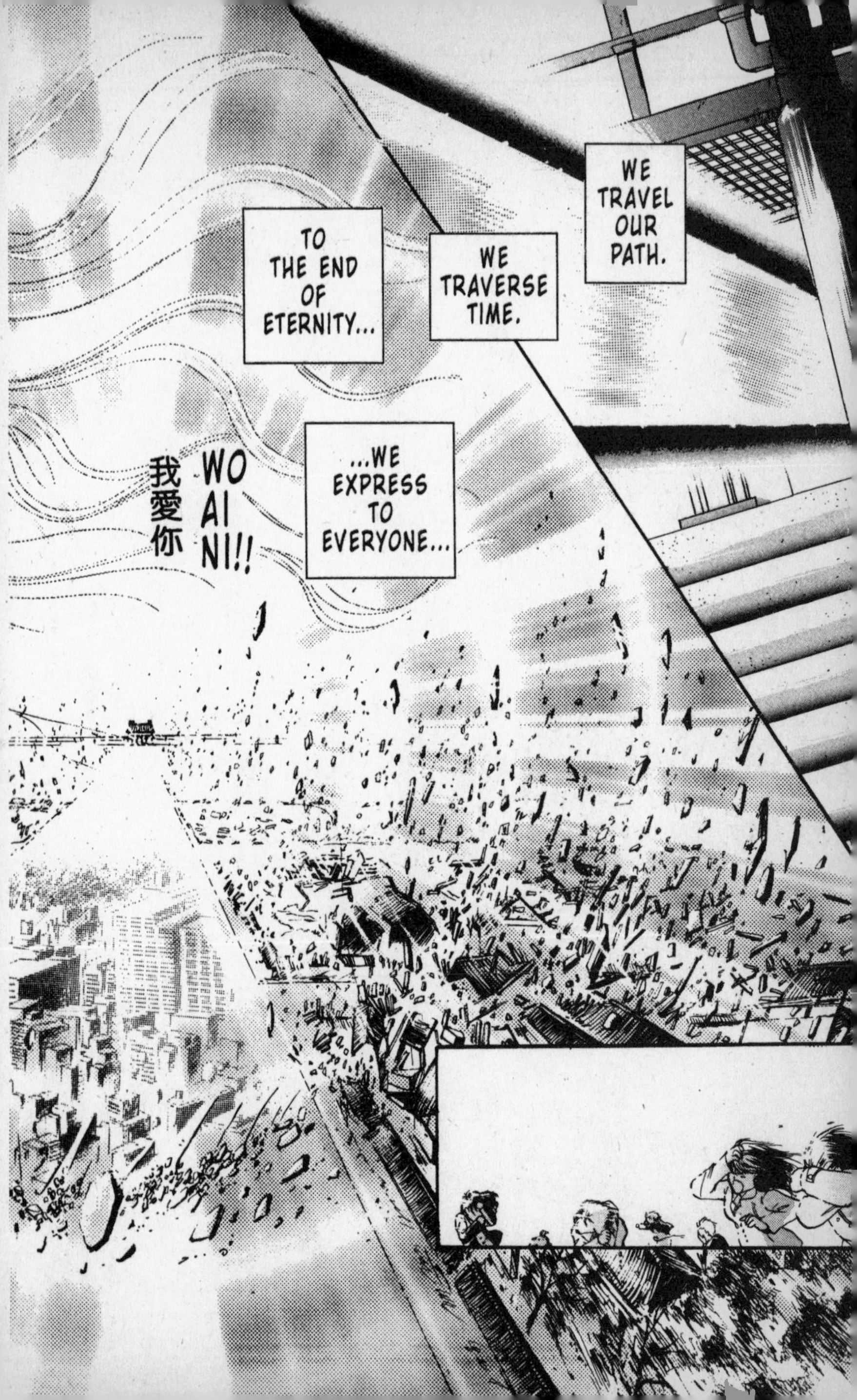

WE TRAVEL OUR PATH.
WE TRAVERSE TIME.
TO THE END OF ETERNITY...
...WE EXPRESS TO EVERYONE...
WO AI NI!!
我愛你

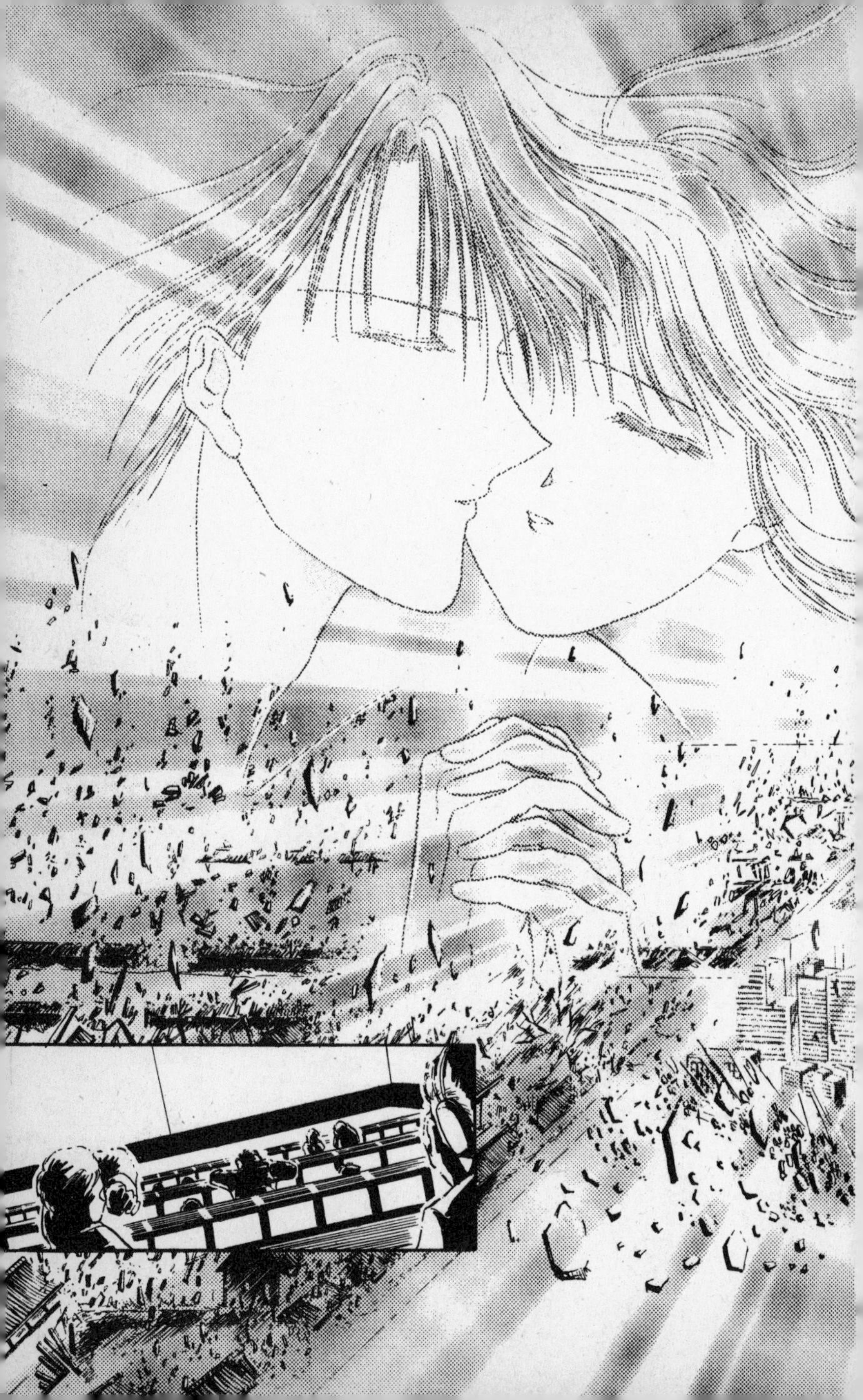

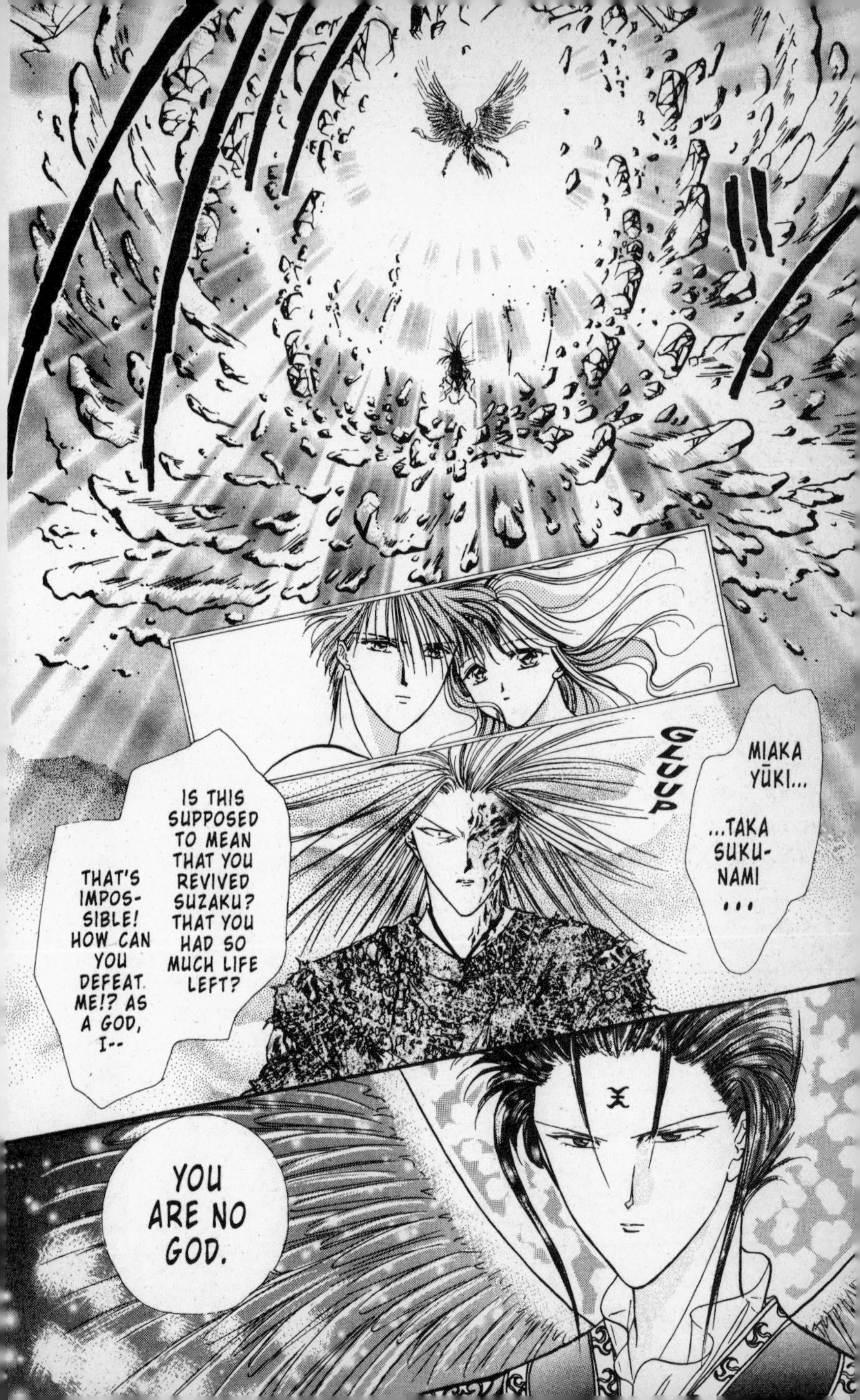
MIAKA YŪKI... ...TAKA SUKUNAMI ...
GLUUP
IS THIS SUPPOSED TO MEAN THAT YOU REVIVED SUZAKU? THAT YOU HAD SO MUCH LIFE LEFT?
THAT'S IMPOSSIBLE! HOW CAN YOU DEFEAT ME!? AS A GOD, I--
YOU ARE NO GOD.

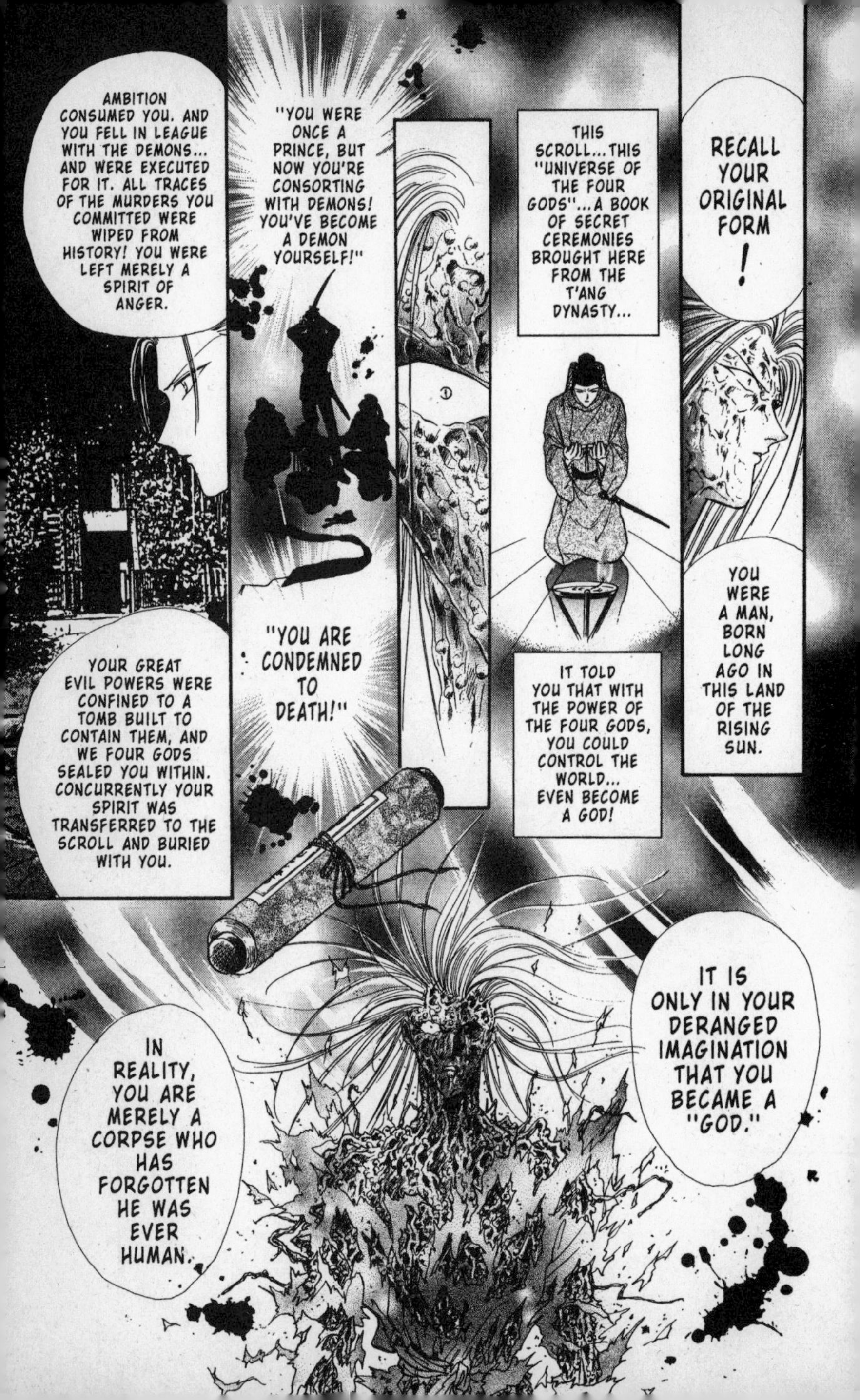
RECALL YOUR ORIGINAL FORM!
YOU WERE A MAN, BORN LONG AGO IN THIS LAND OF THE RISING SUN.
THIS SCROLL...THIS "UNIVERSE OF THE FOUR GODS"...A BOOK OF SECRET CEREMONIES BROUGHT HERE FROM THE T'ANG DYNASTY...
IT TOLD YOU THAT WITH THE POWER OF THE FOUR GODS, YOU COULD CONTROL THE WORLD... EVEN BECOME A GOD!
"YOU WERE ONCE A PRINCE, BUT NOW YOU'RE CONSORTING WITH DEMONS! YOU'VE BECOME A DEMON YOURSELF!"
"YOU ARE CONDEMNED TO DEATH!"
AMBITION CONSUMED YOU. AND YOU FELL IN LEAGUE WITH THE DEMONS... AND WERE EXECUTED FOR IT. ALL TRACES OF THE MURDERS YOU COMMITTED WERE WIPED FROM HISTORY! YOU WERE LEFT MERELY A SPIRIT OF ANGER.
YOUR GREAT EVIL POWERS WERE CONFINED TO A TOMB BUILT TO CONTAIN THEM, AND WE FOUR GODS SEALED YOU WITHIN. CONCURRENTLY YOUR SPIRIT WAS TRANSFERRED TO THE SCROLL AND BURIED WITH YOU.
IT IS ONLY IN YOUR DERANGED IMAGINATION THAT YOU BECAME A "GOD."
IN REALITY, YOU ARE MERELY A CORPSE WHO HAS FORGOTTEN HE WAS EVER HUMAN.

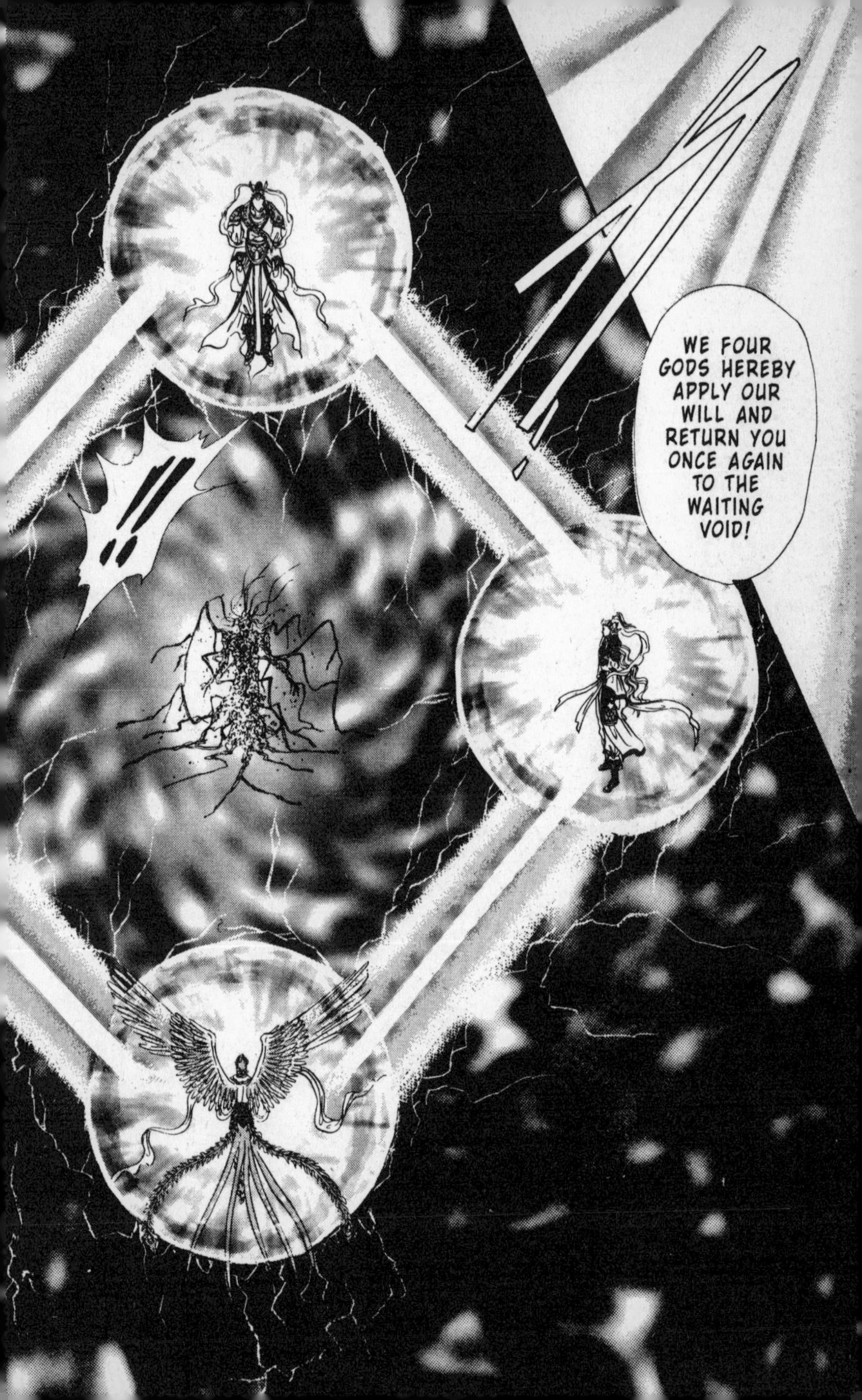
WE FOUR GODS HEREBY APPLY OUR WILL AND RETURN YOU ONCE AGAIN TO THE WAITING VOID!
!!

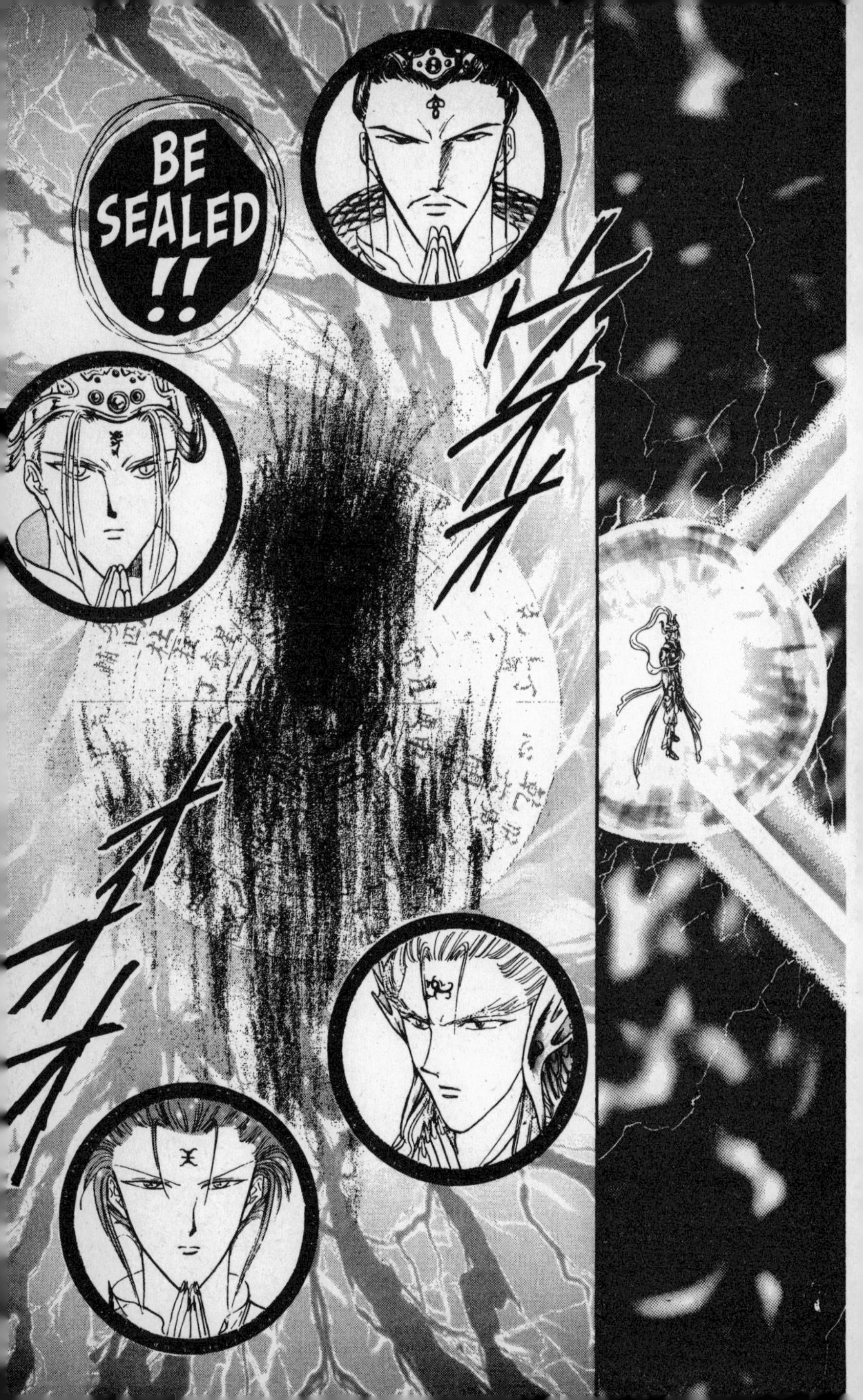
BE SEALED!!

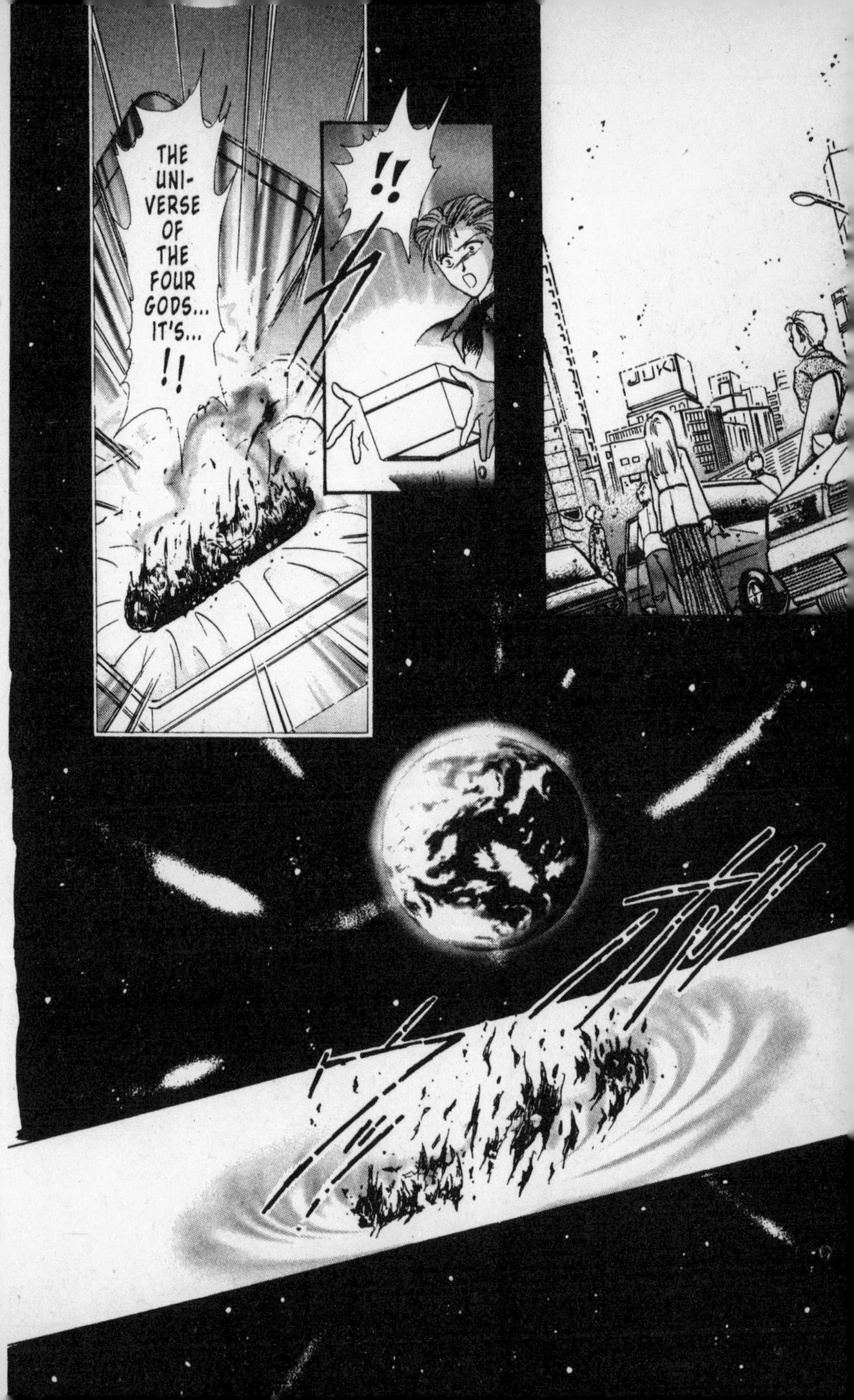
!!
THE UNI-VERSE OF THE FOUR GODS... IT'S... !!
JUKI

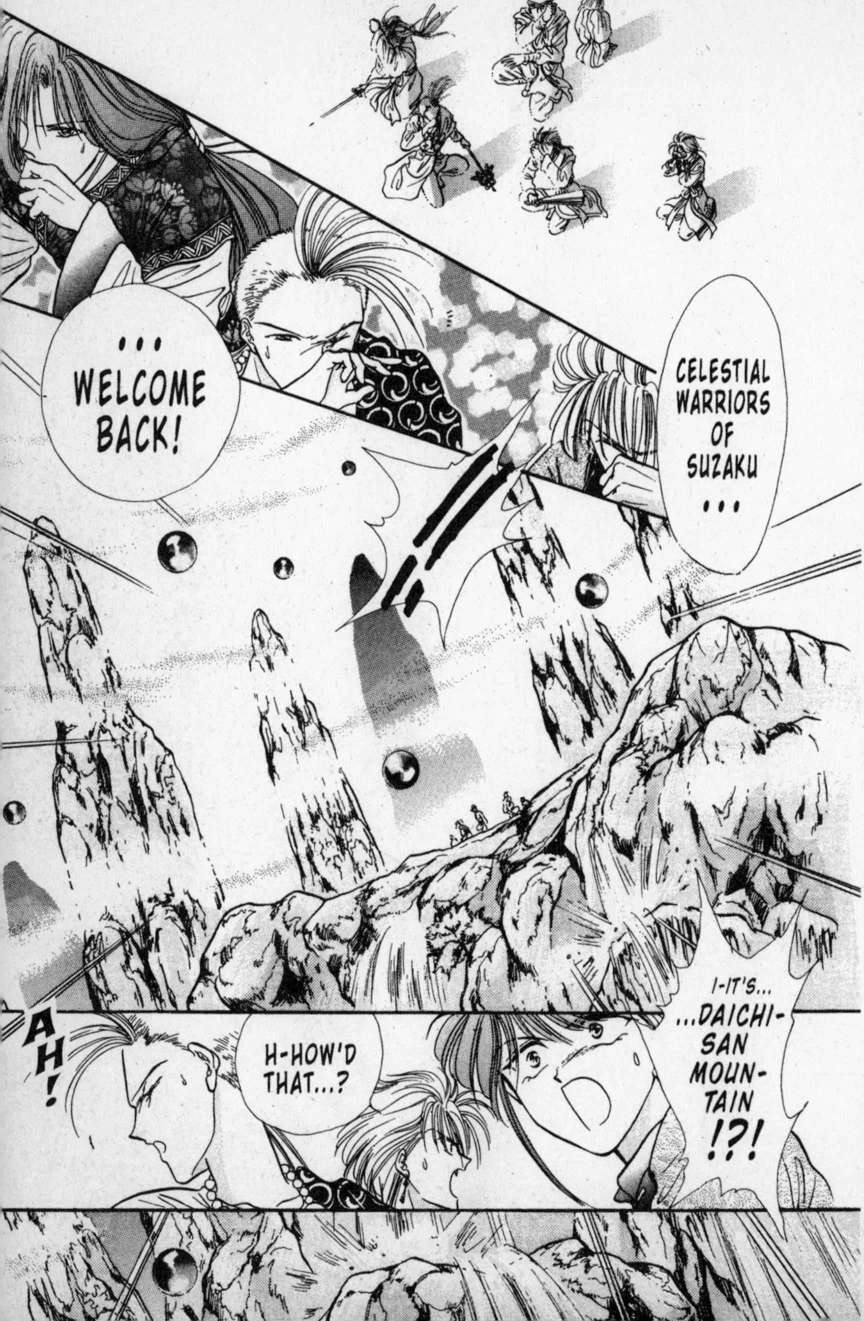
CELESTIAL WARRIORS OF SUZAKU ...
... WELCOME BACK!
I-IT'S... ...DAICHI-SAN MOUNTAIN !?!
H-HOW'D THAT...?
AH!

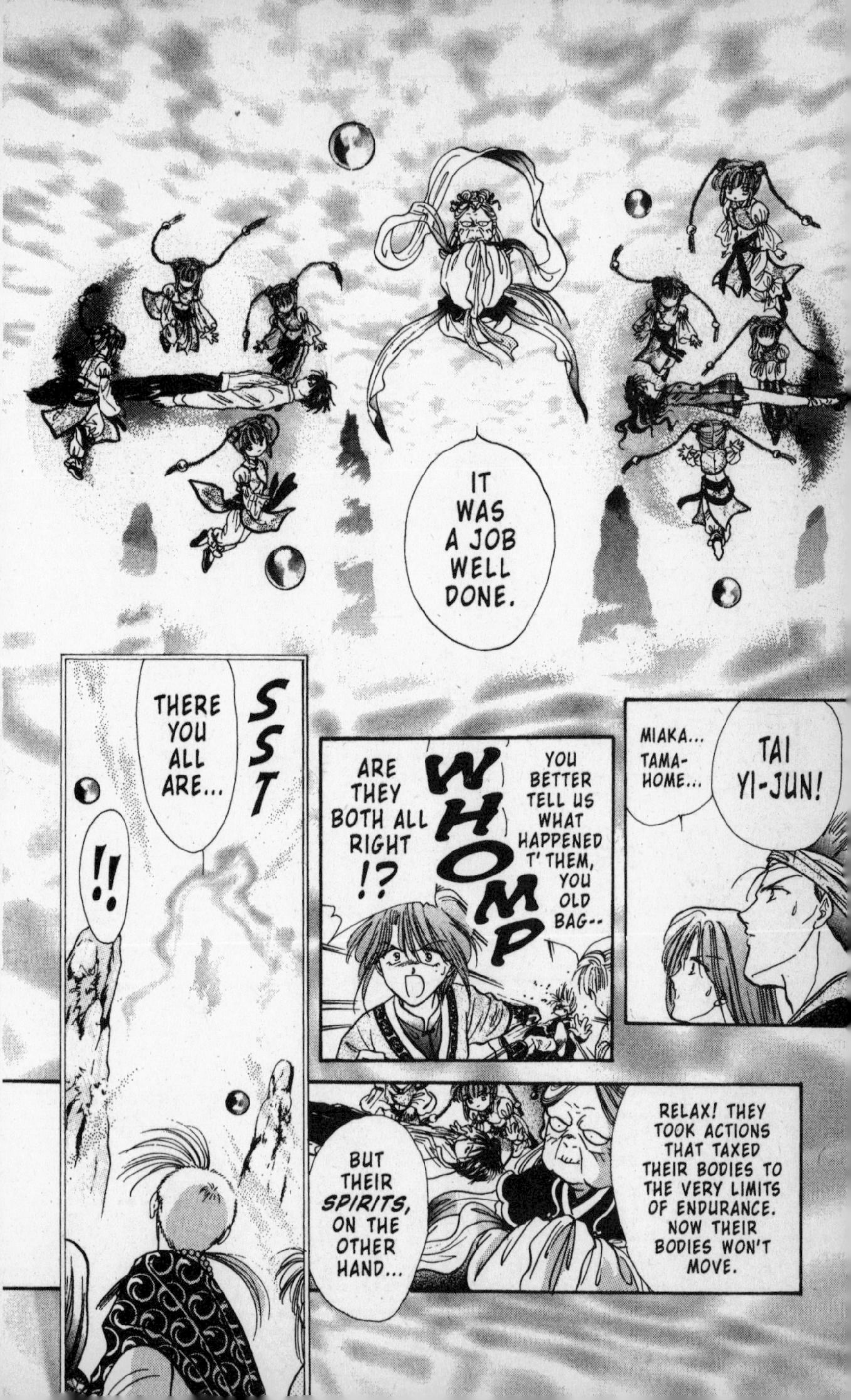
IT WAS A JOB WELL DONE.
TAI YI-JUN!
MIAKA... TAMA-HOME...
YOU BETTER TELL US WHAT HAPPENED T' THEM, YOU OLD BAG--
WHOMP
ARE THEY BOTH ALL RIGHT!?
RELAX! THEY TOOK ACTIONS THAT TAXED THEIR BODIES TO THE VERY LIMITS OF ENDURANCE. NOW THEIR BODIES WON'T MOVE.
BUT THEIR *SPIRITS*, ON THE OTHER HAND...
SST
THERE YOU ALL ARE...
!!

Bride

Now... Of all the deviations from the original story, the greatest one happened at the end of Part 1. And now I'm willing to tell you about it!
From the moment I started the series until there were only five or six chapters left, *I HAD PLANNED FOR MIAKA AND TAMAHOME TO SPLIT UP AT THE END.* My reasoning was, "Look, this is a story about how the main character views reality, and she could never wind up with such an ideal fiction of a man!" And for three years, the story was totally rooted in that concept. But... my editor at the time ♀ was dead-set against it. And more than that, my own heart began to change... You remember, around Chapter 70... I probably started to change my mind around the time Tamahome began to realize that he was a character out of a book and not a real human -- when that shock started to take hold. (The date they went on was supposed to be their last hurrah.) But I lost. I, the creator, tried to face down my own characters, Miaka and Tamahome, and lost.
Now I'm glad that I lost.
The way I see things, it's only natural for two lovers to see nobody but the one they love. They always want to be able to see the other's face... to hear the other's voice everyday. When the other isn't around, it's lonely and painful. That's deep love -- the feeling that you'd like to become one with your lover. Those who don't understand that will just have to fall in love themselves, right? And when something like that happens, one feels grateful to the entire world for making it happen. That's how Miaka and Taka felt about it. But if you try to put their relationship from Part 1 in the context of reality, their love really is the "puppy love" of young men and women. Love is different from that. *Ha! A single woman saying all this!* In much the same way, all of the Celestial Warriors, who are full of love themselves, ended up happy. I'm pretty sure of that. Even the ones who died will be just fine in the next life. Yeah! Considering that Part 2 is a manga with so many complications, it's interesting that I drew it with such an amazingly quiet heart. Yep! ☺

For Volume 18's background music, any of these will do, so give them a try!
- Hiroko Taniyama: Kyūka Ryokō ("Holiday Trip") & Hitomi no Eien ("Eternal Eyes")
- PSY.S: Earth
- TMN: "Self Control" & "We Love the Earth"
- Daisuke Asakura: "D-Trick" & "1000-nen no Chikai" ("1000 Year Vow")
- Akemi Satō: "Itōshii Hito no Tame Ni" Album Version ("For the One I Love") from the CD Book.
- Yōko Ueno: "Sayonara wa Iranai" ("There's no Need to Say Good Bye") & "Sennen no Chigiri" ("Pledge of a Thousand Years")
I listened to this during Vol. 13 too!

"Landing Time Machine." I've been listening to this ever since Part 1! *Especially Track 8! Highly Recommended!*

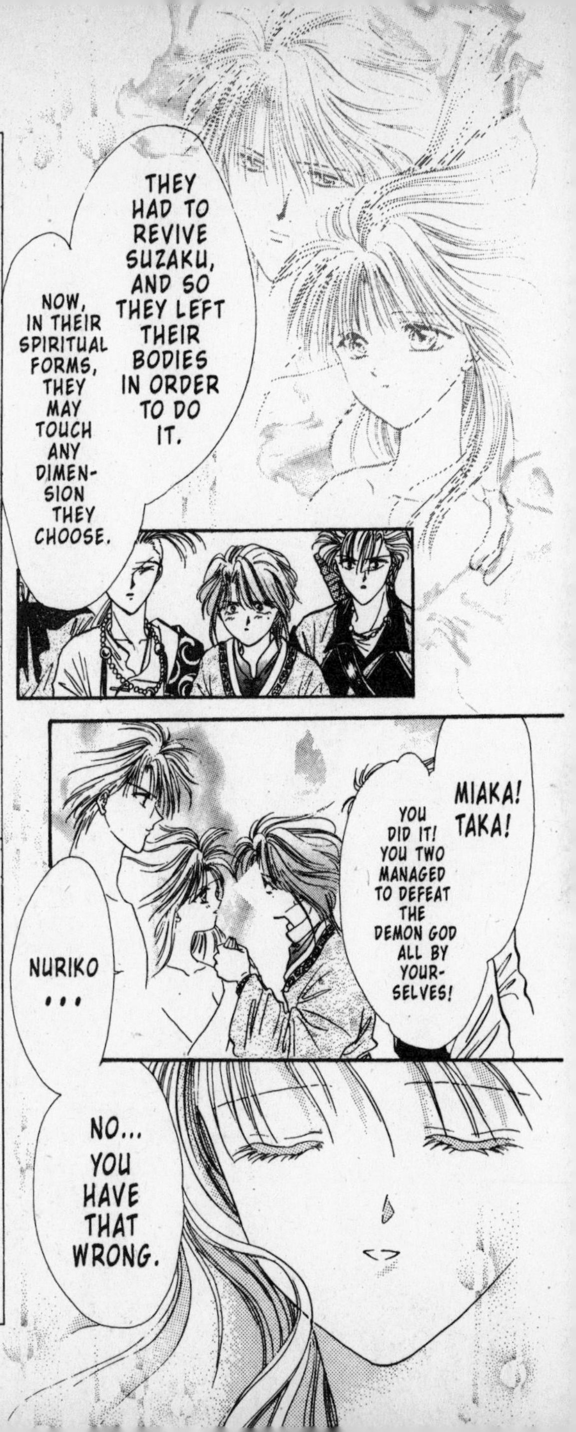
THEY HAD TO REVIVE SUZAKU, AND SO THEY LEFT THEIR BODIES IN ORDER TO DO IT.
NOW, IN THEIR SPIRITUAL FORMS, THEY MAY TOUCH ANY DIMENSION THEY CHOOSE.
MIAKA! TAKA!
YOU DID IT! YOU TWO MANAGED TO DEFEAT THE DEMON GOD ALL BY YOURSELVES!
NURIKO...
NO... YOU HAVE THAT WRONG.

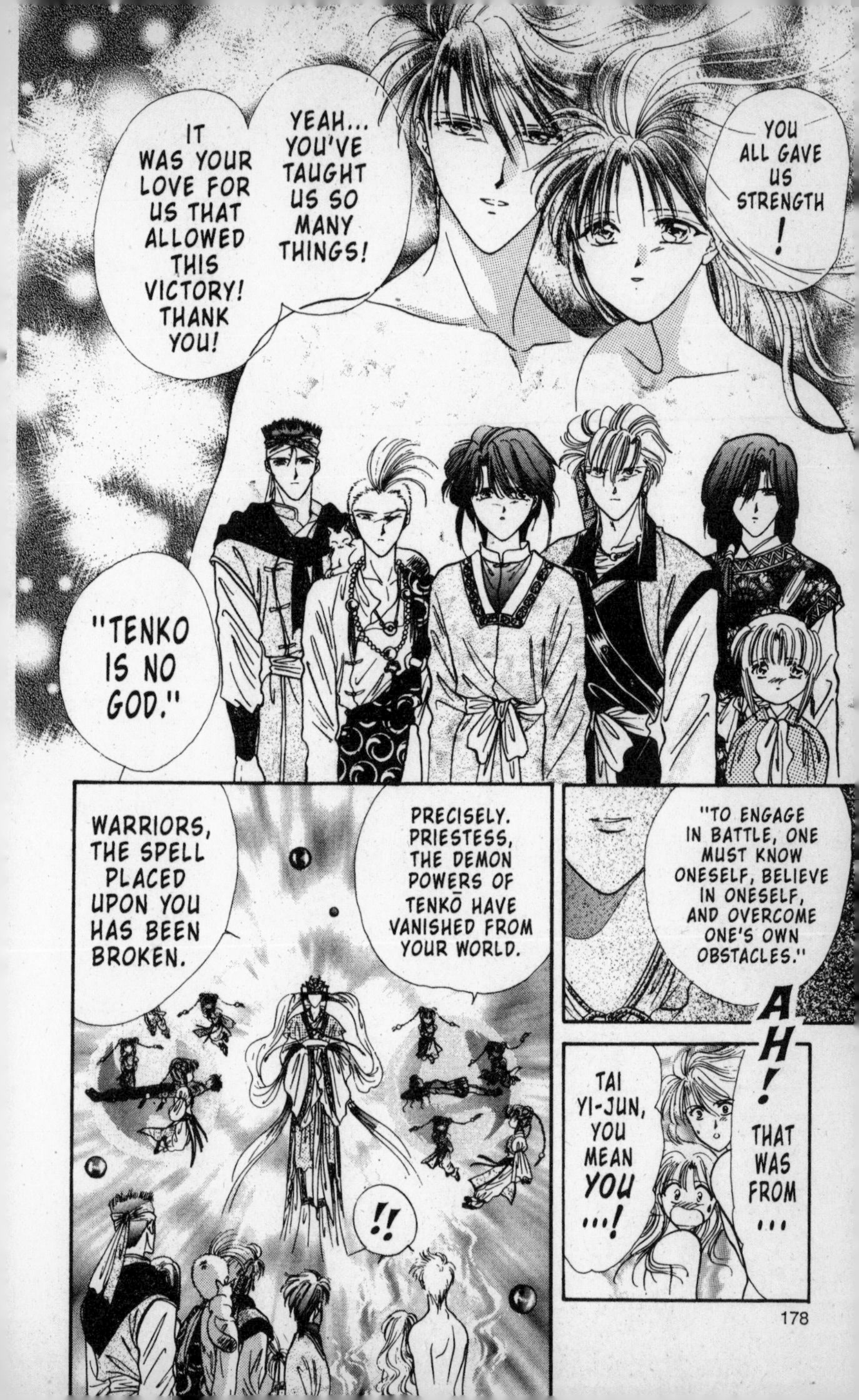
YOU ALL GAVE US STRENGTH!
YEAH... YOU'VE TAUGHT US SO MANY THINGS!
IT WAS YOUR LOVE FOR US THAT ALLOWED THIS VICTORY! THANK YOU!
"TENKO IS NO GOD."
"TO ENGAGE IN BATTLE, ONE MUST KNOW ONESELF, BELIEVE IN ONESELF, AND OVERCOME ONE'S OWN OBSTACLES."
AH!
THAT WAS FROM ...
TAI YI-JUN, YOU MEAN YOU ...!
PRECISELY. PRIESTESS, THE DEMON POWERS OF TENKŌ HAVE VANISHED FROM YOUR WORLD.
WARRIORS, THE SPELL PLACED UPON YOU HAS BEEN BROKEN.
!!

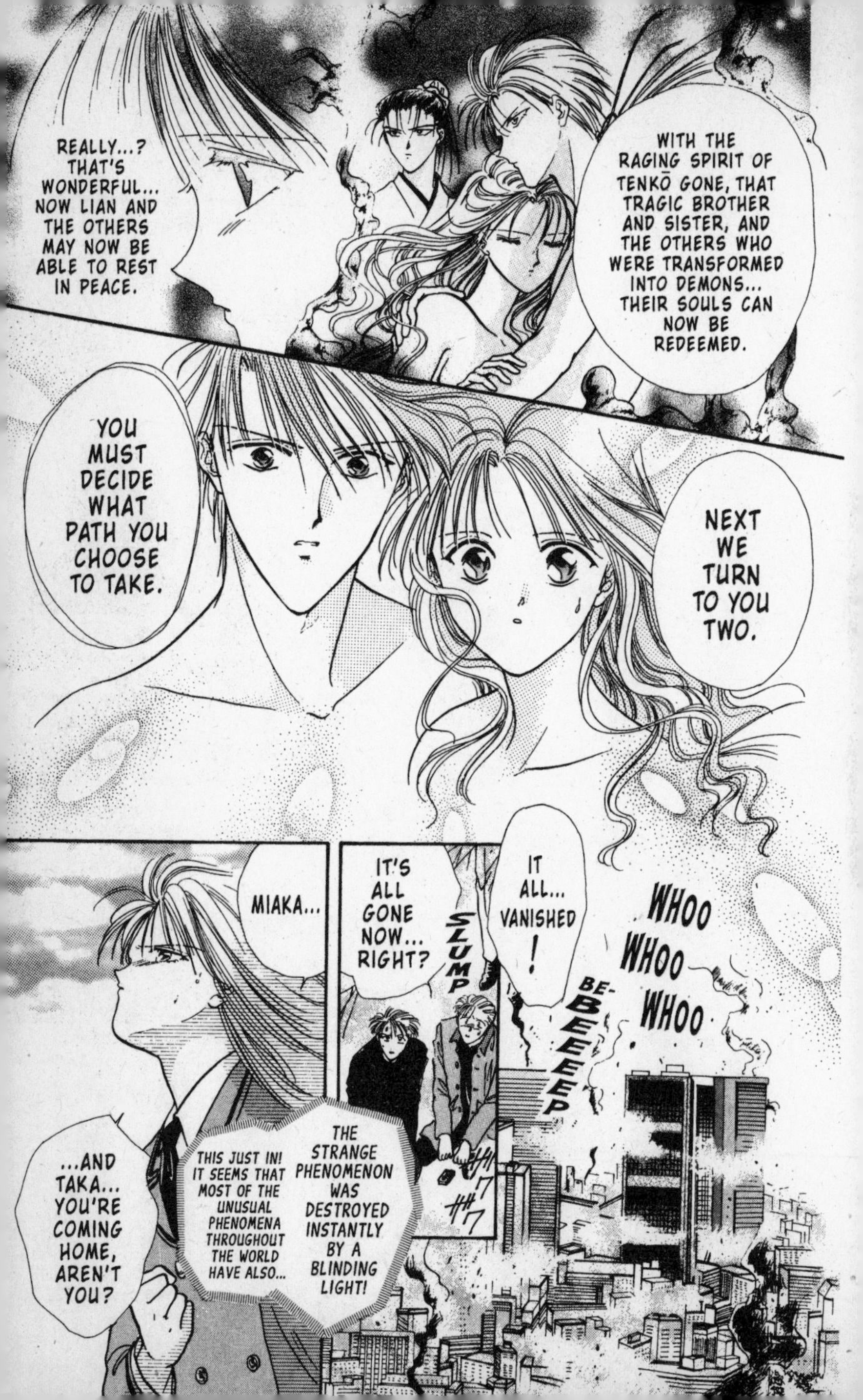
WITH THE RAGING SPIRIT OF TENKŌ GONE, THAT TRAGIC BROTHER AND SISTER, AND THE OTHERS WHO WERE TRANSFORMED INTO DEMONS... THEIR SOULS CAN NOW BE REDEEMED.
REALLY...? THAT'S WONDERFUL... NOW LIAN AND THE OTHERS MAY NOW BE ABLE TO REST IN PEACE.
NEXT WE TURN TO YOU TWO.
YOU MUST DECIDE WHAT PATH YOU CHOOSE TO TAKE.
WHOO WHOO WHOO
BE-BEEEEEP
THE STRANGE PHENOMENON WAS DESTROYED INSTANTLY BY A BLINDING LIGHT!
THIS JUST IN! IT SEEMS THAT MOST OF THE UNUSUAL PHENOMENA THROUGHOUT THE WORLD HAVE ALSO...
IT ALL... VANISHED!
SLUMP
IT'S ALL GONE NOW... RIGHT?
MIAKA...
...AND TAKA... YOU'RE COMING HOME, AREN'T YOU?

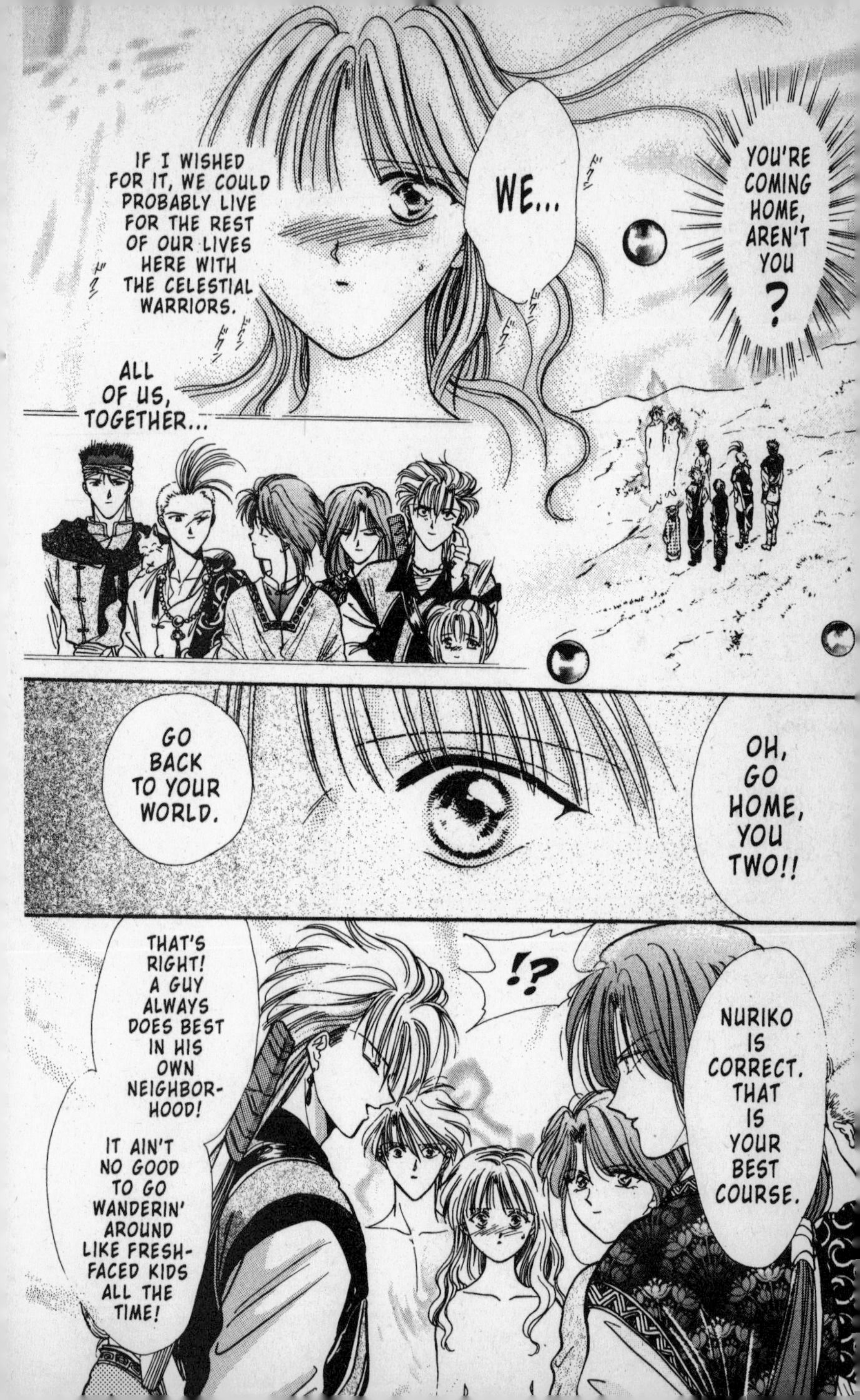

YOU'RE COMING HOME, AREN'T YOU?
WE...
IF I WISHED FOR IT, WE COULD PROBABLY LIVE FOR THE REST OF OUR LIVES HERE WITH THE CELESTIAL WARRIORS.
ALL OF US, TOGETHER...
OH, GO HOME, YOU TWO!!
GO BACK TO YOUR WORLD.
NURIKO IS CORRECT. THAT IS YOUR BEST COURSE.
!?
THAT'S RIGHT! A GUY ALWAYS DOES BEST IN HIS OWN NEIGHBOR-HOOD!
IT AIN'T NO GOOD TO GO WANDERIN' AROUND LIKE FRESH-FACED KIDS ALL THE TIME!

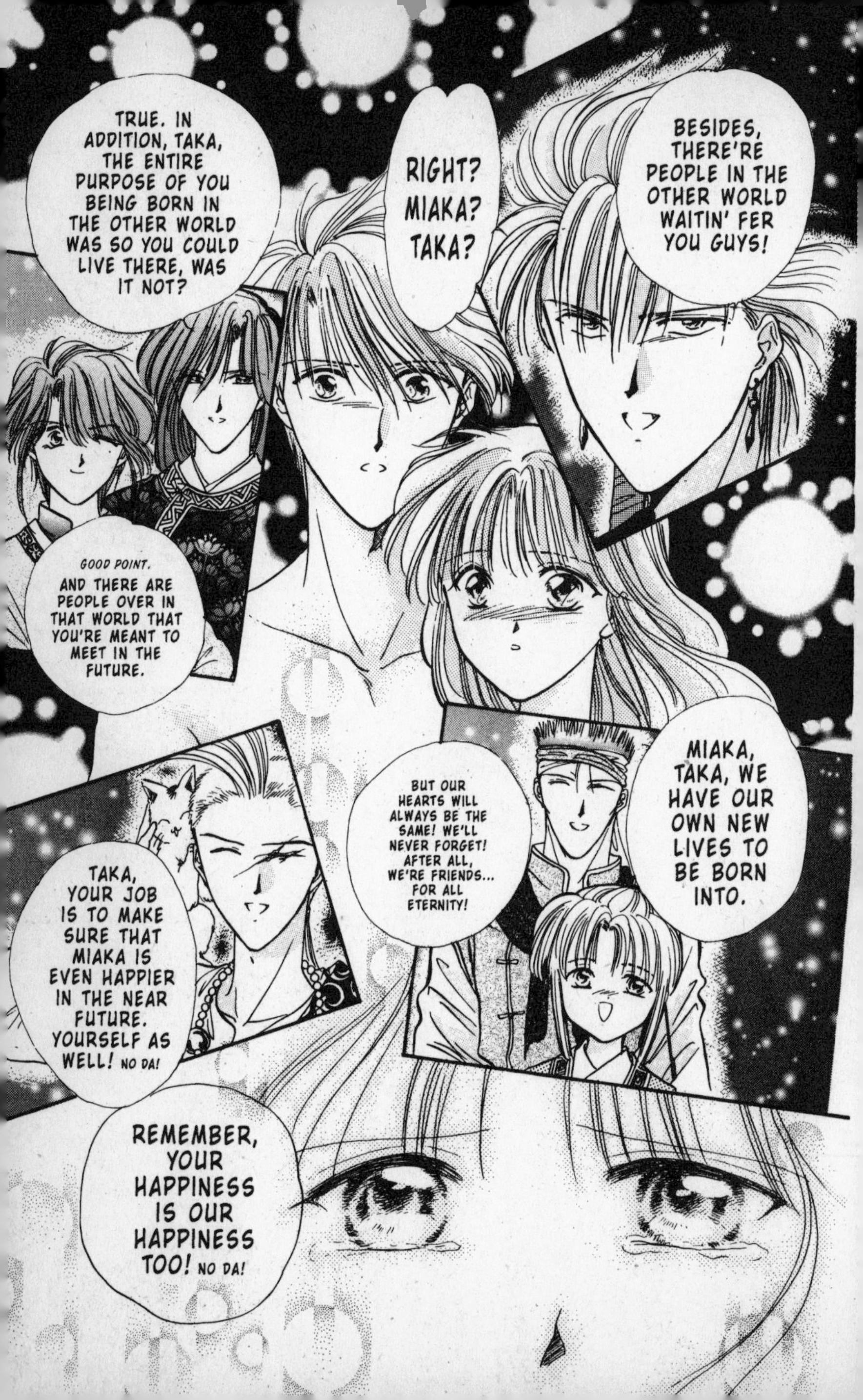
BESIDES, THERE'RE PEOPLE IN THE OTHER WORLD WAITIN' FER YOU GUYS!
RIGHT? MIAKA? TAKA?
TRUE. IN ADDITION, TAKA, THE ENTIRE PURPOSE OF YOU BEING BORN IN THE OTHER WORLD WAS SO YOU COULD LIVE THERE, WAS IT NOT?
GOOD POINT. AND THERE ARE PEOPLE OVER IN THAT WORLD THAT YOU'RE MEANT TO MEET IN THE FUTURE.
MIAKA, TAKA, WE HAVE OUR OWN NEW LIVES TO BE BORN INTO.
BUT OUR HEARTS WILL ALWAYS BE THE SAME! WE'LL NEVER FORGET! AFTER ALL, WE'RE FRIENDS... FOR ALL ETERNITY!
TAKA, YOUR JOB IS TO MAKE SURE THAT MIAKA IS EVEN HAPPIER IN THE NEAR FUTURE. YOURSELF AS WELL! NO DA!
REMEMBER, YOUR HAPPINESS IS OUR HAPPINESS TOO! NO DA!

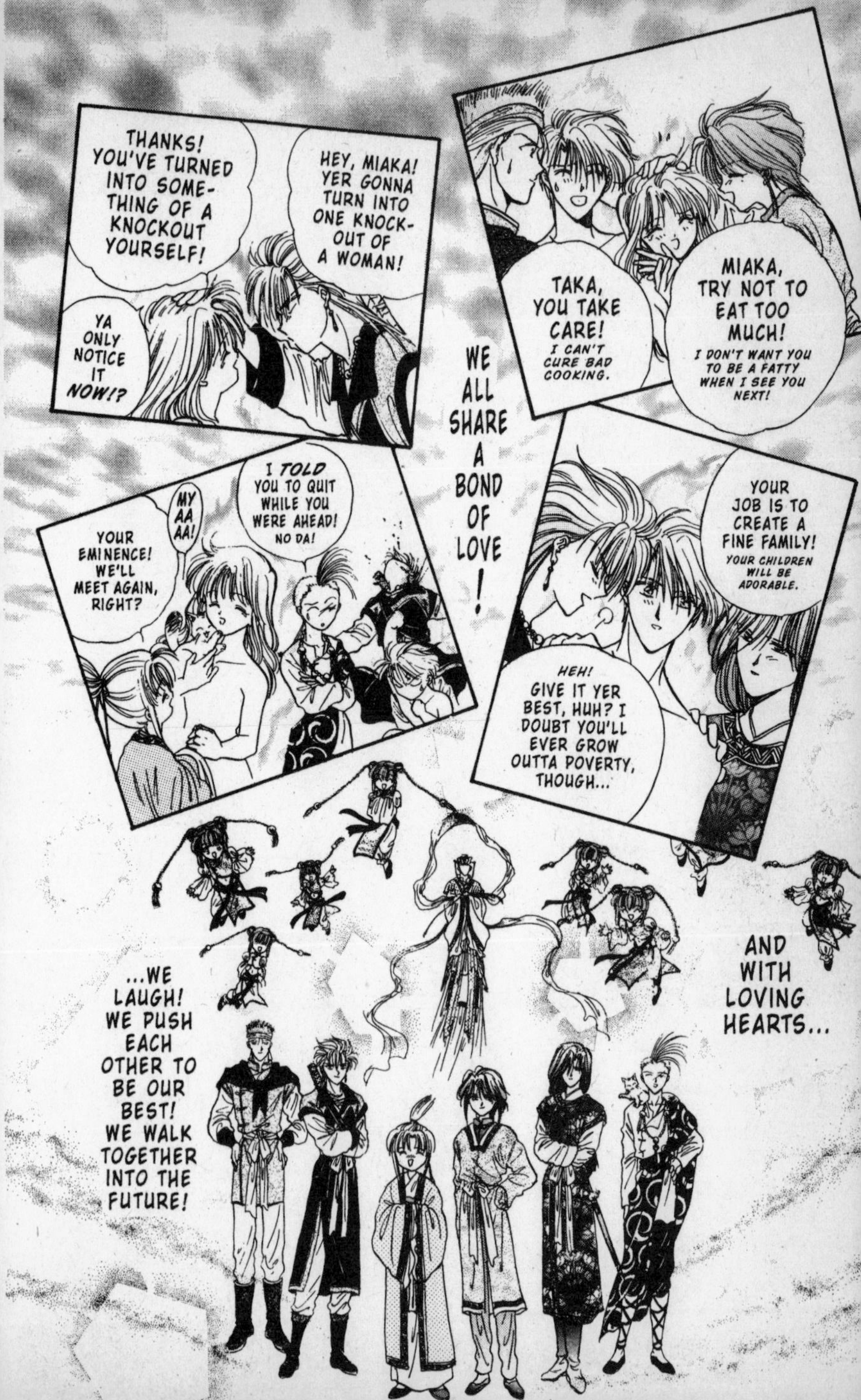
MIAKA, TRY NOT TO EAT TOO MUCH! I DON'T WANT YOU TO BE A FATTY WHEN I SEE YOU NEXT!
TAKA, YOU TAKE CARE! I CAN'T CURE BAD COOKING.
HEY, MIAKA! YER GONNA TURN INTO ONE KNOCK-OUT OF A WOMAN!
THANKS! YOU'VE TURNED INTO SOME-THING OF A KNOCKOUT YOURSELF!
YA ONLY NOTICE IT NOW!?
WE ALL SHARE A BOND OF LOVE!
YOUR JOB IS TO CREATE A FINE FAMILY! YOUR CHILDREN WILL BE ADORABLE.
HEH! GIVE IT YER BEST, HUH? I DOUBT YOU'LL EVER GROW OUTTA POVERTY, THOUGH...
I TOLD YOU TO QUIT WHILE YOU WERE AHEAD! NO DA!
MY AA AA!
YOUR EMINENCE! WE'LL MEET AGAIN, RIGHT?
AND WITH LOVING HEARTS...
...WE LAUGH! WE PUSH EACH OTHER TO BE OUR BEST! WE WALK TOGETHER INTO THE FUTURE!

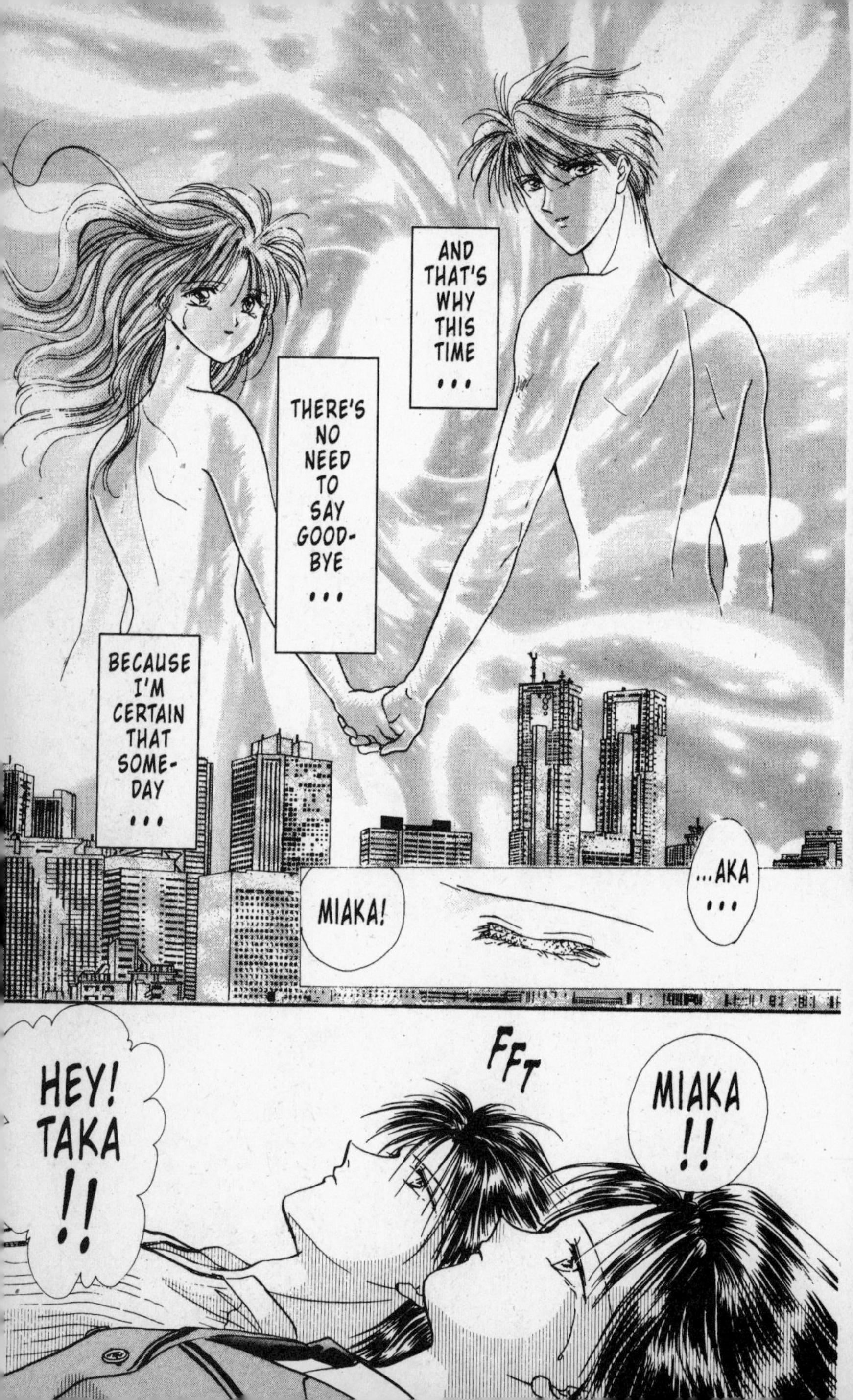
AND THAT'S WHY THIS TIME...
THERE'S NO NEED TO SAY GOOD-BYE...
BECAUSE I'M CERTAIN THAT SOME-DAY...
...AKA...
MIAKA!
MIAKA!!
FFT
HEY! TAKA!!

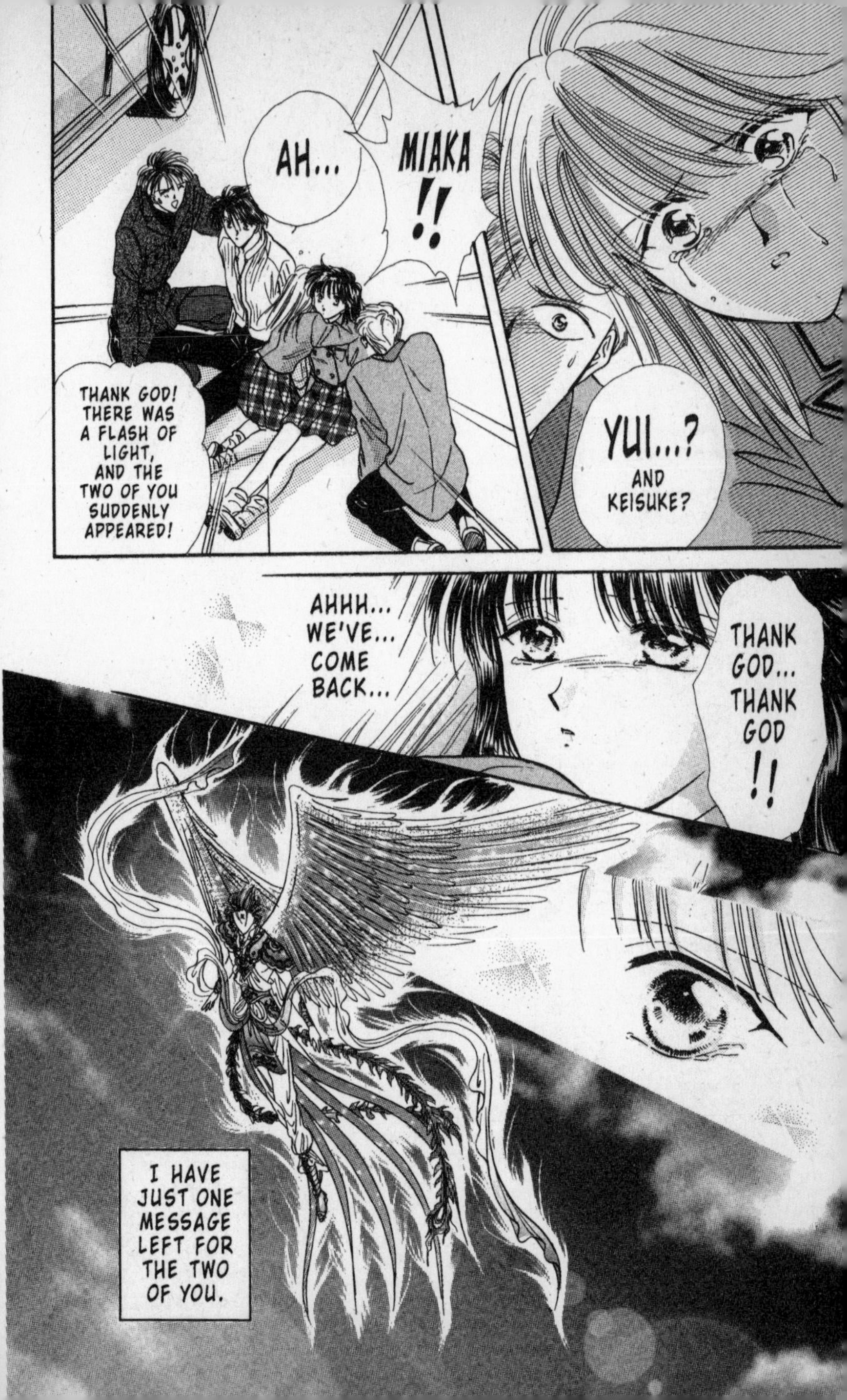
YUI...? AND KEISUKE?
MIAKA!!
AH...
THANK GOD! THERE WAS A FLASH OF LIGHT, AND THE TWO OF YOU SUDDENLY APPEARED!
THANK GOD... THANK GOD!!
AHHH... WE'VE... COME BACK...
I HAVE JUST ONE MESSAGE LEFT FOR THE TWO OF YOU.

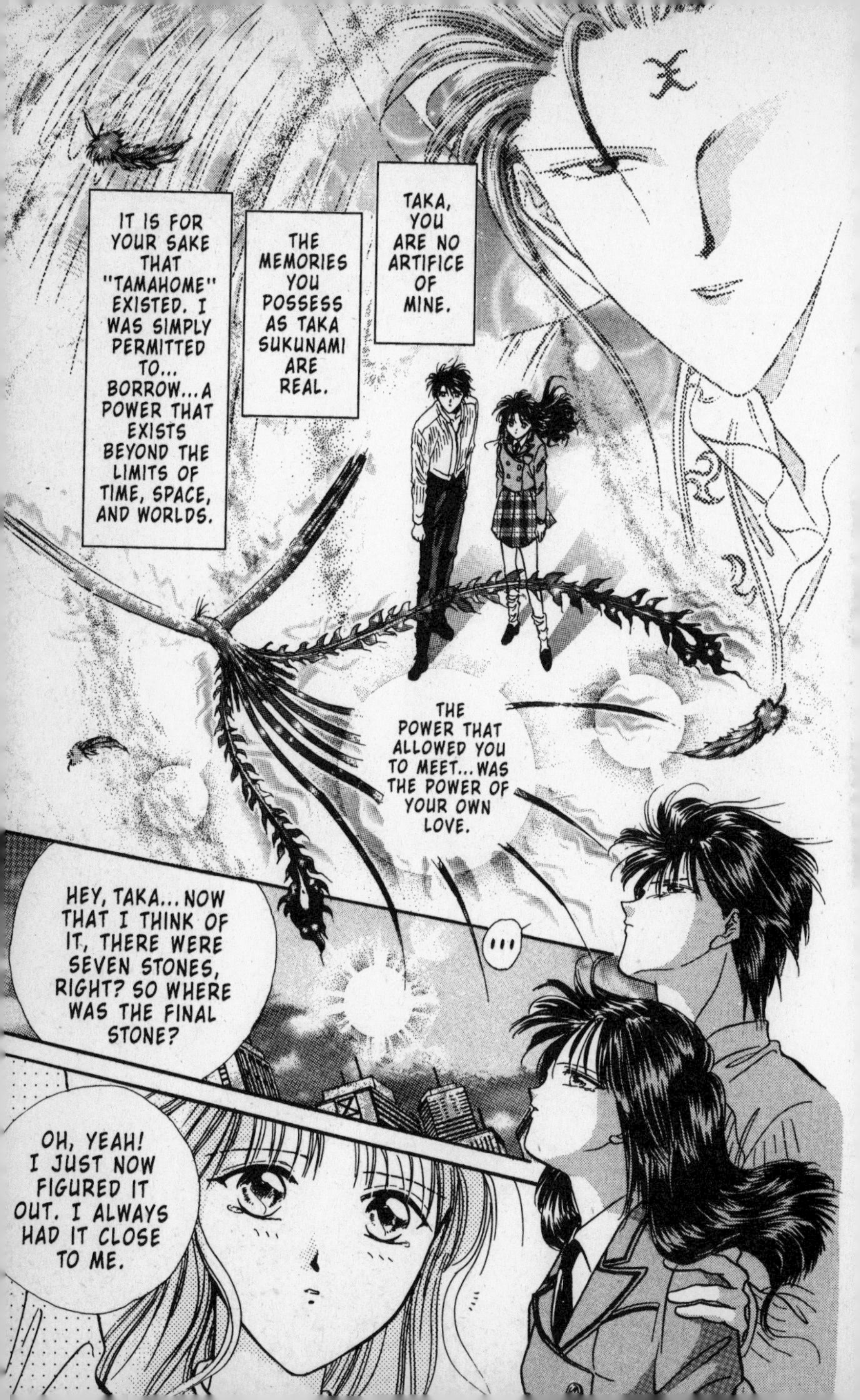

TAKA, YOU ARE NO ARTIFICE OF MINE.
THE MEMORIES YOU POSSESS AS TAKA SUKUNAMI ARE REAL.
IT IS FOR YOUR SAKE THAT "TAMAHOME" EXISTED. I WAS SIMPLY PERMITTED TO... BORROW... A POWER THAT EXISTS BEYOND THE LIMITS OF TIME, SPACE, AND WORLDS.
THE POWER THAT ALLOWED YOU TO MEET... WAS THE POWER OF YOUR OWN LOVE.
...
HEY, TAKA... NOW THAT I THINK OF IT, THERE WERE SEVEN STONES, RIGHT? SO WHERE WAS THE FINAL STONE?
OH, YEAH! I JUST NOW FIGURED IT OUT. I ALWAYS HAD IT CLOSE TO ME.

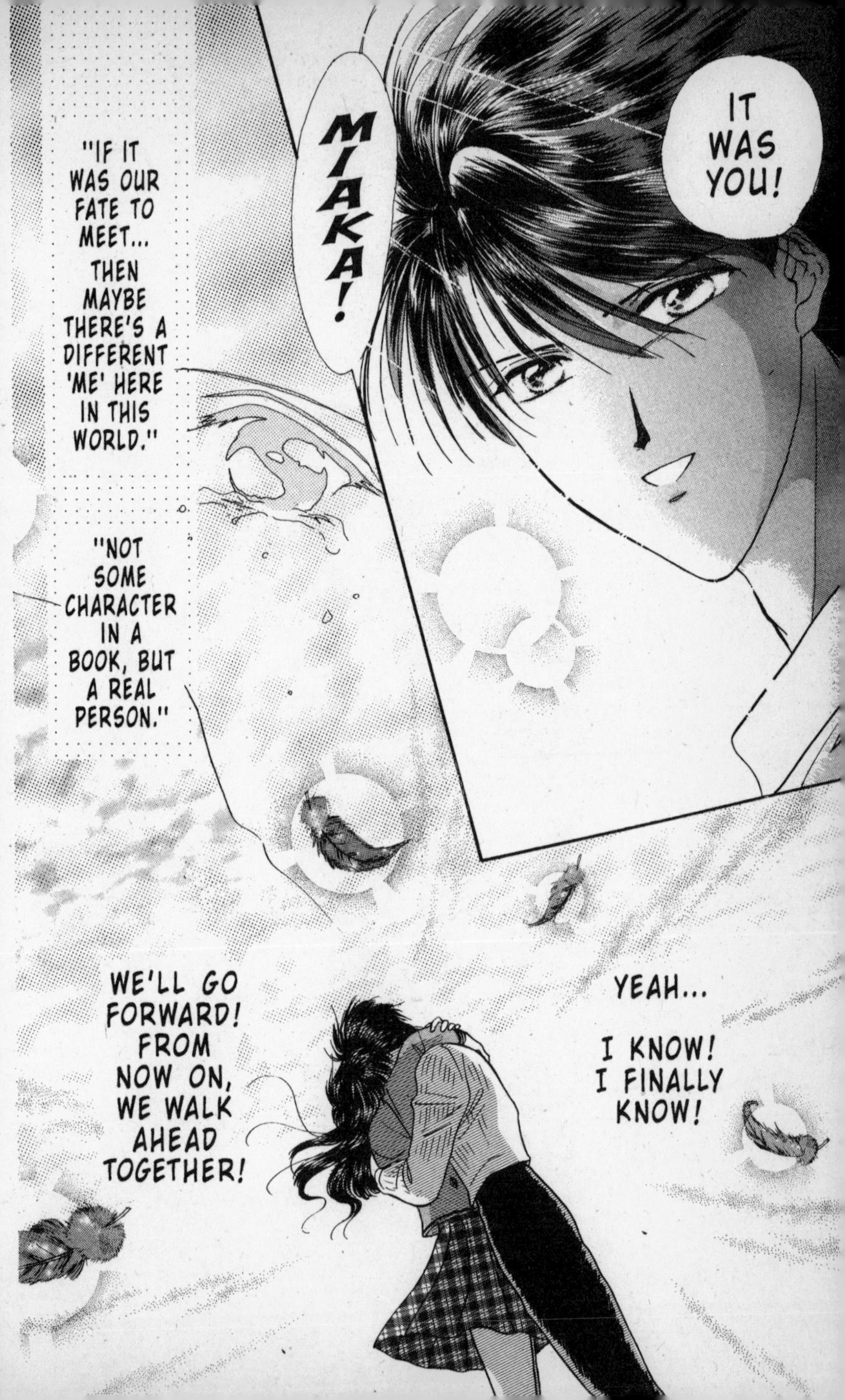
IT WAS YOU!
MIAKA!
"IF IT WAS OUR FATE TO MEET... THEN MAYBE THERE'S A DIFFERENT 'ME' HERE IN THIS WORLD."
"NOT SOME CHARACTER IN A BOOK, BUT A REAL PERSON."
YEAH...
I KNOW! I FINALLY KNOW!
WE'LL GO FORWARD! FROM NOW ON, WE WALK AHEAD TOGETHER!

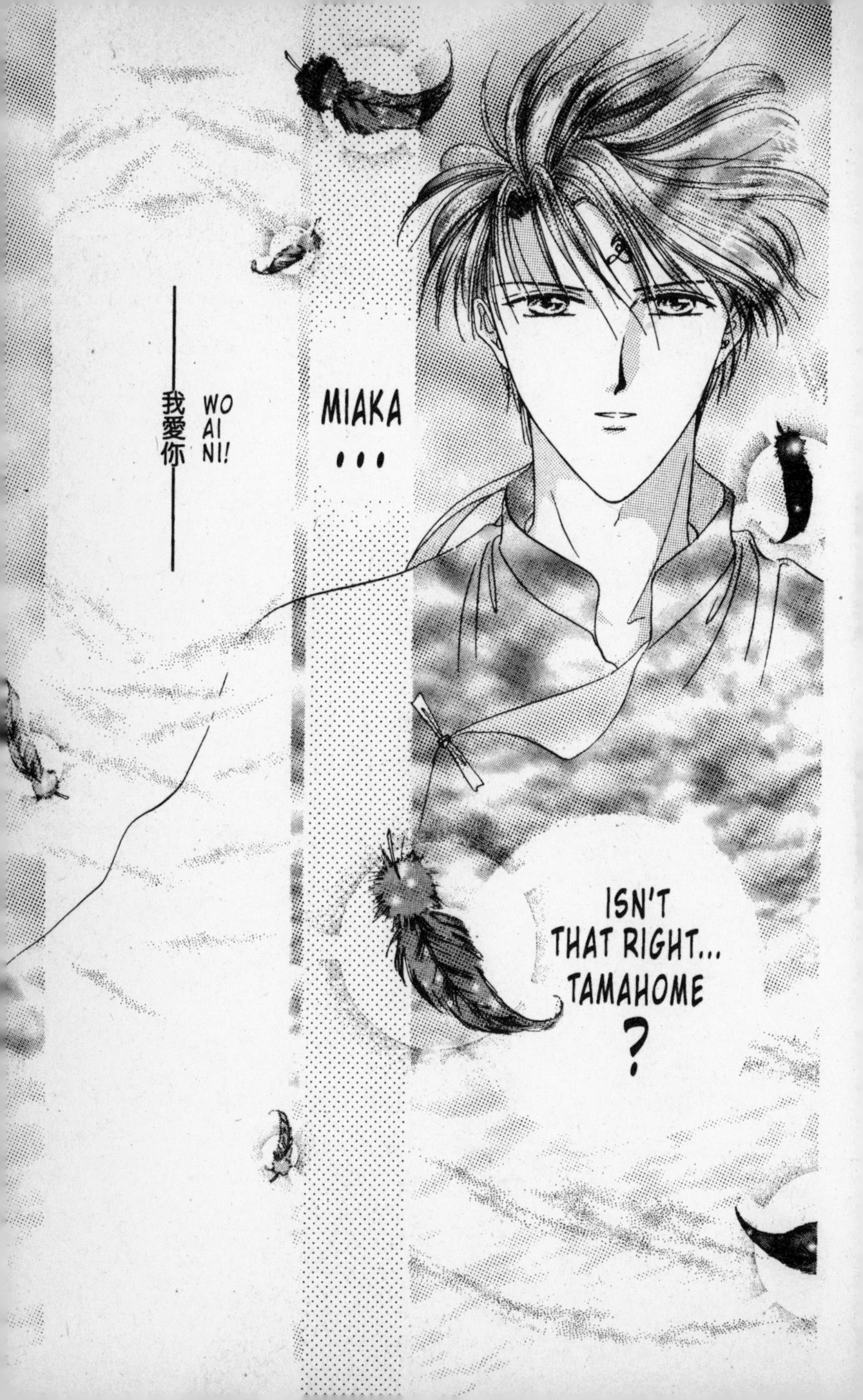
ISN'T THAT RIGHT... TAMAHOME ?
MIAKA ...
—我愛你— WO AI NI!

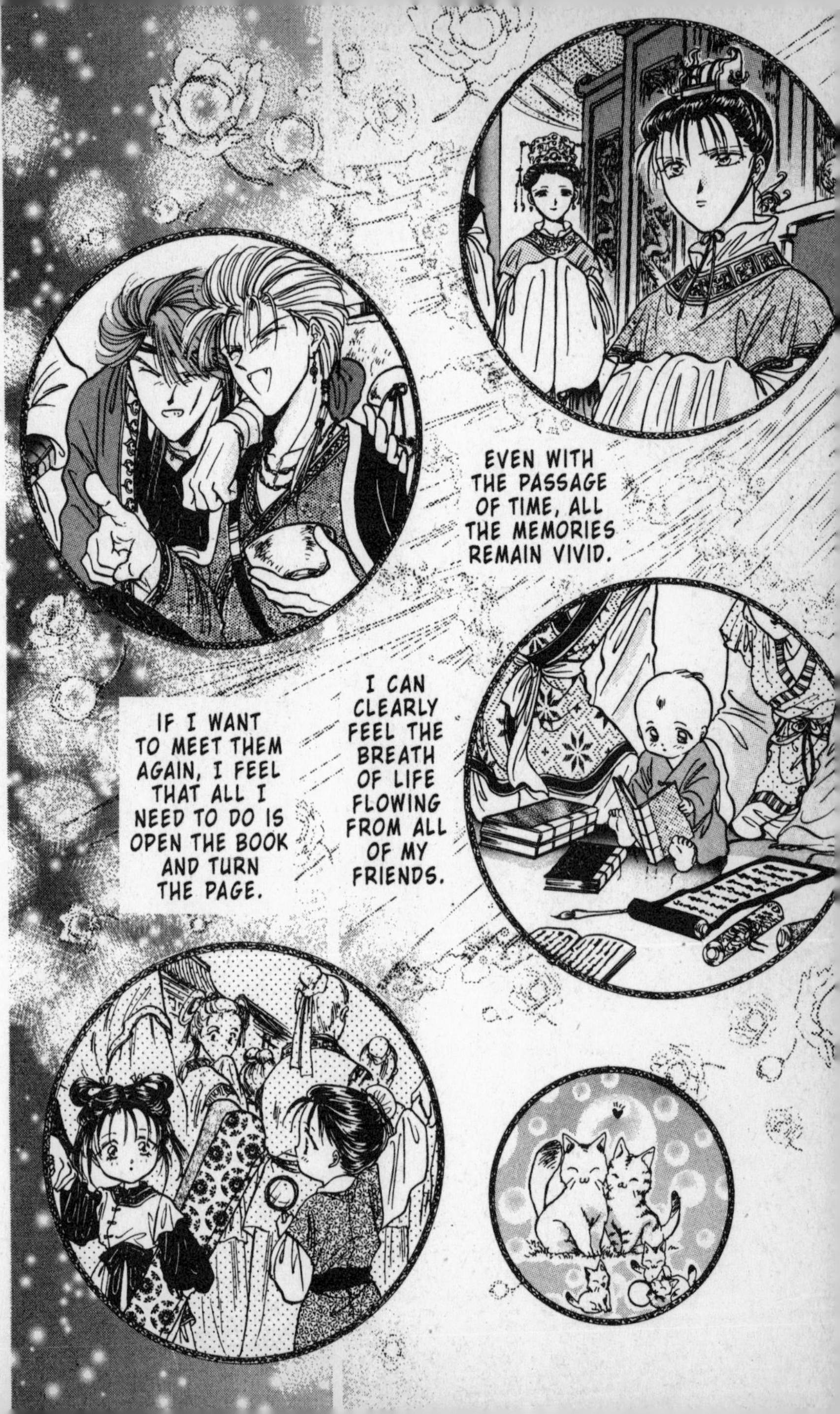
EVEN WITH THE PASSAGE OF TIME, ALL THE MEMORIES REMAIN VIVID.
I CAN CLEARLY FEEL THE BREATH OF LIFE FLOWING FROM ALL OF MY FRIENDS.
IF I WANT TO MEET THEM AGAIN, I FEEL THAT ALL I NEED TO DO IS OPEN THE BOOK AND TURN THE PAGE.

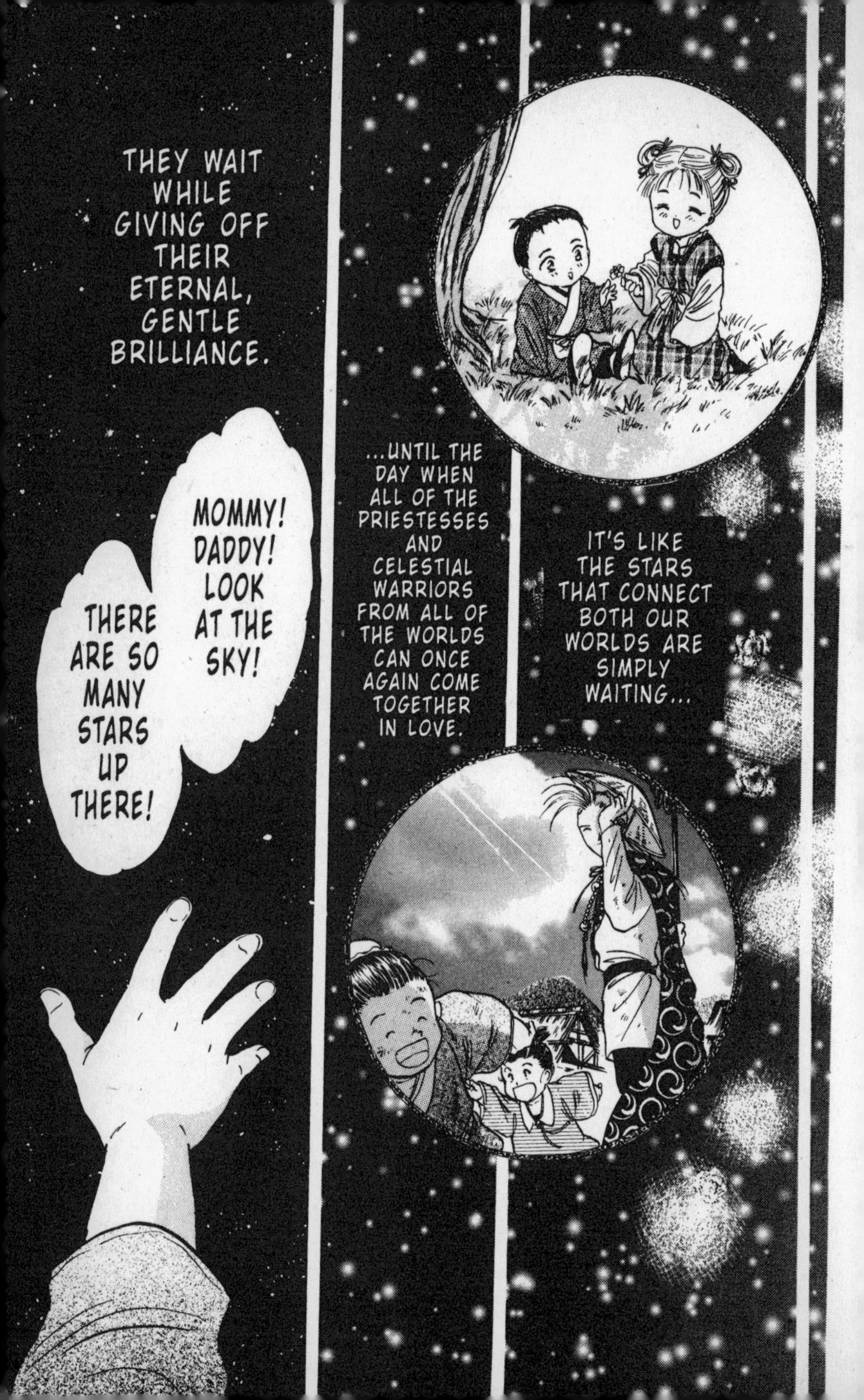
IT'S LIKE THE STARS THAT CONNECT BOTH OUR WORLDS ARE SIMPLY WAITING...
...UNTIL THE DAY WHEN ALL OF THE PRIESTESSES AND CELESTIAL WARRIORS FROM ALL OF THE WORLDS CAN ONCE AGAIN COME TOGETHER IN LOVE.
THEY WAIT WHILE GIVING OFF THEIR ETERNAL, GENTLE BRILLIANCE.
MOMMY! DADDY! LOOK AT THE SKY!
THERE ARE SO MANY STARS UP THERE!

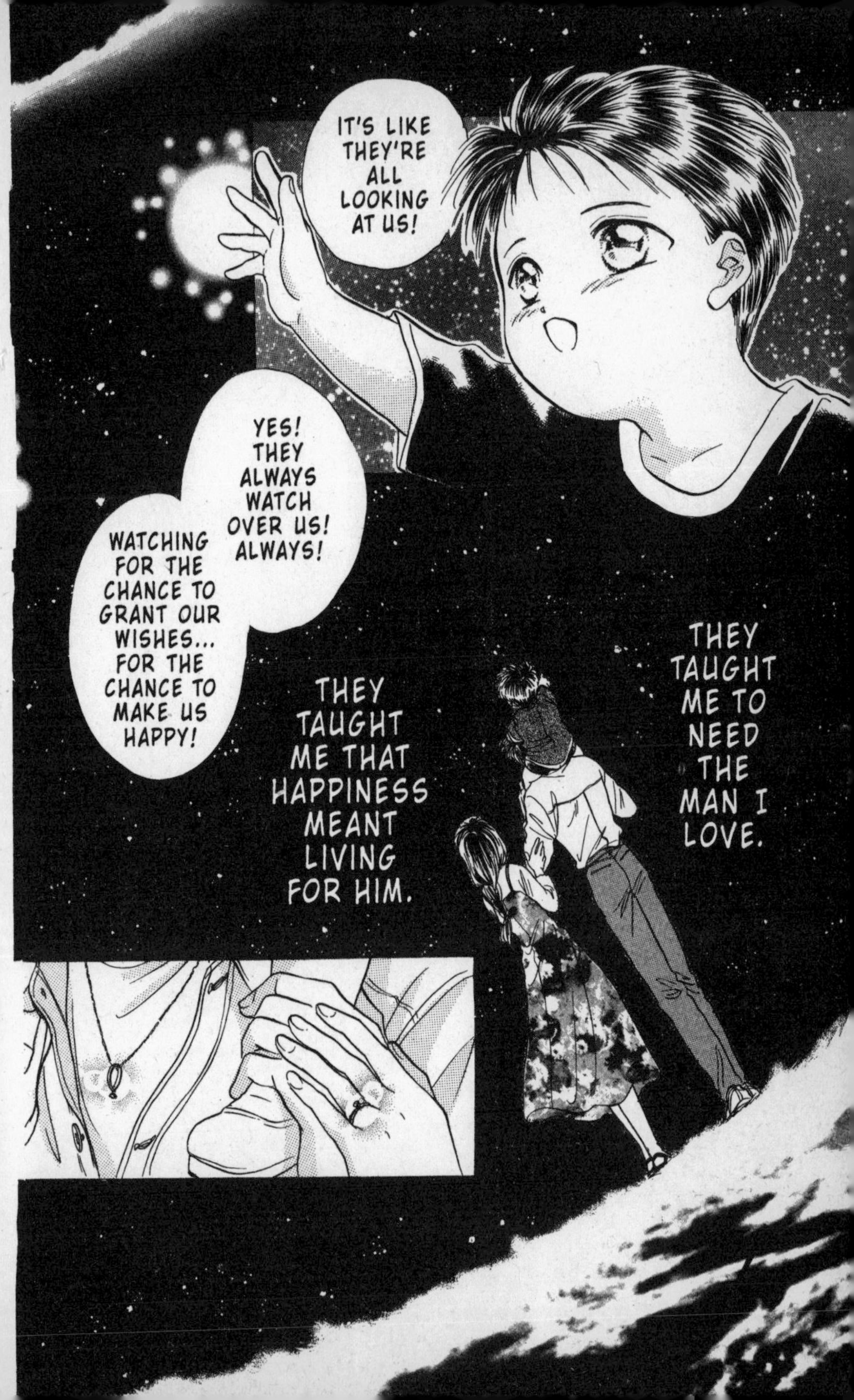
IT'S LIKE THEY'RE ALL LOOKING AT US!
YES! THEY ALWAYS WATCH OVER US! ALWAYS!
WATCHING FOR THE CHANCE TO GRANT OUR WISHES... FOR THE CHANCE TO MAKE US HAPPY!
THEY TAUGHT ME TO NEED THE MAN I LOVE.
THEY TAUGHT ME THAT HAPPINESS MEANT LIVING FOR HIM.

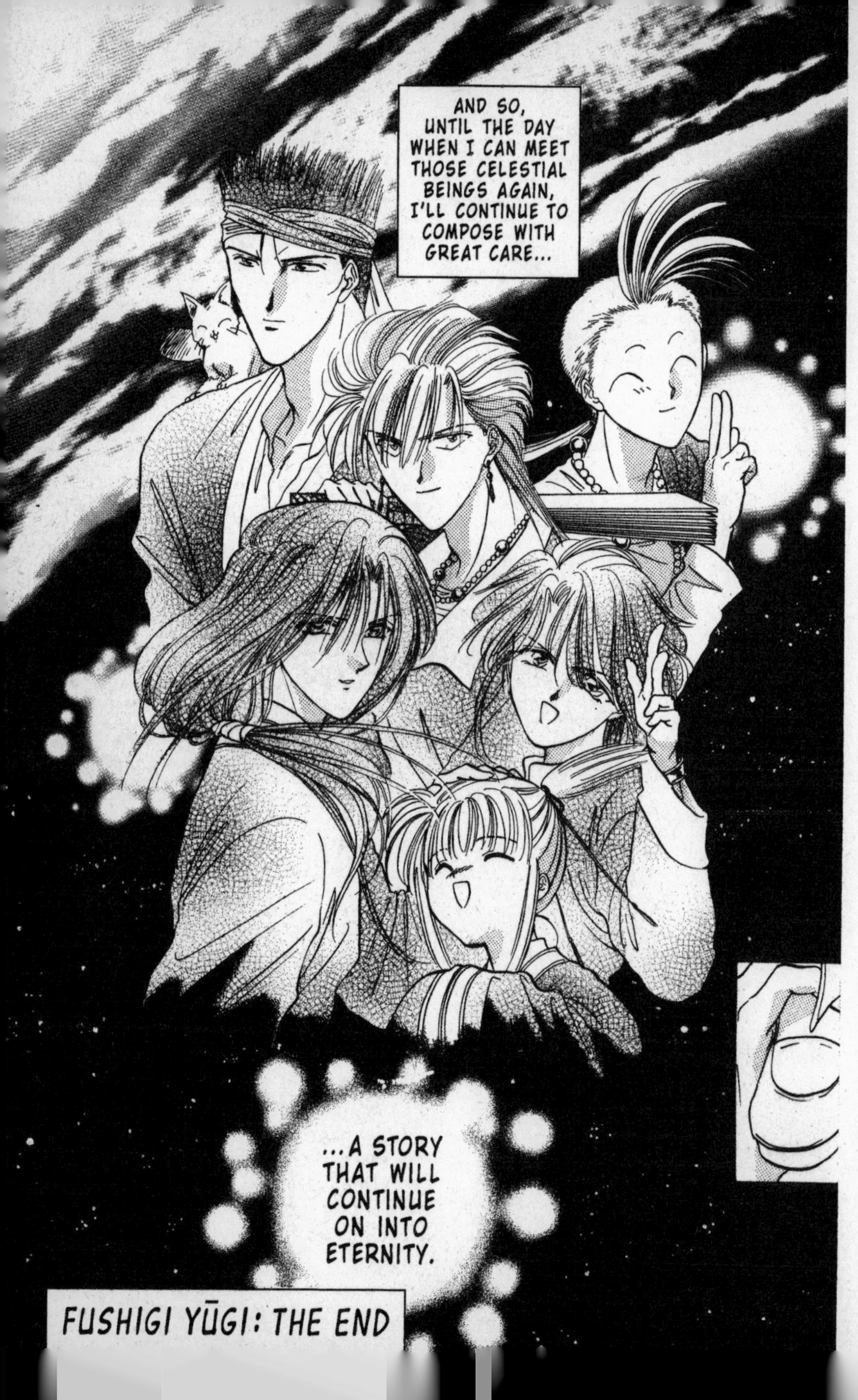
AND SO, UNTIL THE DAY WHEN I CAN MEET THOSE CELESTIAL BEINGS AGAIN, I'LL CONTINUE TO COMPOSE WITH GREAT CARE...
...A STORY THAT WILL CONTINUE ON INTO ETERNITY.
FUSHIGI YŪGI: THE END

THANK YOU SO MUCH!
…謝謝你

The day we begin our new journey… I suppose I can call it that. Rather than call it the ending of a continuing story, it's like everyone is leaving the nest. That's the feeling I get. I think that I've raised all of the Celestial Warriors… All of them have grown into fine, upstanding men (in their own ways). And the reason I was able to continue it this far is truly thanks to you readers. There were so many letters, and they constantly cheered us up when we were down. They made us cry…laugh…get angry…and there were those that really moved us. About the time when Part 1 ended, we got a letter from a student who was studying for her entrance exams, and she wrote, "I was anxious and scared, but I remembered Miaka's words. Miaka and Tamahome gave their very best, so I know I can take on this challenge with everything I've got!"

"I was filled with envy for Miaka. I mean, I was really jealous! But that inspired me to do my best to make myself into a girl that someone could love!"

"In the manga, when Nuriko thought wistfully about if he were still alive… I had been contemplating suicide. But reading that made me want to hang on instead."

And there were more.

After the last chapter was printed in the magazine, there were so many letters thanking me (Hey! I'm supposed to be the one thanking you!)…

"I couldn't stop crying as I read the chapter over and over." And that letter made me cry too!

"While I wasn't paying attention, Miaka grew up fast and turned into a beautiful woman! I think she passed me and left me far behind," said one girl, and similar sentiments were expressed by a large number of others.

There were a large number of letters from homemakers, many of whom said, "This is the first time in years and years that a shōjo manga got me addicted." That's interesting, isn't it…?

The oldest was from a person who was…45, maybe? And there were men who admitted that they cried… I was so happy to read all the letters!

Fushigi Yûgi was a story with a lot of "fushigi" (mysterious) events surrounding it. In the anime, they needed real-world setting references for the Genbu Cave and the place where Keisuke and Tetsuya traveled. So the director would simply point to a map and say, "Maybe here," and then when they actually went, they'd find a temple or graveyard. It was scary! At least that's what I was told. And the Takamatsu-Zuka Old Mound… I didn't hear about this until the very end of the series, but… it turns out that there's a legend of it sealing up an actual angry ghost! On the day the anime episode about the death of Nuriko aired on TV, a homemaker who had recently lost her mother was fitting her son with a Chichiri costume, and the son suffered a serious wound to his right eye that nearly blinded him! I hope he's okay now! Do you think that maybe the stories that appeared in the "Universe of the Four Gods" have crossed over into real life!?

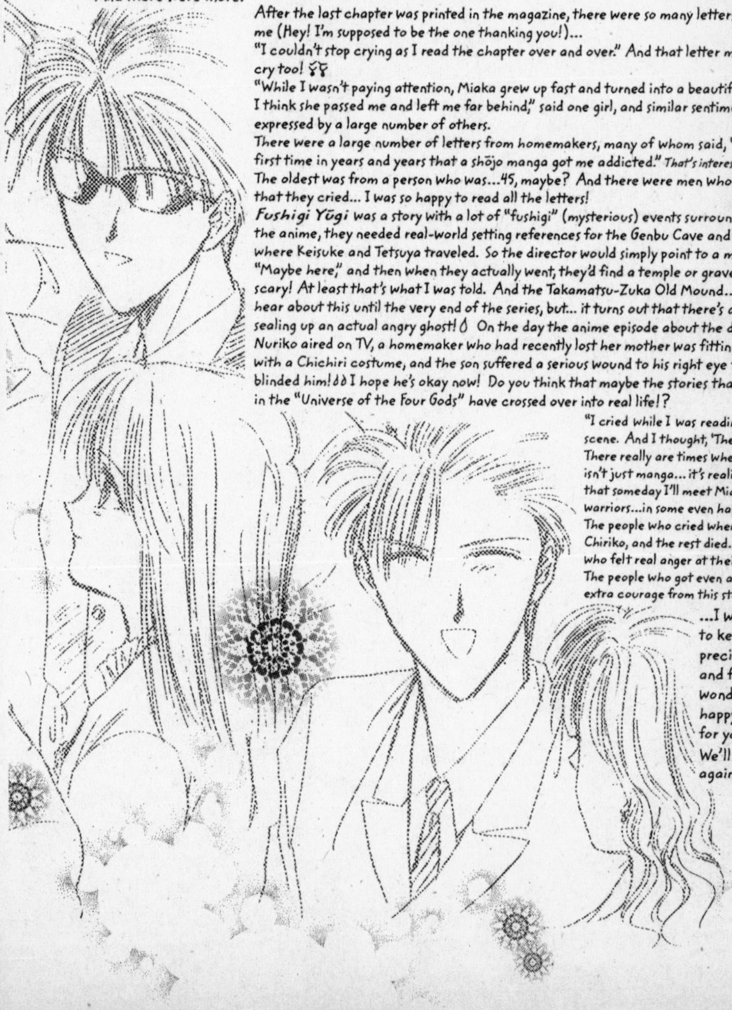

"I cried while I was reading the last scene. And I thought, 'They're alive!' There really are times when a manga isn't just manga… it's reality! I'm sure that someday I'll meet Miaka and her warriors…in some even happier destiny."

The people who cried when Nuriko, Chiriko, and the rest died… The people who felt real anger at their enemies… The people who got even a little bit of extra courage from this story…

…I wish for you to keep that precious feeling, and find a wonderful, happy destiny for yourselves! We'll meet again!

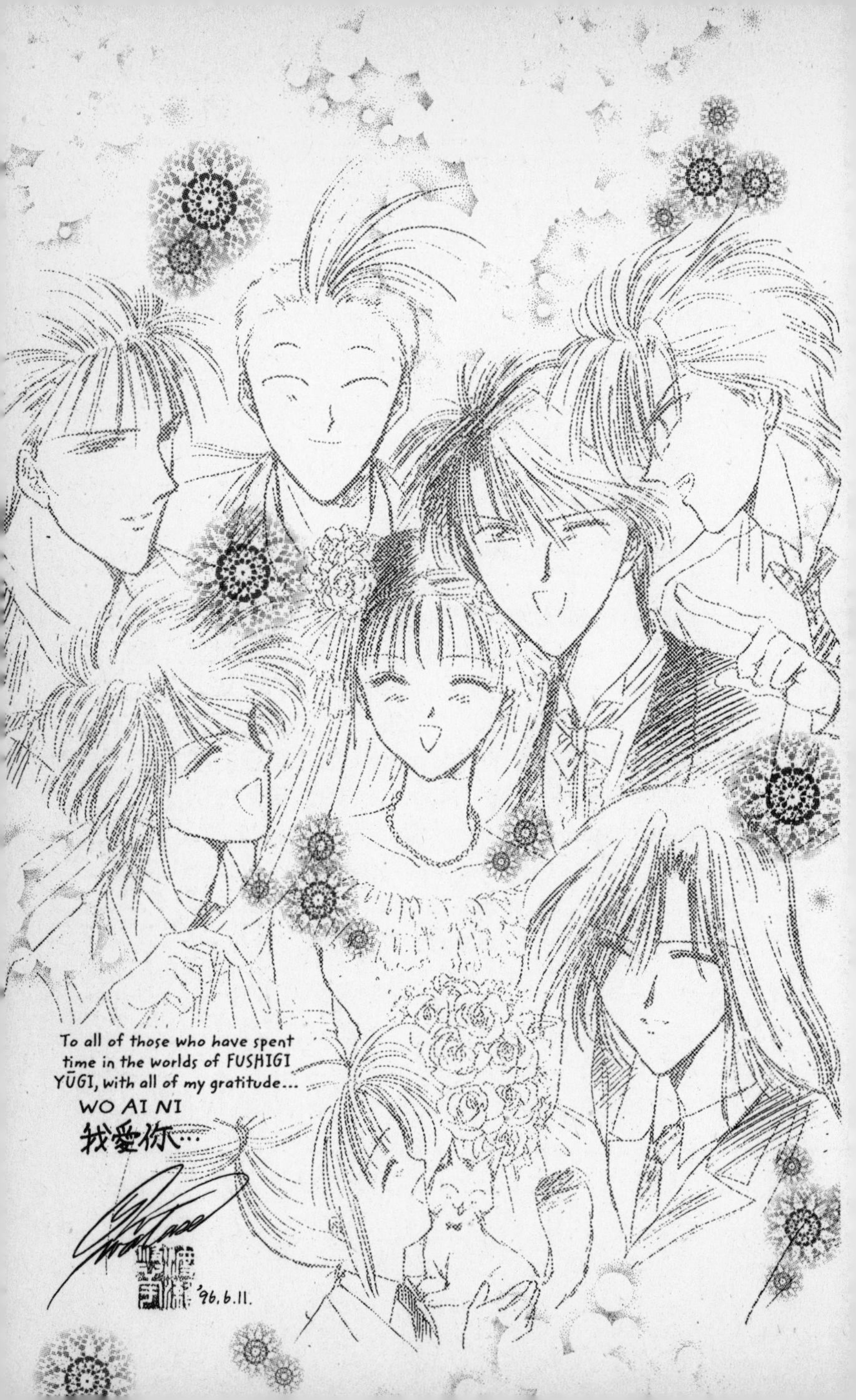
To all of those who have spent time in the worlds of FUSHIGI YŪGI, with all of my gratitude...
WO AI NI
我愛你…
'96.6.11.

ABOUT THE AUTHOR

Yuu Watase was born on March 5 in a town near Osaka, Japan, and she was raised there before moving to Tokyo to follow her dream of creating manga. In the decade since her debut short story, "Pajama De Ojama" (An Intrusion in Pajamas), she has produced more than 50 compiled volumes of short stories and continuing series. Watase's beloved works *Ceres: Celestial Legend*, *Imadoki!* *(Nowadays)*, *Alice 19th*, *Absolute Boyfriend*, and *Fushigi Yûgi: Genbu Kaiden* are now available in North America in English editions published by VIZ Media.

The Fushigi Yûgi Guide to Sound Effects

Most of the sound effects in FUSHIGI YÛGI are the way Yuu Watase created them, in their original Japanese.

We created this glossary for a page-by-page, panel-by-panel explanation of the action and background noises. By using this guide, you may even learn some Japanese.

The glossary lists page and panel number. For example, page 1, panel 3, would be listed as 1.3.

24.5	FX: PON (placing a hand on shoulder)	6.1	FX: ZAWA ZAWA (leaves rustling)
25.4	FX: ZAWA ZAWA (wind in leaves)	9.2	FX: DOOON (dramatic music)
25.6	FX: ZA ZA (footsteps in the grass)	9.4	FX: DOGU DOGU (flowing blood)
		11.4	FX: GASHI GASHI (scratching)
26.3	FX: FU (light shining)	12.4	FX: BIKU (surprise)
		12.5	FX: DOKUN (heavy heartbeat)
27.2	FX: KAAAA (light shining)	13.1	FX: DOKUN DOKUN (heavy heartbeats)
30.3	FX: DA (running footstep)		
31.3	FX: GABA (getting up)	14.5	FX: GABA (pulling at clothes)
32.6	FX: DOKIN (heartbeat)	16.1	FX: DOU (explosion)
		16.2	FX: HA (surprise)
		16.5	FX: GYURURURURU (swirling threads)
		17.4	FX: GIRI GIRI (electric-shock like pain)
		17.5	FX: GIRI GIRI (electric-shock like pain)
		18.1	FX: BA (massive power)
		18.2	FX: DO (explosion)
		18.2	FX: ZUGAZUZU (cracking rubble)
		20.1	FX: ZAWA ZAWA (crowd noises)
		20.2	FX: GYU (holding tight)
		20.3	FX: HYUUUU (wind blowing)

54.2 FX: BATAN (gate closing)
54.3 FX: FURU FURU (trembling)

55.4 FX: YORO (wobble)

56.1 FX: DOO (explosion)

57.2 FX: BA BA BA BA
(sudden appearances)

59.1 FX: PATAN (door closing)

61.1 FX: GAKU GAKU (trembling)

67.1 FX: BURORORO (car engine)

71.2 FX: SARA (fingers through hair)

72.2 FX: GYU (holding tight)

75.1 FX: ZAAN (waves)

76.3 FX: KA (sudden appearance)
76.4 FX: DOOON (explosion)

77.1 FX: BASA BASA BASA
(flapping wings)
77.2 FX: WAN WAN (barking)
77.6 FX: KACHA (door latch opening)

78.4 FX: DOKUN DOKUN DOKUN
DOKUN DOKUN (heartbeats)
78.5 FX: KUSHA (hand in hair)

79.5 FX: BO (blush)

81.5 FX: GACHA (door opening)

82.1 FX: DOKUN DOKUN DOKUN
(throbbing sounds)
82.3 FX: GYU (clenching)
82.5 FX: DOKUN DOKUN
(throbbing sounds)

35.6 FX: GU GU (struggling)

36.2 FX: BAN (slam)

38.1 FX: BAN (explosion)

39.2 FX: BARI BARI BARI
(breaking apart)
39.3 FX: GASHAN (exploding glass)

45.4 FX: FURU FURU (trembling)

46.2 FX: BURORORORO
(engine racing)
46.6 FX: HYUUUUUU (wind blowing)

47.2 FX: HYOOOOOO (wind blowing)

48.3 FX: KYUN (heart pang)
48.6 FX: BA (sudden movement)

49.1 FX: HYUUUU (wind blowing)
49.2 FX: BYOOOO
(wind blowing harder)

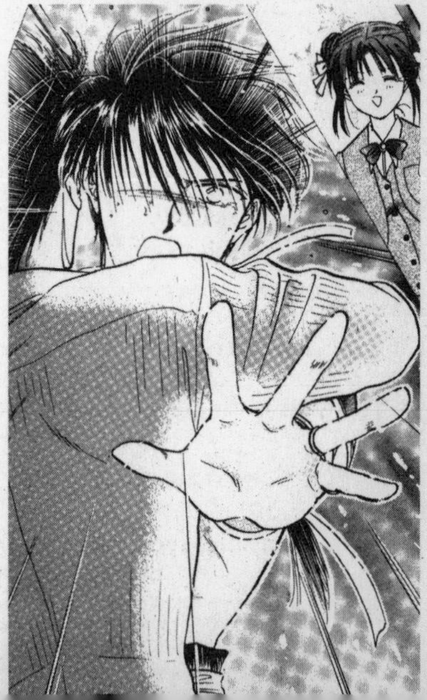

106.6	FX: KA (blush)	86.4	FX: BOO (glowing)
108.1	FX: DOKIN (heartbeat)	90.1	FX: HYOOOO (wind blowing)
108.5	FX: GUSHI (wiping away a tear)	90.3	FX: KA (flash of light)
109.5	FX: KOSO KOSO (sneaking)	92.1	FX: HA (sudden realization)
		92.2	FX: KAAA (flash of light)
110.4	FX: SHAN (rings jingling)		
110.5	FX: PAA (sudden appearance)	95.4	FX: SHULULULULU (unrolling)
111.3	FX: KA (lightning)	97.1	FX: HA (sudden realization)
111.3	FX: BABA BABA (thunder)		
111.4	FX: DO (explosion)	98.4	FX: BA (dramatic movement)
112.1	FX: JIJI (electrified harisen)	99.1	FX: SHULU
112.3	FX: PON (pop)		(throwing off the scroll)
		99.2	FX: KA (flash of light)
113.3	FX: DON (dramatic appearance)	99.3	FX: FUWA (flipping the bo-stick)
113.5	FX: DOKUN DOKUN DOKUN		
	DOKUN DOKUN (throbbing)	101.1	FX: GYU (clenching)
114.1	FX: SHAN (rings jingling)	102.3	Pictures: Huan-Lang
114.1-2	FX: ZUZUZUZUZUZU		(Tasuki's Chinese name)
	(low rumbling)		
114.2	FX: PAPPAAA PAAAA (car horns)		
114.5	FX: PIKU (twitch)		
117.4	FX: ZUZUZUZUZU (rumbling)		
118.1	FX: KA (sudden appearance)		
119.1	FX: DON (explosion)		
119.4	FX: DOOOOON (explosion)		
121.2	FX: KO (a footstep)		
121.3	FX: DO (threads striking)		
122.3	FX: KA KA (steps)		
123.2	FX: ZA (fighting stance)		
123.3	FX: ZUOOOOOO		
	(blast of energy)		

124.2 FX: BA (rushing air)
124.3 FX: DOGU (hitting)

125.1 FX: DOGAGA GAGA (multiple hits)
125.2 FX: DO BASH DO (more hits)

126.1-3 FX: DOSHAA (kick)
126.5 FX: KA (determination)

127.2 FX: KA (power surge)
127.2-4 FX: DOOOOO (explosive power)

134.1 FX: ZUZUZU (rumbling)
134.4 FX: DOOOON (explosion)

135.1 FX: ZUUUUN (smoke clearing)

136.2 FX: VOON (energy burst)

137.1 FX: VOON (energy burst)

143.1 FX: KA (flash)
143.2 FX: BA (explosion)

146.7 FX: KA (flash)

147.2 FX: DOO (explosion)
147.5 FX: ZUUUUU (clearing smoke)

148.2 FX: ZUUUUU (clearing smoke)

150.3 FX: ZUZUZU ZUZU (rumbling)

151.3 FX: BA (explosive energy)

152.1 FX: DOO (collapsing)
152.4 FX: ZA (sudden appearance)

153.2 FX: ZUZU (rumbling)
153.5 FX: ZUZU (rumbling)
153.6 FX: ZUZUZUZU (rumbling)

154.2 FX: ZUZUZU (rumbling)

155.2 FX: ZUZU (rumbling)

156.1 FX: DOOOON (crashing)

158.1 FX: DO (energy)
158.2 FX: BA (attack)

163.1 FX: DOOOOO (fiery explosion)

170.1 FX: BA (explosion)

172.1 FX: KA (flash)

173.2 FX: UOOOOOO (great energy)

174.2 FX: KA (flash)
174.4 FX: BOO (burning)

179.4 FX: ZAWA ZAWA (crowd noise)

180.1 FX: DOKUN DOKUN DOKUN DOKUN DOKUN (heartbeats)

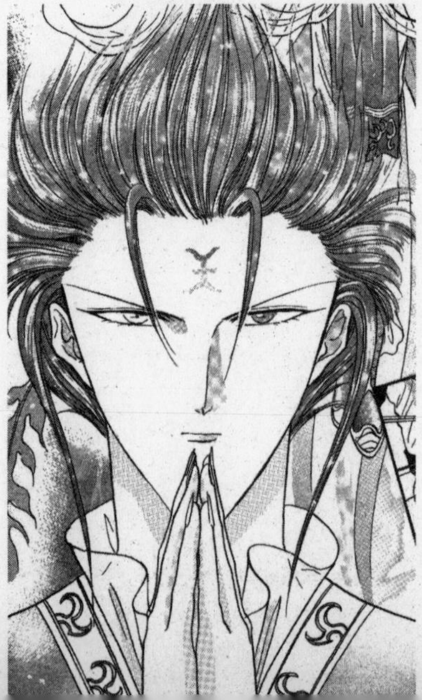

LOVE SHOJO? LET US KNOW!

☐ Please do NOT send me information about VIZ Media products, news and events, special offers, or other information.

☐ Please do NOT send me information from VIZ' trusted business partners.

Name: _____

Address: _____

City:_____ State:_____ Zip:_____

E-mail: _____

☐ Male ☐ Female Date of Birth (mm/dd/yyyy): ___/___/_____ (Under 13? Parental consent required)

What race/ethnicity do you consider yourself? (check all that apply)

☐ White/Caucasian ☐ Black/African American ☐ Hispanic/Latino

☐ Asian/Pacific Islander ☐ Native American/Alaskan Native ☐ Other: _____

What VIZ shojo title(s) did you purchase? (indicate title(s) purchased)

_____

What other shojo titles from other publishers do you own? _____

_____

Reason for purchase: (check all that apply)

☐ Special offer ☐ Favorite title / author / artist / genre

☐ Gift ☐ Recommendation ☐ Collection

☐ Read excerpt in VIZ manga sampler ☐ Other _____

Where did you make your purchase? (please check one)

☐ Comic store ☐ Bookstore ☐ Mass/Grocery Store

☐ Newsstand ☐ Video/Video Game Store

☐ Online (site:_____) ☐ Other _____

How many shojo titles have you purchased in the last year? How many were VIZ shojo titles?
(please check one from each column)

SHOJO MANGA	VIZ SHOJO MANGA
☐ None	☐ None
☐ 1 – 4	☐ 1 – 4
☐ 5 – 10	☐ 5 – 10
☐ 11+	☐ 11+

What do you like most about shojo graphic novels? **(check all that apply)**

☐ Romance ☐ Drama / conflict ☐ Fantasy
☐ Comedy ☐ Real-life storylines ☐ Relatable characters
☐ Other ______________________________

Do you purchase every volume of your favorite shojo series?

☐ Yes! Gotta have 'em as my own
☐ No. Please explain: ______________________________

Who are your favorite shojo authors / artists? ______________________________

____

What shojo titles would like you translated and sold in English? ______________________________

____

THANK YOU! Please send the completed form to:

NJW Research
ATTN: VIZ Media Shojo Survey
42 Catharine Street
Poughkeepsie, NY 12601

Your privacy is very important to us. All information provided will be used for internal purposes only and will not be sold or otherwise divulged.